DUSTY BOOTS
TO BOARDROOM
Follow your dreams

Adrian Stratta

Dusty Boots to Boardroom: Follow your dreams

By Adrian Stratta

Paperback IBSN: 978-1-0684855-0-3
Hardback IBSN: 978-1-0684855-1-0
eBook IBSN: 978-1-0684855-2-7

Integral Growth Ltd, supporting https://dustybootstoboardroom.com

I am proud a percentage of profits will be passed to this veteran's charity to support those warriors from the parent formation that shaped my earlier career.

To 'Top Spotter' Catherine,
for her love, compassion,
determination and resilience
for our African sojourn

CONTENTS

PROLOGUE

'My god, what do I do?' Catherine's scream pierced through the air. We had switched drivers half an hour earlier and were cruising gently along the N7 main single-carriage highway to Namibia. Catherine was fresh and alert, yet nothing could have really prepared us for what we were about to face. My head was down, studying the map, not the road, but Catherine's instinctual scream forced me to look up and see an on-coming articulated lorry being overtaken on the blindside by a 'bakkie' (pick-up truck) round a blind bend. What a stupid, reckless manoeuvre. Whilst Catherine is a very good driver, she had no option. Instinctively, she swerved to avoid a head-on collision with the bakkie. Time seemed to slow down momentarily; there was nothing I could do. Actions beyond our control were already in motion and, given our high centre of gravity, momentum was already shifting Daph's rear-end. Despite her best efforts, there was no stopping the inevitable. With a deafening crash, we slammed into the rock wall, spun and rolled, landing on our side. How she missed a head-on collision with the bakkie, I have no idea.

It all happened in a flash. We were stunned, coming to whilst still suspended like bats by our seatbelts. The event is now etched in our minds, even though we thought we were prepared to expect the unexpected. I could see Catherine lying at an obscure angle, covered in blood. She was conscious but shouting at me. Initially, I was not aware of her alarm, but I soon realised she was terrified by the sight of blood streaming from my head. Instinct took over. I cut the ignition, kicked out the windscreen, through which we both eventually climbed out. Catherine was in pain and complaining about her hand, but I was not able to immediately assess her injuries. She was able to move, which was good, but my mind was spinning and I was worried about the blood. What were those first aid priorities that had been drummed into me? ABC: airway, breathing and circulation. It turned out that the blood covering her was actually mine. A simple bump to my nose was the cause, yet Catherine was convinced I had a severe injury. My immediate worry was the angle of her shoulder, which didn't look right. Thankfully, her breathing was steady as I gently helped her out of the vehicle, but we were both shaken; Catherine was in shock.

The lorry driver thankfully stopped and made a timely call to the police. He also offered himself as a witness. Unsurprisingly, the bakkie driver did not stop, a violation of South African law, as in the UK. The lorry driver had caught a partial bakkie registration, which he shared with the police. We learnt later that the police had an idea who the white driver was, probably a local, but to this day, I'm not sure what follow-up occurred. As in so many areas, never judge a book by its cover...our lorry driver was our saviour and was as much a victim as we were.

But what to do? Catherine was my primary concern. Daphne (our Land Rover) lay on her side, battered, gear strewn all over the road, but mercifully, not obstructing the highway. We were on a bend, but the lorry driver had the situation under control; his hazard lights were on and he was actively controlling traffic from the blindside. I don't recall much traffic, but no one stopped. I guided Catherine to the relative safety of the roadside and sat her on a cushion from Daph, in the shade. I tried to get her to drink but she kept mumbling that she had 'killed Daphne'. It was evident, both from what the lorry driver said and what I recalled, that she had performed magnificently to avoid a head-on collision. The speed on impact was not high, but it was sufficient to bend the Land Rover chassis and 'A' posts. The engine had shifted on its mounting, the bull bar and bonnet were off and the roof rack lay on the road. Thankfully, all the equipment inside the vehicle remained in place; our tie-down scheme had done its job. The sturdy Land Rover chassis absorbed the brunt of the impact and the toughened windscreen and window film had prevented glass flying around the cab; so, kudos to Land Rover.

Impressively, the police arrived in 20 minutes. After an initial consultation with the lorry driver, they quickly pieced together what had happened, having seen many similar incidents. Their medic attended to Catherine, eager to convey her to the local cottage hospital at Garies and assuring me I could follow shortly. Once Catherine was being treated, my primary concern had been addressed. I remained behind to secure the crash site and organise Daph's recovery.

Ashamedly, my first thought was a resigned farewell to Daph and all her gear, which was a poor reflection on the police. I am grateful that the opposite happened; they called a recovery vehicle, started documenting events and gathering our scattered belongings. This proactive response was a promising start, but the recovery truck driver, equipped only to recover cars, not a laden 4x4, was indifferent. Sensing further impending damage to Daph, I assumed directive control, much to the relief of the police. Had I not, Daph and her gear would likely have disappeared for good. The police remained dutiful, ensuring that Daph was loaded onto the recovery truck with decorum, whilst the police van limped back to the station with all of our gear. The new police station at Garies had a lock-up for Daph and a secure storeroom for our personal effects. The police were keen to prove their worth, to my relief, for this was far beyond any expectation. A statement was never requested, but documentation was completed and I was given a police number. I was able to recover anything removeable from Daphne and secure it in the storeroom. The efficiency of the police left a lasting positive impression; the lorry driver's testament was all they required.

Taking our two grab bags, Daph's documents, laptop and camera, I jumped into the car that took me to the local cottage hospital to be reunited with Catherine. Adrenaline had drained me and I started to feel utterly deflated. After so long, the mental and physical effort of getting on the road had been snuffed out by a reckless incident. Goodness knows what was going through Catherine's mind, but her health and welfare were my utmost priority. Once at the hospital, I was left to wait for her whilst the doctors and nurses bustled about. I was taking stock when a nurse came by to clean me up. I thanked her, saying I was fine, yet anxious to know where and how Catherine was. She went to enquire, but first showed me where I could get a wash. It was only then that I looked in a mirror, and it was not a pretty sight! The dried blood spattered across my face was one thing, but my eyes didn't really look part of my face; they were lost and sullen. I too must have been in some form of shock and I was suddenly very thirsty. I needed to pull myself together, but I was tired, very tired; our bubble had been burst. I felt like I had gone ten rounds with Mike Tyson, and it was clear that he had won.

The next shock was seeing Catherine wheeled out in a wheelchair, with her right arm in a sling. She was relieved to see me. She had been cleaned up but looked exhausted, partly due to strong pain medication. The accompanying doctor explained that he had arranged for a transfer to the main hospital in Cape Town. He showed me the X-ray of Catherine's shoulder, indicating a laterally displaced fracture of the distal clavicle; it was broken. Normal clavicular fracture management is conservative and it usually heals with rest; but this was not a normal break. They were concerned that she might need surgery due to the angle of her bone displacement and the fracture being at the distal end. They discussed a possible ambulance transfer to Cape Town the following day, unless we wanted to go directly in a car; we opted for the car.

With three others, we crammed into a car for the next four or five hours. Catherine nestled into me for comfort and reassurance; besides the uncomfortable ride, she was upset about Daph. I kept reassuring her how well she had done; it was just bad luck that she happened to be driving. These things happen and it was wrong for her to start blaming herself. At Northern Cape Hospital, Catherine was admitted to a very efficient trauma unit. It was clearly a busy night, manic even. It looked like a shooting had occurred. Not the first time that day, my heart was in my mouth as Catherine was wheeled away for further X-rays. As she was about to leave, she grasped my hand with all the strength she could muster to say, 'We will carry on, won't we?' with pleading eyes. That sliced straight through and hit me hard. What? Was she mad? There was no way - her health was far more important. Yet my weak body language and mumbled assurances tried to be as positive as possible. I can't have been much good, but Catherine's resolve was clear; we were carrying on, despite our differing opinions.

Dawn on safari is a magical experience. Many who experience the African night sounds, under canvas or not, will be familiar with the varied, strange noises that can keep you awake, regardless of futile attempts to snuggle under a blanket for child-like sanctuary. It's an enduring attraction. With dawn, the night sounds fade and smell becomes the more prominent sense. Pungent, damp air and wet grasses first pervade the nostrils, while a chill permeates the bones. It's a fleeting transition between night and day as the fireball sun rises swiftly. Dampness is seared away by the intensity of the sun, leaving a dry, dusty heat. From dawn's initial glimmer, there is a transient passing from an eerie, grey half-light to bright, strong, full sunlight. It takes less than 30 minutes before the warmth replaces the damp and chill. There is no doubt once it arrives. Footfalls recreate the familiar dust cloud around your boots, previously dampened. Insects start to buzz and irritate again. Bird life feasts on the early morning insects, chattering and squawking as they go. Human noises start up again; gentle humming, smells of wood smoke and strange tongues. The ubiquitous cup of tea is drawn and cheerful voices chatter.

By the late nineties, we had conducted a number of African safaris since our honeymoon. Like many of my military colleagues, I too experienced an earlier African enchantment during a Kenyan deployment. Taking a (calculated) risk, Catherine was enthralled to learn about her first safari during our wedding speeches. She loved our honeymoon to Zimbabwe, Botswana and Zambia. Since then, we had been to the Kruger, Okavango and others before we found ourselves on safari in the Serengeti, luxuriating in a personalised fortnight with our own guide (Winston) in a Land Rover. Personalised is overselling it; we conducted the standard northern safari circuit, with additional wild camping in the Serengeti. Winston was a real charmer, a local Maasai lad with a good education and an excellent grasp of English. We conducted the Eastern Park rotations and the Ngorongoro Crater, where we picked up our cook, Aga, and his camping trailer to head for the Serengeti. It was one of those Out of Africa, 'no effort required' safaris with large, canvas walk-in tents, separate shower/toilet and dining tent/shade.

Whilst being thoroughly spoilt wild camping, Aga served up another fantastic breakfast, easily comparable to those served in any local, fancy lodge. We had tea, coffee, fresh bread and a 'full English'. We needed to pinch ourselves, waking within some kopjes (small, rocky outcrops) within the Serengeti. Aga had just stoked the log fire under his grate, accompanied by his endless, jovial banter about the hyenas' 'tea party' the previous night. Trying to tune in to what he referred to, Winston started pointing out the large, male lion footprints in the sand around our tent. Mercifully, we'd been unaware, but the wildlife would not have been, hence Aga's oblique reference to the commotion. We were told that a canvas sheet acts like a brick wall to the lion (and most predators), which sounds crazy. Make no mistake, had there been a loose tent flap or an errant foot hanging out, it would have been supper for any wild animal. Yet wild animals generally dislike human smells, least of all the tilly lamps, Land Rovers, petrol and so forth, so they tend to stay away. I couldn't help wondering if we were being told a tall tale!

Following a magical day of many game sightings and a balloon trip scheduled for the following morning, we kicked back, lost and alone on Simba Kopje, enjoying a sundowner. We could smell miracles being created over Aga's log fire, whilst enjoying the early sunset. I have no clue where it came from, suppressed within the dark recesses of my mind, but I mused to Catherine that, should I leave the army, it might be fun to drive from London to Cape Town. I had been considering my options about staying in the forces, but I had little expectation or belief that such a statement would ever come to fruition. I should have realised that Catherine heard such a statement as sacrosanct; in her mind, we were going to do it (not that either of us knew it at the time). We kicked back on our kopje, gazing at the emerging Milky Way, just before we were refreshed with another obligatory sundowner.

This may sound privileged, and perhaps there is an element of that. We had worked hard at our divergent careers and were hardly ever in the same place. I was away a lot with the military and Catherine travelled with her medical career. Our holidays and safaris became our precious reconnection, to share joint interests and passions. Life is too short to settle. Back then, we were aware of the environment and its shrinking base, long before climate activism and the planet's associated diminishing resources. How many opportunities in life does one have to reach back into the 'mind's store cupboard' and drag out a long-held dream or aspiration? Life takes over; jobs, careers and family predominate. Before realising it, people are looking at retirement.

Catherine and I met at university where Catherine was intent on becoming a doctor, whilst I was weighing various commercial opportunities. 'Follow your dreams' has always been our vague mantra. To actually realise dreams and ambitions from the dark recesses of the mind is rare. People often tuck their aspirations away on the mental back shelf, never really expecting them to come true. Maybe the barriers within the mind are greater and more significant than the reality? Perhaps then, we are doubly blessed, for I believe this has occurred twice for us; our trans-African journey being our second bite at the proverbial cherry.

Catherine had always dreamed of being a doctor. She attained her medical school place with Arts A-Levels, having to pass her three science A-Levels in her first year. My joining the army (more specifically, the Parachute Regiment) was a revelation, achieving what I thought to be an unattainable dream. I had no conscious plan to join the army - quite the opposite. In my final year at university, I was attending the various career 'milk rounds', for my father encouraged me to 'get a profession'. At the same time, I enjoyed being the Contingent Subaltern at Sheffield Officer Training Corps (OTC), having previously enjoyed cadets and the Territorial Army. In my final year, a couple of renowned 'old and bold' regular career paratroopers at the OTC (David and Alf) encouraged me to attend a familiarisation event at the Parachute Regiment depot; I became hooked. Whether on some unconscious level I was morphing to that figure from my teenage poster of a paratrooper climbing into a helicopter in Radfan, Oman or somewhere, I cannot say. As an ironic twist, nine months after entering Sandhurst, passing P Company and jumps, I was posted to 2 PARA and parachuted into Oman on an Airborne Brigade exercise. It felt like stepping into that poster! It wasn't until my feet landed in the Omani desert, and we'd rallied and scaled our first jebel (hill), that a wave of emotion and achievement hit me like a train. Welcome to the regiment. I wanted to shout it from the roof tops, although clearly I suppressed any such exuberance. For one thing, I was out of breath from climbing the jebel, but more fundamentally, I was just a small cog surrounded by the recently tested war machine from the Falklands. Who was I among such giants?

Part 1
WHY AND WHERE IN AFRICA?

Water pump in Kalahari

oops - whilst doing all the right things

Cape Town Harbour

Cape Agulhas Lighthouse

"The only thing predictable about Africa is its unpredictability."

Brian Jackman

Elephant Sanctuary

Makgadikgadi Salt Pans

Chapter 1
Landing in South Africa on 9/11

Sitting perspiring with twenty or so senior British officers on a hillside in the midday sun, we were being threatened, subjected to a 'full-on' Zulu war cry. We were learning how a Zulu army routed a British Imperial Column. The hairs on the back of our necks were on high alert but we were in no immediate danger. We gawped, listening to David Rattray regaling the 1897 Battle of Isandlwana. The renowned historian was friends with both the Zulu nation and King (then, Prince) Charles III. His bestseller, The Day of the Dead Moon, chronicled the battle's events, whose title came about due to the full solar eclipse during the battle. Contrary to popular myth, the Zulus did not want a fight. The Zulus' word is their bond, not broken at any cost. However, the British severed their agreement by crossing the Tugela River, fracturing the brokered peace, for Lord Chelmsford believed in his perceived imperial superiority. Having crossed the river, the British were being tracked by a 20,000-strong Zulu army, equipped with traditional assegai iron spears and cow-hide shields. The Zulus wiped out the poorly positioned and undefended British column, routing 1,800 British colonial and native levees, plus 400 civilians. The British had the latest Martini Henry breech loading rifles and two 7-pounder mountain guns, but the speed of the Zulu attack overwhelmed and divided the slow, uncoordinated and dispersed British, rendering them vulnerable to being picked off in small pockets.

Our party of British military advisors were staying at David Rattray's lodge on a bluff, just above Fugitives Drift, during our five-day battlefield tour around KwaZulu Natal. Learning lessons from historical events is invaluable. Appreciating the country, their military history and capabilities and contrasting them to modern norms cultivates doctrine, which is core to aligning ourselves and providing balanced advice to South African ministries and service colleagues. In a shocking postscript, five years after our visit, David Rattray was killed during a home invasion by half a dozen attackers. It was a tragic loss of life for one dedicated to helping local people and curating their culture. Thankfully, the offenders were caught and given life sentences, but such events were becoming increasingly frequent.

That same evening, we travelled the six miles to Rorke's Drift. I dare say many readers might have seen the film, Zulu, starring Michael Cain and Stanley Baxter on the silver screen; the famous line most people remember is, 'Zulus, thousands of 'em!' Aside from the actual location, the film is a close portrayal to the reality we heard about that evening, during a quiet and dignified walk through the remnants of Rorke's Drift. Here, 150 men (the sick, lame and lazy of 24th Regiment of Foot) amazingly defeated around 3-4,000 Zulus by their 'last stand' at the Drift. Few survived; eleven VCs were awarded. It is a sad and common feature that those who survive, especially the VC holders, suffer survivor's guilt and their lives spiral down towards a quick and ignominious end. Words were unspoken among us, each lost in their own thoughts as the sun descended over Rorke's Drift. All the military aspects of defence - interlocking fire and support - were effectively employed here, the same principles absent from Isandlwana. Compared to other equally evocative sites of Ladysmith, Spion Kop and Majuba Hill, Rorke's Drift left a proverbial lump in our throats.

When I arrived in South Africa, such battlefield horrors were not waiting for me; shocking news of a different kind was announced as we landed at Johannesburg. Travelling with a fellow officer, Chris, to augment the existing British Advisory Team, the shocked pilot announced the unfolding attack on the Twin Towers in New York. The world spun on a new axis; 9/11 became the modern equivalent of knowing 'where you were when President Kennedy was shot'. People were in shock; there was a 24-hour paralysis as we all tried to wrap our heads around the audacity of the attack. Suddenly, everything changed; Chris and I were sent down to the South African ministries' bunker for strategic reactive planning. Why us? Who thought South Africa was under attack? The country was readying itself for a nuclear exchange. I'm not sure what the biggest shock was; that South Africa thought it warranted a potential nuclear attack; that they had a hardened, deep nuclear shelter; or that we (Chris and I) would be intrinsic in any decision-making. Honoured though that we were to attend their geo-political planning, we emerged a week later, blinking into the glare of the sun, having made friends and established an 'Entente Cordiale' with our new colleagues.

The twists and turns of life constantly evolve, whether planned or happenstance; one can only roll with events and maximise on each opportunity as it's presented. It's how one reacts, and subsequently thrives, that remains important. It was (managed) fortune that I served my final year supporting the FCO in Pretoria. Having made the momentous decision to leave the army, I was keen to avoid a rubbish final role 'running bogs and drains in Benbecular', as the popular euphemism ran (no offence to that delightful part of Scotland). I had reached the first significant pension breakpoint and was delivering 'conscious competency' that 16 years of military service bestows (for one should never stop learning). I loved my three years of command; a Rifle Company on operations and then restructuring Support Company. I was delighted to be appointed 2IC to 3 PARA for my next posting, a great springboard for advancement, but what would follow? I made the decision to leave before the many overseas operations were known about, which I suspect would have offered many more opportunities. Would I command? What would be the future shape of the army? As ever, too many unknowns.

The MoD sponsored my MBA and I wanted to apply the learnings whilst still fresh. Whilst Cranfield qualifications would not secure me a job, it helps establish some credibility. Following a subsequent two-year desk job devising and applying the Defence Balanced Scorecard, I was offered commercial opportunities within Deloitte and PwC that sounded interesting and tempting. But I knew they would send me back into the MoD, so it seemed I was swapping one uniform for another. I was enormously grateful for the support from the general to whom I reported for his endorsement of the South African appointment. I had worked for him before and he was a leader I held in high regard. Presenting him my letter of resignation went something like, 'Sir, with a heavy heart…and so forth….' He said, 'No problem, Adrian,' holding up his own resignation letter, 'I have just written my own.' My face must have been a picture!

The British Military Advisory and Training Team (BMATT) was linked to the Foreign and Commonwealth Office (FCO). Chris and I were part of a new three-man team to establish a new Peace Support Office, designed to assist countries orientate their forces into deploying as Peace Supporters and enablers. A few such advisory teams existed in Eastern Europe and East Africa. In South Africa, the historic 1994 election of Nelson Mandela as president engendered wholesale change to the direction of the state. Chief among these changes was the integration of the six non-statutory (former homeland and guerrilla) armies within the restructured and unified South African National Defence Force (SANDF). This was the primary task for the original BMATT.

Interestingly, South Africa's continued Defence Policy assumed their borders would never be attacked. They wanted to be 'Little Sister' not 'Big Brother', yet they possessed a Blue Water Navy and first generation combat aircraft. Their regional forces and commandos were aligned to the renowned South African Defence Force (SADF) of the past. The military, mainly the army, were used as a social engineering tool to assimilate and utilise (pay) the former irregular forces, to reduce societal instability.

By the 2000s, the South African government was strapped for cash, with the country's wealth largely held by the big corporates or individuals. The ANC was struggling to fund and honour their election pledge of jobs, wealth and housing for the masses. At the same time, the GDP of Gauteng Province on the Highveld was comparable, even higher, than that of Nigeria, the next largest African economy. Mandela sought to leverage his military and obtain UN funds by offering his troops to Burundi, where they could help create the conditions for 'free and fair elections'. Once committed, the UN was delighted that 'Big Brother' was supporting their fellow Africans, so considered it appropriate for South Africa to self-fund the intervention. Mandela was hoisted by his own petard and SANDF had to cobble together an untrained battalion group. The deployment did not go well, nor could the process be repeated. Our PSO team was to advise on the necessary restructuring and training, to create, prepare and (potentially) deploy Peace Support Troops, within the countries' unique restrictions.

If all subsequent military appointments were like this role, I would still be serving today. It was challenging and rewarding, working hard and playing harder. Although I had engineered this role, knowing it was my swansong, my commitment remained. Yet, being my last appointment, I needed to take control of my subsequent career path. Whilst I thought it empowering, it was equally daunting. I knew what I did not want to do, rather than what I did. During my service, there was scant choice in what you did. We were there to do a job and there was not much wiggle room (although latterly, after Regimental Service, this was changing). I now had to find my own direction, which was a new concept to me. I had completed some resettlement training, which left me trying to align my skills to future roles. There was not much call for parachute assaults over the city of London, however appealing this might have been in some circles. I needed to focus on my second career move and decide what was appropriate.

Chapter 2
What Is Overlanding – Why Africa?

My last military appointment in South Africa was fabulous, although I couldn't have asked for a better career start. I mentioned parachuting into Oman only a few weeks after my arrival in 2 PARA; the pace continued. In these first two years, we deployed to Kenya, Belize, the Far East, Canada and Cyprus, to name a few, and my feet were rarely in the UK. Dealing with the unexpected became the norm. We worked hard, always seeking to go further and push the envelope, with the airborne dynamic. Yet Kenya seemed different - we saw Africa up close, villages and the people - it was visceral. I was not alone in being seduced by Kenya; it remains a critical training facility for the military today and many of our cohort returned, in varying roles or guises.

You can only imagine the delicate nature for some of the assembling advance party at 6am on New Year's Day, 1987, at our Aldershot Barracks. Only a couple of weeks since returning from Oman, this would be the first African exposure for many. There were a few old hands; I recall one captain with family in Kenya. He planned to propose to his girlfriend during a game-viewing flight. 'How romantic,' we thought, except we learnt he put the plane into a vertical dive mid-flight to pop the question. I'm guessing she said yes, although I am unaware as to the tenure of their marriage. The advance party was a real safari around the training options; we ended up in the Aberdare National Park that I don't recall revisiting. Our training was outstanding, mostly live firing.

Being in the jungle on the lower slopes of Mount Kenya was inspiring, with many laughs. I have vivid memories of creeping around the bush whilst being shadowed by a bull elephant that passed between us like a ghost. And the rats. Oh, the rats - they were the size of beavers! The boys tried to trap the rats one night whilst in our defensive position; the rats won. None were caught. Worse, their teeth bit through equipment and into tinned food. The traps predictably attracted other beasties. Our training demanded 'hard routine', meaning no sound, lights or fires, and sentries throughout the night. Nothing new here; each section protects the central platoon

HQ, manning the radio within a triangular layout. Before the dawn stand-to, my sergeant, Brummie, and I woke to a line of army ants munching straight between us, and the boys gone! Defeated by the rats, they silently repositioned themselves, leaving HQ as sacrificial lambs to the slaughter. At least we knew the boys could move silently.

After company live firing at Dol Dol, one evening we were permitted to bathe in the local river. We posted an armed sentry and embraced the cool, refreshing water. Ahh, it was lovely, a truly cleansing swimming. One brave soul clambered out on the far bank to read the sign beside the dilapidated footbridge, which said 'BEWARE, crocodiles'. The hairs on everyone's necks stood up as we all stampeded for the bank. I still shudder to recall it, and the palpable relief to escape, less so for the poor chap on the far bank. We spent a week tactically trekking across a mountain range, playing hide and seek. One company commander had just returned from Hereford and suggested that each company should replicate one of their exercises, so we played Sherpa Tenzing. It was hard graft, but great soldiering. The final battalion action was live firing at Archers Post, near Marsabit. We sought to complicate matters with a parachute insertion and a live advance to contact. Predictably, the weather and RAF managed to exacerbate the challenge. Exceptional heat, high winds and insufficient aircraft meant we needed three waves of company drops; my company went first at dawn. The thermals and turbulence were appalling; the Hercules aircraft were tossed around like proverbial corks, guys being sick everywhere. Thirty minutes before the drop, we fought to stand up, preparing for the jump, in the maelstrom. I was jumping first, so I was beside the para-door; crucially being able to sniff fresh air and watch the Kenyan bush passing at 600 feet below. Poised in the door, longing for the green light to initiate my escape, excessive winds over the drop zone (DZ) meant they scrubbed our jump. Nightmare! It meant more time being thrown around the 'washing machine'. Back at Lakipia airstrip, we were exhausted and deflated, lacking adrenaline. A third of the company suffered with diarrhoea and vomiting (D&V), such was our dehydration. The winds eased around midday, allowing the other companies to jump, requiring us to try again at dusk. Most parachuting is conducted at night, but for safety, the RAF wanted this completed before dark. The winds were still bad (marginal) as we jumped on to Shaba DZ, an inhospitable DZ. It was an exceptionally hard, lunar landscape of small hillocks and acacia thorn bushes. I passed by one sergeant major from an earlier drop who'd become painfully impaled upon an acacia thorn bush. They were still struggling to extract him; yet another reason why the acacia is called the 'wait a while' bush. Surviving the drop was just the start; now we started our night advance to contact, with the apex animals awake and ready to play.

After 48 hours of frenetic activity following our no-sleep parachuting malarkey, we were exhausted. So, imagine the good humour when the following radio message came from the commanding officer: 'This is Sunray; no one is to sleep on the ground; there are anthrax spores!' What? Should we just stand for a week? We had just been crawling in the dust, simulating battle, so lying down could hardly make any difference. But this was real; tragically we lost a soldier from anthrax. The poor lad had been putting out targets the previous week. Anthrax basically decomposes the body's internal organs. He collapsed and deteriorated rapidly, despite being young, fit and healthy. Thankfully, there were no more deaths and we continued to bomb and shoot all manner of things, manoeuvring our way towards three focal hills. Once our firing was complete, three Masai warriors in full regalia, brandishing spears, came running towards us from 'down range' and through our positions. We were all open mouthed; how did they survive? There were only three now; how many started out? Either we were useless soldiers or something amazing just happened. Apparently, it's their party trick; they know when the exercise ends before we do.

As UK ambassadors, 2PARA held a cocktail party for the local 'great and good' overlooking Lakipia. This was a reciprocal invitation; the Muthaiga Club held a similar reception for the battalion in 1981, before the Falklands War, and sought to show their appreciation to the regiment. The guest list was extensive, including the actress, Stephanie Powers, who farmed locally with her husband, William Holden. He had sadly died a few years earlier, but they were determined to continue their Wildlife Foundation. Also invited was Digby Tatham-Warter; he famously commanded A Company 2 PARA at Arnhem Bridge in 1944. Sadly, he was unable to attend. Already a serving officer in India by the late 1930s, Digby served in North Africa before he joined 2 PARA, arriving with a fearsome fighting reputation. His company were the first to reach Arnhem Bridge, where Digby engaged tanks with a bayonet charge. Reputedly, he stuck the point of his umbrella through the driver's slit and into the driver's eye of a German armoured car and sought to shield a casualty from bullets with the aforementioned brolly - some brolly. The suggestion that he could never remember the password (hence, carrying the umbrella to suggest 'only a bloody fool of an Englishman' would carry one into battle) is the stuff of films, but never let the truth interrupt a story. We were lucky enough to meet him; as young officers, we were summoned to his ranch for an audience. Still quite a character and curmudgeon, he held court with tales of pre-war tiger hunting and pig sticking. He died in 1993, aged 75, at his ranch on the Lakipia Plains, called 'Utrinque Paratus' (meaning 'ready for anything', the motto of the Parachute Regiment).

Everyone is shaped by their experiences; my Kenyan exposure partly inspired our honeymoon, which spawned further safaris. But an overland expedition is a quantum step-up from a safari. My decision to leave the forces meant Catherine and I were at a crossroads. Maybe I should have had a sharper focus on my subsequent career path, yet 'carpe diem'; the lure of my final South African appointment allowed us to 'dream'. For Catherine, following our 'Serengeti Accord', she was more than ready. The charms of Africa were seducing us from afar. All trips require the traveller to make their own luck, yet events can be just that, good and bad; what matters most is how people react.

The classic definition of 'overlanding' relates to a self-reliant overland trip in remote locations for an extended period, using motorised off-road transport and frequently crossing international borders. It implies more than just moving from A to B; frequently there is some purpose or task to be completed. The more classical form began post-war, with the advent of commercially viable four-wheel drive vehicles and trucks. In 1949, Colonel Leblanc drove the first brand-new Land Rover 80-inch Series 1 from Britain to Abyssinia. The same year, the Automobile Association of South Africa published a guide, Trans-African Highways; A Route Book of the Main Trunk Routes in Africa. It suggested vehicle types, where to stop or source provisions along whichever route. However, in 1955-6, the genre-defining classic was the Oxford and Cambridge Far Eastern Expedition between London and Singapore. Half a dozen Oxbridge graduates caught the spirit of adventure by blagging two brand-new Land Rovers to explore. Tim Slessor documented their adventures in his First Overland book, about 'Oxford' and 'Cambridge' (the two named vehicles) that were suitably painted in college appropriate shades of blue. Their adventure summed up the hopes and aspiration as much as the bon vivant of the times; anyone who labels their water jerry cans 'Gin and Tonic' are not going to be shrinking violets! Their galivanting film footage caught the imagination and heart of the media, and the blessing of a young David Attenborough.

In 2019, arriving in the UK just before a COVID lockdown, a team recreated the reverse route (or as close to it as currently possible) propagating a book, TV rights and social media splash, envisaged by adventurer Alex Bescoby. It is a wonderful story. Alex connected with 86-year old Tim Slessor because the original 'Oxford' Land Rover was found on the island of St Helena. Not to spoil the Last Overland, their fleet of enablers and modern Land Rovers replicated the return journey that Sir David Attenborough implied 'could no longer be done'. Indeed, Tim Slessor himself was set to (partially) participate, but a last-minute health scare intervened, thrusting his grandson, Nat, to be his replacement, leading to a joyous reunion of the pair at Dover.

By the 1980s, the Camel Trophy event elevated overlanding challenges for the next twenty years, adopting the sub-title of 'The Olympics for 4x4s'. Commercial overlanders started to operate from the 1960s. Using trucks, groups plied the Cape to Cairo, Asian and North African routes, depending on global security. Today, the internet is awash with information, forums and travel options. Our journey sought to explore the slow road, as we were fascinated by the geology and both the flora and fauna of the continent. Initially, we thought to trek areas and the core peaks, as well as explore the more challenging routes between remote areas. I cashed in my return flight so our route remained flexible, sustained by our shared vision.

Inquisitiveness and exploration to push our boundaries is innate within the human DNA. Early man emerged from Africa, migrating through Arabia, before splitting east and west to Asia and Europe. There were no roads or predecessors to guide them. Today, people like Elon Musk and others want to commercialise space or colonialise Mars. The 18th century monk, Malthus, ventured his theory that 'war, death and pestilence' would keep the world in check. As I draft this, in another COVID lockdown, his insights appear increasingly pertinent. The World Wildlife Fund (WWF) charity publish an annual Living Planet report, implying that the world is consuming 'three times its own resources annually', with little appetite to curtail consumption.

But why Africa? Individual perceptions of the African continent will vary significantly, depending on experience, exposure or life's value set. The modern trend of championing singular issues, to redress perceived historical inequalities and/or diversity are being fanned through social media. Some look to redress the inequalities of slavery, colonialism or exploitation; each admirable and understandable, although perhaps they ought to be seen within the context or mores of the day. Perhaps it's more important to 'play what is ahead'. We may rail against colonialism, yet China has quietly been acquiring the majority of raw materials across the continent, whilst the West frets about the cost of empire, the rise of the mega city and immigration. There is a modern-day scramble - China and Russia, under the guise of 'outreach and support' from the Wagner Group, seek to influence or permeate instability. The vacuum post-colonialism breathed life into non-state actors, such as AQIM or the Islamic Front. The Arab spring revolution arose from populist issues that destabilised and overthrew established authorities, legitimate or otherwise.

What was and remains key to us, in this book, is not to judge, but to observe and comment; akin to author and presenter, Simon Reeve, who states in his Step by Step book, that he seeks to highlight the 'light and shade' of an issue or place. Readers can then judge or reflect against their own belief systems and knowledge. This was never more apparent than Catherine's father, Brian, who looked upon Africa as 'the dark continent'. His frequent saying was, 'Nothing good will ever come from it.' More's the pity, for our own view was one of positivity; the continent remains a vibrant and dynamic region, however challenged, populated by amazing people co-existing alongside unique and stunning flora and fauna. All parts of the globe are under both climate pressures and the exponential rise of humanity; change remains a constant.

Perhaps Catherine and I grew up under a 'Hollywood' veneer and innocence about the wonders of the world, compared to today's darker, more gritty social media construct. We had no wildlife programmes like Frozen or Blue Planet; just Tarzan, Daktari or Born Free, although Jacques Cousteau inspired us all to become marine biologists. Our education remained focused on British medieval kings and queens, or glacial U-shaped valleys and oxbow lakes. Ironically, we witnessed the same Cambridge syllabus being taught at a Kenyan school in 2002, ignoring their own rich and diverse history and culture. African history changed with the arrival of Westerners with their gunpowder. Times have changed and self-determination rightly grows. Today's Africa is dominated by climate, population and health issues. Survival remains at the extremes; subsistence is a limited tool to ward off famine, Ebola or AIDS.

The internet delivers so more information now, both for communications, research and chronicling events; more than a bunch of National Geographic or Land Rover International periodicals that we had. Empty spaces on the map (terror incognito) do not exist. Most overlanders usually have a journey or goal in mind, getting from A to B. One could race London to Cape Town (or anywhere) and get flown around the gnarly parts. We read about a grandmother, who in 2016 drove from South Africa in her Toyota Corolla to 'take tea with the Queen at Buckingham Palace'. Some choose motorbikes or cycles; I recently read Helen Lloyd's 2009 enlightening cycle from London to Cape Town in her Desert Snow – One Girls Take on Africa by Bike. Some trips are very private; others seek to show off or raise charity funds, indeed both. Recently, a 26-year-old man from Worthing, self-named the 'hardest geezer', has just run a marathon a day to be the fastest running between Cape Town to Cap Blanc in Tunisia. Russell Cook undertook the challenge to turn his life around; as a self-confessed fat bloke with gambling and alcohol issues, someone will beat his record.

Our overland story was a personal journey to realise our dream, partly self-discovery and exploration. It was also a reconnection between us, having been separated through work. We can all erect the mental barriers, articulating great reasons why we should not do something, but if the pull or justification is sufficiently compelling, people can achieve so much. For anyone who knows Catherine, once she sets her mind to achieve something, she is rational, yet unstoppable.

There are a number of reasons why I have put pen to paper now, aside from the raft of coalescing activities and incidents. Although we kept diaries and wrote a website as we travelled, ostensibly to help others on the road at that time, we were fascinated by the people we met along the way. The extended time gap between our trip and today, the relevance and inter-related links within our Hampshire village became too strong to ignore. Other people's trips have commonality, yet each trip is individual, personal and different. The year of travel matters little (other than major global events, technology and equipment may vary), but the physical effort of being on the road, seeing new things, places and people never dims. The politeness and helpfulness of strangers never ceases to wonder, no matter how cynical one is.

The yearning to write this book has been a need to scratch that itch. The more I was reading other stories and trips about the African continent, the more it increased the desire to share our experiences. We wanted to share the thoughts from people we met along our route, and how ours and other journeys inter-relate. Our travels have become the cordial thread along which we interweave the shared travel events. These recollections are ours, from our diary, yet remain liable to personal interpretation and fragility or misinterpretation in storytelling. Clearly, the global 'pause' of lockdown was the precipitous event that generated the first draft; and then a second event, relating to the death of Catherine's father, made us reflect on the depth within people, compared to what we see on the surface.

We had read many classic overlanding tales. A few books stood out, like Charles Jacoby's classic, In Search of Will Carling. He travelled with a crowd of rugby fans, cavorting through west and southern Africa in time for the 1995 Rugby World Cup in Cape Town. Already a writer, with an editor chasing a manuscript, it must have been an easy clincher to publish his book, unlike Paul Marketos. Paul's 1998 book, Malachite, A Journey in Africa, documented a bunch of 'green' students working it out on the road in their Bedford lorry. Their route interestingly took them up through Algeria, a country that was synonymous with early overlanders, but later became closed to foreigners. Many journalists end up writing books; they are sent to interesting places, have an inquisitive gene and honed storytelling skills. They also have access to editors and the industry. Seminal among these are Tim Butcher's Blood River or Alec Russell's Big Men Little People, both insightful books of their genre. Celebrities already have their following, but it can be a risk to veer away from what they are renowned. Yet celebrities open doors, have enablers to ensure their transit and often have a TV crew capturing their persona. Michael Palin has become synonymous with travel journalism; ironically he was travelling around North Africa at a similar time, as were Ewan McGregor and Charlie Bormann, who embarked on the Long Way Down a few years later.

There is no single answer or solution for career changes from the forces, for it reflect a microcosm of society. The mix of skills are as broad as the people; a nuclear engineer on submarines is unlikely to have the same outlook or skill set as say a tank driver or an air traffic controller. Neither does the aviator have to continue flying once they've left and the demand for tank commanders or gunners in commerce is likely limited. Aside from tangible skills learnt, all military have undergone some form of selection. Anyone with a length of service has considerable, intangible competencies around leadership, problem-solving, adapting and thriving in difficult, convoluted issues on operations, with people and clients. Most are team players. You might be forgiven for thinking it, but not all paratroopers become adventurers. That said, our competitive cohort does breed people who overachieve. In recent years, rowing the Atlantic has become the latest endurance challenge. I was recently reunited with Peter Ketley (sadly, at a funeral) who, with Neil Young, undertook the 2018 Talisker Whiskey Atlantic Challenge. These regimental, super-achiever grandads were sponsored across the 3,000 miles, emulating the earlier spirit of 1966 of Captain John Ridgeway and Sergeant (now Sir) Chay Blyth, or Tom McClean a few years later. Or today's younger explorers, Ed Stafford and Levison Wood who emerged to acclaim. The regiment does select and imbue those with a determined spirit, relevant for both business and adventure.

Mike, a regimental friend, has run a monthly business networking group in a London club for many years. Being an infrequent attendee, one event in 2013 caught my eye, for a young captain who was leaving and was drumming up support for his 'Walk the Nile' adventure. I dug out my copy of Lost Lion of Empire; The Life of 'Cape-to-Cairo' Grogan; Ewart Grogan DSO, 1876-1976 to give to him, to support him and wish him well. Grogan had been quite a character: a soldier, explorer, pioneer, entrepreneur and politician extraordinaire, his life needs no enlarging or exaggeration. Shunning an expected Cambridge education and early political connections, Grogan scarpered to Africa to fight alongside Cecil Rhodes in the Matebele War (1896). He sought to prove himself and win the hand (or rather, paternal approval) of his intended fair maiden, so Grogan walked the length of Africa, from the Cape to the Nile. He was fêted by the press, the youngest man to address the Royal Geographical Society and presented a Union Jack flag to Queen Victoria. He went on to become the 'Churchill of Kenya', topping his glittering East African colonial career as the Governor of East Africa after the Second World War. Critically, he secured his intended's hand in marriage.

Entering the club, there was quite a crowd. The usual bonhomie prevailed when Mike tapped me on the shoulder and said, 'Adrian, I've got to shoot off to a meeting; can I ask you to introduce Levison?' 'Sure, no problem.' I ducked into the library to introduce myself. Lev was a confident fellow and fully aware of Grogan. During my introduction, I handed him the book, wishing him success on his mission and to win the hand of a fair maiden and plaudits. It appears I was correct; years later, it is wonderful to see Levison Wood flourish, with a pantheon of books, films and media. As for the ladies, I think Lev has that covered.

Land Rover has a strong brand recognition and heritage that enthusiasts relish, whilst seeking to 'tread lightly'. Land Rover is synonymous with country folk as our utilitarian workhorse. So why would we choose an alternative vehicle for our trip? The military were swift to adopt and adapt Land Rovers. Once old enough to reach the peddles, a Land Rover was the first vehicle I drove in the Army Cadets. Catherine's father learnt to drive as a national serviceman in a Land Rover after the war in Germany and later used them for his field study work as a scientist with the Ministry of Agriculture and Fisheries. His constant refrain when teaching Catherine was, if he could drive a Land Rover in boots or waders, then she should be able to drive a car. I'm not sure how much that helped, but Catherine had driven many Land Rovers since.

Land Rover owners appreciate that their vehicles have foibles. As a newly promoted captain in 2 PARA, I assumed command of the patrols platoon that came with six half-tonne lightweight Land Rovers. The average build date for these vehicles was in the mid-1950s. Yet two stripped down Land Rovers could be 'piggy backed' on a parachute frame (Medium Stressed Platform, MSP) and parachuted from a C130 Hercules aircraft. But they were seldom used, so we thought to test them whilst training at Otterburn, some 350 miles north of Aldershot. Three never made it out of camp, one broke down at the camp gates and another on the M25! The final go-cart arrived and performed admirably, yet clearly could not carry 50 odd blokes. So much for the 'cutting-edge' of the British Army; as expected, we tabbed. When questioning their age and suitability, the response was, 'Well, if you do throw them out of aircraft...'

After commanding a rifle company years later with no mobility, I then assumed command of support company, 2 PARA, where I had too many vehicles. We received the brand-new Wolf Land Rovers and the new, much prized Pinzgauers for the mortars. Unsurprisingly, we were not allowed to parachute these vehicles unless for 'operational use'. We set about trialling a new concept of operating, conferring an element of mobility and firepower and an opportunity to play with Land Rovers.

The MoD has always equipped the last conflict. Whilst UK forces were engaged in Iraq and Afghanistan, Snatch Land Rovers were again under the spotlight. The Urgent Operational Requirement (UOR) acquisition process brought upgrades, usually too late. To be fair, the airborne brigade did OK, although I know the Falklands' veterans sought better equipment, if only better boots. During this UOR period, I recall walking the dogs over the sand dunes at Broughton Burrows in Devon with Catherine one weekend, five or so years after leaving the forces. Suddenly, a Jackal came roaring over the dunes. 'What the .... was that?' Then a voice shouted, 'Hello boss, want a go?' Having left, one of my lads was working with industry and was responsible for UOR testing on the Jackal. What a great mobile weapons platform, suitable for the proposed hot destination, yet there was absolutely no protection from the elements - no change there then.

It is a perennial challenge to provide equipment for every environment or mission. Industry charge premium prices for cutting-edge technology, as you cannot buy a battleship, combat aircraft or submarine off the supermarket shelf. Once visiting the MoD procurement centre at Abbey Wood, I learnt that a basic, commercial Land Rover needs thousands spending on it, to align it to MoD specification. The spec required a fully-laden vehicle and trailer to travel at 30 miles per hour cross-country and 50 miles per hour down a motorway. So, after removing the aircon, radio, commercial items, reducing the bake and suspension capacity to match the design specification, and then fitting various communications or operational needs, it overlooks the user mentality. Imagine the end of training; everyone wants to get back to base, clean up and disperse. The military commander, who likely has been awake for days, inevitably nods off after telling the driver to take it easy. Most Land Rovers obey the speed limits, but when failing to do so, and the tired driver hit the brakes at anything over 50 miles per hour, the Land Rover would (and did) flip. Thankfully, contracts have been rectified, but nothing should be taken at face value. Today, I am horrified to learn that Land Rovers are no longer used by the military; I now see hired white Ford

Transit vans tactically trying to hide themselves on training areas as we walk our dogs.

Prior to our African trip, Land Rover was already losing market share to Asian competitors. Around 2002, Land Rover introduced the new TD5 Series, with smart electronic ignition and engine management. It improved starting and cruising on highways, providing more power, better emissions and grunt to engage the rough stuff. We benefited from a freebie TD5 90 in Cape Town and loved it when running around town. Whilst aimed at the US market, should there be a technical breakdown, a factory computer reset was required. Evidently this would preclude 'bush repairs'; Land Rover were not going to drive to the breakdown site in the Kalahari. The African solution was to retain the traditional Rest of World (ROW) 300 series TDI engine.

By 2006, we were living on the west coast of America, when fuel prices doubled to less than half that in the UK, to great uproar. Land Rovers were pricey then and needed adaptation to stringent US market regulations. You couldn't buy diesel variants, for any vehicle, as there was no diesel. In Seattle, we joined the North West Pacific Land Rover Club (NWPLRC), whose owners had a fine range of pre-owned American Land Rovers. One chap's lovely Porsche 911 was cheaper than his mint Land Rover 90. I'm delighted to report that brand recognition is alive and well in the US, with considerable waving and headlight flashing. I wanted to buy an old Country Range Rover Classic but had to settle for a Series II Discovery. This came with a stock American 4-litre petrol engine that transformed the vehicle, delivering greater power over a diesel. Ironically, having bought the Disco, our friend, Mason, finally relented and offered us his mint Country Range Rover, lovingly restored and re-engineered (sorry Mason, too late). We headed into the Rockies back country and, on more than one occasion, we were up to our necks in deep snow. We got a wonderful PR picture with a LR 90, a Range Rover and our Disco, should the media/PR folk at JLR be interested?

Chapter 3
Daphne gets her kit on

Speaking to Catherine from Pretoria, who was still working in the UK, I announced that we had a new, white purchase on the driveway. 'Wonderful,' she beamed over the phone, 'you've bought Daphne.' Following a prolonged silence and probably my delayed, 'What?', I received the only too logical explanation that Daphne was to be our 'ship of the desert'; she therefore had to be female. To see us through our various trials and tribulations, she should be named after the ever capable 'Daphne' from the TV sitcom, Frasier. A husband knows there are those occasions when he cannot argue in the face of predetermined logic.

Johannesburg has a vibrant second-hand 4x4 market. Purchased from a private seller, Daphne appeared to be a well-maintained, cherished vehicle. Now our trip became tangible and real; no more talk or aspiration. Catherine was still finalising her work in the UK, whilst pulling together our administration, documents, visas and medical requirements. This was no small task, as visa information alone (in those pre-digital years) was a minefield. Gathering the required drugs for an extended period was another challenge, especially anti-malarials. In the military, the regiment practically lived on paludrine and nivaquine, although for one tour we were given larium. Many had unwanted side effects. We sourced malarone in South Africa for our trip. Catherine's biggest (and self-imposed) challenge was creating our website. Before commercial web packages were available, Catherine taught herself HTML and wrote the site framework. Neither of us are especially technically minded but we were both amazed with the outcome.

Daphne was a 1998, white Land Rover 110 Defender County, 300 Series Tdi, Rest of the World (ROW) export model. Complete with air-con (an unexpected bonus that was never used), she was one of the last base 300 Tdi series, prior to the TD5 electronic engines. Of the many configurations between double-cab or Crew Cab, our classic 4-door County Station Wagon variant offered the optimum layout and visibility. A surprising and welcome phenomenon arose immediately; we had joined the 'Land Rover fraternity'. We initially wondered why every other Land Rover out on the road was flashing their lights and waving at us. Did we have a problem? Had something fallen off? Land Rovers are common in the UK as opposed to just having a leisure-orientated focus, and we had not experienced this ownership/brand fanfare.

First, we needed to assess Daphne's mechanical health. It was fully conceivable that Daphne would be more than competent to complete our trip in her 'vanilla state', including getting off the beaten track. Vehicle choice is always a balance of compromise, although Toyota (both the bakkie and Land Cruiser) and Land Rovers score highly on any such list. Toyota's dominance in South Africa (at Land Rover's expense) along with Isuzu, was credit to their extensive dealer networks, pricing and reliability, although Land Rover, for us, still retained the pedigree and familiarity we sought.

Daphne quickly proved her mettle; one of her foibles was the slow, wet drip onto the driver's foot during and after rain. We were satisfied that we had a robust, basic Land Rover. An expedition vehicle must reliably carry a load and sustain the crew for an extended period in remote areas; we did not want a flash weekend warrior that needed a recovery for the next trip. Daph had a reliable engine, a strong core frame, with superior axel articulation and suspension, conferring a superior ride. The absence of body plastics or mouldings facilitated a wide range of after-market accessories, although the true merits of each addition is a minefield. Sorting through these takes both experience, research and a huge dollop of savvy. The after-market options in South Africa were in excess of anything in the UK and included Australian products. After a month in South Africa, my colleagues wanted to visit the annual Outventure Show in Johannesburg, where all travel and related vendors promote their wares. I was delighted; it was a great show. Southern Africa offers a wonderful playground for adventurous travel, ranging from family getaways and mega-luxury, through to bare bones travel, coastal or bush adventures. Outventure markets the full gamut of options and for me, the 'extras' after-market. One could go bonkers; thankfully I had done my research.

Aside from my Land Rover experience, I was guided by two seminal books, Tom Sheppard's Vehicle-Dependent Expedition Guide and Chris Scott's Sahara Overland. Both remain as relevant today as then. Tom's later RAF career focused on testing and exploring the globe's remote areas (lucky fella) to teach survival and mobility. His book was precise and prescriptive about what was good and bad. It was not his opinion, but his experience, backed by science. Now a Land Rover brand ambassador, Tom has driven all marques and types over the years. His book focused on the planning and execution of a vehicle-based expedition. Not everything was relevant for us, but the vehicle aspects were excellent, notably, the daily vehicle check routine. Chris Scott's book was wonderful, based on experience and objectivity and more focussed on motorbikes in the desert. We were not (then) planning on a Sahara crossing; maybe we should have paid more attention.

Our copy of Tom's book was written in 1998 and much of the technology facts related to 20th century kit and equipment. Modern technical advances do not invalidate basic principles; the insight to fresh water in the Sahara has not changed since the 10th century, no matter how advanced a computer might be - the science is the science. Rest assured, Tom's 2020 edition addresses all advancements, notably swapping radios for mobile and satellite solutions. Today, the internet is awash with how to pimp your ride, but the core fundamentals do not change; good equipment will make or break an expedition.

I do not intend to replicate these books here, but our transit was mainly dry bush, savannah and latterly desert, with some wet tarmac at either end. Our website (https://daphneoverland.co.uk) was written as we travelled to guide and support other travellers at the time, although it includes our vehicle's additions in detail. We added our considered top ten tips, as well as the bottom ten, for we did not get everything right. We knew we were carrying too much stuff, given our starting circumstance, yet people have a tendency to fill the space. In the Parachute Regiment, if you couldn't carry it, it didn't go, hence the 'travel light, freeze at night' maxim. Catherine was far too sensible; she enjoys camping, yet hates the cold and sensibly likes her comforts.

With the confirmation of Daphne's health assured from Land Rover, we thought about augmentations. First, we shipping the alloys home; alloys are vulnerable off-road. Whilst light to reduce weight, one pothole can ruin an alloy rim. The stronger Wolf steel rims can - critically - be repaired. Good tyres are also essential; we fitted new tubeless BF Goodrich ATs. We learnt that tubeless tyres could be repaired with a rubber 'bung', plugged through the hole with appropriate glue, like threading a needle. But tubed tyres need the inner tube repairing, and 'breaking the tyre bead' off the rim is a massive undertaking without the powered machines used in tyre shops. Reinflation also becomes an issue; most after-market compressors are incapable of asserting, or popping, a new tyre onto the rim. Whilst you can use the 'lighter fuel and fire' method to blow the rim back on in extremis, it's a lot more hassle compared to the five-minute plug system, especially if you want to retain your eyebrows. Quality and robust tyres are key; prevention is the best cure with careful driving. Daphne came with Blistein shocks and standard OME springs. Blistein are a quality after-market shock, although Land Rover wanted to uprate the rear with OME 130 heavy duty shocks and springs. The Land Rover's rear door is vulnerable, so fitting a rear swing-away arm to take the spare wheel weight alleviates stresses on the door and enhances protection. We learnt of a new latex product called 'treadseal' which, when pumped in through the value and spun, it's supposed to reseal small holes and thorn punctures, plus it assists with retaining tyre pressure; we thought it helped.

Our Land Rover mechanic linked me to Heine at B'rakhah 4x4, local to me in Pretoria. Heine and Kobus were passionate about the big outdoors and loved escorting customers into the bush. They also had a dive shop; I was sorely tempted to join their latest Mozambique jaunt. Heine was a huge bloke (an 'Oak' in the local parlance), probably too big to prop for the Springboks. He had a very gentle manner and naturally preferred larger vehicles, as was evident when he squeezed himself in behind the wheel of Daph for a test drive. His knees straddled the steering wheel and there was insufficient headroom, forcing his neck to bend sideways. Yet he stated he preferred the Land Rover's superior off-road agility and comfort; hard to reconcile when seeing him squashed in the driving seat. Very business focused and analytical, Heine rightly refused to spend money on gadgets that didn't work. This was reflected in their own range of products, made to a high quality at competitive prices.

The B'rakhah roof rack was lightweight, solid and common with all racks, is bolted within the drain gully. Carrying weight high runs contrary to the overarching principle of maintaining a low centre of gravity (CoG). Tom Sheppard is vociferous about this, yet most expeditions erroneously pile weight high. If you must have high weight, use a (internal or external) roll cage to transfer the weight onto the chassis. Cages are expensive, add extra weight and can be obtrusive. It's best to pack the weight inside and low, leaving light, bulky items on the rack. Sleeping high in the bush has advantages; one avoids the creepy crawlies, snakes and discourages lions, especially with the bonnet up. A roof tent keeps the bedding safe and clean, tucked inside the folded tent. Once flipped open, a full, firm double mattress and headspace is revealed with elevated views. They are quick and easy to erect and are self-supporting with an integral flysheet; no poles or guys ropes to trip over. In the morning, it is a quick reversal by pushing the ladder up, the tent concertinas and tucks neatly away. Despite the extra weight and increased centre of gravity, they are a real game changer; we loved it. Catherine was sold straight away and we plumped for the gold standard Eezi-Awn. We ratcheted our aluminium camping table (inside its bespoke sleeve) over the roof tent to further condense the profile and wind resistance.

Before buying the Eezi-Awn, we tested Heine's alternative during our test run, sleeping in a free-standing, geodesic tent up on the B'rakhah rack. The tent was easy to flip up, but we considered it cramped and the surface firm. It worked for short trips. B'rakhah's integrated awning was simplicity itself: two light, aluminium arms swung out from the rack and were self-supported. It only took a minute to unfurl and replace, although an inertia reel system would have been cleaner. Shade could be adjusted by moving the vehicle. We fitted a double gas bottle holder on the rear. Southern Africa uses a low-pressure gas bottle system unlike the European higher-pressure alternative, upon which we could screw a diffuser plate, forming a simple but very effective cooking platform.

Fuel and water are heavy; Tom Sheppard believed both should be stored low, inside the vehicle, but this can leave fumes inside the cabin. To avoid confusion, especially in the dark, we used green metal jerry cans for fuel and black plastic cans for water. Four water cans slotted snugly behind the passenger seats. Daphne had a standard 80-litre fuel tank and B'rakhah fitted an integrated extended 45-litre tank behind the right rear bodywork that was fabulous and faultless. This enabled around 1,000 miles range of bush travel. On the rack, I fitted two double jerry can holders, retaining four (empty) 20-litre jerry cans locked down by rubberised baskets to prevent wear and rattling, for emergencies only. I discussed the notion of hanging jerry cans either side of the rear windows, to reduce our CoG; a simple foot bracket along the ledge at the base of the backside windows could take the weight. The cans would also protect the vulnerable rear windows at the same time. Heine loved the idea and set about manufacturing a trial bracket. It marginally increased the vehicle width, protruding no more than the rear-view mirrors, but we did not pursue it in the end.

B'rakhah fitted a National Lunar split charging battery system that managed a secondary auxiliary battery, fitted under the passenger seat, with a monitor on the dash. Both batteries are charged when running; when static, all power was drawn from the spare, preserving the engine battery for starting. When the spare battery is drained, it alarms. It was an excellent system and powered our reliable 40-litre National Lunar fridge. We fitted six additional Hella plugs throughout the vehicle, including an external plug above the rear door for a rear spot lamp or a power shower system. Finally, we wired a Bush Buddy air compressor under the bonnet for tyre inflation.

We stripped out the rear bench seats and replaced a single jump seat behind the front passenger seat, should we need to carry a guide or in an emergency. We mounted the fridge centrally, behind the cubby box, with access from both the front and driver's side door. We sat the fridge on a small, raised platform over the footwell, under which we fabricated a second safe that was hidden under carpet. A more obvious safe was under the raised cubby box between the front seats. We recarpeted, for this was cheap and needed doing. We forged an aluminium frame with a cargo net to stop items flying forward from the rear area, but could also poke long items through if necessary. A tie-down net held items in place. In first, we packed four black 20-litre water jerry cans, ratcheted down behind the fridge. Next, the six plastic Wolf Pack boxes slotted in neatly, over which chairs and extra equipment laid, under the net. Our packing system constantly evolved but the basic idea was sound and worked throughout.

We debated underbody protection which, to me, added unnecessary weight; we were not planning to rock-hop down canyons. Daphne came with a protective steering bar and bull bar. A sump guard would probably have been helpful, but we went without. We ditched the tow bar and fitted high tensile JATE bolts through the recovery points, front and rear. The rear passenger windows had a tendency to slip down, as the window handles can get progressively nudged. I thought to remove the handles but Heine held them in place with strong rubber bands that worked amazingly well. The rear sliding windows are a major weak point and can easily be jemmied, even when a stick or something is lain within the internal window frame gully.

We covered the windows with an aluminium mesh frame, which would have worked with the hanging jerry can concept. Heine recommended a simple seed net. He had spent hours picking seeds from his radiator to get home on a 'long' Botswana trip, so was a big fan. Driving at night is best avoided but Daphne came fitted with two 100-Watt Hella spotlights mounted on the bull bar and integrally wired to the full beam headlamps. When camping, we carried head torches, but rarely needed them as we had a portable light wand, powered from the auxiliary battery, that was excellent. It had a long cable to hang it remotely and illuminate a wide area, plus a yellow film covering emitting a soft, yellow light that did not attract the bugs or mozzies. We removed Daphne's internal light bulbs to avoid an open door draining the battery erroneously.

A front-mounted electric or hydraulic winch is a classic pimp product. We thought long and hard about the Warn electrical winch and integral front bumper. More nose weight would require reinforced front suspension and longer hydraulic brake cables. Plus, 60 pounds more front-end weight would only increase our propensity to get stuck. We settled for a hand operated Tirfor winch with a 10-metre steel cable that was excellent. We carried a Hi-Lift jack on the front of the bull bar, which could double as a Tirfor-style winch along with its core lifting function. Hi-Lifts are great, but they have a tendency to bite back nastily on the unwary. We found a natty set of track mats instead of traditional sand ladders; these were light, metal rolls akin to a rope ladder that proved equally effective as sand ladders. We carried standard recovery straps, snatch straps, pulleys and shackles and two shovels, plus a useful panga for wood chopping and general use. Snatch straps are excellent, as they have elasticity and kinetic energy to pop a stuck vehicle out of its predicament. They need another vehicle, something we were lacking, but on the premise it gave us extra reach, it offered the ability to use another vehicle should one present itself.

Spares were a whole other world. Tom Sheppard's list of spares was comprehensive, yet it felt excessive. Parts would be available en route, and in any event, on a reduced list, you could guarantee the part you needed would be the one you omitted! Further, if you assumed X or Y was weak, so carried a spare, again, Sod's Law would apply and the non-obvious part would break. Weight and space on a single vehicle trip is a factor. Mechanical knowledge or ability can be mitigated with knowledge and tools; your average bush mechanic is very resourceful. We hoped that the indispensable Haynes Manual would see us through. A stout canvas bag contained tools that packed well and prevented rattles and abrasion during transit. Spares and fluids were packed under the driver's seat and within a Wolf Pack box. Prevention is better than repair, as drummed home by Tom. We carried a small fire extinguisher in the front and a larger one in the rear. We knew we had too much stuff. We had a complete box full of books and walking/mountaineering gear which we didn't use in the end. We had small grab bags and immediate access items with our clothes, packed within a small, squashy duffel bag, plus a set of best. These bags were behind each other's respective seats as personal space, which worked well. Accessible water was important. We found a five-litre container that slotted neatly behind the passenger's seat, with our 'immediate box' containing lunch/snacks, plates, cutlery and so forth, making any admin stop slick.

Tom's book scared us about water and the need to purify everything. In the military, we used sterilisation tablets or boiled it. Steri tabs always left an unpleasant taste; we carried loads but didn't use any. We had a camping kettle with a whistling cap for the gas burner that was fabulous, boiling frequent cups of tea. We carried a storm kettle; a cylinder within a cylinder, where the inner chamber burns kindling that rapidly boils water in the outer cylinder. As the name suggests, it works in all weathers. Developing the prevention theme, near B'rakhah, I found Tommy Dent and his shop, H20, selling home kitchen water purifiers. Tommy was ex-military and excited about our trip, so I asked him to fashion a filter system within a Wolf Pack, with pumps and hoses that could run on vehicle power. We had a couple of trial versions, each one smaller and more powerful. In shower mode, it would have consumed our available water in seconds. Sadly, when we tried to use the product in anger in Tanzania, it failed – sorry Tommy, I am sure version five would have been better!

Part 2

SOUTHERN AFRICA

"In Africa, you have space... there is a profound sense of space here, space and sky."

Thabo Mbeki

Elephants at Etosha

Dune 45, Sossusvlei

Top of Sani Pass

Deadvlei

Fish River Canyon

Bloedkoppie

43

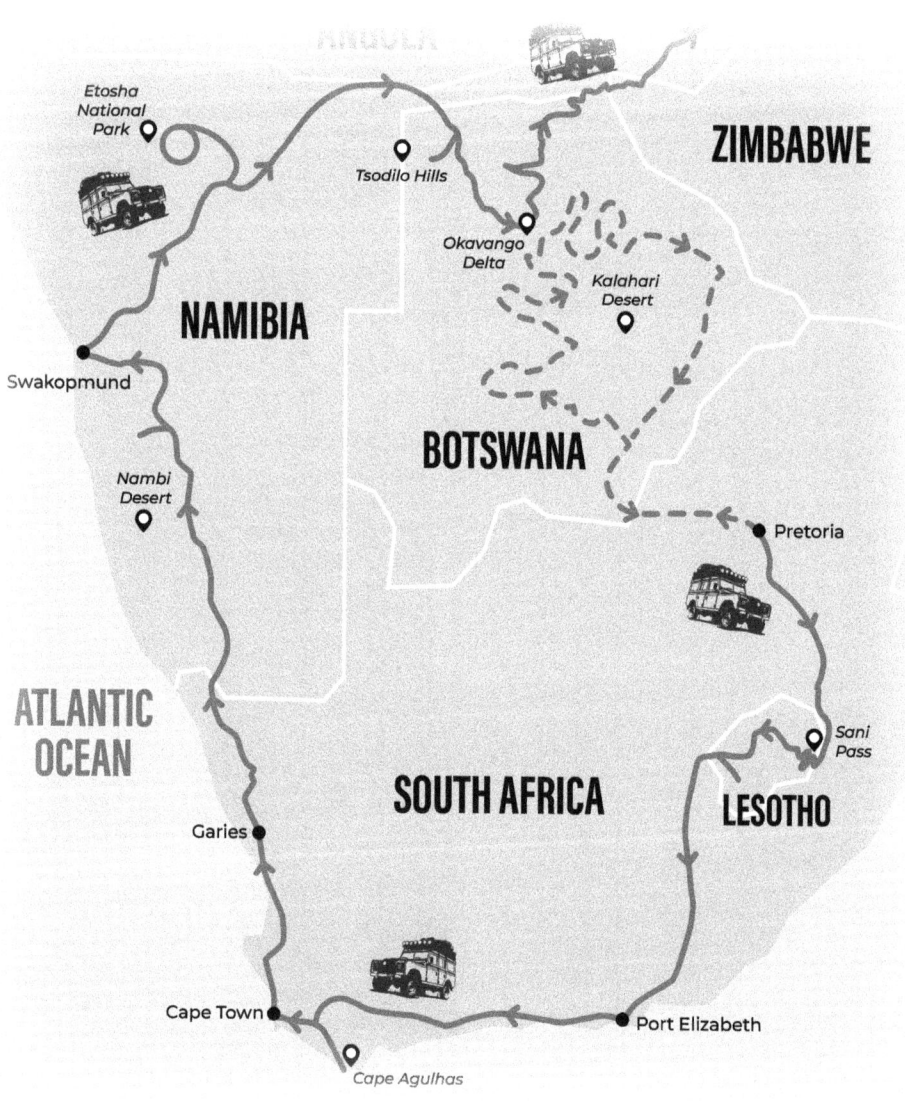

Etosha
National
Park

Tsodilo Hills

ZIMBABWE

Okavango
Delta

Kalahari
Desert

NAMIBIA

Swakopmund

BOTSWANA

Nambi
Desert

Pretoria

ATLANTIC
OCEAN

Garies

SOUTH AFRICA

Sani
Pass

LESOTHO

Cape Town

Port Elizabeth

Cape Agulhas

Chapter 4
Kalahari rehearsal

'Brake!' I cried, sitting in the passenger seat, stamping on the imaginary brake pedal. 'OK, don't shout at me,' Catherine snapped back, still hurtling up a steep mud ramp. The idea was to stop just before the peak, but I (and our 'white knuckled' instructor in the back) had visions of us careering over the top, Dukes-of-Hazard style, in a Land Rover. Thankfully, Catherine stopped at the crest to execute the practice manoeuvre at the off-road training centre, just outside Johannesburg. The prescribed emergency drill ('failed ascent procedure') uses engine braking from a stall, to enable a controlled reverse recovery, should you have insufficient power or momentum to crest a hill. We assume modern car brakes would be sufficient in such circumstances, but for a laden 4x4 on a steep ramp, applying the brake on a descent could flip the vehicle. Catherine is an excellent, focused driver with Land Rover experience, although like most of us, not under extreme circumstances. The expected rebuff for me to shut up came; Catherine engaged reverse, released the hand brake and lifted her feet away, allowing the gears and gravity to recover the vehicle; it takes a leap of faith. It is invariably hard for a close relative, especially a spouse, to teach their partner anything; numerous skiing arguments reminded me of that. The course was a no brainer - aside from some fun and practicing those rarely executed procedures, completion of the course reduced our vehicle insurance premium. Run by a British couple who drove south ten years earlier, the course was packed with ideas and tips. We loved getting stuck in swamps, wading through rivers, assessing routes whilst rock hopping, building confidence in Daphne and ourselves; basically doing all the things we hoped to avoid.

Catherine and I bicker at the best of times, each assured we are 'correct', but how would this play out over six months? We needed a test-run to acquaint ourselves with Daph, our gear and, critically, our own ability. But where to go? The southern Africa options were endless. Europeans invariably head for Morocco as it is sufficiently different, is only a ferry trip across the Mediterranean and drivers remain covered on their EU Green Card. In one of life's ironies, we have longed to visit Morocco, yet years later, it still remains on the growing aspirational list. We knew Heine and Kobus were diving Mozambique's coast over Christmas and whilst welcome to join-in, their recommendation was of sterner stuff – Botswana's Central Kalahari Game Reserve and the Makgadikgadi Pans. Perfect! We had to cross borders and endure the hot summer, where conditions were exacerbated by unseasonal rainfall, causing excessively tall grasses. As South Africa practically closes down for their summer December holidays, the majority of the (predominantly white) population descend upon the Cape. We needed to move fast to secure options over the enforced two-week break, and crucially Heine's contacts and knowledge secured a brilliant itinerary in the nick of time.

Botswana is amazing for the adventurous traveller. Our last visit was full-on luxury, flying in and out of the Okavango Delta, so naturally we loved it. But this trip was not about comfort; we needed to know if we could function and thrive on the road. The Kalahari Desert covers around 80% of Botswana and is reputed to be the single largest desert expanse on earth - larger than the mighty Sahara. The Central Kalahari Game Reserve (CKGR) was established in 1961 and covers 52 square kilometres. Conflict between farmers and game hunters led to the erection of veterinary cordon fences, to control the spread of foot and mouth disease and rinderpest. The reserve was extensively explored, largely by De Beers, for diamonds and mining potential, so remained closed for many years. Today, the Central Kalahari offers refuge for the indigenous San people to continue their hunter-gatherer lifestyle, although only around 1,000 bushmen pursue their traditional way of life - a dwindling, disenchanted number.

The geological shift split of Gondwandaland, around 100 million years ago, left the Kalahari as one of three major water basins within the newly formed African continent. Subsequent glacial drying from Antarctica (five million years ago) left the area dry and barren. Two million years later, after more geological faulting, it left two great lakes, the Okavango and Makgadikgadi. Faulting 20,000 years ago caused these lakes to drain north, then east, flooding the Zambezi River, the resultant outflow gouging the Victoria Falls Gorge that we recognise today. The geological link from this draining was the Boteti River, now a mere trickle after thousands of years drying. Today, the Makgadikgadi are the largest salt-water pans in the world.

As Catherine flew in from the UK, we had a wedding anniversary to celebrate. Located on the Magaliesberg Ridge that runs west from Pretoria, near Hartbeespoortdam, is the Elephant Sanctuary. It is rearing five orphaned, wild female African elephants, rescued from hunters from the Tuli Block (Botswana) that sadly had taken their herd. I had arranged our first night at the Sanctuary which educates visitors about elephant behaviour. A few selected guests are permitted to walk with, feed and groom the elephants and, as Catherine has held a long fascination and love for these majestic, intelligent animals, she was thrilled. On arrival, we walked with, then fed and brushed down the elephants, before bedding them down. They knew the routine and slept in a giant, stone hut. After a few sundowners and a delicious meal in the boma, we too settled down and listened to the rumbling and breathing of the elephants on the other side of the stone wall.

At first light, we woke the sleepy heads. The door to their quarters had a huge, steel sliding gate that required at least three men to manhandle it shut at night. Not so the following morning; the keeper slipped the chain before standing back. Clearly a party trick, one Nelly simply flicked open the gate with her trunk as though it was a matchstick. Still juveniles, these were powerful animals. Walking with them was special, but grooming them was amazing. The hairs on their leathery skin were like receptive piano wires, the backs of their ears emulating the softest chamois leather. That was a very memorable stay.

The next day, we needed to cross the Botswanan border. En route, Daph's speedo cable snapped. Having replaced this in the service, it was irritating but we ignored it; it gave us a chance to play with our new handheld GPS, for which we started frantically reading the manual. Unlike modern smartphones, the route-finding clarity was rubbish; it was basically a compass, but as a substitute speedo, it was fabulous. Eventually, down a dusty track, we arrived at the Lobatse Gate and minutes later, after a scant review of paperwork, we were in Botswana. We planned to reach Gaborone, but the day was fading, as were we, so we sought to stay in downtown Lobatse. Applying potluck, we checked into The Cumberland Hotel that transpired to be the oldest establishment in Botswana. It was quite a night; despite the obvious dilapidations and former grandeur, inside there was a distinct party vibe underway. It had secure parking, a reasonable steak supper and a comfortable bed. Apparently, there was considerable (human) nocturnal activity throughout the night, although we were oblivious as we'd crashed out. In the morning, the Cumberland looked like a party war zone with bodies everywhere. We skipped breakfast and headed for Gaborone, a burgeoning metropolis of glass towers emerging from a quaint, colonial past. Gaborone was thronging with people on the move, so we didn't hang around; we needed to get to the park, for thanks to Heine's recommendations, we had an exacting itinerary that left little scope for slippage or misadventure. Over Christmas, the expensive campsites are heavily subscribed.

To visit the Kalahari, one needs to be totally self-sufficient; it is a pristine wilderness, unfettered by trappings or tourist paraphernalia. We were late entering the Khutse, the park's southern gate. Validating all our permits and documentation took an age, leaving an hour of sunlight for a sprint to our allotted campsite at Khankhe Pan. No time for game viewing or deviating from the path, though that was not possible; the soft, rutted sand tracks meant slow progress and the grasses were window height. Our campsite was a lone tree by a pan and little else. The silence and darkness were amazing, shivers of excitement keeping the hairs on the back of our necks alive. Familiarity and experience precludes any faffing about in the fading light, but thankfully, our lighting system worked well, notably the yellow film. Khutse translated as 'place to kneel down to drink'. The reeds surrounding us implied water in the vicinity, yet the ground was bone dry; we were astride an ancient water system that previously fed the Makgadikgadi Pan. Small, isolated pans around were abundant and attract game throughout the year. We had no idea how many eyes were looking back at us from the blackness, licking their lips as we pitched camp and made a meal.

Our next campsite was Piper Pans. The guidebook and Heine implied this would be a real struggle to make the distance in a single day, so we got moving early. The myriad of tracks that emanate from the De Beers mining concessions were poorly defined and frequently contained soft, heavy sand. We passed many abandoned San settlements, with only Mothomelo being occupied. We checked with the locals about our onward track, as the map and guidebook did not relate. It was a sobering insight into the plight of the San; these legendary, diminutive hunter-gatherers once roamed southern Africa, at one with their environment. There are few, if any, truly 'wild' bushmen remaining, the majority having resettled into villages and towns. Some have rebelled and sought refuge in their traditional life, but like those we met at

Mothomelo, they live a hybrid life between two cultures. The listless locals smelt of drink and cigarettes; it was not a hopeful sign. Dressed in tatty, Western garb, they were very friendly, spoke only a smattering of English and were insistent in demanding cigarettes, rather than Pula. Yet they were honest and helpfully pointed out our track, being nothing but courteous.

Our slow progress towards Piper Pans could have resulted in us being held overnight at the western Ranger Gate at Xade, but thankfully the park staff insisted we push on the last 70 kilometres to Piper Pans in the final hours of daylight. This was refreshing, although strange, especially when they reminded us that night driving was prohibited. If the road was as bad as the last stretch, we'd not make it, but it wasn't and we made Piper Pans in time. We arrived, tired and dusty, on Christmas Eve. We had two days to relax here in the centre of the Kalahari. Our pitch consisted of shade from a large acacia tree, under the vast expanse of clear African skies. The long reeds and grasses continued to frustrate game viewing; we heard lions calling throughout the night and saw scattered game at a distance. Apart from what looked like an old, empty nest in our acacia tree and remnants of a burnt-out fire hearth, the campsite appeared devoid of any other inhabitants. We gathered some firewood, erected our larger table and chairs and made Christmas more comfortable, enjoying a satisfying supper and welcome bottle of wine.

The morning view from our tent was fabulous and we were in for a surprise. The old, empty nest a metre away had a large egret perched upon it, being watched by nervous parents maintaining their vigil from a nearby tree. We shifted Daph as far away as we could so as not to intrude, for a few hours later, the second egret popped its head up. The Kalahari was very hot, airless and listless; little was stirring by day. Once dark, we turned in, only to be woken by a small convoy of vehicles screaming past on the tracks at around midnight, headlights on and horns honking. It was extremely disconcerting. The 'no driving at night' rule clearly meant nothing, but was impossible to enforce. This appeared more than getting from A to B - they were either hunting, smuggling or just joyriding. Who knows, but thankfully they didn't stop. We were silent and blacked out, so not readily visible, but we were not hidden; our light reflectors would have bounced back from any passing headlight. As is typical in the bush, any violent disruption and action soon settles down to calm silence immediately after.

On Boxing Day, we moved north to Deception Pans, where Mark and Delia Owens researched lions and brown hyenas, as documented in their book, Cry of the Kalahari. The expansive valley was littered with grazing ungulates, but apart from a fleeting glimpse of (what we hoped were) brown hyenas, the predators remained elusive. All very frustrating, as the spectacular, black-maned lions are reputed to be the finest in Africa. The airstrip was clear and functional, and offered the best location for longer game viewing. Our last few nights were spent at Sunday Pans within the northern valley. Being on a small ridge, this campsite was delightful as it offered a vista and caught a slight breeze. The expected abundant herds of gemsbok and springbok in this northern area were not seen, but this did not detract from the wonderful, wild experience.

The Kalahari was magical; it was one of the harshest and most desolate 'bush' experiences we've ever had. Our trial run was a success; we were still talking and felt some measure of achievement. Daph and our gear were thriving and we managed our resources well. We had sufficient water, but at Sunday Pan, we found a well pump that we thought could alleviate our dwindling water supply. The motor was simple enough, reminiscent of my father's old petrol motor mower. Fuel was in the tank; the plugs were engaged; we needed to cranked the handle to compress the motor that drove the belt to draw water. That was the theory, but after a sweaty hour of tinkering and cranking, nothing - apart from a higher consumption of existing water.

We exited the Northern Gate to transit into the Makgadikgadi Game Reserve and restock at Gweta, a small settlement of huts. We found the recommended Gweta Lodge somewhat dilapidated, although previously it had been a private hunting lodge for a wealthy owner. Vestiges of finery and past opulence existed, but our room was reasonable, as was the food. Clearly the pool clearly had not been used for many years, although we understood that later on, the Top Gear TV production crew centred themselves here for their Botswanan Challenge, as did Levison Wood, who walked through the Makgadikgadi to the Okavango on his 2019 Botswanan Walk with Elephants programme.

Lev Wood's trek was very evocative, stimulating delightful memories, but we thought he visited the area prior to a significant elephant phenomenon. Botswana has the greatest concentration of elephants in Africa, but in 2020, it was reported that 350 elephants had mysteriously died en-masse in the Delta. Elephants of all ages and sexes were affected, many allegedly walking in circles before suddenly collapsing on their faces and dying. Most remaining elephants fled the panhandle. Similar events were reported in the Kruger National Park and Zimbabwe, although only with 22 deaths. There is little evidence among the many theories and rumours for the cause. The suggested human/wildlife conflict has been discounted, as cyanide poisoning would have caused other scavengers to die and elephant tusks were found in situ; the carcasses were tested clear for pesticides and anthrax.

In Gweta village, we found supplies like bread and milk from a small, basic grocery outlet. Catherine sent me to another shack for milk, where she had seen a group of men drinking from cartons. Merriment was high when the mzungu (foreigner) asked for milk; they were consuming maize beer, a particularly evil concoction, so it's no wonder they were convivial.

The Makgadikgadi salt pan is the largest, covering an area bigger than Switzerland. These pans only hold water for short periods after the rains, as evaporation leaves a salty, sucking mud, with a hard-baked, thin crust that 'should' sustain the weight of a light vehicle. But, break the crusty surface, and it's 'goodnight Vienna'. Any chance of recovery, especially without a back-up vehicle, is negligible. During the wet season, around 35 - 75,000 zebra and wildebeest are estimated to migrate around these pans - Africa's second largest migration. Predators like lions, leopards, cheetahs, hyenas and wild dogs, amongst others, are attracted by the spectacle. Millions of flamingos, feeding around the water's edge, creates that characteristic pink hue, reminiscent of East African lakes. Entering via Njuca Hills, we challenged ourselves by taking the difficult, sandy riverine route along the Boteti River. This supposed testing route was no more challenging than we'd already undertaken, and we saw little game and no hippos. Reassuringly, Daph took it all in her stride and eventually, as we crested a slight rise, we came across a vast herd of grazing zebras and wildebeest.

Like the early settlers in 1860s, we visited both Chapman's and Green's baobabs, which had been significant waypoints. Aside from navigation, they also functioned like a post office, or 'social media' of the day. The need to communicate has always been present; on my first trip to Nairobi in the eighties, the Thorn Tree Café had messages pinned to the eponymous tree, such as, 'Stayed for a few days but headed to Mombasa' scribbled on scraps of paper, postcards or whatever personal marker came to hand. Similarly at Green's, inscriptions were carved into the 25 metre-round trunk from notables like Livingstone, Selous, Rhodes and Grogan during the Matabele wars, and the forebears of Captain Lawrence Oates, the Antarctic explorer who took the ultimate, lonely walk in 1912. Near Chapman's, we stumbled upon the secluded luxury of Jack's Camp - if the pan tracks were safe for Jack's, they would be fine for us. I read in 2016 that the largest tree in Africa, Chapman's Baobab, had finally fallen.

Nxai Pan was a smaller delight; the reeds and grasses were less dense, allowing a better viewing. We settled into our allocated campsite on New Year's Eve, fixed a meal and relaxed as we watched the sun go down on a lovely day. It was a serene spot which we had all to ourselves, although just after dark, an Italian couple in a rented 4x4 bowled in, animated from a recent, dramatic game viewing. After a brief and cordial meeting, we each settled in for the night, only to be woken hours later by a surreal experience. Shortly after midnight, it was like the sun had been rekindled; the new moon shone so brightly like a rising flame-red sun, low on the horizon; it caused us to get up. So we celebrated the coming of the new year again with our European friends over a convivial bottle of Chianti. Who knows what the animals made of such natural phenomena?

On the pan at Nata Bird Sanctuary, on the north of Sowa Pan, the shimmering horizon and emptiness highlighted the vast expanse of sky: simply breathtaking. Our growing confidence in Daph led us to follow the veterinary cordon fence track, inland of Sowa Pan down to Kubu Island, to witness evidence of early habitation. An enclosed, circular stone wall akin to that of the Great Zimbabwe Empire has been dated to around 1250 AD. But access is quite another matter: enclosed by pans, driving on them requires a balance of momentum, to 'float' lightly over the crust. Any sinking is bad news. The guidebook was quite specific; when approaching from the north, follow the game cordon fence. After a couple of hours, the conditions deteriorated as the water levels gradually submerged our sandy track. Daphne was labouring in the cloying mud, although ahead, the track appeared to improve. Confident we had traction and momentum, we pressed on, until we suddenly sank on one side and became hopelessly stuck, unable to go forwards or backwards. Yes, it was a swamp. Oh my god! Where the hell were we and how could we get this thing out? Received wisdom suggests not to panic; put the kettle on (or have a cigarette, for those inclined) whilst you assess the wider situation. Sod that, I needed to get this thing out! Thankfully, the engine was still running, with the exhaust out of the water, but only because the front left wheel was sunk into a hole. Daph had a disconcerting lean as I fought to clamber out, but not before Catherine was able to reach across from her side to lightly depress the accelerator to maintain Daph's tick-over, preventing a stall and water being sucked into her engine via the exhaust.

I surveyed the immediate area, wading forward to check the track ahead and to the sides. The prospect of retracing our steps was not welcome, yet it appeared the only option. There was a track ahead, but getting there was uncertain and what lay beyond that was unknown. We were less than a third of the way to Sowa Pan. Trying to remain calm and logical, I calculated that the only firm anchor point was a tree (of sorts) behind Daph that was only just in reach of our Tirfor winch. So backwards was the logical extraction. The next task was to get the recovery gear from the back of Daph, which was quite a mission. I made a mental note to ensure the recovery gear would always be on hand when you least demand it. It was a relatively simple, straight rearward pull; the anchor strap was around the base of the tree, securing the Tirfor winch cable to the JATE bolt on the chassis. As I started to winch, I was impressed by the torque of the Tirfor. After a couple of hard, resisted movements of the lever arm, it broke the suction of the mud and then pulled strongly and easily. I was more worried about the desiccated tree holding out, which thankfully it did. The hand winch proved a great option. With Daphne half out and in a position to be powered free, suddenly half a dozen, young locals appeared from nowhere, running towards us from our intended direction of travel. There had been no signs of habitation en route. In broken English, they gesticulated that it was best to turn back. They were already pushing Daph back as I winched. Recovery achieved, I rewarded them with the dodgy maize beer, which appeared to go down exceptionally well. A very muddy Daphne returned along the cordon fence, with slightly dented pride. But we had made the right call and extracted ourselves without significant help. Pressing ahead would have been nice, but it wasn't essential. It turned out to be a positive experience; we were in one piece, as we headed down to Francistown, where we overnighted at an opportune lodge.

Botswana is a very friendly and peaceful society, with a stable currency and political climate. However, on our last day driving back to South Africa, we were stopped twice for speeding, which we found ironic in a laden Land Rover. Both incidents are noteworthy for their humour rather than the offence committed. Considering the poor repair of most vehicles and the roads (although still better than the UK at present), the police being hot on speeding made it more crazy. Daphne still lacked a speedometer so, when we were stopped for doing 88 kilometres per hour in what we believed was an 80kph limit, we felt like congratulating ourselves. Then we were informed this was a 60kph stretch, which I should have realised, regardless of the demise of the earlier 60kph speed restriction sign long ago. The friendly banter was made all the more humorous when two more vehicles were similarly caught, each proclaiming there was no speed sign. I was pleased we were all fined the same amount for our innocent misdemeanour and the mzungu was not unduly ripped off. I was satisfied that my £10 equivalent was helping the local community, however cynical I was about the strategic placement of the blatant speed trap to catch the returning tourists 'speeding' home to South Africa.

During the second, more irritating misdemeanour, I was joking with the constable about the muddy state of Daphne and how we'd got stuck, when a hapless local driver behind me was similarly ensnared and severely castigated for his excessive 67kph. The policeman took no prisoners with the local driver, shouting and proclaiming him to be 'a suicide bomber, responsible for the death and mayhem on Botswana's roads!' Despite the obvious and recent 9/11 reference, the miscreant was crestfallen and started to claim that he had lost control of his car. To my mind, this admission was a far more worrying statement, yet it was either ignored or lost on the policeman, who completed his full repertoire of tried-and-tested abuse, with a further tirade about speeding and its ills on society. I don't know what happened to the poor chap: a roadside fine, a summons or let off?

We loved the Kalahari and our trial; Daphne and her equipment performed well. Her character was developing nicely, and thus far, she was not yet answering back. Critically, Catherine and I felt more ready for our challenge, as we had managed and resolved potential setbacks and were more than excited for our forthcoming adventure.

Chapter 5
Prior preparation and planning...

'Charlie 172, this is the tower, you are clear to land.' 'C172, clear to land, Roger, out.' Executing the final turn, I flew down the glidepath. If there was one thing I mastered early on, it was the landings, yet with Catherine beside me as my first passenger, I was bouncing down the runway. 'Were you meant to do that?' she nervously asked, which didn't really help, but she loved her flight and handling the controls. Aside from always wanting to learn, we hoped to find ways to use my qualification during our trip, perhaps snagging opportunities to fly over the Okavango Delta or the Maasai Mara.

The club at Wonderboom was a friendly bunch of enthusiasts and those cramming for their commercial 'ticket'. South Africa has the weather and affordability to gain a (UK compatible) pilot's licence and many of my colleagues were similarly learning. A PPL is governed by visual flight rules, so we had to avoid adverse weather and definitely not fly in cloud. So naturally, the first thing my instructor (a fast jet pilot and Cheetah instructor) exposed me to was the discombobulating effect of flying in cloud. He was trained to fly totally on instruments but I found the absence of reference points mesmeric; the sound was muted, and everything appeared to slow down. It was a salutary lesson to trust your instruments and avoid the fluffy stuff. Further incidents with him included being chased down the main Lanseria runway by a scheduled commercial jet whilst conducting a training 'touch-and-go' landing. 'Mr Cheetah' had a habit of popping up and surprising me; on my solo test, he buzzed me wing to wing in his plane. 'Where the F*** did that come from?!' I guess he realised I could handle it, or he was bored. The RAF's parachuting school motto of 'Knowledge dispels fear' rang true; being able to think calmly and manage the situation logically is a valuable life lesson, for every occasion, and one I still leverage at work today.

As we were packing to depart South Africa and begin our safari, time became condensed. By the end of the tour, I reflected that we had achieved a lot, both for and with our South African colleagues, as much as preparing for our adventure. Naturally, there was some trepidation; we were stepping into the unknown, both for future jobs and our adventure, but this added to the excitement too. The African sights and sounds are very different to Europe, but for me, the smell is the most evocative sense. Ten years or so after our trip, I was excited to find myself back in Johannesburg, with my nostrils stirred by the smell from the jacaranda trees. In spring, these trees droop with the weight of their vivid, purple blossom, releasing their sap and pollen. Like on our road in Pretoria, the jacarandas in Rosebank (near the head office of the business group for whom I ran the European operations) were similarly carpeted. I enjoyed being back in South Africa, even if it meant presenting the EU trading and growth plans. Whilst there, I was able to revisit the fabulous Sunday craft market, still held in the local car park. On a subsequent trip, we conducted our business planning at one of the group's community-sponsored wildlife concessions at Madikwe Game Reserve. We worked by day and each evening, we bonded over evening game drives and in the boma.

The Limpopo Reserve is malaria-free. It has been nurtured to now host the 'Big Five' (lions, leopards, rhinos, elephants and African buffaloes) and offers sanctuary for both white and black rhinos. During a sundowner pause on an evening game drive, there was an almighty commotion nearby from a clash between a black and a white rhino. The irascible rhino has poor eyesight, so bumping into each other at dusk caused predictable mayhem. Greater excitement was to follow, for we came across a dramatic wild dog pack pursuit. A small group of endangered wild dog had been reintroduced in 1994, where their survival was considered marginal; yet they flourished. Our guide glimpsed them lolloping along, so we tried to follow. As an indication as to the advances in communications, whilst driving to Madikwe (from Johannesburg), I received a call from an old army chum. Bryan, a white Kenyan, was calling from the UK to persuade me to participate in his 'Arch to Arc' charity event. He refused to believe we were driving to the Limpopo. We used to run together and play golf whilst studying for our MBA, but now Bryan had the adventure racing bug. As a worthy nod to his heritage, he started running events for Save the Rhino charity (he was that chap running the London Marathon or the Marathon des Sables inside the large rhino head). On this latest Arch to Arc jaunt, Duncan Goodhew, the Olympic swimmer, took my place. By relay, they ran from Marble Arch to Dover, swam the channel and then they all cycled to the Arc de Triomphe in Paris. An amazing effort, but full credit is extended to Duncan. The team was exhausted and floundering off the French coast, unable to breach the French tide, so he ploughed himself through heavy current to 'land the team'. He certainly was a far bigger PR draw than I could ever have dreamed of, especially as I swim like a proverbial brick.

During our preparations, we were asked countless times what weapon(s) we'd be carrying. This was quite a disturbing question, as we never considered it. We assumed the question arose from their perception of the risks, or they were simply responding to my military background. Maybe they expected our Land Rover to be sporting James Bond-style machine guns, sidewinder missiles and flares shooting from every orifice as we 'fought our way north'? Prevention is the cornerstone to every response. Be careful and alert, and avoid putting yourself in compromising or dangerous situations. At the same time, one needs to be confident and wise; if you walk and behave like a scared rabbit, then people are likely to treat you as such, or they will assume you have something to hide. With Daphne, we sought to present a grubby workhorse, rather than a daily washed and pimped wealthy vehicle. If there is escalation in conflict, it remains important to take the initiative and control a situation. Culturally, Africans rarely hold one's eye, so making deliberate eye contact demonstrates authority, but it's critical not to overplay the situation or make it aggressive. Smile and widen the eyes to show no malice, only friendliness. Small measures are far more important than ramping up the aggression stakes. Subtleties apply; it is key to read the situation and take avoidance measures first. The military refer to this awareness as 'combat indicators', sensing what is out of place, the absence of the normal, a change in behaviours, something being too quiet.

Maintaining self-control is vital. If you're armed, then the (subconscious) mind is constantly worried about when and how to use your force. If you reach for a gun, you have to be committed and must follow. Yet being unarmed, you have to think directly of de-escalation measures; talk or manage your way out of the situation. Let's face it, if shit is going to happen, chances are you'll be faced with more than one assailant, most likely a few armed with the ubiquitous AK47 automatic rifle, or similar. Then you are in the poo, with or without a weapon, and at best, you might carry a pistol. If you adopt an attitude of 'Hey you (with an appropriate insult), get out of my way', you're hardly engaging with the people or country you wish to visit. But a softer 'Hi, how are you?' with an immediate question or something to shift their present thought process (hence conferring some advantage) might be a more viable approach. If it boils down to a shooting match, the aggressive acceleration and stance from an overladen Land Rover (or whatever you drive) means you'll be screwed. By all means use the vehicle as a weapon, but a laden 4x4 is hardly an effective getaway vehicle. We saw no value in being armed.

What about the authorities? Well, in most cases, it would be 'What authorities?' They are never there or empowered sufficiently in the first place, which is why others are taking arms into their own hands. In many places, the authorities are part of the problem; they too are looking for an advantage or 'un petit cadeau'; something to augment their meagre income or convert their advantage. This might appear a bleak picture, but we had some countermeasures. The nuisance threat was a greater concern than armed attackers swarming our vehicle. But we hoped this was all academic… we'd have to wait and see.

Chapter 6
Who knew? Forming the Holybourne Sand Club

It's strange how events unfold. Ten years or so after getting home, we carried on working hard. We then got dogs (a long story) and I began cycling with fellow villagers; life took over. Like most of our generation, as kids we grew up with bicycles – it was our freedom. My abiding memory of the road home was always uphill with the wind against me, making me even later than I already was. The arrival of carbon bikes and new equipment around 2010 spawned a resurgence in cycling (triggered by 2012 Olympic efforts). Now the 'MAMIL' (middle-aged men in Lycra) brigade represents the older face of rugby. My creaking knees were slowing me on the hills, making me an unwitting founding member of the White Hart Vuelta's (WHV), our village cycling cohort; a club without rules. Of the twelve 'originals', most remain today, with our club name acknowledging the village sponsor where essential rehydration occurred most Friday evenings. There still are some excellent riders, a few qualifying to ride in British (pro-am) colours. It was a wonderful way to become further inculcated within village life. On one ride, whilst chatting with David, who recently volunteered to chair our Village Association, he was on a mission. David had grown up in the village, where his mother was a retired local GP (albeit at a different practice to Dr Christopher Everett, another retired, local GP). After the ride, David sat in our kitchen, drinking wine, not leaving until I had assumed the organisation of the village remembrance service. I prolonged making any decision for as long as I could.

I have been organising the Holybourne remembrance service for over ten years now, and each year, we draw a great crowd. We are wonderfully supported by the village and local dignitaries, including the Deputy Lord Lieutenant for Hampshire, Alan Titchmarsh, along with our local MP, past mayors, plus the many generals and veterans I have asked to speak. One year, we had the honour of General Sir Huw Pike to speak on a significant Falklands anniversary. Not only had he been one of my earliest commanders, in turn I commanded his son in 2 PARA. As the Pipes and Drums struck up to lead the parade, the sight of the full Highland regalia made him comment,

'Blimey Adrian, this is all a bit Hollywood.' If only he possessed a monocle popping out at the same time, it would have been rather apt, for he was right - we do put on a splendid village event.

An evening or so later, I was sitting in the Old Vicarage with Christopher and Geraldine, whiskey in hand, amongst their packing boxes. Immediately, it was, 'Are you able to organise the parade?' Yes. 'Good, then let's talk Africa.' I was unaware that Chris, with five fellow Westminster medical school students, had toured the Belgium Congo in 1958 for their 'elective'. I recall Catherine initially thought to do her elective in Nairobi, before adjusting to Belfast, given the then high preponderance of gunshot wounds. An elective allowed the trainee doctor to experience hospital work for a few months: on-the-job training. Chris and his chums were 'stretching' their elective somewhat, even for the 1950s, conducting work experience in African hospitals.

In a further twist, Chris was moving closer to family, leaving the village where they had lived for most of their adult lives. He was selling their vicarage to Paul Aichroth, the chief instigator of their Congo trip. Chris and I formed the 'Holybourne Sand Club' that evening once we discovered we'd driven the same route across the Sahara, albeit 44 years apart. His 1958 buccaneers had remained firm friends, enjoying annual reunions, but it was not until their 50th

anniversary meeting that Paul's secretary had transcribed his diary for the team. As Paul expressed, he was the only one with the energy to keep a diary. Thank goodness he had, for a copy was passed to me, with Christopher's blessing, to publish. At the time, I only thought to read it. Events precluded us ever meeting (it is still pending), yet the diary offers a wonderful glimpse into their trip's character, attitude, colonialism and what was then understood about the continent, as well as a vague transcript of their transit.

'So, what did you do in your fourth Michaelmas term at medical school, Chris?' He was the last, and late to join the party, owing to someone dropping out. In a junior year to the others, Chris grasped this opportunity. Paul had been instrumental and influential at attaining favours and pleading for (amazing) commercial support. They leveraged help, with letters from their college dean, who introduced them to the president of Shell Oil. On the college board of governors was Lord Nathan, who had recently been appointed president of the Royal Geographical Society (embraced by Royal endorsement), along with other 'movers and shakers' offering in-country contacts, visas and connections to a series of Nigerian and Congolese hospitals. Contingent on their academic commitment, they collected plants for the Royal Marsden Hospital that inevitably decomposed and stank in their transported polythene bags. They took soil samples for antibiotic analysis for pharma companies, plus plants, fruits and insects they observed being used in native medicine. Capacity in their vehicles must have been a premium; in our meeting of the Cambridge2CapeTown (C2C) crew in Chad, we watched these six-foot plus lads folding themselves into their Land Rover. Paul's ultimate coup was the loan of two Land Rovers (a Short and a Long Wheelbase) from The Rover Company. Shell sponsored their fuel, Avon their tyres, spares from Lucas and crucial maintenance training from Soutter Developments. Despite this, each member had to contribute £50, acknowledging this was a considerable sum in those days. They had done fantastically well; we secured zero interest or sponsorship before we travelled - how the times and attitudes have changed.

African transit routes and options are constantly evolving. The 1958 boys travelled before independence in many countries, so colonial rule (only just) held sway. Interestingly, their transit through Europe was harsher, although help was probably more readily available. Following the Second World War, European empires retained their colonies, to varying degrees. They initially transited French-administered countries of Morocco, Algeria, Niger, French Equatorial Africa and French Cameroon. Crucially back then, the border between Morocco and Algeria was passable, making Gibraltar their obvious Mediterranean crossing, via Tangier. Belgium still ruled the Congo, whilst Britain administered Nigeria, British Cameroon, Sudan, East Africa and parts south. Their adventures broadly transcribed a figure of eight route through Africa. In Algeria, they went down the main N1 highway (euphemism for a marked track), often travelling at night to avoid the heat. They described an exceptionally long piste-traverse, accompanying a lorry, navigating between water wells, where our routes coalesced (although driving in opposite directions) between Tamanrasset and Zinder in Niger, which took us a fraction of their time. They battled for eight days through harsh desert storms and endured bad 'fech fech' conditions, a fine, powdered sand that offers little to no cohesion. Fech fech appears as though it has a hard surface crust but delivers an unfortunate surprise to the unwary driver as they collapse into a quicksand-like substance.

We had circumvented Lake Chad after Ndjamena, to avoid insurrection in northern Nigeria, but the 1958 team were able to carry on south at Zinder. Nigeria then was still a British colony and the team had arranged to work first at the Katsina hospital. Thereafter they headed east across northern Nigeria to Fort Lamy (in Chad), known today as Ndjamena. Between 1910 to 1958, French Equatorial Africa consisted of modern-day Chad, Gabon, French Congo and Ubangi-Shari, a colony administered from Brazzaville. On 1st December 1958, the French Congo and Ubangi-Shari were granted independence to become Central African Republic (CAR). Interestingly, Chris and the team reported no insurrection or disquiet whilst passing through only months earlier. After Fort Lamy, where they were admirably hosted by the Chambre of Commerce and strangers, they went south towards Stanleyville (modern-day Kisangani) and worked at Yakusu hospital. From Stanleyville, they toured the Congo and Great Lakes, starting in the south, with Lake Kivu. Today, Kivu straddles the Rwandan border; Rwanda was then part of German East Africa. Rwanda gained their independence a year later in 1959. Heading north, via Lakes Edward and Albert, they came level with the Rwenzori Mountains, ending their Congo tour at Goma. Goma was of interest to me, which I mention in our Ugandan chapter, and still today there is an appalling refugee crisis of greater proportions than the Ethiopian response of the 1980s, yet in DRC, now there this little or no world attention.

Starting home from Stanleyville (Kisangani), the 1958 team initially went west to Yaoundé, then north towards Bamenda, through the respective French, then British Cameroon colonies, expressing their view that the French half was more ordered and organised. Entering Nigeria via Jos, they conducted their last hospital stop at Kaduna; thereafter heading north via Niamey. They followed the Niger River up to Gao, then paralleled the western Algerian border, finally crossing a freezing Sahara on the N6 track; they were amazed at the uncomfortably low temperatures, exacerbated by night driving. On Christmas Eve, they were 'detained' by the French military (roughing it in the officers' mess) at Reggane, where they partied on cognacs to Christmas Day. Apparently they were arrested for being in an unauthorised area, so they produced their 'royal laissez-passer' from The Duke of Edinburgh (indirectly via Lord Nathan), to scarper north, and home. Unbeknown to the team, the French were preparing the first of 17 nuclear tests for the next six consecutive years from 1960; four air atmospheric tests were released around Reggane and 13 further underground tests in the Hoggar Massif nearby in Ekker, just south of Tamanrasset. That the team blundered into a controlled area embarrassed the French for a lack of control, but this was hardly the team's fault. For sure, the French were looking for local terrorist activists, striving for both independence and objecting to the impending atomic testing, so the boys were wise to escape north (using their trump card) to Gibraltar. Like my parents, who flew their car on honeymoon to Jersey, the team flew their Land Rovers from Le Touquet to Lydd airport, on the Silver City Airways flight and back to Westminster.

Paul's diary offered a glimpse into the bon viveur of their trip, and enabled comparison with our travels and today. Paul referenced their equipment and their mindset, for they travelled at a time when the shackles of colonial rule were being resisted, yet questioned. They were able to appreciate Africa as a European playground, receiving essential and much appreciated support (as well as offering essential medical assistance). The 1960s saw considerable rebellion and change, still rippling today. There was a sad, yet inevitable footnote from their diary transcript, as friends at Yakusu hospital (in the Congo, downstream from Kisangani) were murdered, some beheaded, within the bloody independence uprising of 1964. These folk were providers of welfare and medicine, regardless of creed or stripe. In 2002, the Congo and CAR were no-go areas, still suffering post-conflict chaos. In the 1970s and 1980s, many independent travellers were transiting the Sahel areas and reporting extreme travelling conditions, especially in CAR. Prominent among these were the huge mud sinks, generating excessively long hold-ups, whilst overladen lorries and other freight sought to disentangle themselves from mud wallows or pay bribes at frequent 'police' checkpoints. None of this was experienced in 1958, yet these issues were something we sought to avoid. Maybe the 1958 team was still in a period of relative worldly innocence, still recovering from the privations of the war, but in Africa? For example, after obtaining fuel from the Mediterrane-Niger Company at Gao, David, for some inexplicable reason, placed his passport on the bonnet of the Land Rover. When driving off, Paul was subconsciously aware of something flying off, and later David realised it was his passport! At the same moment, a lorry following them and stopped to recover the passport and drove on to return it to David. I wonder if that would happen today?

Only one of the team had experienced National Service in the RAF. Conscription was ending before the remainder were eligible, yet the majority of their equipment was basic military surplus - that was all there was. They had a canvas tent strung between their vehicles, not unlike today's military 9x9 derivation used with Land Rovers. Being cumbersome, they rarely bothered with it, unless it was raining. They preferred to kip in sleeping bags on camp beds or inflatable mattresses. From my experience of modern camp cots, they are more bother than they're worth, and few inflatables have air remaining by morning! They always used mozzie nets and were careful about malarial prophylactics. The only real constant was the huge climatic range that all transits endure; tropical and dry heat, humidity, through to freezing. They too crossed the Sahara in late autumn when the night temperature plummeted, but they experienced snow on the southern Atlas near Tindouf on their return, prompting them to acquire Arab blankets for extra warmth.

At least their military surplus work clothing was cotton so it could absorb sweat, but they also referenced quite a number of parties and receptions, beyond the periods of hospital work. These included hobnobbing with senior figures at events like the governor's reception in Gibraltar, or the consul general's office in Algiers. Formal attire, at least jacket and tie, was de rigueur for such events, although I read that they sported college cravats to cut a dash. They had support throughout their transit, such as in Gibraltar, where mail was always waiting for them. On their arrival at The Rock, they were picked out by customs, not for anything unduly wrong, other than they were three days late in reporting to the Governor, Sir Charles Keithley. Sir Charles wanted to proffer the benefit of his desert wisdom for their onward journey. Given that they were six blokes living on top of one another, with limited water, they remained relatively healthy.

One thing that intrigued me was their daily physiological tests. I latterly understood this was part of a unique, published experiment into how the body adapts to heat stress when moving from a temperate to tropical climate. Whether it was a conditional part of their academic assessment, I'm not sure, but half the team conducted a Standard Work test in the heat of the day, observed by the other half, before they rotated. Wisely, they suspended the tests in the depth of their Sahara travails, but conducted them everywhere else, even in the humidity of the Congo. These tests undoubtedly hampered their time/distance and were beneficial to their health and fitness. Indirectly, I felt these tests induced their penchant for night driving, to cover the distances. The combination of work rates and fatigue could not have been aided by night driving, for sage advice implies driving at night is inherently dangerous. But I acknowledge that it is much cooler, being nearer to the equator; the ambient moonlight is often sufficiently bright for driving and there were fewer locals wandering about. It's a reminder that all travel is a balance of risk.

Crossing the Sahara, and navigating between known wells, they adopted local goat-skin water containers in addition to their (leaky) jerry cans that provided cool drinking water. The team used a Berkerfeld chlorine filter with silver ion impregnation, akin to the more modern derivation we tried to fabricate, thus ensuring a supply of drinkable water. They had a few gippy stomachs, coughs and extreme tiredness, but their digestion adjusted to regional bacteria, which by and large was the same for us. One member suffered poor guts in Gibraltar and another contracted Red Congo fever in Stanleyville from a small, black biting fly. This second chap was indisposed with a severe rash and a very high fever for three days, but otherwise, the team stayed in reasonable health.

They carried sufficient food, cooking en route. They had no fridge but interestingly, they were 'testing' a special margarine designed for the tropics; regrettably, there were no reports as to its quality, desirability or longevity. They received food supplies at designated points en route, along with mail, that surprisingly arrived. One wonders if such system would be reliable today? They cooked on an efficient paraffin primus stove, making frequent hot brews and munching biscuits as they travelled. They tested a lot of experimental dehydrated foods for the Ministry of Agriculture and Fisheries that proved popular, notably enjoying a rehydrated steak in the Sahara! Dehydrated food had an obvious weight advantage, provided they had sufficient water. In airborne forces, we also preferred the individual 24-hour Artic Field Ration packs, as they were high in calories and (critically) lightweight, and water rehydration was never an issue.

With a team of six, consecutive tasks could be delegated. They rotated the driving and cooking, although the two designated mechanics, Chris and Bryan, often drew the short straw for repairs. Their breakdowns were manageable and amazing, given each vehicle was weighed down to their spring stops. They had constant fuel filter issues and assorted dust failures, although the main breakdowns were three broken (leaf) springs and a rear axle ball race failure. They had spares for everything except the ball race, yet they sourced a solution at a local garage. Each vehicle covered around 14,500 miles and they were still viable on return to Land Rover. Like the Last Overland discovery of 'Oxford', the team's renovated short wheelbase Land Rover was recently spotted for sale in 2022.

Chapter 7
The highest country in the world

The endless packing and re-packing is a nightmare, but we needed to move out of our Pretoria digs at the same time as starting our adventure. It forced a deadline upon us, which can be useful. As we said our goodbyes, the thunder clouds gathered and the heavens opened. It stayed like this all the way down to the Drakensberg Mountains. Passing through the Midlands Meander - a rural scene of agricultural beauty on gentler secondary roads - it made us feel we could be anywhere; rural Somerset or Surrey, France or Germany. We stopped in Mooi River to resupply, picking up local, fresh vegetables, bread and milk. Travelling south, the tar road became gravel, as the sun appeared and we started to climb. Settlements came and went, featuring huts with their distinctive, thatched, conical roofs. Right on time, hordes of school children came streaming down the roads. Whilst the majority were bare foot, they all had a school uniform, satchels, shorts or skirts and all wearing a crisp, white shirt. I challenge any reader to tell me where in the Western world you can find school children in uniforms, let alone in immaculate, white shirts at the end of the day. Especially considering where they come from, their bush walk to school, without pavements or school buses. This classic African scene was observed in most countries up to Kenya, where thankfully, education was prioritised, enabling the next generation.

The dark, characteristically flat-topped Drakensberg Mountains, with their sheer, imposing ridges, increasingly dominated our skyline. We'd holidayed at Cathedral Peak before, an aptly named area known as 'Little Switzerland'. The farming methods had altered the terrain, with more cattle than sheep and large, man-made lakes and dams, stocked with fish and other wildlife. The Boers were canny farmers, appreciating water flow, conservation dams and header pools to ensure optimal irrigation and water management. The shadows were lengthening as we arrived at Sani Pass Hotel, at the base of the infamous eponymous pass. Its faded glory was common among many domestic hotels. Under apartheid, international travel was not possible, so most whites were content to holiday within South Africa; they had sunny weather, fabulous destinations and a well-developed tourist infrastructure.

Now post-apartheid, the dynamic has flipped. Those who can afford to travel do, those who can't, can neither support the indigenous home market. Getting on the move and the mountain air must have impacted us, for after a meal, we crashed out, prior to our first border crossing.

Lesotho is a landlocked, mountainous country, criss-crossed by a network of rivers. Known as the highest country in the world, the elevation of its lowest point is 1,400 metres. Formerly Basutoland, a British protectorate, Lesotho is a democratic sovereign and independent country today that is uniquely and totally surrounded by its neighbour. During my time there, the capital, Maseru, was 'off limits' due to high crime, rioting and political insurrection since the 1998 military coup.

Cresting Sani Pass was never in doubt and the view was fabulous, but the graded track travelling up had suffered considerable erosion. Some washaways made the sharp, hairpin bends and switchbacks interesting. Daph pulled confidently which, given the numerous wrecked lorries and vehicles that hadn't made it, was reassuring. The eponymous sign at Sani Top (2,865 metres) was by a small border post hut. We noted the temperature drop at this altitude, not helped by the biting wind. The border hut was warmed by a log stove, with a small black and white portable television (powered by a car battery) looping a 'prevention of AIDS' tape. Further anti-AIDS posters and health information leaflets were plastered around the walls - remarkable, considering that 40% of the population was suffering and the South African Government had yet to acknowledge AIDS.

As we arrived, a small convoy of wonderfully restored classic Series I and Series II Land Rovers, each emblazoned with the 'Conical Hat' company logo, were just starting their descent. Conical Hat is an exclusive travel experience company offering escorted tours into remote parts of Lesotho. We stopped for a pint at the Sani Pass Top Chalet, aptly named 'the highest pub in Africa'. We initially planned to climb Thabana Ntlenyana (3,482 metres), the highest point in southern Africa. Thabana demanded respect on our initial 'Roof of Africa' sojourn, even if it was just a walk in from the highest pub. A few months prior, I had walked to Thabana, which had started as a challenge at a braai with my military team colleagues. Colonel Tim, an experienced hillwalker, challenged Steve (a medic with the longest service and probably the most medals amongst us), who foolishly confessed he had never properly rough-camped, let alone been up a mountain. This was too good to ignore; Steve was up for the challenge. I volunteered to adjudicate fair play and join the fun. We cobbled together some gear and set off, with vague details of a route. Stopping for an essential rehydration at Sani Pass Top Chalet, Tim and I found an invaluable sketch map of the route, hanging on a wall. Naturally, we didn't tell Steve! As part of his education, we gave him the (unmarked) map and set off from Sani Top at around midday. Following goat tracks along a ridge sounds simple enough, but we were already feeling the effects of altitude on our pace and distance.

After a couple of kilometres, Steve gave up any pretence of map reading, becoming content to follow. A further six kilometres on, we were joined by some young boys tending their flock. It was an African classic; no obvious civilisation for miles around, yet suddenly, these boys popped up, offering help. Each was similarly dressed in blankets and welly boots, as they strolled lazily and laconically beside us, whilst we stumbled over the grassy tussocks. These honest and inquisitive lads were veritable mountain goats, and smart; they knew the white mzungu presented a meal ticket. Food, cash, cigarettes, watches or GPS, whatever they thought they could get (and monetise). They were not shy, offering to carry our packs and show us the way. We were polite and stuck to our task; had we given them a pack to carry, they could be off like a dose of salts and we'd have no chance of catching them. We gave them some food, then separated. The slope was not severe, but the altitude was slowing us down and the weather started to close in with nightfall. We stopped a kilometre short of the summit under a sheltering outcrop. Comforted by a warming brew, we watched the sun go down over the remote, stunning views. The temperature dropped like a stone and the wind started to whip up. Steve was loving his first 'boy scout' night under the stars. With something hot to eat, we rigged up a shelter for Steve, whilst Tim and I snuggled down in our respective bivvy bags. But it was cold - very cold. Poor Steve picked a choice night; howling cold winds and a full-on celestial rainbow. I am not sure Steve got much sleep, but as so often happens in such situations, the sunrise was glorious, calm and warming. We stowed our gear and to warm up, we raced the kilometre to the top for the obligatory sunrise photo, before retracing our steps, collecting our gear and heading for a late breakfast at the pub. Steve was ecstatic; after 30-odd years of service, he had never enjoyed such an outdoors experience.

Back in Daph, Catherine and I were bouncing along the A3 highway to

Thaba Tseka, on a single carriage, hardcore track. The Lesotho plateau is at altitude, for Daph's power was down. The sun was strong but once it set, we knew it would be cold. Children occasionally ran considerable distances to intersect us on the road; many were tending herds and some were on horseback. We later learnt that where there was any schooling, it was often allocated to the girls since most of the boys were working on the land. Catherine always said, 'Teach a girl and she will teach the family.' Most locals wore the same welly boots, some sort of woolly hat and a colourful blanket draped around their shoulders. The main crop here is maize, grown on steps or terraces cut into the mountain sides. They make pap, where maize is pounded before 30 minutes' cooking, and it's occasionally eaten with vegetables or milk, rarely ever meat.

The altitude and twisting terrain drastically slowed our progress. We needed to reassess our plans and find somewhere to camp. We had been advised against rough camping beside the road, but had scant option. It took us some time to find a hidden spot, but within a gorge we found a gravel pit that was hidden from the road, once Daph was safely inside. Getting her in was another matter, but the judicious application of low ratio eased her in. We used our dome tent on the ground to retain a low profile and thankfully passed a quiet, if somewhat chilly night. After easing Daph out the following morning, I found an oil leak. 'Here we go,' I thought. The pulse started to quicken with all the mechanical demons mustering in my head. So soon? Daph had just been serviced in Pretoria. Stock advice for any such mechanical issue is to retire to the nearest rock, relax and have a fag! Not being smokers, we went one better and made a cup of tea. I wondered if we had struck something getting in or out of our camping hollow, but there was no evidence. Stranger still, we were losing oil at a high rate. All we could do was top up the oil and monitor the situation.

On arrival at Thaba, the oil light came back on. It was Good Friday and not the sort of place to find a garage or mechanic. At the BP fuel point, there no oil, or mechanic. We topped up with our remaining spare oil that predictably only got us three kilometres before the oil light reappeared; we turned back. Arriving again at the BP garage, the locals said, 'Aah, we knew you'd be back'; the three kilometres oil streak giving us away. Still observing anything obvious (the oil filter, pipes and fittings appeared sound) and having consumed our spare engine oil, we had a problem. More stilted discussion with the garage guys failed, when a lady living next door appeared with her son. Both spoke reasonable English; she offered to find some oil and if possible, a mechanic. Catherine volunteered to go with them on this epic quest, armed with the vehicle handbook and the empty oil bottle. The lady sought to assure Catherine that everyone in Lesotho was taught English at school rather than Afrikaans, yet few were speaking English. They drove around numerous places, some of which looked like shops, others that definitely did not. Critically, no oil of any sort was found, let alone the right specification. Despite it being Good Friday, this lady appeared to be some sort of celebrity, for everyone they met seemed to know her, each time necessitating considerable social interaction. Keeping in mind one of the principles of African life, that nothing can be hurried, Catherine kept smiling and waited patiently. During their tour of Thaba, Catherine had asked several times if it would be better to just try and find a mechanic. Eventually, the lady turned to her and asked, 'Do you not think it would be a good idea to get the mechanic before finding the oil?' 'Yes, that's a very good idea,' Catherine replied enthusiastically.

Around more 'garages' and, after the mandatory social chatter, one mechanic agreed to come to our aid, along with what appeared to be the correct oil. Back at Daph, the mechanic jabbered away in Sotho to his crowd of supporters, pushing and pulling the same things I had. He tightened the same nuts and bolts, proclaiming that the severe road vibration will loosen joints, so leaks occur when under pressure. We topped up some oil and started Daph to test his repair, only to watch the last of our oil stream out again. More tinkering and more oil inserted, he then pronounced the problem fixed. Time would tell, but it emphasised the fact we were fortunate to not have broken down on a remote stretch. Catherine took a picture of our mechanics and the gathering support crew. Our lady saviour expressed to Catherine how difficult it must be in a strange place and to not speak the language; how did we cope? She saw it as her duty to help us, for which we were grateful, affirming our experience of the kind and gentle Lesotho people.

A further few hours driving across the wild plateau, we passed a lodge, nestled in a valley, called Marakabei Lodge, so we stopped. The lodge was a delight; the people were very welcoming and camping in their ground was cheap. There were a few others staying too, so we flipped open the roof tent. Just before dark, a solo lady arrived on an enduro Honda motorcycle from Sani Pass. She was very well-equipped and was destined to take part in the forthcoming Paris-Dakar rally. Although polite, she sought to keep to herself. Eating at the restaurant, we were introduced to Lesotho's South African High Commissioner who was also staying there, prompting another late evening of genial chatter. As we left Marakabei Lodge, we passed the Mohale Dam, a hydro-electric power project to feed Johannesburg. This was the first of a few similar projects which ironically benefited us as they had tarmac roads.

We descended Bushman's Pass into Lesotho's lowlands, making for Malealea Lodge, renowned for wonderful trekking and horse riding. We passed through the 'Gates of Paradise' (with a photoshoot across the stunning vista of the Malealea valley), before arriving and meeting our new hosts, Mick and Di. Both wonderfully welcoming, they offered us a vast array of hiking, hunting, chilling, trekking (on horse or foot) or 'challenge 4x4 trails'. We rested a few days and explored the Bushman rock art in the riverine valley below. We left Lesotho via Van Rooyen's Gate on the western border; it was a Sunday and hundreds of migrant workers were swarming to get back to Johannesburg after the Easter holidays. Most migrant workers had a temporary passport and were queuing for company buses waiting to pick them up on the South African side. We started to queue, but were waved directly through, assuming we were South Africans, given Daph's registration.

We had a great experience in Lesotho, but interestingly, weeks later, Lesotho declared a state of emergency. It was one of six countries, according to the World Food Programme (WFP) in Southern Africa, to be critically short of grain, enabling them to claim relief from developed countries. Today, Lesotho suffers the highest murder rate in the world, worse than Central America. Poverty reduces people to the 'haves and have nots'; people assume they can escape crime if there is no law to prevent it. Weapons were freely available; if there is violence, it is quick and brutal. With so many men working in abhorrent mining conditions away from home in Johannesburg's deep mines, maybe too many returning workers are overly institutionalised.

We immediately felt the benefit of a wealthier country in South Africa. The roads improved and the towns were actual settlements, as opposed to dwellings strewn along the roadside. Wepner was the first settlement we came across; it had seen better days. Most houses remain unchanged from the Victorian/Settler era, just wooden frames and rusty, corrugated roofs. Being a Sunday, most shops were closed, but thankfully, we stumbled across a local store that was about to close. This would have been treasured in Lesotho, but here, so close to the border, the quantity and range of convenience goods on sale was impressive. The store was a testament to an effective distribution network and franchise of convenience stores, plus graft from a grateful, self-sustaining (in this case, Indian) community.

We journeyed on and camped at a health spa in Aliwal North. The hot, sulphurous spring implied healing properties, the South African equivalent to Buxton in the UK's Derbyshire. Like the Sani Pass Hotel, this was another example of 'yesterday's heyday' and the need for funds and customers. Unlike the modern, ultra-glam palaces-to-spa-luxury, Aliwal retained the noxious, sulphuric air and braai-and-beer culture. It was fine for us, being the first time in a while to shake ourselves out. We passed a comfortable night with our neighbour, a cheerful, Belgian chap, resplendent with his fully-kitted VW Kombi. He and his wife were travelling around southern Africa and regaled us with their previous trans-global journeys.

Continuing through frontier country, we headed to the coast. Back in the 1820s, many English families were duped by the then government who led them to believe they were arriving in the land of plenty. Instead, they were thrown into conflict and competition with the existing Boers and warring Khoisan tribes, for which most settlers were ill-equipped. Many of the emergent towns became fortified, rather than the perceived trading posts and farms. Queenstown was built around a hexagonal, central fortress and sadly, we passed through a struggling, rundown mixed community. Unexpectedly, just beyond, we came across Hogsback; a lush mountain village with an atmosphere reminiscent of a faded Indian hill station or plantation. On the back roads between Queenstown and Beaufort West, the Amathole mountain range is a lush, verdant ridge above the arid Ciskei flatlands and rumoured to have inspired South Africa's JRR Tolkien's The Hobbit. The quaint cottages, shaded, trickling waterfalls and deeply sunken roads were quite picturesque, yet somewhat out of place, marking Hogsback as a natural tourist spot. The hotels had soft, gentle names like 'Away with the Fairies on Hydrangea Lane'. Absolutely delightful.

Juxtaposed to Hogsback was modern South Africa. The town of Alice was predominantly a black town, where many key figures from the Independence Movement had acquired their tertiary education. The University of Fort Hare was the alma mater of Nelson Mandela, Oliver Tambo, Zimbabwe's Robert Mugabe, Zambia's Kenneth Kaunda and Tanzania's Julius Nyerere. Founded in 1916 as the South African Native College, it has fostered its academic reputation within the indigenous community. Prudently, we did not stop and travelled on to Grahamstown. With its dark stone and Victorian layout, this regional town was reminiscent of St Andrews or Perth in Scotland. Adverts and flyers were displayed everywhere for the annual Grahamstown National Arts Festival and its associated fringe, a southern version of Edinburgh's fringe festival. Grahamstown was the capital of Settler County, and the beautiful, old buildings suggested a 'safer region'. Today, Grahamstown is renowned for the large Rhodes University campus.

I had been to Grahamstown a few months before, visiting the army's new 'ready and deployable' battalion. The sprawling military base was on the outskirts of town, in and among two large settlements; an ever-present reminder of different times and economies. It remained an indelible feature of our time in South Africa that the known towns and cities marked on maps reflect the pre-apartheid demographic, yet the vast bulk of the population still lived within settler communities, unmarked outside of major towns. At the time of our journey, the defined, two-room brick house promised to all in the 1994 ANC landslide election was now being challenged. Over the years, such houses had morphed with whatever building materials were available; brick, mud or corrugated iron extensions fostering all manner of 'grand designs'. Prosperity and awareness meant people refused to be defined as 'good-enough-for-two-rooms'. Most people expressed a capitalist desire to reflect their efforts and reward.

We initially thought to avoid both Port Elizabeth (PE) and the fabricated luxury, malarial-free 'safari experience' of Shamwari Game Reserve. The less exclusive neighbour, Addo Elephant Park, had a herd of over 600; we watched a waterhole with about 50 elephants frolicking and many babies scrabbling to keep up with their mothers. Interestingly, many of these elephants were tuskless; we were unclear if it was a natural genetic reaction to poaching or conservation. I decided to tackle Daph's recalcitrant driver's door lock, but after my careful ministrations, it completely gave up and refused to open. The required balletic efforts to climb in were not really an option - it's always the little things! The Addo staff suggested a Peugeot franchise in PE that previously had the Land Rover franchise. It was easily found and their retained, qualified mechanics loved checking Daph over. They fixed the door and refused any payment; quite unexpected, but delightfully welcome. PE was lovely, reminding us of a faded Eastbourne, the Victorian, English seaside town. As with many places today in South Africa, they are being renamed; Pretoria is now called Tshwane and PE is to be called Gqeberha, a Xhosa word for the eponymous, local Baakens River.

The Garden Route is South Africa's core tourist strip along the southwestern coast, stretching from PE to Cape Town. The terrain passes through mountains, semi-desert to the north (the Karoo), indigenous forests and stunning, wave-lashed coastlines with expansive sweeps of sand. This area has been domesticated by agriculture and viticulture, and now tourism. All manner of adventurous activities and sports exist here, from world-renowned golf courses to kayaking, cycling and caving, through to coastal walks and whale-watching, attracting both domestic and international travellers alike. I appreciate the irony surrounding the domestic tourist claim as the area has become a largely white playground. We drove through a blinding thunderstorm and driving rain, forcing us to omit the delights of the Tsitsikamma National Park, instead stopping at a B&B in Knysna. This town has become synonymous for travellers and senior citizens, noticeably European and expatriates, due to the year-round great climate, ironic given our weather experience. The following day, on Wilderness beach, the weather cleared and we gazed over the outstanding views of the Indian Ocean, stunning beaches and inland up the Outeniqua Mountains.

We tackled the Outeniqua Mountains, driving inland from George up the Craddock Pass. What used to be a three or four-day slog, with extra oxen trains to ascend the Pass, took a mere 15 minutes on smooth, fresh tarmac. The terrain was rugged and dramatic, offering more outstanding views. The Klein Karoo is a semi-desert, which initially presented an impenetrable barrier to further inland exploration. We arrived at Oudtshoorn, renowned for ostrich farming, with some amazing caves, and the start of the Wine Route to Cape Town. I had been here before as it was also home to their Infantry Training Battle School. We lunched on a huge ostrich omelette, bought some ostrich steaks and headed to Cape Town, after dwelling in the delightful Franschhoek and Stellenbosch wine country.

Chapter 8
Africa's iconic city and coastline

Bullets started pinging off the armoured police car to our front. This was not in the schedule outlined earlier at Silvermine, the Regional Command in Cape Town. As military advisors, we were touring Mitchells Plain (Cape Flats) in an armoured car, escorting (following) the police. British doctrine would have 'boots on the ground', to speak and engage with the locals as part of a peace-making, police support patrol, a 'hearts and minds' approach to law-enforcing. Interestingly, such lofty thoughts vanished the moment the lead police car became engulfed in automatic gunfire.

It was a fleeting incident; we were secure inside our snazzy, V-shaped, mine-resistant, armoured monolith, watching the police car getting hit. The sergeant escorting us grew up and still lived and patrolled here for the last 10 years. He was rightly proud of his country - a poster boy for the Cape. A charming chap, full of facts and free with his wide-ranging views, with which I had no difficulties. Thankfully, the police car was armoured. My instinct sought action; a response; to identify the firing point, win the firefight and exploit in depth. But no. 'Let's wait and see what happens,' said the quiet, passive sergeant. Being a guest, I was shocked at the passive stance. It was police primacy, so we watched. 'Err, are we not going to help?' I suggested. Sitting here, with all the weapons and firepower to strike back, the response was 'Oh no, if we were to do that, we would become embroiled in the problem and then they would shoot at us too.' I was wrestling with this concept; what was the point of us being here? As soon as it started, it was over. We moved on like nothing had happened. No secured firing point or preservation of the scene of the crime. The reality was black-on-black, a drug-related crime (or a battle for supremacy) that was a daily occurrence. They knew who the protagonists were; the Nigerian drugs trade there was a problem in the tourist areas around Green Point, near the V&A Waterfront. Aware of the irony, we later enjoyed a delightful meal at the Waterfront that evening.

This minor fracas occurred several months before our arrival with Daph as we drove past the airport along the northern side of Cape Flats. Around four million black and coloured voters were 'shipped' into Mitchells Plain to swing the ANC vote during the key 1994 Western Province election. Violence is not foremost for most people visiting Cape Town, one of the world's most iconic cities, like Rio, Sydney, Singapore or London. As we nudged Daphne through the heavy traffic in light rain, the unsightly and makeshift Cape Flats' housing, jammed against the roadside fence, was thrust in your face; hardly the tourist board's dream image. I appreciate Rio (as elsewhere) has their favelas, but this was the first impression tourists get on arrival from the airport. I accept people are not looking for poverty as they head for the beaches, glamour and 'high life'. This reflected the housing dichotomy we witnessed in Grahamstown. Cape Town had its own way of managing the issue, for as soon as we rose out of Mitchells Plain, the old town and modern environs took hold. We were staying with some friends, for any camping options were far outside city limits. Our friends ran a very successful guest house in a colonial, Dutch house in the nook of Table Mountain, in Oranjezicht.

The history of Cape Town, both old and recent, is amazing, and there are so many things to see and do; for all tastes. Staying centrally was fantastic. Around the corner was District Six, juxtaposed to the expensive hotels and central area. Johnny was able to squeeze Daph into his secure, off-street parking; petty car theft is rife. From Oranjezicht, we were able to run up Table Mountain, Lions Head or walk down to Kloof Nek Road and down to the Waterfront. The Waterfront and the V&A are wonderful, vibrant places especially as the 'Volvo Ocean Racing' village and teams were arriving for their Cape stopover.

Knowing locals makes such a difference, as opposed to simply being a tourist. They generally want you to see their town through their eyes and can short-cut and enable a great stay. Cape Town was the last shakedown before our trek north and we had booked Daph into Cape Town Land Rover for a service. Situated near the top of Kloof Nek, it was a convenient location. Johnny allowed us to unload most of our gear into his garage temporarily. We were well received at Land Rover; they loved Daph. We felt reassured when they said they would 'make a plan'. I should have known…

Rain cannot dampen Cape Town, so whilst Daph was getting her therapy, we watch the live broadcast of the Queen Mother's funeral in London, a solemn, sad event in which the locals were fascinated. We revisited the planetarium; Cape Town is part of the Dark Skies programme. Here, one lies back and gazes at the roof as they explain the stars, alignment and evolution. When I looked up at night's sky in Africa to see the Milky Way and bright lights that are obscured in the Northern Hemisphere, I just wished I could recall half of what was explained.

All countries celebrate their regional differences. Hitherto, we were told the Highveld (Gauteng, the plateau environs around Jo'berg and Pretoria) featured the 'real' South African cultural of hospitality and warmth, as opposed to Cape Town's laid-back, 'English' vibe. We found the hospitality in Cape Town as open, but language still applies. In Cape Town, people predominantly spoke English first, whereas in Pretoria it is Afrikaans. Cape Town was different; a more cosmopolitan, global place, but here more than before, we noticed phrases like 'howsit' and 'lekker' (meaning pleasant or enjoyable) were more prevalent. Helpfully, there is an explanatory frieze at the Waterfront that tells baffled tourists the essential language differences.

South Africa has eleven official languages, including English and Afrikaans. Our military team ultimately reported to the Chief of the Defence Staff, who spoke most languages, Xhosa (spoken in clicks) being his native language. Abbreviations sometimes confuse; pronouns are frequently dropped, for example, 'take with us' becomes 'take with'. English words sometimes convey different meanings too, leading to humorous outcomes. Depending on the tenor of the voice and context used, a word may have a double meaning. The classic being, 'shame hey' meaning 'it's a pity', but 'ag shame' is a positive affirmation. So, 'ag shame' means a baby is cute, whereas 'shame hey' implies the opposite! Time is also a factor; if someone says they will do this 'just now', they mean that the task will be done eventually (if at all), but certainly not now. Similarly, if the phrase implies they will 'make a plan', they do not mean they're considering and proposing a solution for action; far from it. It's more mañana - they may or may not get around to it. Recently, when cycling with mates, our tame South African had a mechanical issue with his wheel, so we all stopped to help fix it. After some tussling, he stated he would 'make a plan' and promptly got on and rode off, leaving us all agog and me in stitches.

Hence, we were not so amused when we returned to Cape Town Land Rover two days later to find little or nothing had changed on Daph, despite being presented with a bill. The embarrassed workshop manager emerged. It turned out he knew the PE boys and was contrite. He cancelled the bill and quietly directed us to LR Services, south near Plumstead. These guys knew Land Rovers and sorted Daph immediately, effectively and for significantly less cost. They also had a selection of great after-market add-ons and vehicles for sale, akin to B'rakkah in Pretoria. Their chief mechanic, Steve, was English, and had driven down from London years previously. He had loved the journey so much that he stayed. Steve provided some valuable insight, but basically told us to just get out there. We also found nearby Just Done It, who provided fabrication services and a range of expedition-ready Land Rovers for self-drive.

A number of ex-military live around Cape Town, and although many were out of town during our visit, we met Simon Mann through a mutual contact. Simon was happy to meet but was very cagey about the location. I knew a few lads who had worked with him during his Sandline adventures in Sierra Leone, but aside talking about mutual friends, I mainly wanted to discuss flying. After some cloak and dagger activities, we found ourselves in a diner, enjoying a beer, when in slipped Simon. He was charm personified and started chatting about the military, flying and driving through Africa. He was heading out of town, but if we waited a month or so, he offered us a flight around the Cape on his return. Critically, he gave us the name of Hammy, his mechanic, down in Muizenburg, who maintained his Range Rover and our friend, Robin's Land Rover. And with that, he was gone, leaving us little or no clue as to the imaginary shadows tailing him.

We visited the Cape of Good Hope (the demise of too many early sailors) and Cape Agulhas, the continent's most southerly point. The Cape of Good Hope at the bottom of the Table Mountain peninsular is frequently mistaken for being the southernmost tip. The lighthouse perched precariously on the rocky promontory at the Cape of Good Hope looks considerably dramatic. Named by the Portuguese 'the Cape of Needles', it looks every bit rocky and dangerous. Geologically, the warm Agulhas current rotates back eastwards, warming the beaches of KwaZulu Natal, whilst the cold Benguela current, drawn from the Antarctic, flows up the western and Namibian coastline. This split here of ocean currents generates notorious winter storms and mammoth waves, up to 100 feet high, with the obvious shipping impact. The lighthouses built around the coastline to alert shipping were invaluable.

We visited Hermanus, despite being out of whale-watching season, and we were lucky to see a pod of Southern right whales frolicking in the bay.

The following bright and clear morning brought out the 'whale man' ringing his hand bell, announcing the whale's arrival. September hosts Hermanus' annual whale festival. Whale watching is passive, compared to the mad shark baiting and cage diving adventures offered there. The Southern right whale is huge, distinguished by callositiy deposits on their head. The thick layer of blubber under their skin, essential for Antarctic waters, make it impossible for them to cool down, partially explaining the curious tricks and shapes they perform to cool off. Cape Agulhas was not so dramatic. The lighthouse (built around the mid-1850s) provides stunning views along the coastline. We had not planned a 'toe to tip' transit of Africa initially, but it seemed daft to omit the southernmost geological feature whilst here.

It was time to move on. Cape Town is a wonderful place; easy to live, relax and enjoy oneself, but our mission was to drive the slow road home. Had we stayed any longer in Cape Town, there was a growing possibility we might never leave. Our wonderful hosts, Johnny and Sharron, could not have been more helpful. But the Cederberg Mountains were calling, for we had arranged to meet some old friends there, Gary and Sarah, whilst they were supporting the 'Across the Divide' adventure operation, where we all met in Namibia years earlier. They were at an overnight stop at the Algeria campsite. Talk about turning the clock back when we arrived; owners Mark and Karen were there with their new baby, with their Namibian crew (and many of the same guides) plus Gary and Sarah. Tales were told into the evening whilst the trekkers were set for their pre-dawn departure up the mountain. They planned to capture the sunrise on the next mountain top and suggested we join them for the sunrise, before returning to Algeria and Daph. We had a wonderful evening and enjoyed the catch-up, but gracefully declined; we had Namibia to explore. We made arrangements to see Gary and Sarah in Swakopmund, although I must admit I felt a twang of regret as the walkers departed. However, we were up early, packed and prepared for our own trek. After our goodbyes, we pressed on. We enjoyed the Cederbergs as we wove our way to brunch in Clanwilliam. This town was a glimpse back in time, replete with traditional Cape Dutch settler heritage, nestled in their surroundings astride the Olifants River. A major wine and citrus producing region for Western Cape, we passed acres of lemon, orange, apple groves and vineyards. The air was crisp and clear; it was a lovely day and we felt refreshed, rested and eager to experience the adventure ahead of us.

Chapter 9
We can rebuild you

That night, following the accident and leaving Catherine in the hospital, it's time like these that friends come to the rescue; bless Johnny, he picked me up and placed a metaphorical arm around me. I initiated the travel and vehicle insurance in the morning, grateful at being covered. Catherine was the priority; she was receiving immediate care, X-rays and could be released the following day. The A & E consultant was also an orthopaedic doctor; he explained her injuries and said she might require surgery. For now, the bruising was too severe for immediate treatment, so she was released with painkillers and her shoulder immobilised in a sling. This was not the National Health Service (NHS) - only immediate services were provided and anything else had to be paid, usually via insurance.

The thing about contingency plans is that you never really believe they are needed; plan for the worst, hope for the best. The military mind expects all outcomes to be considered, with potential actions aligned. We had discussed some, outside the obvious hijack or attack, but now, in the 'shock of capture', we were managing our way through. If you have to, Cape Town must be the optimal African location to recover; it has excellent communications, medical facilities and we were grateful for friends and colleagues. Vehicles can be replaced, but bodies cannot. Catherine was relieved to be out of the hospital; she believed the doctor's diagnosis but sought a second opinion. Her shoulder was causing the most concern, despite the pain in her hand. Our insurance company only wanted to repatriate us to the NHS, where Catherine understood it would involve plates and shoulder screws, leading to probable life-long discomfort, further operations and limited limb movement. We refused to be rushed. Catherine was not sure how, but in her mind, she was determined to carry on with our trip. This was madness to my mind, but I understood this was her coping strategy.

Catherine's greatest concern was confessing the accident to her parents. Her father, a dominant character, had always been against the trip. His dire protestations that 'no good will come of it' were now ringing true. His negative perception of Africa was dark, foreboding doom and gloom and now, here we were. Yet he, more than most, understood that once Catherine's mind was set, that would be it. As he dropped her off at Heathrow for her last flight to Johannesburg, he asked her, 'How much would I have to pay to persuade you not to go?' Of course, Catherine was having none of it; thankfully, he relented and gave us his blessing. But only now, here in Cape Town, was I learning of all this angst. To be fair, when she phoned her parents, they were great, offering any necessary help. This provided considerable solace; Catherine would not have wanted to admit defeat to her father, let alone to herself. Years later, writing this, I appreciate the worst aspect for Catherine was breaking the news to her parents. She should not have worried.

It was Johnny and Sharron who came up trumps. They knew a doctor, Dr Joe DeBeer, who ran a private clinic locally. He was a shoulder expert - not just any expert - it turned out he was the shoulder expert for the Springboks rugby team. Johnny had arranged an appointment for the following day. It was an outstanding meeting. Dr Joe said, 'Welcome to the third world,' yet both Catherine and he knew the medical options here were superior to the NHS. Dr Joe explained the nature of the break, a complicated fracture at the distal end making it challenging to 'plate and screw'. Dr Joe sought to fix the joint with dissolvable tape and, if necessary, a bone graft from Catherine's hip, offering a full restructure and movement. He was confident that we would be back on the road within six weeks, provided Catherine completed the full physio regime. We were gobsmacked. This was music to Catherine's ears, whereas I just wanted her well. Dr Joe explained his fees would be covered under insurance and offered to speak to the insurance company himself. The physio was crucial to Catherine's recovery, and part of the fees. He recommended Cathy Chambers, who was used to sports injuries, having played and supported the South African hockey team herself.

This gave Catherine the impetus to carry on. Unsurprisingly, our insurance company was not happy, leading to an inevitable ping-pong, but once a final price was disclosed, the best health outcome prevailed. Cape Town was becoming a health destination because of the quality of medical and practitioner care, the climate and the recovery environment. Catherine got settled in her private room, with attentive nurses and good facilities, an uninterrupted view of Lion's Head, being situated next to the Mount Nelson Hotel, one of the world's premier hotels. Meanwhile, I was in the basement, filling in forms and signing my life away. Dr Joe and his team were thoroughly professional, diligent in all the follow-ups. When Catherine came round from the operation, Dr Joe, his anaesthetist and the hospital physio were by her bedside to discuss her aftercare. Dr Joe was delighted with the operation and there was no need for a bone graft. Catherine's ligaments now needed to heal.

The day she came out of hospital, unbeknown to us, Sharron and her friends threw Catherine a 40th birthday party; we were very touched. During these celebrations, Catherine received a text from her father to announce the birth of her nephew; Julie had given birth to their first, Ben, that same day. Catherine's father sent a text that read, 'Congratulations, u r now an ANT.' Yes; it took a little interpretation! A week later, I too found out that I was an uncle again; my brother's wife gave birth to their daughter. Catherine was determined to carry on. Still reticent as to whether it was the right thing to further jeopardise her health, we were already taking action. Word was out about the accident and we were getting constant messages and best wishes from back home. Thank goodness social media was not around then to plague us. Among the comical suggestions for a 'Daphne replacement', special mention is extended to Gary and Sarah for their creativity and natty imagery that we posted on our website.

A couple of days after the accident, I travelled to Garies police station to reclaim our gear and arrange for Daph to be recovered for insurance purposes. The police were satisfied that they had all the necessary details; they knew of the perpetrator, but thus far had not apprehended the bakkie driver. Unsurprisingly, nothing ever happened. Whilst Sharron looked after Catherine, Johnny lent me his VW Kombi and a mate to recover our gear. What we thought we were going to do with the recovered gear remained questionable. Setting off before dawn, we made Garies just after breakfast time and were able to strip any salvageable items off Daph before the salvage truck arrived. The police were very efficient, having itemised and secured everything in their lock-up. It's worth repeating what a great job these chaps had done; I was both grateful and humbled. Daph had not been tampered with, so we removed the extended fuel tank, the dual battery charging system, fridge and everything else that was recoverable.

What is it about recovery chaps? This one marked his card on arrival by almost reversing over the roof rack and Eezi-Awn. I appreciate that Daph was scrap in his eyes, but there is a difference between incompetence and professionalism; the police were more annoyed than me! To compound Mr Recovery's inadequacies, he was woefully unprepared for his task; he had no straps or ability to carry anything other than a small vehicle. I called the insurance company who were dismayed and apologetic. Interestingly, having given the recovery guy my straps and rachets to fulfil his task, the insurance company told me that ARC in Cape Town had acquired Daph at auction for 23% above her scrap value. Later, a lad in Pretoria sent us pictures of a stripped-down Daphne shell, replete with the original decals, languishing in a Land Rover graveyard. Who knew that people were following us? We just managed to load the remaining gear into the Kombi, including the rack and roof tent inside, and returned to Cape Town.

Bruce Willmore and his colleagues at Cross Country Insurance were outstanding. Our 'All Terrain' policy was underwritten by SA Eagle, providing cover up to and including all southern African countries to Kenya and Uganda (minus Angola and CAR). Their policy was unique in that it also covered vehicle accessories. Bruce used a raft of 4x4 accident data to prove his offer to Eagle; over 80% of 4x4 accidents happen on normal roads under normal conditions, so the marginal, extra off-road cover was minimal. Most 4x4 drivers are unaware that their vehicle is 'top heavy' or unstable with knobbly tyres, making them more prone to on-road accidents; but manufacturer statistics imply that these vehicles are better maintained, serviced and more survivable in accidents. Finally, with off-road driver training and enhanced awareness, it should reduce potential accidents, thus reduce premiums whilst offering more extensive cover: a win-win. Bruce knew we had closed our South African bank account, so when Daph was written off within 14 days of the accident, Bruce held payment until we decided what to do. In fact, it was through Bruce's network that we found our replacement Daphne. Bruce conducted the financial transactions and transferred our insurance and Carnet onto the second vehicle. We cannot thank Bruce and his team enough.

Perhaps I've just let the cat out of the bag. Catherine was determined to carry on, obtaining Dr Joe's endorsement, confident of his six-week prediction that the shoulder would be healed. I was sure there were a million and one reasons not to press on, but we had come this far. Besides, given my experiences, it's not the knocks one takes, it's how they are managed; the same wind blows upon us all, it is how you set your sails.

Before Bruce found Daphne II, I was unenamoured by the alternative options available in Cape Town. Cape Town Land Rover sought to sell us a new vehicle, further depressing my expectation from them, but I should not be too harsh, for they lent me a new Land Rover 90 TD5 for a week. South Africa had been the global launch, at Bushman's Kloof in the Cederberg, for the new engines, models and Range Rover. The TD5 was great around town, with more power and torque, but it was fundamentally unsuited to our needs. LR services had scant stock, although I did consider a Series II, 200 series tdi Discovery.

I got a call from Simon Mann. He invited us for lunch and was sorry to hear about the accident. He loaned us his pristine V8 Range Rover County. This was 'Paris Dakar' ready. I loved it; it had that lovely V8 rumble. Loan aside, he suggested if we didn't find an alternative, we should use it for the trip. This was so tempting, a real heart v. head matter. The redoubtable Tom Sheppard is a big Range Rover fan, after all, the Range Rover has the most capable chassis on the market. But there were a number of concerns; this was petrol not diesel, doubling our fuel consumption, halving our range and the associated high risk of fuel contamination. Not to mention speed that could well get us into more trouble. A Range Rover needs constant and qualified maintenance; way beyond my competencies with 'half a spanner and a Leatherman'; the electronics alone are notoriously tricky. We would need a major rethink for our gear, not least the roof tent. Range Rovers already have a high centre of gravity and are prone to rolling, so a roof tent on top (even with a roll cage) would not help. I was sorely tempted, and we were running out of options. But to potentially break or lose someone's precious plaything might be one thing, but this was verging on irreplaceable. Plus, finding dodgy diamonds at Dover Customs welded within the chassis that you didn't know were there, would be quite another! Clearly, I'm joking on the diamond point, but one never knows. Still, we had a few lunches with Simon, and more than a few beers and laughs about Wonderboom airport. Ironically, it was at Wonderboom that his subsequent Equatorial Guinea escapade started to unravel, before being arrested at Harare airport. Again, I was grateful he never offered me a job.

When Bruce called about a Land Rover of similar spec, age and condition to Daph at Midrand Land Rover, I asked him to place it on hold for me to check it out. It had been an ex-safari vehicle, so had some miles on the clock, but was in fine condition. A few days later, I was on an internal flight to Johannesburg to check it out. Coincidentally, Gary and Sarah were also in Johannesburg to inspect the work for their 10-seater Land Cruiser safari wagon, all stripped down and doors off. Lovely, if a tad pricey. They agreed to pick me up at the airport. As I wandered through arrivals, I saw them immediately; Gary had gone native, not having worn shoes for six months or more. To cut a long story short, the vehicle was fine, although it had the inevitable oil leak. Not again! We agreed a price, including some work, allowing me to pick it up the following day. Great work, Bruce, who covered the bill and insured it immediately. I was able to return to Cape Town the following day, my birthday, driving away with Daphne II. It came with some extras like a roof rack, front bull bars, a snorkel and its own second split-battery charging system, but there were a few extras I sought this time around. The garage fixed a bonnet mount and strengthening kit to carry a second spare wheel, along with the one on the rear swing-arm. Most Kenyan rear swing-arms carry two spare wheels; we opted for a balanced approach that worked well.

That night, I caught up with Chris and the boys back in Pretoria; they wanted to hear about the crash and find out how Catherine was. It was great to see them again. For the second time departing Pretoria, I rose at 4am to hit the road. Eighteen hours later, I was in Cape Town, having taken the direct route via Kimberley, Beaufort West and Paarl. It was a long slog and I was knackered. The last most attractive part through the Hex River and Worcester was in the dark, it was raining and I was too tired to really notice. I was aware I needed to stop, but Daph pulled well, not missing a beat, thank goodness. I had arranged for LR Services to check her over, where she received a clean bill of health. She had low compression on one injector, yet it was pronounced manageable. We fitted a new cambelt tensioner, fuel lift pump, new brakes and discs and readjusted the diesel timing. Now Daphne II was mechanically sound and raring to go. More good news from Dr Joe; in our second-week check-up, he pronounced Catherine on track, although he wanted further healing before starting physio with Cathy, to strengthen the ligaments.

Daph II went to Hammy, Simon Mann's mechanic, and his A-Team to get our recovered extras fitted. Hammy had trained on a Mercedes scholarship in Germany after his father was forced off their farm in Zimbabwe. He ran a garage near Muizenberg, south of Cape Town, but his passion was rallying. Challenging at best, given he was a large 'Oak', easily six and a half feet and built like the proverbial, I'd like to have seen him squeeze into a rally car. He had a workshop in his home garage too, which is where he and I, with some of his lads, 'spannered' for many hours, re-assembling Daph II. I managed to recover the side window grilles, but also fitted some expensive Mantec rear window protectors as the rear door and side windows were a security weak point.

Hammy's contacts fitted window tints to protect the glass from shattering and deter prying eyes in the rear, along with a carpet trimmer to replace the existing threadbare stuff and conceal the hidden safe, on which we refitted the fridge. I had the trimmer replace Johnny's Kombi carpet whilst Hammy gave it a service. Hammy's electrician had a nightmare with the electrics and the split-battery charger; it became easier to refit our recovered system. A local tent company, Christies, patched the Eezi Awn, after which, another company, Just Done It, fitted our roof tent and awning to the rack, along with new jerry cans and gas bottle holders. Daph II gradually morphed into the original Daph.

Johnny was getting interested and wanted to visit a new off-road shop in Cape Town, so we tagged along - fatal! We certainly didn't need any more equipment, but we saw an excellent Australian tent that enabled one person to erect it with one arm in seconds; no guy ropes and two people could stand upright inside. The Oztent (original name!) with its awning could connect to the back of the vehicle, enabling us to administrate ourselves undercover in inclement weather. We sold the dome tent. At two metres long, the Oztent was a proverbial pain to carry. Eventually, we hung it internally along the roof line, so it poked through into the driver's cabin, without being intrusive. Ironically, we rarely used it, but when we did, it was fabulous.

We walked to Cathy's place for Catherine's physio and learn the stretches and movements for recovery. The girls bonded and her shoulder became a strong repair, retaining a full range of movement. Catherine still uses many of the same stretches. Every morning thereafter, Catherine religiously completed her routine, afraid she might get a frozen shoulder, so she waved her tin of beans or used an exercise band to strengthen the joint. Dr Joe discharged her at the six-week point, although he advised initially to avoid driving, especially off-road, in case of a sudden wrench. In fact, from here on, poor Catherine didn't drive on the trip, or really lift much, so her active participation was limited from her perspective. This was a massive blow, for it had been Catherine's dream to actively drive through Africa. She adapted fantastically, took on the administration, documentation and writing up our website as we went. All too soon, it was time to leave Cape Town again. We said our goodbyes as we inched the fully-laden Daph off Johnny's excessively steep driveway. Thank you all in Cape Town; you have been wonderful.

We took it easy to start with and used a B & B in Clanwilliam. The Scottish owner was worried for Catherine, although at the same time excited, as much for our trip as the impending emergence of the wildflowers that appear once every ten years in the barren, local Namaqualand desert. Taking things slowly, we dawdled up to Springbok, our final night in South Africa. That evening, Johnny called for a progress report, bless him; I guess he feared we might reappear.

Chapter 10
Dark skies over the Namib

Namibia has an excellent road network spanning the country, making it accessible with a car, even the non-tar roads. But an SUV offers more comfort and potential to explore deeper into Damarland, Kaokoland or eastern Caprivi. That said, the corrugations vibrated Daph, making it uncomfortable for Catherine. Corrugation driving is both an art and skill; one has to find the right balance of speed, sufficient to glide over the top of the corrugations, yet retaining control; what Tom Shepperd calls this finding the 'harmonic speed'. Our friends, Gary and Sarah, were extolling the virtues of their bigger, more powerful (and thirstier!) 4.2 litre Toyota Landcruiser, yet Daph pulled well. I understood Gary was experiencing excessive punctures, but we were sure it had nothing to do with Gary's heavy left foot! We plodded on, enjoying yet more Land Rover brand recognition and head-light flashing.

We arrived early at the Namibian border, but struggled with officialdom. The pointless farce took the majority of the day. Our paperwork was correct, except the girl behind the desk said, 'Computer says no.' There was no reasoning or recourse; at one point we returned to Springbok, to get a police inspector to jemmy open a filling cabinet with a large hunting knife, to then laboriously transcribe the right ('unnecessary' - his words) data. By late afternoon, back at the border, 'our girl' stamped our clearance form without a blink! The Namibian side also struggled with the Carnet, but we corrected their error and prayed this was not indicative for all borders.

Our initial intent was to camp at Hobas, above Fish River Canyon, but even allowing for the time difference (we had gained an hour by crossing the border), this was no longer feasible. The Fish River flows through southern Namibia, down to the Ai-Ais/Richtersveld Transfrontier Park, where it joins the Orange River. Over the millennia, the Fish River has carved a gigantic, horseshoe-shaped canyon, a miniature version of the American Grand Canyon. Classically, it takes hikers five days to walk the 100-mile length, descending 550 metres to the river. Reassessing our options in the fading light, we headed to the walk-out point at Ais-Ais, a hot springs site at the base of the canyon. We planned to camp, but by the time we had paid for the hot springs and facilities, it was just as cheap to check-in at the lodge, which bought us more recovery time for Catherine's shoulder. The hot spa was very therapeutic; we felt excessively hot and heavy when we finished wallowing in the sulphur pool like a couple of hippos.

Following a decent breakfast, we re-emerged from the canyon into the hot, dry heat on the plateau. A strong headwind blew as we battled against it around the canyon rim to view the horseshoe canyon in all its glory. As we drove north, the heavy corrugations were vibrating Catherine's shoulder; she never complained as there was little we could do about it. The Land Rover is a cushioned ride, although the air suspension on the new Range Rover would have been nice! The headwind continued to make it feel like we were getting nowhere; Daph's engine was labouring so I started to worry that there might be a turbo or fuel filter issue. But no, it was just the wind. It reignited Gary's Land Rover versus Toyota debate, not to mention Simon's Rangie. We found fuel and supplies at the small settlement of Bethanie, where we learnt this was the oldest settlement in Namibia, founded by German missionaries. Their stone Lutheran church remained.

We were transiting the breath taking Namib Rand Nature Reserve under its vast, open skies, scrub and sand gravel planes. The majority of southwestern Namibia is covered by the oldest desert in the world, the Namib Desert. We passed signposts for the recently established, uber chic and scarily expensive tented eco-lodge of Wolwedans. This was around 60 kilometres south of the classic dune formation at Sossusvlei, our destination. The huge photogenic sand ridges around Sossusvlei have been formed by the sun, wind and rain, and attract thousands of visitors annually. Wolwedans, and others, seek to capitalise on the growing demand for high-end, discerning visitors, striving to relax within iconic yet remote locations. By contrast, we were looking to rough camp when, quite by chance, we came across the Balloon Safari Lodge and campsite. This place was being set up by a French couple who apologised that they were not ready for visitors, but they took one look at Catherine with her arm in the sling and invited us in. We said we were more than happy to rough camp, we just sought a quiet space. This caused a huge French discussion about the fact they were not ready to offer the full 'Le Dinner' that we had not asked for!

Paul and Fifi were fabulous; they insisted that we stay and test one of their walk-in, en-suite safari tents, on a notional deal with a spaghetti bolognaise supper thrown in. Fantastic - the deal was secured with a bottle of French red from the back of Daph that they had not tasted in years. Paul was a trainee balloon pilot, preparing for trips across the Namib at dune height, with back-up vehicles offering game drives in support. Wolwedans clients were apparently clamouring for slots. Originally French, they were refugees from the Belgium Congo, where Paul had been a tobacco farmer. They were effectively driven out of the country, partly due to the market collapsing, as much as by corruption and intimidation. They were relieved to escape, although they had grown up with the 'African problem', yet the scale and threats to them and their business proved too much. They claimed to have found peace and harmony here in this small slice of delightful Namibia.

They were the usual have-a-go experts that the country relies upon. Fifi was a wonderful cook, had a good eye for dressing and decorating the lodge, offering a warm and inviting space. The ever-practical Paul could fix anything and was relishing his balloon flying. We were offered a freebie flight, but they were waiting for a gas resupply and the current high winds made flying unsafe, sadly. Interestingly, their balloon was made in the UK (Bristol) and their panels were decorated with bushman art. They were fascinated by our trip, wished us well, yet were saddened by the accident. Never once did Fifi question Catherine's decision to travel; she would have done the same in a heartbeat. Hardy African people.

A significant attraction for this area is the vast, open skies, both day and night. This region is part of the Dark-Sky Association of the International Dark Sky Reserve. The absence of light pollution makes this area brilliant for observing the full splendour of the night's sky, the Milky Way and more, except for us, unusually, it was raining. Never mind, we were cosy and warm in our safari tent. After a delightfully lazy start, saying a lingering goodbye to new friends, we wished them well for their new adventures. Conducting my morning checks on Daph, I noted she was burning oil. I topped her up, but again I could not detect the cause. After Lesotho's oil-dumping experience, I was aware of what to monitor. As we hit the rain-dampened roads, it reduced the dust. The clouds were still with us, creating a fantastic light and dramatic sky; at one point, we saw the most vivid rainbow arc across our path. The slightly damp air also helped Daph's turbo to breath more efficiently. At Sesriem, the entrance to Sossusvlei, the road became tarred. Had we pressed on for a further hour the previous night, we would have hit these lodges and camping facilities, although there was no question that we had been far better off at Paul and Fifi's. We drove through wet sand to Sossusvlei.

The salt and clay pan of Sossusvlei is surrounded by huge dunes that have become the poster image for Namibian tourism. Sossusvlei is the most accessible part of a huge, sand-sea dune desert that stretches 300 kilometres along the coast and nearly 150 kilometres inland, smothering over 32,000 square kilometres of western Namibia. It is estimated that these dunes are growing by over 400,000 cubic metres a year. The sand was swept from the Kalahari around three to five million years ago down the Orange River, and now, the Benguela wind and currents are blowing it back along the Namib coast and inland. These dunes are among the highest in the world, many being over 200 metres high. The older dunes are dark red in colour, the lighter hues denote more recent activity. Named by numbers, Dune 45 is the one that most tourists are photographed ascending. The Namib Desert is watered very occasionally by rain, but most moisture comes from the huge fog banks that roll in from the temperature inversion from the cold Benguela current hitting the warm desert air. Subterranean, seasonal rivers feed the pans; these ephemeral flows leave a white salt deposit of evaporation and residue. Animals love it, licking the salts.

Both Dune 45 and the clay pans, with the desiccated, camel thorn tree skeleton framed against the dunes, called Deadvlei, frame the classic tourist photograph. These trees died around six or seven thousand years ago from insufficient water. Now, they have become scorched black from the intense sun, so are not petrified as most believe; the wood cannot decompose due to the intense dryness. The unusual, intense rain we travelled through left puddles in the sand, drying at an astonishing rate. The clay pan was bone dry, leaving a crazy-paving pattern. Rain or not, we were delighted we had made the effort to visit, for like the Fish River Canyon, the place was magnificent.

We headed on north towards the Namib Naukluft National Park. The Namib is considered to be the oldest and driest desert in the world, comparable with the Atacama Desert in South America for age and aridity. The inland gravel plains have scattered mountain outcrops and stunning canyons, such as the Moon Valley system. While most of this area is rocky, sand dunes exist. The Namib has been mined for minerals, revealing tungsten, salt and diamonds. Several rivers and ephemeral streams exist, but few reach the ocean. Without water, the Namib cannot sustain human life, forcing the very few, small settlements and indigenous pastoral groups to its northern boundary.

I had been to the Namib before, whilst working to the MoD a few years previously. It was one of those drink-induced challenges where I picked up the gauntlet to compete in a nascent extreme charity event. What I thought was a 100-mile race through the Namib Desert turned out to be so much better; a thoroughly enjoyable five-day trek for MAG (Mine Advisory Group) International, a de-mining charity. MAG are dedicated to clearing up post-conflict zones and assisting communities, enabling the local populous to resume a semblance of normality, without fear of getting their legs blown off by unmarked ordnance. Many charity challenges and events outsource the in-country administration to third-party companies to run the events. For mine, it was Across the Divide (ATD), run by Mark Hannaford. Aside from being a nice bloke, Mark was a sharp cookie. Whether he was a chum of Bear Grylls or not, Mark similarly cut his teeth with the London Territorial SAS. ATD combined his adventurous spirit, whilst tapping into the corporate social responsibility programmes and burgeoning charity quest for alternative fund-raising activities. ATD supported a network of global events managing the in-country support (accommodation, food, medical supplies and transport) and directing the guides with en route challenges. I have to say, mine was seamlessly delivered. When I last looked up ATD, they were running Global to Local challenges in the Arctic, plus supporting the BBC's Rickshaw Challenge. Such challenges are open to all, and to sweeten the pill, celebrities are signed-up to spice up the fundraising activity. It was rumoured that Richard Branson was signed up for the Namib event, but this turned out to be a morale booster, with a group satellite call halfway to Richard, sweating in his office. The actress, Amanda Redmond, was sadly a no-show too (probably because I offered to carry her bags at the event briefing), but we did have Trevor Bayliss (he of the wind-up radio) and Paul Burrell, the ex-butler to Lady Diana. It was here that I met Gary and Sarah, who were within my walking group. This was all new to Gary and Sarah, who were so taken with Namibia and the ATD challenge that Gary subsequently sold his business and relocated to Namibia, to run a tourist camp and support ATD, which is how we re-connected.

I was able to show Catherine many of the features that we'd traversed. The MAG challengers first met at Heathrow for the flight to Windhoek, where they were picked up by coaches and dumped in the desert as dusk fell. 'Leave your kit there and walk that way'…for a few miles in the semi-dark to our tented camp. Great icebreaker. Thereafter, groups of 20 were guided each day through the hot, dry desert and rocky terrain. It was great, except that Air Namibia lost my bag on the way out, so I was as I stood. Thankfully, the old soldier's metaphor of 'never get separated from your kit' meant I had sufficient essentials in my day sack and was wearing my boots on the flight. Frankly, I didn't need much more, so when I was reunited with my gear, I simply enjoyed a wash and fresh clothes, before replacing the bag on the baggage belt for the return trip. We camped at Bloedkoppie one night, Namibia's answer to Australia's Ayers Rock (now known as Uluru). As we walked towards it in the evening sun, it glowed red, and in the chilly evening, it radiated heat.

With Daph, I thought to camp at Bloedkoppie after Sossusvlei, as I also wanted to show Catherine the strange Welwitschia plant, but we never made it. Instead, we bush camped in the Kiseb Valley once darkness rolled in. We enjoyed the Oztent, alleviating Catherine having to climb the step ladder with her sore shoulder. The following morning at Bloedkoppie, we rambled up the kopje, with the heat still radiating out. There was a track to a viewing point for the Welwitschia, with a sign proclaiming this example to be the oldest such plant. Given that they were a wild plant, this was a big claim. Whilst not a cactus, the Welwitschia grows two strap-shaped leaves each, about a metre long, that become gnarled and weather-beaten. It sucks up moisture from the fog banks. These plants appeared to be in league with a local swarm of bees that were unrelenting and most unpleasant. Thank goodness for Tabard, the local mozzie repellent, which worked a treat. All life here is adapted for the dry; they tend to be smaller animals like jackals and rodents, although zebra and the classic gemsbok roam freely. The oryx, here referred to as gemsbok, are so well adapted to the dry that it's thought they can exist for months without water. They use nasal panting to keep their brains cool while the rest of their body temperature soars; they draw air rapidly over their nose. Cool air molecules over numerous blood capillaries in the nose send cooled blood to the brain. They do not sweat either, so moisture is not wasted.

Since our arrival in Namibia, we had been reading the most amazing story of desert survival in Sheltering Desert by Henno Martin; a true story of survival and immense friendship. We were both moved by their tussle and the primeval hunting instinct. At the outbreak of the Second World War, these two German geologists, Hermann Korn and Henno Martin were facing internment, so they ran and hid in the desert, with their faithful dog, Otto. They had to adapt to their surroundings through observation and trial and error; the desert gradually revealed its secrets. They sought to extract both beauty and significance from ordinary things - the hunter and the hunted. I would not dare pre-empt the ending, but it is a great read and a sharp insight into humanity.

We pressed on to Swakopmund, in the hope and understanding that we might catch up with Gary and Sarah; sadly, they were not responding. Once out of the Namib, it was tar road all the way to town. We checked into a cheap B & B, in part to rest Catherine's shoulder, to remain central should we get comms with Gary or Sarah, and to securely park Daph. Swakopmund retains a German feel, thriving as a beach resort. The town was captured by a German gunboat in 1862, as a challenge to the British fleet, unable to react at anchor in Walvis Bay. Our B & B owner was of German heritage and expressed concerned about African politics, especially events in Zimbabwe. In contrast to Paul and Fifi, all she could see was government corruption and potential land grabs against the 'whites'. Not wanting to be drawn in, we took an evening stroll along the beach that was surprisingly cold from a stiff, coastal breeze. We took shelter in the Old Tug Boat pub on the sea wall, which was delightful and very friendly. They directed us to a local restaurant that offered the choice of 'croc in a pot' or 'ostrich stroganoff'; both were fantastic.

Catherine's shoulder was getting stronger each day. She religiously did her exercises to strengthen the muscles each evening to ensure she recovered full movement. The corrugations were not helping, so it was a relief to depart Swakopmund on tar roads via the main highway to Windhoek. We climbed inland to the edge of the Namib, up which Daph really struggled. It was a gentle, relentless climb and she should not have strained. Again, it was the strength of an exceptional headwind; I was blocking out Gary's voice. 'Should have bought a Toyota!'- no way!

We considered chasing the desert elephants further north in the Damaraland, but we knew we would see them at Etosha. En route to Etosha, we booked a stay at Okonjima Lodge. Okonjima (supporting Africat) had a similar vibe to the elephant sanctuary; a conservation initiative that offered great comfort and insight. In the sandstone Omboroko Mountains, the farming area of thick acacia thornveld is renowned for leopards, brown hyaenas and pangolins. AfriCat, founded in 1991, is a non-profit to ensure the survival of Namibia's predators in their wild. Working alongside local farmers, they help educated and resolve conflict between farms and predators. Initially, they trapped and removed predators encroaching on farmland, but gradually, through education (their second pillar), they seek ways for harmony. The foundation seeks to redress the evolutionary balance ruined by encroaching intensive farming; the predators' natural prey is reduced, forcing them to hunt sub-optimally on cattle.

That evening, we witnessed a special treat; we were in a hide near the 'dinner table' of the leopards, where meat bait was left. We watched the male leopard eat, then heard growling from behind; MJ, the young female, was being darted, so her radio collar could be enlarged. Dave, a British qualified AfriCat representative (and apparently a wildlife filmmaker) had MJ laid out on a truck tailgate and was inserting an ID microchip and administered a contraceptive injection that would last a year. This area would not support more cubs and MJ was 18 months old, so ready to have cubs. Dave loosened her collar, making sure that she could not pull it off or get her jaw caught. We were allowed to stroke and touch MJ whilst she was sedated. Her fur was wonderfully soft and velvety - no wonder leopards glide so silently. By comparison, a cheetah's fur is coarser and wirier. MJ's retractable claws were very sharp, with blood on them from the meat she had just eaten. She was in prime health and an awesome apex predator.

We were still buzzing from the leopard experience, when on our return to the lodge, the loudest eating sound erupted that we'd ever heard; a porcupine had got into the lodge refuse bins and was chomping his way through the food waste - talk about a noisy eater! Our evening of surprises did not end there. The chap of the young couple with us, on holiday touring in a hire car, was the son of my first Parachute Regimental colonel, who had recruited me. Not only that, he planned to meet a young captain (whom we both knew) from 1 PARA that had left years earlier to work in Africa, based in

Cape Town. As if on cue, in walked Robin. Both wives rolled their eyes as if it was a stitch-up; but no, it was pure serendipity.

During the following morning's game drive, we were being driven along the game fence when we came across some orphaned cheetahs. Having been caught by farmers and handed to AfriCat, it was not feasible to release these cats into the wild, as they had become too dependent on humans, so were unlikely to survive. It was wonderful to be so close, when one executed its party trick. Despite only having three legs, it hopped onto the bonnet of our stationary Land Rover. This was an open-top vehicle, with no windscreen, but 'everything was safe' - apparently? I'm sure our eyes were out on stalks. We knew that cheetahs needed the 'pounce for prey' stimulus, so sitting still was the best thing to do; however, knowing and doing are seldom the same. Of course, this was a party trick, for we were not aware of the food stashed within the front tyre on the bonnet - phew!

After a great breakfast, we continued to Etosha and checked in at Okaukuejo Park HQ. The park was exceptionally dry, forcing the game to congregate around the limited water holes. Etosha means 'Great White Place', a large salt pan. This saline desert, with its characteristic white and greenish algae on its surface, was formed around 10 million years ago when tectonic plates created the Kalahari Basin; Etosha became isolated as it sat within an endorheic basin (a geological feature that has no water run off). The water had to evaporate, leaving a salty residue, and crazed crusted pan. We preferred the more romantic folklore explanation of Etosha's derivation, handed down orally within the Heikum. Their fable tells of a group of travellers passing through the area, when they were surrounded by local hunters who put the men and boys to the knife and spear, sparing only the women. One of the captured women sat weeping under a tree. Her tears were so copious that they formed a vast lake. When the salty tears dried out, it left a barren wasteland. Today's national park is one of the largest game parks in Africa, including numerous satellite pans. These artesian springs support a rich diversity of flora and fauna. Mopane trees grow around the pans, with dense scrub and grasslands. Most of the Big Five are seen here, but not buffalo. There is a profusion of ungulates and bird life, notably the black-faced impala and the Damara dik dik (Africa's smallest antelope). The critically endangered black rhino are reported to survive at Etosha, but typically, we were unable to confirm or deny their presence.

Etosha is a wildlife photographer's paradise; it was easy to get wonderful shots of elephant herds reflected against water, or giraffes, zebras and other ungulates drinking in unison. The man-made water holes by the lodges attract the animals and foster 'no effort viewing'. It's easy to be critical of this intervention, but wildlife numbers are recovering here since rinderpest devastated both cattle and wildlife at the turn of the last century. Water resources are in conflict with increasing cattle ranches since the 1970s, when the then government in Pretoria decided to fence in the park. This created mayhem, cut traditional migration routes and led to a severe decline of blue wildebeest. A similar decision in the 1970s meant lions here were injected with contraception measures. Today's prides are now suffer inbreeding, canine distemper and feline AIDS, given pride isolation and poor mixing of the gene pool (a continental issue). Man has interrupted the natural ecosystem.

We transited the park west to east, spending our second night centrally at Halali. This area was dense with gemsbok, black-faced impala and springbok, each competing with more than 30 elephants at the same water hole. Our third night we spent inside the Fort at Namutoni, a white, mini-castellated structure at the Eastern Gate. Originally built in 1897 by the occupying Germans as a border post, they slaughtered large numbers of cattle in the northern territory trying to control both the locals and rinderpest. This sparked local rebellion that wrought severe reprisals upon the Herero nation. A further act of rebellion in 1904 saw 500 Ovambo warriors attack the few Germans at Naumtoni. The Germans initially held their ground, but eventually torched the place and retreated to safety. A year later, under a local negotiated peace, they rebuilt the fort. As for our night's stay, it was very comfortable. I checked under Daph and sure enough, I found traces of a transmission leak; we had grease on the prop-shaft. More to add to the watch list.

At Popa Falls, just short of the Botswanan border, we were led to believe we'd see a series of cataracts where the Okavango River falls four metres down a cascade. We were there at low water and could only just observe a faint ripple in the water. No matter, this location suited us for access into Botswana and it was a delightful campsite. We thoroughly enjoyed Namibia, the country and the people, with so much to see. Catherine's shoulder was getting stronger and less painful. The corrugated tracks around the Namib were uncomfortable (for us all), and we hoped they would become less prevalent as we entered the mighty Okavango Delta.

Part 3

AN EXTENDED CLASSIC SAFARI

Drive into Tsodilo Hills

"You know you are truly alive when you're living among lions." Karen Blixen

Kazangulu Ferry

Camping on the Banks of the Zambezi

Victoria Falls

Camping on Lake Malawi coast

Khwai River Crossing

101

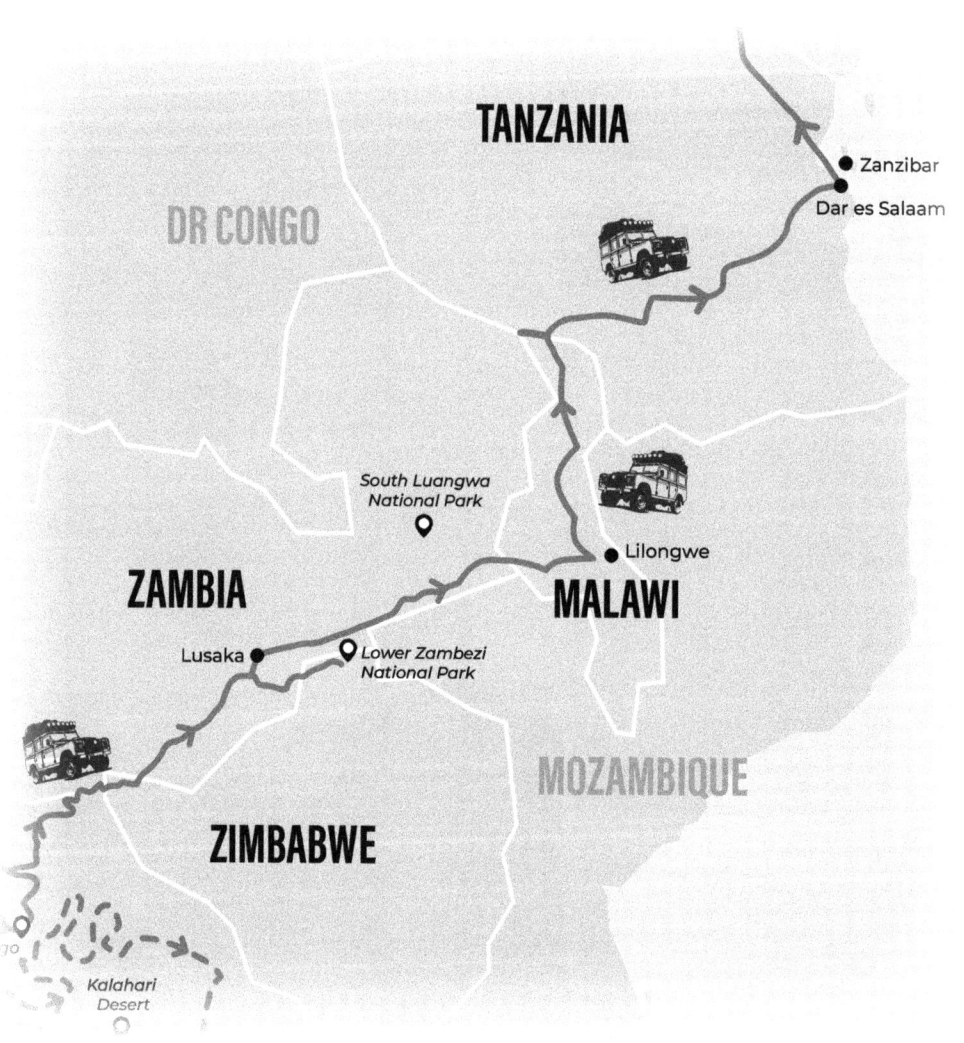

Chapter 11
The Okavango ecosystem

A military escort was required to visit the Caprivi Strip, which we did not relish. Government forces were still seeking remnants of belligerent, irregular Angolan forces. Any game would have scattered or worse, be in the pot, so we avoided conflict and headed to Botswana. Just before the Mohembo Gate, we passed a new, cheap and convenient Shell station. We topped up and filled two of the four jerry cans. The Namibian border administration was swift, but the Botswanan officials started to question the Carnet. As all these countries are within a single customs area, we recognised a revenue ruse and ignored it.

Outside, I noticed a group of officers were all gathering around Daph, peering in, waving their long sjamboks (heavy, leather whips). This required a distraction, so in an overly cheery cry, I extolled the virtues of the Senegalese football team. Senegal were the last African team in the 2002 World Cup, heading for the quarter finals in a few days, so now, all Africans were Senegalese. I threw in a few 'David Beckham's' for good measure, which worked; it generated chanting, dancing and shuffling amongst the officials. Using the distraction as my chance to escape, I was just caught by those immortal words, 'You have fuel?' Despite more David Beckhams and dancing from me, I replied, 'Of course' and tapped the bottom of Daph. This seemed to satisfy the officials, except their apparent leader. He nodded and pointed at the jerry cans on the rack; obviously, they knew about the Shell garage. Playing the game, I bluffed by tapping the outside can. 'Empty,' I said. He smiled and tapped the other outside can and said, 'Empty,' which thankfully, it was. With grins all round and a few more Senegalese cries, we were off - did it matter who was fooling who?

We were heading for Tsodilo Hills, the spiritual home for the San people. Tsodilo Hills are a unique record of human settlement over the millennia, with over 4,500 rock paintings. But the San people believe these hills are the birthplace of all life. This would be the same San people we encountered in the Kalahari Game Reserve; these hunter gathers return here to ask their ancestors for a good hunt. Just south of the border, our guidebook implied the three routes off the main road were challenging due to heavy sand. Reducing the tyre pressures, we plumped for the middle route, but Daph laboured. There was a myriad of criss-crossing tracks, each implying better going, until we battled across to find it was just as bad. This was the softest sand we had encountered. Only a year earlier, UNESCO recognised Tsodilo Hills, the 'Louvre of the Desert', as a World Heritage Site and created an airstrip, a visitor centre (hut) and marked some trails through the hills. The four distinct hills are known as Male Hill (the largest and the highest point in Botswana) and in descending order are Female, Child and North Hill. It was Laurens van der Post (the adventurer/soldier, writer, historian and intellectual) who championed the culture and folklore of the San. I was reading his book, The Lost World of the Kalahari, documenting his discovery of Tsodilo Hills, where he has a rock art panel named in his honour.

After a couple of hours bashing along the tracks, we passed through a small Bantu village before reaching the visitor centre. The informative centre had only been opened by the president of Botswana in 2001. We registered and Catherine wanted to walk the Rhino Trail because it limited the clambering for her sore shoulder. It was nice to walk and stretch our legs, and Female Hill contained most of the rock art we had come to see. Drawn mostly in a red pigment, a few, including the rhino panel, used a white pigment. As we neared the top of the scramble, we came across a medium-sized, greyish-green snake. I froze. For the record, I hate snakes. Irrational, I know, but I've had sufficient (mental) scares from snake incidents around the world that I was relieved to see the shy green mamba slink away. I realise that they want to avoid our contact and are reluctant to bite, but we were in its backyard and, considering they are one of the world's most deadly, I was not up for testing the theories. Besides, I understood they usually move around in pairs; where was that other one?

We eventually found the van der Post panel, depicting a giraffe with other animals, as the path was indistinct. We needed to cool down, so we drove around to our allocated campsite nearby. Rumbling in the back of my mind was a tale from a few years back by a previous commander of mine. Some years earlier, as a team leader from Hereford, he was sent to cross-train with the Botswanan Special Forces. They found themselves at Tsodilo Hills to climb, abseil and so forth. They heard the San tale of protection and needless taking or loss of life; a warning not to anger the gods. Folklore implied that, if a life was taken beyond what was needed for the pot or survival, the gods would exact their revenge. Not dwelling on the matter, the team went exploring and climbing. One of the team went hunting and shot a monkey to try some bush meat. Whilst not strictly kosher, it could be argued this was survival training and 'living off the land'. That said, the poor, barbecued monkey had his revenge, for it was apparently very tough and gave them all the trots. The subsequent day, when climbing, the hunter who was securely belayed and pinned correctly to the rock, appeared to be ejected bodily away from the rock wall and fell. He missed his climbing partner below, whose own rock pin took all the weight of the falling hunter and held them both. The hunter's pin failed, despite being safely secured by a previous climber. To be forced violently away from the rock was quite bizarre and the lower pin and climber were saved, despite taking excessive weight. I don't recall the 'hunter' dying but he suffered head wounds and needed evacuating.

This tale was rattling in my subconscious. We gathered firewood to add to the partially burned wood in the hearth and eventually managed to get a fire and a nearby log to glow, for it had turned quite chilly. This local wood was exceptionally hard and heavy, likely it was a lead wood, explaining its reluctance to burn. As the sun faded, the wind really picked up. There was a definite 'air' and spookiness blowing about; it was quite eerie. We were all alone, or so we thought, for we saw nobody else around. We cooked our meal and listened to the silence after packing everything away, absorbing the night noises, drinking our tea. It was getting colder, so we retired to the roof tent and zipped ourselves into our cosy sleeping bags. I had pulled the log from the fire; it would soon extinguish itself.

Somewhile later, as we were dozing off, we heard running hooves, with puffing and snorting nearby. Strange, given our isolation, but thinking little of it, we snuggled into our safe, elevated cocoon. Dozing off again, we heard repeated snuffling and hooves, but this time it sounded as if a herd of animals was circling around Daph. Sound is magnified at night, but this was unusual and disconcerting.

We had discussed a vague plan for 'incidents' but here and now, it reinforced how limited our reactive capacity really was. We hung a rape alarm from the roof tent, hoping the high-pitched shriek would create a distraction. Further escalations included a flashlight or firing small signal flares; anything to respond in an unexpected way. Any such response would be slow, for one still had to get one's head out to see. Then we felt something brush against Daph, gently rocking the Land Rover. This was too much so I unzipped my sleeping bag (noise), scrabbled for my torch and unzipped (more noise) the roof tent door that to me telegraphed any intention. By the time I actually got my head out to look and make sense of the dark, I saw nothing. The wind was blowing dust about and again, I felt a shiver down my spine. Clearly my mind was playing tricks on me. The moon was bright, although occasionally obscured by passing clouds and dust in the wind. I waited in ambush for a bit, but got cold, so did the decent thing and bravely slunk back under the protection of the sleeping bag, having re-zipped the tent shut. Just as I was dozing off, again we heard the trampling of hooves.

This time, I tried to hurry to get the door zip open, but again, I couldn't see or hear anything. Flashing the torch around caught nothing. I'd hoped to see at least the reflection within the eyes of the predator, or monster, threatening our peace. This was getting weird and I began to assume the worst; people were herding animals towards us to cover their mischievous intent. I readopted my ambush position at the door; torch in hand and the door unzipped, just the Velcro closure. Just as I was dozing off, I felt the vehicle start to rock again, so I sprung my trap, whipping out the torch to see a cow using Daph as a scratching post. Then I saw another cow astride the burning log, the embers warming its udders, quite unperturbed. After all that, it was just cows rumbling around at night to keep warm and benefiting from our fire. No big drama, no hunting predator or malicious human movements, although now we were wondering where the cows had come from!

After our sleepless night, I was happy to get a brew on and warm up. The eerie wind had abated, and the blue, gin-clear skies were warming up. I couldn't see any evidence of cows; did we dream it? The lead wood embers were still warm, hot even. As we checked out of the small visitor centre, we asked if there were people (with cattle) about, but the warden denied any presence. He recommended the southern-most route out; although longer, it was marginally less sandy. We saw two safari vehicles from local lodges on the western fringe of the Delta; they enjoyed higher clearances, fatter tyres and were considerably less laden, so were zipping around with abandon. We came across an old Toyota truck stuck in some very soft sand, so with a quick tug on the snatch line, we popped it out. A few hours later, we turned towards Maun and headed for the Delta.

The Okavango Delta covers a fifth of Botswana (around 16,000 kilometres) a third of which is designated the Moremi Game Reserve. This island and its rivers support a rich, diverse ecosystem as bountiful as any in Africa. Rain from the Angolan Benguela Plateau collects between 1,200 and 2,000mm of water flowing ultimately into the Okavango River, then creating one of the largest inland deltas in the world. Most of the water evaporates or becomes absorbed by vegetation. Only during exceptional years will water reach the far end and feed the Thamalakane and Boleti Rivers. Occasionally, in exceptional years, water can flow northeast into the Savute marshes via the Selinda Spillway. Geological faults have left an interlinked ecosystem between the Chobe, Linyanti, Savute and Okavango rivers and the Makgadikgadi salt pans. Access into the Delta is via Maun, known as the 'gateway' town on the Thamalakane River. Translated, Maun means 'the place of short reeds'. Having shed its former 'wild west' reputation, today Maun supports a growing regional airport shuttling wealthy tourists into the luxury lodges of the Okavango.

One of life's rare privileges is to fly over the Okavango Delta in a light aircraft. One minute you are gazing across endless Delta views, the next dropping within the vegetation, landing at one of the many dirt airstrips. Long sightlines are lost as the senses switch to sounds and smells of the bush. Botswana's policy is to support low volume, high value tourism to protect the delicate Delta ecosystem. The light aircraft provide access to the luxury lodges and camps, despite considerable ire from the environmental lobby, but compared to a highway trashing this pristine wilderness, the aircraft make sense. That said, the most environmental and romantic mode of entry would be a mokoro canoe trip from Maun.

Maun has the government offices for the northwestern district, including Botswana's parks' booking office. Like most African administrative systems, doing something away from the norm stretches the system, so 'computers say no.' We received a prompt, efficient service when we booked our Christmas Kalahari run, but now we were told flatly it was not possible to enter the Delta. All the campsites were fully booked and there was no negotiation. To lick our wounds and assess our options, we headed for a recommended campsite. Maun is awash with choice, but Audi Camp was the recommendation for independent travellers. On the river, just north of Maun, it is run by the friendly couple, Jack and Eve Drew. They were accustomed to travellers with similar frustrations arising from the intransigence of the authorities. It was a local source of grievance, caused when large tour operators are guaranteed block camp bookings, as they offer unfettered access for high paying clients. Whilst appearing understandable, these big tour operators are only achieving a 60% occupancy rate, at best. The remaining space is left vacant, at the expense of the local community who rely on the associated spending from tourists.

Jack and Eve ran Delta trips themselves and offered excellent camping suggestions just outside the park. Refreshed from a beer and updated information, we erected the Oztent and ventured back into Maun for supplies. The idea of poling silently along in a mokoro, brushing through tall grasses and reeds, floating past eye-popping birdlife like lilac-breasted rollers, malachite kingfishers and carmine bee-eaters, is the stuff of dreams.

Our pitch was allocated next to a retired British couple, Austin and Una, who were driving an adapted five-tonne Iveco Italian army ambulance. Their modifications were excellent, with all their needs adapted inside the comfort and security of the ambulance box body. Whilst not the fastest of vehicles, they had supreme cross-country ability and taking the slow road was their want. They could survive in the bush for up to a month should they need. Of greatest importance, they were heading in the opposite direction, so we could swap notes. Austin had grown up in Tanganyika and spoke fluent Swahili. Just as well, for after lavishing years of love and preparing their Iveco in the UK, they shipped it to Mombasa. The ambulance was too large to fit inside a container and, despite all appropriate security and assurances, when they met the ship at Mombasa, they were devastated to find an empty shell once the vehicle was unloaded. It was a brutal shock to Austin that everything had been taken. Most poignant for him was the loss of his father's cherished toolset. It was a heart-rending story, but one of great resilience. Mombasa port is renowned for such theft and pilfering (how they got into the Iveco remains anyone's guess), but whilst most people might have given up at this point, they set about refitting the ambulance and resumed their travels. Austin and Una were thriving in this environment, verifying that one is never too old for adventure. We were still swapping stories and details at 3am; they were a mine of useful information, and we were able to reciprocate with our experiences.

My daily checks on Daph continued to monitor a transmission leak, which I thought prudent to repair before we got too far into the wilderness. Jack directed us to Lesedi Motors, the local Land Rover dealer in town. Botswana is big Land Rover country; Lesedi Motors service over 7,000 Land Rovers in government service (for an annual three million Pula contract) that excludes their work on the Botswanan defence force fleet. Naturally, they were delighted to see us (even on a Sunday) and got Daph onto a hoist immediately to diagnose our problem. I assisted a young lad from Zimbabwe, who demonstrated excellent knowledge and care, although it still took five hours to replace a seeping O-ring on top of the transmission, all for a very reasonable rate. During this time, the office manager and staff were fascinated by our trip and Catherine was able to update and upload our latest web post. We got back on the road just in time to reach the South Gate National Park entrance before dark. Using Jack's recommendation, we camped at a delightful spot by South Park, near a village called San-ta-wani. It was a serene camp under the mopane trees, with clean showers and latrines. The local Tawana people were exceptionally kind and gentle, at ease within their surroundings, and the place was better maintained than the scruffier and more expensive official sites we glimpsed later. The caretaker provided us with plenty of firewood and a kerosene lamp, an unnecessary yet very welcome touch.

Moremi Game Reserve is frequently referred to as a 'Garden of Eden' as it provides excellent, year-round experience, amidst a stunning photographic savannah, floodplains, lagoons, dense forests and winding rivers. The Big Five are all here, having successfully reintroduced white rhino, together with the full gamut of ungulates, elephants and other wildlife. It is an ornithological paradise too. Notoriously difficult to spot, wild dog numbers are recovering here. We paid our park fees at South Gate and headed towards the Third Bridge. Early morning game drives here were wonderful. We witnessed a herd of impala fight back against a leopard who had been compromised while descending from a tree; the herd gathered tightly and spat at the leopard to warn him off. This was at odds with the expected impala flight instinct. We also watched a healthy lion pride frolicking, replete and content from the night's hunt, lolling listlessly with stretched bellies. People don't normally recognise lions to be endangered, but there are less than 18,000 free-roaming wild lions according, to the International Union for Conservation of Nature (IUCN) in 2002. They list them as 'vulnerable', one stage away from endangered, as 90% of lions have feline immunodeficiency virus (FIV), an HIV equivalent that weakens their resistance to viruses; similar to the recent tuberculosis epidemic in the Kruger Park or the 1994 outbreak of canine distemper that killed 1,000 lions in the Serengeti.

Further research is examining the impact of smaller lion gene pools to maintain healthy reproductive rates. Only the Delta, Kruger and Serengeti groups are sufficiently large and diverse to maintain survival. Scientists believe lions are essential for survival, reigniting the hunting debate. Botswana previously viewed hunting as a balancing process for the ecosystem. The hunting lobby is lucrative, vocal and powerful. This lobby queries the policy and wants to manage the trophy males rejected from prides that are beyond reproductive value. But, this is being questioned in a new study – for it is the pride lionesses, aside from the leading the hunting, that decide on their choice of mate! Young males are ejected from the pride until they are ready to take on their own pride, won through violent clashes that result in infanticide of the outgoing male's cubs. As induced ovulators, lionesses require sex to release their eggs. Males are observed to copulate 3,000 times for each cub, once every 20 minutes. New evidence suggests that on the fifth day, when the lioness is ready, the poor male has exhausted his sperm count. Further evidence suggests that lionesses are sneaking off to young males on the edge of the pride for illicit trysts to ensure impregnation, whilst continuing to associate with the pride male, reinforcing his belief that he is the father.

At the Third Bridge, a different story emerged about accommodation and availability. Despite being told the campsites were full, it was evident that there was plenty of space. The Third Bridge campsite had only one vehicle. We enjoyed a wonderful drive through mopane trees, watching numerous forms of wildlife, although predator sightings were low. In 1998, we flew into Camp Xakanaxa, so we went there to see if we could get some lunch. We also needed to deliver a message to Bob and Flo, the most charming white Africans owners one could ever meet. On one of our last days in Pretoria, we had a delightful encounter with Mike and Hazel at the local Land Rover dealership. Mike had been a chief of police for the South African borders and they had recently returned from a trip to Kenya. After a long lunch together, we learnt they were great friends with Bob and Flo, who were still running Camp Xakanaxa. This was too good to pass up, and Bob and Flo were delighted to see us. But it transpired since our previous visit, a fire had gutted most of Xakanaxa. Thankfully, no one was hurt as it occurred during the low season, but all their records and many valuables were lost. Having rebuilt Xakanaxa, Bob and Flo insisted on showing us around.

Maintaining their orientation west along the Khwai River, they rebuilt the main boma from local timber, reed and thatch. They had renewed the classic Meru-style, canvas, walk-in safari tents, replumbing the en-suite facilities. The Amarula tree survived for Bob and I had a chuckle as I recalled the drunken elephant incident one evening after supper. Seeking the Amarula berries, the elephants had trampled the protective perimeter electronic wire, the same wire that was now retaining them inside the camp. Bob immediately got all the guests to safety before attempting to 'shoo' the elephants away! It was such a crazy notion that I joined him. Drunk or not, they could easily trample a tent if spooked, yet they were carefully tiptoeing around the canvas tents as though they were concrete structures. After some noise and encouragement, the elephants got bored and departed. Whilst it was not as severe as the story implies, Bob replaced the electric wire with a string impregnated and studded with chillies, which proved a far more effective deterrent. He got the idea from a charity supporting Kenyan Maasai to protect their crops.

Bob and Flo are fine examples of their generation's resilience. Being forced to leave their native Zimbabwe (like Mike and Hazel), Bob tried to settle in South Africa but was not legally allowed to stay, so he ended up at Xakanaxa. Tourist numbers were down, having been affected by the lack of Americans and Europeans not travelling after 9/11. The high park fees were discouraging South Africans. Bob was frustrated at the intransigence of the administration, and was a strong advocate of setting up a wireless booking system (in those pre-internet days) to resolve unused capacity. The park management was neither helping the safari operators, the park nor those supporting the preservation of wildlife.

Walking within most African game reserves is strongly discouraged, especially without the right precautions, guide and/or training. Maybe it's a testament to how far man has evolved that walking in wild nature is no longer instinctual. An experienced guide can really amplify a walk.

Back in 1998, we took a boat/skiff from Xakanaxa to an island for a bush walk towards dusk. There were eight of us, of varying ages, nationalities and fitness, with a guide. Had I been with Bob, I would not have thought twice, but our guide was something else. I was still deciding if he was the 'cool dude' that he tried to convey or 'less than the full shilling'. He was a local lad, this was his backyard, so there should not have been an issue. But how much did he realise about the relative incompetence and fitness of the average, aging Western tourist, out of their milieu? I was confident the guide would be OK. He told us that guides here in Moremi were not allowed to carry guns, which I thought strange, so I asked if he had a radio. 'No,' he said, 'but I have a knife.' Catherine's nail scissors were larger! It was a beautiful day and we were keen to explore, so into the boat we clambered and paddled to our walking point. Half-way into our short walk, we saw a herd of grazing springbok. How lovely. But why are they barking and alerting? 'Must be a mating call or something,' the guide proposed, yet they appeared to be warning something away. 'Err, OK, so what would their main predators be?' 'Well, most of the big cats, hyenas and maybe wild dogs, but they are not here, as this is an island; they don't like water,' he told us. 'Oh, OK,' Catherine said, 'I thought cats could swim?' 'Yes, but not here, this is an island!' It was at this point that top spotter Catherine helpfully pointed out the pride of lions sunbathing in line of sight to the springbok, placing us between the prey and the lions. 'Oh, they're back,' said the guide, unreassuringly. 'They will not be interested in us.' But his demeanour had changed and he seemed flustered. 'If we stay together as a large group, like the springbok, err, the lions will think we are too large to be of interest to them,' he hesitantly ventured. 'Err, OK, then we ought to wait for those two elderly ladies over there to catch up,' I replied. I waited and helped the ladies, who were breathless and hot, so slowing down. 'Hurry now, keep together,' encouraged our cool dude, striding ever further away. As the old joke goes, nature targets the weak and more infirm, so I guessed my speed against the old ladies might sway in my favour as I helped them along. Again, Catherine ventured, 'Where are the lions now?' 'Oh, just resting in the trees, I expect,' responded the guide. Well, we have all seen David Attenborough documentaries and lions stalking their prey; no one was fooled. Besides, the springbok were no longer barking and had settled down to eat. The lions obviously had much sweeter prey in their sights.

The boat couldn't come quickly enough. As we clambered aboard, it was a sombre paddle back.

We had a lovely lunch, during which Flo proposed we should stay at Mankwe Camp, which was outside the reserve and en route to Savute, where we were heading. Flo called Mankwe while Bob came to check out Daph. He was reassuringly impressed and delighted to learn that we'd been to Lesedi Motors, for his son, Dean, was the manager who helped with our website. Africa is a small world. With such positivity, we set off. Whilst signing out of the Reserve Gate, I saw oil dripping from the engine bay…here we go again. On closer examination, it became clear that the problem was the same that we encountered in Lesotho; the oil coolant pipes had vibrated loose at the union with the radiator. To fix this would require the removal of the engine fan and housing. It was 4pm and I was considering camping locally and attempting a bush fix, or Mankwe Camp, but common sense prevailed. We limped back to Maun to revisit Lesedi Motors in the morning.

So, back to Audi Camp to surprise Austin and Una, who hadn't moved. Austin wanted to get his spanners out there and then, but the engine had to cool and we needed spares. In the morning, Dean was even more surprised to see us, especially having spoken to his parents the night before. Bless him, he addressed the repair straightaway and by the afternoon, we were heading back north for Mankwe. Or so we thought, for just after Maun, Daph was still not happy. She had a strange, wheezing sound coming from under the bonnet. After poking under the hood, Lesedi had overlooked the reconnection of the water hose from the radiator. Some quick fiddling and job done, so we carried on. Daph was taking it all in her stride. The track was sandy but manageable as we passed South Gate, towards Mankwe Lodge.

We were struck by the serenity of the drive; sunlight dappling through the trees and birds singing. I had a flashback and thought we could be motoring around the Sussex countryside, except for the fact that I was in southern Africa, grinding through sand with big game all around, ready to feast. It was about this time that we started to be plagued by 'earworms'. I have nothing against Blondie - I like her songs - but in my head, all I could think of was 'One Way or Another'. Catherine was equally battling the recurring theme tune to 'Animal Magic' that still haunts her to this day. This emergent issue pestered us all the way home. In essence, a song (or part of a song or rift) starts rattling inside your brain. It's not sung, for it's a subconscious, repetitive refrain in the head. Regardless of the song, good or bad, popular or otherwise, it usually has a catchy 'hook' that beats away in the back of the mind, on constant repeat. Like a background hum, chiming chords riff, a pattern of sound; regardless of genre, it occurs when you least expect it. Not knowing or remembering the words is irrelevant, that just adds depth to the frustration. It's in the subconscious, for the harder you try to think of something else, the more it infiltrates; stronger and more powerful than ever.

But, it can be usurped by another tune, especially when transferred from someone else. Song transfer is an evil thing. Imagine the scene: you are travelling along, alone in your thoughts and you have, for argument's sake, a Beach Boys song rumbling around, when someone else informs you they cannot get rid of their song, perhaps David Bowie or Beethoven's Fifth. The power of suggestion causes the other person to recall the new tune, which supplants the old refrain with the new suggestion. So, whilst the transferee song may have been considering 'Life on Mars', you are left wondering why 'Daddy took the T'bird away'. This is song transfer.

Worse, if you try and manufacture a ruse or trick, it is never effective; it has to come from the unconscious mind. The more sticky and immoveable a song, the more invasive it becomes for the victim. Worse, the more annoying the song, the more persistent it is! You cannot be mean with song transfer, for if you try to go on the attack and think of an annoying song to poison others, the retribution rarely sticks, and often backfires. Driving through the Okavango, I was even foot-tapping the accelerator to Led Zeppelin at one point, until Catherine finally cracked; 'The levee broke!' she barked. Poor Catherine was tortured by the 'Birdy Song' throughout the Serengeti.

Perhaps a radio would have been simpler? We had a CD adapter, although I cannot recall using it. The natural ambiance and wild soundtrack was enough. We still suffer song transfer today; all one has to do or say is, 'Oh no, I can't get X or Y out of my head.' As soon as it's said, the afflicted one is liberated and the other one is infected. If it's Kylie, that's a killer, but apparently there is some science behind it. A recent study suggests that certain songs and tunes have catchy and infectious beats and rhythms to make them contagious.

It was a serene drive to Mankwe, but due to our delay, they had no camping spaces left. The staff asked us to wait for Dempsey, the head guide, to get back. No problem, we were going nowhere, so we enjoyed a sundowner on their deck. Presently, a tall, barefooted, 'grizzly bear' alpha male, wearing only shorts, a hat and carrying a rifle, bellowed, 'Who has that awesome truck outside?' We knew Dempsey was announcing his arrival. He was unaware of our mechanical, but having spoken to Flo, he was a great chap who went out of his way to help us. That evening, he had just returned from tracking a roan antelope with his guests. Lucky guests, for roan are notoriously elusive. He insisted we join him for supper, after which he would show us a spot. He had checked out Daph on his way back to camp, so knew we were all set to camp. Mankwe was a delight, having been established with government and NGO support as part of an initiative to encourage an alternative income and employment for indigenous people. Its aim was to attract and educate the locals away from hunting or poaching, to retain and apply local knowledge, whilst championing local culture and crafts. The profits were directed to the community for education and training, rather than filling commercial safari company coffers. Dempsey showed us to a beautiful spot under a tamarind tree. In the roof tent, with the doors open, we could see a clear moonlit night right across the Savute. Dempsey had pointed out the track for the morning, allowing us to head off when we were ready.

The Savute Marsh is a relic of a large, inland lake, not unlike the Makgadikgadi pans, although its water supply was cut a long time ago. Now, the erratic Savute Channel flows north. In 1982, when the Savute completely dried up, the event was captured by naturalists, Derek and Beverly Joubert, in The Stolen River, showing how wildlife struggles without water. The erratic water supply has left hundreds of dead and desiccated trees along the channel, whilst the extensive savannah and grassland support a dynamic wildlife ecosystem. The Mangwikhewe sand ridge and the Mababe depression feed the Savute Marsh. In the wet season, it's almost impossible to transit this region, yet the marsh area is generally teeming with wildlife. In the dry season, game viewing is easier due to the shorter grass and sandy tracks. Predators here have adapted to their extreme, dry conditions; lion prides have been known to take down large elephants in extremis. Wild dogs fair well, as they have the space to roam and chase down their prey over distance. This is a truly wild area, less frequented by tourists, hence our interest.

A leisurely breakfast followed a comfortable night, and we pressed on to the Khwai River. Pausing on the swollen bank to assess crossing options, we met a South African couple from Pretoria, with their brand new TD5 130 Land Rover, doing the same as us. One needs to be careful when wading a river, and it's best to know what lies below the surface before crossing. Sage advice suggests wading through first with a pole, in advance of any vehicle – a brave manoeuvre inside an active game park stacked with lions, leopards and crocodiles, to name but a few challenges. The synchronicity of meeting these guys was reassuring, for it's always best to cross rivers with others. As if on cue, a passing local lorry ploughed through, showing us the way. We both had raised air-breathers and while the water was easily bonnet-height in the middle, the River Khwai was no issue. We stopped on the far bank for a quick chat and discussion about plans and routes. They were heading back towards Pretoria but were enthused by our trip. Just as we parted and drove a few yards along the Khwai riverbank, we saw a pride of lions sitting in the bushes, just by a lovely picnic spot. I imagine that was their thought too.

Entering Savute through the Mababe Gate, we followed the western Sandridge north. Now in the dry phase, the hard-baked, sand track was especially harsh and bumpy, irritating Catherine's shoulder. Better than the wet, sticky, black cotton soil that becomes unnavigable; these tracks frequently become submerged and undrivable. We drove around the floodplain and thick salt bush and eventually came across Savute Lodge, a luxurious camp. It was previously known as Lloyds Camp that uniquely offered elephant back safaris. The lodge overlooked a man-made waterhole that attracted a continuous stream of elephants. Such opulence was juxtaposed to the surroundings, so we sought a cup of tea. Desert and Delta now run Savute Lodge, one of a number of exclusive, high-end lodges across southern Africa. We bumped into the managers, Tanya and Johann, on arrival, whom we asked over high tea about Lloyd's Camp next door and the tale of a very unusual African elephant, Abu.

Riding a horse (or elephant), one can get closer to game without a disturbance. They are conducted in Linyanti for competent riders; the Lloyd's project sought to offer the same experience, but with an African elephant. Unlike their Indian cousins, African elephants cannot normally be tamed or habituated. However, Abu was an East African elephant relocated to Texas in 1960 whilst young. Being uncommonly friendly, he was used as a ride attraction in a 'wildlife park' in Texas. He was introduced to Botswana in 1990 to lead the 'Abu' herd as the first elephant back safari in Africa. It ran until Abu's death, only some months prior to our arrival. Lloyds Camp was temporarily closed whilst the project management was hoping that the herd's matriarch, Cathy, similarly born in East Africa and habituated in Canada, might assume the lead.

Tanya and Johann were enthused by our trip and had heard of Bob and Flo at Xakanaxa. Desert and Delta were similarly suffering reduced tourist numbers and their company was hurting. Tanya showed us around and offered such a low price for the night's stay that we could not refuse. We joined the evening game drive, for their guide knew the most likely viewing spots. It's rarely a precise art and we felt vindicated that we were not doing too badly ourselves. They drove top-of-the-range, adapted V8 Land Cruisers that had power and quiet idling, yet it was still bouncy and uncomfortable for Catherine's arm (worse than Daph, she said). All game drives include the mandatory sundowner at a picturesque spot, conducted with flair and elegance comparable to a Western five-star hotel. Whilst enjoying a G & T, we watched a herd of elephants descending to a waterhole under a glorious sunset. Just at that moment, the guide was informed of a leopard stalking its prey over the radio, so off we dashed to find the satisfied leopard wandering off with its supper.

Our room at the lodge was magnificent. It had huge, sliding glass patio doors overlooking the waterhole. The air-conditioned luxury was almost too much, more than Out of Africa. The four-poster bed was draped with the softest, finest white cottons and the full safari paraphernalia; we slept magnificently. Thankfully, we had some clean, presentable clothes in which to enjoy a smashing meal on the fire deck, explaining our journey with the (mainly wealthy) American and Swiss travellers. Over supper, Johann wanted to know more about our travels. We learnt that this area was home to the second largest zebra migration in Africa, similarly determined by the summer rains when the zebras migrate from the northern rivers, south, in search of the rain-induced grassland, triggering the symbiotic predator following.

Tanya and Johann were wonderful hosts; they had even prepared a packed lunch for our onward journey. Later that morning, at the Savute Park office, we bumped into Peggy and Richard. They had a wealth of knowledge, having driven south along the majority of our proposed route. These Americans were in their splendid 1982 petrol 3.5ltr Range Rover, with an automatic transmission, sporting Saudi plates. Peggy had just finished 12 years' working in the lucrative Saudi hospital system in Jeddah, so Richard enjoyed early retirement to tinker with his Rangy and got lost within the local deserts. It was quite a passion of his, for their 'rig' was fully desert adapted. Along his front bumper was a huge, compressed air pump to change a tyre in seconds. They were heading south to Cape Town to ship themselves back to the States. Little did I realise at that time, I would find myself working in Riyadh some years later. Being both American and living in Saudi, they could get access to Egypt and came down the Nile. They too endured horrendous administrative hassles we'd heard about at Aswan Dam, for we still needed to find a way to get Egyptian visas and Carnet.

The track to Savute North Gate (Ghoca Hills) was passable, although the game viewing was limited. The area between Savute and Chobe was notorious for its soft sand, yet after the border with Caprivi, by the park entrance, we found the most pristine tar road in all of Africa, funded by the European Union; how very nice of them. We dived into the western boundary of Chobe National Park. The northern park boundary is defined by the Chobe River, equally forming Botswana's northern border with Angola, Namibia, Zambia and Zimbabwe. Our first visit here was during our honeymoon in 1997; we stayed at Chobe Game Lodge, the only lodge then permitted within the park. Since that visit, we noticed two significant changes: wide-scale devastation from the huge concentration of elephants upon the woodland vegetation, and secondly, the increase in low value, high impact tourism, especially when compared to the southern parks.

Chobe Game Reserve was Botswana's first official park in 1960. Seven years later, it was declared a national park. There were several industrial settlements in the park, especially at Serondela, managing timber, mostly mahogany, teak and other hardwood. These settlements were gradually removed, although it was not until 1975 that the whole park was exempt from industry. Given its proximity to Victoria Falls, the Chobe Riverfront is the most visited area. Kasane serves as the main gateway, with the majority of lodges, guest houses and infrastructure. Huge river barges and cruise boats plough up and down, watching the game concentration and magnificent birdlife. The river attracts huge numbers of carmine bee-eaters nesting in the river cliffs and when in flood, spoonbills, ibis, all manner of storks, ducks and other waterfowl flock here.

We sought to avoid the hordes on our honeymoon at Chobe Game Lodge, whilst emulating the then golden couple of the 1970s, Elizabeth Taylor and Richard Burton, who also honeymooned at the lodge. No doubt there were many changes since, but the Arabian-inspired theme of Persian carpets, Moroccan lanterns and heavy, ornate, wooden doors prevailed. Here, the game drives, sundowners and river boat safaris were just that bit deeper into the park for exclusivity. We were sharing our honeymoon experiences with many Japanese tourists also staying at the lodge. They were wonderfully charming and courteous, until it came to mealtimes, where we had to get smart rapidly. The food service, to cater for the numbers, was not the silver service of old, but a buffet tsunami. Our oriental friends descended upon the food like a plague of locusts. Some started with the sweets and worked backwards, inwards and all over at such a phenomenal rate; hesitate or be polite and all the food was gone. They were eating Kudu steaks with soup, salad with Victoria sponge and custard as one! It was a clash of cultures and quite an education, given these were the well-educated and wealthy Japanese. They didn't do queuing, like the reserved British. Still, calorie intake on safari is a sport in itself!

Chobe was a massive anti-climax compared to the southern parks. Whilst we enjoyed fantastic long views out towards the Linyanti swamps, spying herds of nervous elephants and red lechwe, we saw no buffalo as seen previously on Puku Flats. The shabby lionesses we saw were radio collared and very dopey. Driving into Kasane did little to lighten the mood as we tried to understand the justification for the level of foreign EU investment here. We recognise that the EU should help countries to be more stable and develop, but given Botswana is already wealthy, with a strong and stable currency, and the third largest diamond exporter with a non-invasive environmental plan, why choose Botswana?

Chapter 12
Boy scout was a revelation

The avarice of a few has long led to the downfall of many an African country; sadly, Zimbabwe has been no exception. This is wonderfully illustrated in Alec Russell's book, Big Men Little People, where he examines the continent's dictators and acquiescence by the masses to these tribal chiefs. We are not judging; our journey is a reflection of our observations, as a snapshot from each country. We were extremely privileged to honeymoon in Southern Africa, primarily in Zimbabwe and gracing both Botswana and Zambia. Then, travel to and within Zimbabwe was easy and welcomed. We enjoyed a privileged encounter, met the nicest, kindest, brightest and most gentle Africans (of all backgrounds) ever. The subsequent change and devastation for the people of Zimbabwe cannot be justified by politics, race or culture. The destruction of a well-managed, prosperous, mineral-rich and viable farming country is criminal. The West (however complicit) could only watch the disintegration of lives and potential; for the flora and fauna too. As Alec Russell observes, this is not new, as we watch Ukraine and Gaza fragment.

Why can humankind not learn from historical lessons? We acknowledge such comments will attract criticism and we will be labelled with white privilege. Even if this were true, with the evidence thus far in Zimbabwe, we do not observe the new regime doing well or behaving altruistically either. Our concern is that the majority of Zimbabweans (of all creed and colour) have lost so much, with the ramifications spreading across the continent. History will judge; we just observe. Having worked alongside many a proud Rhodesian/Zimbabwean, most, if not all, have lost livelihoods at best. Douglas Rogers' 2009 book, The Last Resort, is about his parents' endurance and survival under the violent, intimidating Mugabe regime of land repossession, intimidation and then far worse.

Avoiding Zimbabwe, we took the Kazangulu ferry across the Zambezi, direct to Zambia. No longer the small, back door entry, this access point has become the main route for trade today. It looked like the ferry would sink at any moment, or worse, break free and flow over the Falls. We were lined up in a small queue and thought we were next, when a large fuel tanker was loaded from behind us; very African. The tanker appeared to fill the ferry, or so we thought. But no, they crammed a few small cars on behind a double articulated tanker, for good measure. Lorry drivers can wait for weeks for their passage, yet smaller vehicles are swift, almost instant, slotted around the lorries. The ferry operated a chain link mechanism to align and power it between each bank; it was slow, but efficient. We were guided on by a chap in his flip-flops as far as we could go. Once Daph's front wheel collapsed into the broken plank hole, we were deemed parked. Another car was wedged in behind us, before a final lorry was loaded. We set off at a sedate pace.

Writing nearly 20 years later, I was amazed to learn the African Development Bank and others have funded a £185 million gleaming, shiny, curved bridge to replace the ferry. At 923 metres long, built over the last five years, this route is now the main highway for trade from ports in Durban to Dar es Salaam. It is part of an African-wide trade deal to abolish 90% of trade tariffs across Sub Sahara Africa, a scaled-down, African version of the Chinese Belt and Road project. With an expected 250 lorries a day, we just hope the roads either side are maintained to justify the bridge. Unloading was just as efficient and we were ushered to the police post to pay our road tax. On both sides of the ferry, the customary hawkers were jostling for our attention to change money.

But borders are never simple; we had to haggle about our third-party vehicle insurance. We knew we had to have a Zambian-recognised insurance document (equivalent to the European Green Card) but were unable to get a Comesa Yellow Card in South Africa. We already had third-party insurance through our comprehensive cross-country policy, but whether the police at the roadblocks would accept such a document was another matter. In the event, we settled on US$15 for Daph, for police peace of mind, for we understood that Zambian roadblocks could be problematic. That said, we were only stopped once and the police could not have been more polite throughout our time in Zambia. The tar road to Livingstone was appalling - severely potholed. The future of the new glass bridge doesn't bode well. Livingstone, the original capital of Northern Rhodesia, had the air of a town long past its glory. In 1935, the capital shifted to Lusaka to be closer and aligned to the northern copper belt. On arrival, a throng of locals clamoured for our attention to wash Daph, watch her, show us where to go or to change money. Once we were polite but firm, they (amazingly) left us alone.

Victoria Falls, or the 'Smoke that Thunders,' are breathtaking; utterly timeless. Despite previous viewings from the Zimbabwean side, we felt that the Zambian view had more magnitude; you get closer to the Falls, thus feeling the awesome thunder of the water. We experienced high water, so the spray obscured our view and made photography more challenging. Crossing a small footbridge (called Knife Edge Bridge) we stood on the Falls' edge - it was palpable. Apparently, at low water, they allow swimming in a small cataract above the Falls, where you can hang over the edge, or even take 'high tea' on a small island that emerges there.

We could see the Zimbabwean side and watched the adrenalin junkies throwing themselves off the railway bridge, with only a large elastic band for safety. We met many travellers walking back who had been across to the Zimbabwean side to bungie jump; they reported brisk trade and a good exchange rate, despite the embargo. Apparently, petrol or diesel was plentiful and cheap there, yet the tourist industry in Zimbabwe has taken a massive hit. The Zambians have not been slow to capitalise. A year before our honeymoon visit to Victoria Falls (in 1997), 2 PARA sent B Company to Botswana to train. Whilst there, they were allocated a few days off for rest and recuperation (R & R). The company commander believed the lads would head to the bright lights of Cape Town or somewhere, so he and his sergeant major, Spike, went the opposite way for some peace, to Victoria Falls. On their arrival, the boys were lined up on Railway Bridge, waiting for Spike and the company commander to step off first; 'After you, Sir.' Then, they were all in the 'washing machine', shooting down the rapids as they rafted the white water down the mighty Zambezi; naturally, they loved it. It was only a few months after their return that I assumed command of B Company myself.

In 1997, we checked into the Victoria Falls Hotel having flown from Harare. It was a surreal and very colonial experience. On arrival, we enjoyed a magnificent 'high tea' on the terrace, overlooking Railway Bridge, in line of sight of the Falls. Later that evening, we were invited to a dinner dance, for which we were not prepared. I needed to borrow a tie from the maître d' who - unfazed - opened his lobby store, retained for such eventualities. It was such a marked difference from our earlier, more relaxed time in the Eastern Highlands of Zimbabwe, staying at Troutbeck and Leopards Rock Hotel, playing golf in both locations. It was a gentle and wonderful experience, in such contrast to the current political and economic meltdown. In 1997, we enjoyed a helicopter tour above the Falls for a fantastic perspective, yet quite unthinkable later.

Back in Livingstone, we tried to recreate the high tea experience at the exclusive, new Royal Livingstone Hotel, modern competition to the Victoria Falls Hotel for the upscale tourist. We bluffed our way in, where all the staff were resplendent in smart uniforms, especially the lady on the gate. She was loving her job, and had the broadest, widest smile (although missing a few front teeth) and great salute to each and every passing car. It was all very pleasant, but failed to capture the romance and shabby elegance, or history, of Victoria Falls Hotel. Run by Sun International Hotels, they operated a casino option, rather than a dowdy dinner dance.

The road from Livingstone to Lusaka was tarred, yet badly potholed. Long stretches were being repaired, which meant that we were often diverted onto temporary gravel, which was preferable. We were transiting to Lower Zambezi and South Luangwa national parks, having decided to give Kafue National Park a miss, despite it being the second largest park in Africa. Kafue is very spread out, flat and marshy, thus game viewing is challenging. There are large lion prides here and they have reintroduced wild dogs successfully. Kafue is renowned for the huge bird populations, especially in the winter months, when a large swathe of the park floods.

Driving to Lower Zambezi National Park, we had a crazy notion that we could transit east along the Zambezi to Luangwa. There were no references to imply this was possible, just an old map eluding to it. Zambia's south-eastern border with Mozambique is along the lower, narrow gorge section of the Luangwa River. Where the Luangwa meets the wider and deeper Zambezi, a flood plain has formed, on the apex of which is a small town called Luangwa. Current access is only via a single road paralleling the Luangwa gorge and Mozambique border. Assuming we could transit the park, this road was our exit north. Luangwa town holds strategic importance; there is no ferry across either river to Zimbabwe or Mozambique, yet there have been many incursions, notably during the independence wars, with pursuing Rhodesian or Portuguese forces chasing.

Heading south down the Great North Road to Churindu, we transited through uplands before the border with Zimbabwe. This highway between

Harare and Lusaka (and on to the northern Copperbelt) was in an appalling state of repair. Heavily laden trucks were passing both ways, with many broken down and some partially blocking the road. Churindu itself was just a mass of HGVs waiting to be processed to cross the rail or road bridge, over the Zambezi. The embargo with Zimbabwe clearly was not being observed here.

Just before Churindu, we turned east towards Lower Zambezi National Park. The park entrance was a further 75 kilometres along a graded, poorly marked track; we were struggling to make the distance in daylight. We stumbled across a campsite at Gwabi Lodge, on the bank of the Kafwe River, just before nightfall. Gwabi Lodge was some form of outward bound-type school and Zambia was starting a four-day bank holiday to celebrate independence. Gwabi was crammed with kids and families. The lodge owner was unaware of a transit route through the park but warned us of the tough, two-hour drive to reach the park entrance.

The next morning, we had to negotiate the small ferry to cross the Kafwe River. This was a hand-cranked, chain-link ferry, grinding along a twisted and fraying steel hawser. We passed villages on the banks of the river, with a continuous stream of people washing clothes, dishes and themselves. Our ferry was jammed with locals and cars, but only we were heading into the park. Up until 1983, the wilderness area referred to as Lower Zambezi National Park used to be the private game reserve for the president, so was spared the ravages of mass tourism and poaching. Today, it remains one of the few pristine wilderness areas left in Africa. The park slopes gently from the Zambezi escarpment (a remnant ridgeline from the Rift Valley) down to the Zambezi River. The upper slopes are mainly mopane woodland savannah down to the southern floodplain. Opposite, on the Zimbabwe side of the Zambezi, is Mana Pools National Park that has suffered enormously under the ravages of the Mugabe regime, from the loss of visitors, human encroachment and poaching.

The Lower Zambezi Park itself is ringed by a much larger game management area (GMA), with no fences segregating them. There are no roads and you are very unlikely to encounter another tourist. Tourist numbers are minimised as access demands advanced 4x4s and driving skills, only at certain times of the year. Most tourists access either by boat up the Zambezi or light aircraft into the airstrip. Or, as we did during our honeymoon in 1997, we arrived by floatplane from Lake Kariba, flying down the mighty Zambezi and landing on the river at Kayila Lodge. We stayed in a treehouse overhanging the river that was a pure delight. We canoed down the river, walked the escarpment and enjoyed many game drives around the floodplain. The escarpment geology has contained many animals between the ridge and the river, fostering a unique domain. We understand wild dogs were being reintroduced where they continue to flourish, same at Mana Pools, although we sadly failed to see any.

Our treehouse in 1997 was serviced by the lodge close by. Lion, leopard and elephant footprints were frequently seen in the dusty ground each morning around the base of our tree. Surrounding the base of the treehouse was a small, brick open shower and toilet wall; hot water was provided by a fire lit each morning under the water pipes. One morning, I was joining a dawn bush walk, so had just popped down to use the porcelain facility. Then I heard rustling outside, with my trousers around my ankles and armed with a toilet roll. The rustling came closer; tension (fear) was mounting when around the corner and into view came the large eyes of a small dik dik, the camp's semi-tame 'deer'. Once my heart rate recovered at the relief of not seeing something more wild, hungry or aggressive, I joined the walk. The friendly dik dik maintained a respectful distance away within the more open terrain, but once the terrain became more dense, he shot in between our walking group for protection; very smart, wild animal.

Negotiating Daph off the Kafue ferry and past the settlements, the graded track ended. Hereon in, we wrestled the track over humps and streams, beams and washaways. For me, it was exciting, twisting and turning and maintaining momentum, shifting between high and low ratio, but I was acutely aware that Catherine was only enduring it. I understood she wanted to also drive and relish the challenge, but with her injured shoulder, we dare not risk it. I wouldn't say I was a bad passenger (naturally), but I was glad I was driving. Daph performed wonderfully; the flexibility and articulation of her chassis really came to the fore.

The environs started to look familiar and then we recognised Kayila Lodge; we practically drove past the front, so we called in. This was happenstance - we had not planned to stop. As we arrived, a boatload of guests were also arriving, from the speedboat thrill. Back in 1997, we left early morning by boat, which was blinking freezing. Despite our unannounced arrival, the lodge's managing couple, Dave and Elspeth, were fantastic and so welcoming. They insisted on including us in their welcome drinks with their other guests. They had been running the camp for nine months and, after hearing our story, they were keen to show us around. The lodge (or lapa) was as we remembered, although it had been rethatched with reeds. It retained its unique upside-down boat shape, with the thatch extending to the ground over each sloping, retaining end-pole. This formed the distinctive, arch-shaped access points around the lapa. I had forgotten about the huge baobab tree beside the lapa, yet it remained, and inside, the flushing porcelain toilet was still there, replete with its green door. Our treehouse had been refurbished and due to guests being present, we didn't invade their privacy. I was relieved to note that the facilities below the tree had been improved!

We camped at a site further along the river, but before we departed, we asked Dave and Elspeth if they knew of a track to Luwanga. They did not, so Dave went to find out more. Meanwhile, Elspeth spoke about their background and showed us a picture of their old 1920s Morris Oxford. Originally from Kenya, her parents had settled there after the Second World War, having driven through Europe in the Morris. I ventured how brave that was and implied it must have been much harder to travel in those days, but Elspeth suggested the opposite. Post-war, everything was in short supply, except labour. People were on the move and she said if you had a British passport, everyone wanted to help. Even if you were stuck in the mud, in those days, the cars were so light they could be lifted out of difficulty. It certainly put our journey into perspective. Getting through Europe then was harder than the African transit; now, bizarrely, it was the reverse. Dave and Elspeth themselves were fugitives from Zimbabwe where they had been farming for many years. Like Bob and Flo, they spoke of the 'African problem' rather than anything specific, citing bureaucracy, red tape, bribes and corruption more than physically being driven off the land, as some of their friends had been.

Dave connected us to a couple of local experts, but neither Roddy, a local guide and ex Selous Scout, or Chris, running a nearby lodge, knew of a route. Both were extremely helpful but doubtful such a transit could be done. Roddy unsuccessfully tried to find a route a while back, so the theory was correct. The track would be so overgrown, an army would be required to cut a way through. As expected, we'd have to retrace our steps. In a twist, a young couple helping Chris run his lodge was Phil, and his wildlife artist wife, Julia Cassels. Fed up with corporate law, Phil joined WWF-UK around the similar time as me, a year or so after we got home. After a year of strategising and planning with WWF, I moved on, but Phil stayed and latterly has been supporting the David Attenborough team to deliver the Blue Planet series. I came to know of this recently, for not only were we living in close proximity in Hampshire, we watched, quite by chance, the same Lions rugby match in my local pub, where England defeated the All Blacks in such fine style and against the run of form.

We settled at a fabulous bare campsite that evening, alone on the banks of the Zambezi, to watch a glorious sunset, enjoy a meal and a sundowner. We listened to the growing night calls and watched the stars emerge. For anyone interested in the night's sky, the view from anywhere in southern Africa, especially in the bush, away from light pollution, is quite breathtaking. We slept well in the roof tent, with the windows and vents open, and woke to the sound of a bull elephant grazing along the riverbank. He was quite unperturbed by our presence, although we could see he was in musth. This is like being drunk; the tell-tale secretions behind the ear can be characterised by highly aggressive behaviour and a rise in reproductive testosterone levels; on average, 60 times greater than normal, although in some individuals, it can be higher. Even with the most placid of elephants, the slightest provocation can engender highly violent behaviour toward humans and other elephants during musth. A bull elephant would think nothing of lifting and trashing a Land Rover in seconds like a tin of beans, with or without a human inside. We lay in the roof tent and kept as still as possible. He was clearly not interested in us as he feasted on the trees and bushes in front of us. It was fascinating, although I did wonder if he was alone.

After an hour or so, as silently as I could, I snuck down the ladder on the elephant's blindside, opened the driver's door and only inserted the keys. We wouldn't really stand much of a chance if things turned nasty, but at least I'd want that chance. We could drive with the tent up and the awning out if we had to; clearly damage would ensue, but that might be better than being sat upon and gouged. If (and it was a big if) we escaped, the damage would be superficial and hopefully repairable. So, we continued to wait and watch in silence. He was alone - maybe he had been jilted and wanted some company?

All we knew, he stayed for two hours and we had the honour of watching and appreciating him as silently as possible. Catherine was enthralled.

Once he moseyed off, we packed away and headed slowly back to the Kafue ferry and Lusaka, via a game drive through the park. Watching the elephant was such an unexpected pleasure; nature is strange and wonderful. Within one of my last jobs in the UK, I had partial involvement in a board of inquiry into the death of an Oxbridge student, who was with a military-sponsored expedition to Africa. The student had wandered out from camp early one morning, alone in the Kenyan Masai Mara, eating an orange. Breaking all the 'rules', his worst offence was the orange, for sadly he was appallingly trampled by an elephant. Oranges are catnip to elephants and they go wild for the smell. Reportedly, they open cars and trucks like tin-openers to access a jar of marmalade. Thankfully, we had no such nectar in our fridge, although I do like a drop of marmalade.

The main draw of this area is the Zambezi River. Whilst it may not be the longest, wildest or deepest, it is flanked by wonderful, remote wildlife areas. In a wide, shallow flow, it has created a maze of meandering, forest-lined channels, spotted with sandbars and islands. Canoe safaris are popular along these stretches and we enjoyed half a day drifting and guiding a canoe from Kayala Lodge in 1997. The wildlife is not threatened by the presence of the boats, so we were able to float past hippo pods, all spluttering and yawning, and huge crocs slithering into the water from the banks at a close, yet respectful distance.

The game in Lower Zambezi was more plentiful than we remembered; we saw huge buffalo herds, more elephants and some hyenas hunting, whom we initially hoped, at a distance, were wild dogs, but no. The bird life was amazing and more extensive than we were able to recognise. As we left the park, we acknowledged that the park fees were significantly higher than in Botswana, but they have fewer visitors. How they control who is in or outside the GMA remains a mystery, but we came across an NGO's Land Rover who were tracking radio-collared wild dogs. They had reintroduced a pack and sought to follow them but were unsurprisingly struggling to keep up in the dense vegetation. We would have loved to stay and assist. We pressed on back to Churindu, where again Daph performed admirably on the rough stuff. She seemed to prefer this to potholed tar that we endured on the Great North Road to Lusaka; I know I did.

Lusaka emerged during the construction of the Cape to Cairo railway in 1906. It became the centre for colonial administration in 1930 and then subsumed Livingstone as the capital. Approaching Lusaka from the south, we entered a modern, monolithic glass and steel skyline, common for most cities these days. There had been a financial boom around the time of independence in 1964, just prior to the country's economic collapse. We arrived on Zambian Independence Day, another public holiday, so the city was quieter than normal. The city centre was very shabby, deserted and run down as we carried on via the East Cairo Road towards Pioneer Campsite, near the university. En route, we passed Mander Hill that had a new, American-style shopping mall, so we were relieved to buy provisions. It was clear that Western aid was gradually improving the city, claims supported by big signs extolling the virtues of Japanese funding for a road and cycleway project along the Cairo Road and at the university. It did not escape our attention that most vehicles were brand-new, white aid 4x4 Toyota Land Cruisers, each with a driver, steering straight through the potholes; clear evidence on their return-on-aid-investment? This was in 2002, and it would be interesting to know what state it's in now.

That evening at Pioneer Camp, we ate our supper at the communal rondavel. Present were a bunch of aid workers staying and one young, bright, articulate American girl, just out of college, who was banging on (endlessly) about her aid project and the value of education for all. Her project acquired old computers and sought to train kids to become computer literate. Fantastic, utterly laudable; we are all for education and helping people acquire new skills. But as the tales and aspiration were becoming increasingly saccharine, we slipped away, not wanting to cause offence or stifle ambition. At that point though, someone helpfully suggested it was a good idea, but where and how were the local kids going to get the money to buy these old (probably broken) computers when they couldn't afford them and had no access to electricity to run them? We continued to walk away (faster) before our guffawing became too loud.

Most guidebooks imply that it takes eight hours to reach South Luangwa National Park, via Chapata, along the East Cairo Road from Lusaka. Apparently, the East Cairo Road had been improved and was billed as 'the best road in Zambia'. The road we experienced had good tar, until we passed the impressive Luangwa Suspension Bridge. Thereafter, the road deteriorated. It was so badly potholed, we considered it the worst tarred road we'd travelled. Slow, over-laden lorries were avoiding the potholes, whilst being over and under-taken by other road users; it was a free-for-all. Consequently, we only reached Chapata half an hour after nightfall. Our self-imposed rule not to drive after dark was now challenged, for Chapata was a Wild West town, with people swarming everywhere. Whilst we had extra lights, to use them could well have made us a target. We were not directly concerned about our security, but it was virtually impossible to see or read any road signs in the dark. Thus, it took us over an hour to find our recommended campsite, the Yellow Chicken. The campsite on the edge of town was an oasis of calm amongst the chaos. The owners were extremely helpful and directed us to a local farm shop selling excellent fresh meat.

One of the world's most pristine and undisturbed rivers, the Luangwa River, rises in the Mafinga Hills (up on the Rift Valley plateau) of northeast Zambia, flowing down to the Zambezi. Around Mfuwe, the gradient flattens sufficiently for the river to meander across a 10 kilometre-wide floodplain, astride which is the eponymous South Luangwa Park. This is a seasonal park due to flooding; the roads are impassable in the wet season and the temporary lodges are washed away. Most visitors come in the dry season, largely attracting a wealthier guest who is prepared to pay a premium for a remote, pristine wilderness and to experience outstanding walking safaris. South Luangwa Park has a long history of wildlife protection, although sadly not from man. The Rift Valley, creating the Luangwa escarpment, has protected and isolated wildlife here, fostering subspecies. In 1904, protection was sought for the Thornicroft giraffe, and subsequently for the Cookson's wildebeest and Burchill's zebra subspecies. Still today, there is increasing conflict between farmers and conservation. In the 1930s, vast elephant herds were devastated by hunting; indeed, by the 1970s, poaching was endemic. Only a fraction of the original 100,000-strong elephant population survived. By 1950, the white hunter, Norman Carr, proposed a conservation scheme for the locals to derive a benefit, leading to the creation of many of today's national parks. A hunter turned environmentalist, Carr was nominated an MBE for his conservation work, although Carr politely suggested it should have been awarded to the Tsetse fly. In areas where the Tsetse fly was vanquished, people and cattle followed, but where the fly remained, wildlife flourished.

Catherine was reading Mark and Delia Owens' sequel, their 1994 book, Survivor's Song. It picks up the thread of their deportation from Botswana, arising from their open criticism of the government's soft stance on conservation. They found refuge at a Zambian research station (in North Luangwa) to find endemic elephant poaching. So began a long struggle to raise conservation awareness among the officials, who themselves were found living off black market ivory and villagers depended on elephant meat for food. Mark's obsession with catching the poachers led to vicious confrontations and fostered an intense strain on their relationship. Given Catherine's love and affection for elephants, South Luangwa was always on our visit list. Sightings of the Big Five are common, especially leopard, but it is doubtful whether any rhino remain. Most camps and lodges are situated along the Luangwa River, especially the pop-up luxury lodges, to capitalise on the huge, basking hippo pods and large crocodiles. Here, walking safaris are renowned; knowledgeable guides and game scouts are available for all walks, not just the premium Robin Pope or Norman Carr walks.

The graded road from Chipata to Mafuwe took a couple of hours, half the time suggested by our guidebook. Whilst driving along a relatively benign stretch of track, my driver's side window suddenly shattered for no apparent reason. It was akin to being shot at, such was the bang, and the window disintegrated. Thankfully, the only casualty was the glass, mostly collapsing into the door housing. The clear safety film kept the shattered window partially together and no injury arose, but now we had an issue; not being able to secure Daph. We decided it was best to press on to South Luangwa, as opposed to returning to Chipata, for our theory ran that there would be at least one Land Rover game vehicle roaming without a door, hence increasing our chance of finding a spare window. The Yellow Chicken had recommended Wildlife Camp and, on arrival, we met the owners, Herman and Peggy, a wonderful white African couple, both born in Zambia. We explained our window dilemma to Herman, who was doubtful that anything could be done. Our theory was correct, but most people here drove Land Cruisers. However, to Herman's utmost delight, half an hour later, he appeared from his workshop with an old window to fit.

We arranged a dawn game walk with a local guide, Peter, and a game scout, Cassius, with his rifle. I admit that first impressions were not great, yet boy, was I wrong! Cassius had a typical casual, laidback, slightly bored-by-the-affair demeanour, with his rifle acting more like a prop or walking stick than a weapon. It appeared he'd more likely hurt himself. But when it mattered, he was acutely tuned into his environment and moved like a cat. But Peter was a revelation; a young, preppy boy scout, his English was perfect, his enthusiasm was off the charts and his knowledge was endless. Plus, he was such a polite, young lad. Amazingly, the two worked well together. We have always enjoyed bush walks, but this took game viewing to a whole new level, enabling all the senses to come alive. Animal smell and hearing is far superior to ours, as they use them in a more primary (unconscious) way than we use sight. Once you tune into these senses, it's a revelation, like seeing the natural world with a new set of eyes. Peter loved his big cats, all the ungulates and birds, but quite unlike other guides that trot out the facts and observations, Peter had a fascination with what he saw and applied amazingly rich context to his image painting. But his real passion was plants and insects. Like most with his knowledge, it was quite technical and scientific, but his manner was soft, gentle and very engaging. His mission was to exchange as much information in as short a time as possible, so we could see with his eyes and senses. The backdrop of the Luangwa Park bestowed his storytelling with vivid images.

We experienced the whole gamut of game, predators and more; if we didn't see it, we discovered their prints and markers. We saw Thornicroft giraffe, some mating leopards up trees (you couldn't miss them for the racket they made) and passed elephants and hippos at close range. Two hours into the walk, we stopped on the banks of the river overlooking a pod of hippos, while Peter pulled out a thermos of tea and his mother's muffins; bless him. Cassius sloped off for a fag. Just beyond the sandbanks was a pod of hippos, practically lying on top of one another. One moves, they all shuffle and bustle about, causing the oxpecker birds to flutter, hovering until the hippos settle again and they re-land. Off to our left were a couple of young bull hippos offering each other a challenge. They advanced, stopped and repeated the process towards each other, offering the classic yawn threats, until one bottled it and broke off into the water. We moved on as a huge croc slipped silently into the water. Cassius flicked his butt away and led us back to camp.

We encountered huge herds of puku and Burchill's zebra and had to divert our course several times due to grazing elephants. Thanks to Peter, we were buzzing. To him, it was another walk in his back yard, for it's no stretch to expect him to behave exactly the same for everyone. Whilst we were free to drive around the park ourselves, we were so buoyed by the morning's walk that we took a guided evening game drive. In an ironic contrast, we saw very little, despite our knowledgeable guide. Over a convivial sundowner, he started describing the vivid night skies and constellations. We saw no predators, just African wildcat and civet, hippo and elephant along with the usual ungulates, plus more Thornicroft giraffe.

Each of our three days were more revealing than the last. Fixing Daph's window solved our temporary security problem, not that we expected an issue at the park. However, it appeared another couple from South Africa were not so fortunate. Apparently, the lady's handbag was stolen. Mind you, whilst it takes all sorts, this couple were so dopey, they were a drama waiting to happen! Peggy and Herman were on it straightaway; incensed that this should happen at their place, for much of what happened here was based on trust. In a flash, Herman rounded up his boys, grabbed a rifle and his dogs and was off in the bush, tracking what he thought was the perpetrator. Peggy was left to manage the camp and start questioning people on what they saw. To Peggy, this was an example of the gradual decline in values in what she again described as the 'African problem'. There were very few incidents of theft or lawlessness in the camps, certainly not from any of the locals, who depended on tourists for income. Herman was pursuing some 'out-of-towners'; it also emerged that he had soldiered in the bush wars (little more was divulged), but he was not a chap to be diverted, and was after his man. The manhunt lasted two days and the perpetrator was handed to the police, but without the evidence. It was likely nothing more would happen, but the chap was clearly rattled and very unlikely to do something similar again. I certainly would not have liked to be caught by Herman, with his boys and dogs, for sure.

Poaching remains a major issue; man versus wildlife and their want to fill the pot. However, here we observed a much healthier balance, with education, related employment and income from tourists redressing the balance. But hunger and famine are strong motivators. We came across the park's own anti-poaching Rapid Action Team (the RATs) who explained their work. They appeared well-equipped, certainly highly motivated and operating largely at night. I suppose time will tell how effective they are. It was interesting that Herman was off doing his own thing rather than calling in the police or the RAT boys.

After a delightful interlude, we backtracked to Chapata, to stock up on fuel and some more of those fantastic steaks that we'd acquired from the farm shop. It was in Chapata that we first saw some albino kids. Albinism is a rare and congenital disorder where offspring have either complete or partial absence of pigmentation in their skin, hair or eyes. Vision defects are common. The lack of skin pigments leads to terrible cancers, which are often related to poor immunity and a greater susceptibility to infection. It certainly engenders a double take, such is the difference to the normal kids. Albinism is a worldwide issue and Sub-Saharan Africa has a greater predisposition, compounded by the persecution of those afflicted. Misinformation is spread by witch doctors and folklore, promulgating the misconception that they are diseased, or being punished, when it's actually caused by a genetic default. Few live beyond their forties. Folklore and traditional medicine imply that use of their body parts in rituals will bring prosperity to the user, so if the albinos have not been ostracized or killed, on the presumption they bring 'bad luck', they are persecuted, or killed and dismembered, with their graves dug up and desecrated for potions.

We needed fuel and wanted to dispose of our remaining local currency, so chose a relatively new Texaco station. I didn't think much of a group of lads hanging around, but as they started to wander across, I got a sixth sense. Thankfully, Catherine stayed (locked) inside Daph, with the money, and I did my best to ignore them. Sadly, this was becoming challenging, as they started rocking Daph and asking pointed questions as I was filling up. I thought the fuel station owners might have a system or something to intervene, but no. This mild (yet annoying) intimidation continued, for us out-of-towners were an obvious target. Something had to give! Eventually, the big fella, and I mean big – nearly seven feet tall, chunky, with half his teeth missing and the largest feet I have ever seen - started to invade my personal space. At the start of my 2 PARA days, I had a Private Morris who had size 18 feet; the army had to make special boots to fit him. Mind you, he could march for days and was a bright soldier. Here, this Big Foot clearly was not the sharpest tool in the box, as he said, 'I want your boots.' I was practically half his size - certainly my feet were. I started laughing and said if he wanted these old boots, they'd have to fit him, and I started to prank about, walking like Donald Duck around the fuel station. It was pure distraction; I had no clue what else to do, but thankfully, his mates started to take the mickey out of Big Foot too. I was never going to be able to fight my way out effectively, nor run away cleanly, so I ramped up the micky-taking and started calling big foot 'Big Foot'. Thankfully, his mates cottoned on, turning their single brain cell amongst them to Big Foot as they bundled him away. Phew; I know it was hot, but I was sweating. I went to pay. The owner was Asian and was intimidated and worried, but not empowered or enabled to take action. It ended up a funny and bizarre event, which on this occasion, had a positive outcome; I guess the Asian owner has seen the opposite. We did not hang about for Big Foot to realise he had been duped; we headed to the Malawi border.

The tar road to the border was pristine, although we noticed the locals burning the side undergrowth. We had not seen this before; it's logical under controlled burning to clear the scrub, fertilise the ground and discourage snakes and other undesirables away. Yet I emphasise the word 'controlled'. Reflecting on Zambia, we had enjoyed our time and would have stayed longer, time permitting. We read about the dire famine predictions in Zambia before our arrival, yet we experienced the opposite. Other than the appalling state of the roads, the police were friendly and helpful, and the locals warm and generous. The worry around famine is a constant concern for poor countries, especially in rural areas where aid is targeted but rarely arrives.

Maize availability is the accepted measure for famine, but there was plenty of other foodstuffs. We saw crops, irrigated fields and lots of food being sold along the roadside. We understood the famine allegations from the press were aimed at the government who, having sold all their maize reserves to Tanzania at a good price on the suggestion of the IMF to 'rotate' their reserves, appeared to have failed to replace that reserve. So obviously, it was now 'hand-out to the West for assistance' with reports of famine. Was it a mismanagement issue? It would be interesting to know what happened to the revenue from the maize sold to Tanzania. Also, one has to question where the maize surplus and rotation might come from. The rural communities appeared to be growing sufficient subsistence crops but they did not have a surplus or income to buy anything else.

The Zambian customs were a breeze, although oblivious to our Carnet.

About 10 kilometres down the road were the Malawian customs and in between, there was a police road block, looking for freebies. Up until now, it had been easy to distract any officialdom and police, but now, for the first time, we were asked, 'What have you brought me?' My stock response to such questions was always a big smile and the offer of 'the hand of friendship'. There was nothing else on offer and we usually rolled past. Malawian customs were more officious; the 'lady with the stamp' slammed her stamp down so hard onto the passports that I thought the table would break! Customs demanded money for the Carnet…here we go. We were told our Comesa Third Party was not valid as South Africa had pulled out of the scheme. More nonsense and opportunistic bribery; we thanked them and left them empty-handed. Attitudes here might explain the high number of money changers and kids running around with thick wads of cash.

Chapter 13
We weren't feeling the 'warm heart of Africa'

The new, smooth Malawian roads were a revelation; we were on edge for a pothole at any second. Immediately, we noticed the constant stream of people walking along each side of the road. In fact, it was nearly impossible to find a quiet place to pull over for a drink or bite, let alone a crafty pee stop. Once we stopped for a quick rest at what we thought was a quiet spot, only to attract a whole village! Feeling guilty, we handed over a half-eaten sandwich (probably the wrong thing to do) and moved on.

Landlocked Malawi is rural and agricultural. Independence was granted in 1964, having been the British protectorate of Nyasaland. This was an extension of Northern Rhodesia (present-day Zambia) and was known as 'The Warm Heart of Africa'. We headed to Lilongwe and stumbled upon another four-day national holiday. Lilongwe Old Town had more character than the shiny, new centre, but as in Zambia, the threat of famine loomed. The expected outcome for Malawi was poor, given their small population and limited subsistence infrastructure. Reports of drought from the south implied severe suffering, but we could not substantiate this. The villages we passed appeared to have available foodstuffs on market stalls. There were the ubiquitous onions and tomatoes, some other vegetables, as well as USAID grain sacks. We couldn't say if the locals had the funds to buy, or were just selling their wares. Interestingly, and uniquely, bicycle manufacturers must have enjoyed a boom here; hitherto we had not seen many (if any) bicycles. In Lilongwe, we saw comparable numbers of bikes as we had seen in China; these bikes were similarly overladen with gigantic loads and passengers that made them unpredictable fellow road users.

We skipped Lilongwe and drove on to Senga Bay, where we found a beautiful, Mediterranean-style coastline and beach. Presiding over the bay was the old Livingstone Beach Hotel, now part of Le Méridian Group. This refurbished hotel was a luxury, all-inclusive expensive resort, but adjacent on the beach was the glorious Steps Campsite, just 20 yards from the crystal-clear lake. It was reminiscent of a Spanish or Greek island, except for the African warning sign: 'Take care after dark, beware hippos.'

We were blissfully unaware of any large mammals roaming the beach, so set up Daph and enjoyed our Chapata steaks. Lake Malawi, by volume, is the fourth largest freshwater lake in the world. It is a meromictic lake, meaning the water layers do not mix. These permanent layers have an oxic-anoxic boundary (pertaining to oxygen levels). We could see that the water was both warm and clear, and knew the central glacial trench was very deep. The locals were not bothered by the hippos, crocs or sea eagles as they seemed to haul out plentiful fish. Monkeys were reputed to be an irritant, but at Senga, we didn't see any. We declined Le Méridian's offer of a boat trip to see monitor lizards on an uninhabited island, unimaginatively named Lizard Island.

Reluctant to move on, our guidebook recommended a 'Caribbean-style, lush, tropical indent' at Nkhata Bay. We drove along smooth roads north with high expectations, unaware that this bay was popular with the overlander routes. Nkhata Bay was described as a backpacker's hippy dropout; 'a cheap delight, with a flourishing arts and crafts market' at Chikali Beach Resort. Perhaps due to the Malawi independence celebrations, it was rammed, and the locals were using the site as a thoroughfare. One entrepreneurial local opened his chalet for campers to use his bathroom facilities, but it was like trying to camp in a crammed car park. It was poor; I was all for moving, but we stuck it out in case we had missed something. We hadn't! We were constantly bothered by locals and boys trying to sell us their collections of batiks, postcards and wooden carvings. They were so persistent that in the end, we said it was not our policy to buy anything on a Sunday - please come back on Tuesday after the holiday (and after our departure); we were more surprised that this actually worked.

We left early the next morning through some attractive, hilly terrain that was reminiscent of a rubber plantation, to arrive at Mzuzu, a local, administrative town. The colonial feel was conferred by the Mzuzu Royal Hotel, something akin to a Malaysian hill station, where we stopped for some delightful, local coffee. Mzuzu is the third largest town in Malawi, trading timber, tea, coffee and rubber. We found a thriving community, a university, all active given that it was a holiday period. As we were stocking up, I saw a car sales lot with a dozen or more (functional) Series II and III Land Rovers and parts; a Land Rover enthusiast's delight! I was prodded on, rapidly. The roads started to deteriorate as we drove north; normal African service resumed. We were heading for Livingstonia, perched high on the Nyika Plateau in the north of Malawi. As we ascended, we started to pass heavily-laden (and struggling) lorries, when suddenly, we were detoured on to a pristine stretch of tarmac, courtesy of a Danish aid programme.

David Livingstone's death in 1873 rekindled British missionary zeal. Party to this was the Free Church of Scotland, who became intent on establishing a mission in Malawi. Their initial chosen location was on the lakeshore near Cape Maclear in 1875. The mission was named Livingstonia, in honour of Dr Livingstone himself, but malaria ravaged these new missionaries. They moved north to a new site along the shoreline to Bandawe, but the same plight was rendered upon them. In 1894, Dr Laws again moved the mission up the escarpment above the lake, but below the Nyika Plateau. Here, he created a little piece of Scotland, with a church and what was thought to be the first stone house in Africa. They added a post office, schools and the David Gordon Memorial Hospital, all of which still stand in some guise or other today.

To reach the mission of Livingstonia, you need to ascend a 15 kilometre rough, gravel track. It was wide enough for a 4x4, but the surface was so badly damaged by water erosion and run-offs, the 20 or so hairpin bends would have been a challenge for any long vehicle. It was steep and challenging in parts, but thankfully, Daph pulled up strongly, in low ratio. We passed a campervan halfway up, taking a breather and letting their engine cool down; they were struggling, but refused assistance. I referred to the track's unsuitability for long vehicles, yet in good African style, long logging trucks were negotiating their way up and down.

At the mission, we were saddened by what we found. The 'Stone House' (a listed building, built for Dr Laws) was being left to rot. Tragic in itself, but the building was also listed as a viable guest house. It contained memorabilia like a museum, with some unique insights, treasures and letters from Livingstone. The Malawian government had decreed the Stone House should be refurbished as a national monument, but there was no money. Bizarrely, we came across a few chaps from Devon's Rotary UK, who thought they were there to give the place a 'lick of paint' and possibly some surface repairs. On examination, they realised this would only paper over the major, structural issues and the paint would not last five minutes. Bless their endeavour, these chaps were frustrated and sought to do more.

We were told that the museum was closed because the 20-year-old custodian had recently died from AIDS. The Rotary boys had the keys so let us have a look around. My parents lived in Devon and were active Rotarians but were unaware of this project when we discussed it once home. To imply this was a museum would be a misnomer; basically, the Stone House had been locked up with all the contents left in situ. It was surreal; the old writing desk, letters and prints just left. The Rotary boys understood there was a plan for the exhibits to be sent back to Strathclyde in Scotland, but by whom and when, no one knew.

Around the wider site, the church was all locked up and in as much disrepair as the David Gordon Memorial Hospital. Catherine was distressed at the state of these essential services. The hospital layout reminded Catherine of the isolation institutions of Victorian England, like those she saw at Lodge Moor in Sheffield when she started her medical degree; she thought Lodge Moor was in desperate need of improvements back then! But here, there was an obvious demand for the David Gordon Hospital; patients were waiting on the grass outside. We understood that many of the male patients had been working in the South African mines and consequently, they and their relatives in Livingstonia were suffering from AIDS at the rate of two diagnosed per week. The 'African problem' was rearing its head again, for there was no management, money or direction; these people were left to manage by themselves and they were not coping. We came across quite a modern ambulance, donated by the Friends of Livingstonia. I guess they would have been shocked at what was left - this vehicle was going nowhere. It had no wheels and the engine, what was left of it, had not seen fuel for many a year. The rear was crammed with wheel-less trolleys and other dilapidated hospital equipment; it was not surprising, but a visceral image nonetheless.

Deflated by the image of Livingstonia, our thoughts of camping here were scuppered when the whole village came out to plead, hands held out. What could we do? With heavy hearts, we moved on. At the top of the escarpment descent, we saw a timely sign to Manchewe Falls and campsite, so we headed down to investigate. This site was at complete odds to Livingstonia; it was a delightful eco-campsite with hot showers and composting toilets. The site was well-maintained by some real enthusiasts who were very interesting to chat to. We bumped into an English couple who were also chancing their luck to stay. They were travelling from Mombasa to South Africa with their young children, conducting their education en route. How brave, and what an education! We wished them well. We followed the sign and walked to the Falls, which would have been a tremendous drop had there been much water beyond the trickle we saw. It certainly verified the vertiginous height of the escarpment and views. The next day, we headed for the border, tackling first the hairpin bends and sheer drops to get down the escarpment.

In Paul Theroux's Dark Star Safari, he returns to Africa to rekindle his first trip after his university days; he seeks to recapture his experiences as a USAID English teacher in Malawi. In his witty, observant and endearingly irascible style, one follows his dubious modes of travel from Cairo, by rattletrap bus, dugout canoe, cattle truck, armed convoy, ferry and finally, train to Cape Town. He was travelling over a similar timeframe as us, comparing his memory by speaking with locals, aid workers, missionaries and tourists, yet it was Malawi and Blantyre that held his greatest aspiration. Sadly, the country (and continent) failed to live up to his high expectations in the intervening years. Our brief transit only offered a tiny snapshot, but we observed a country at odds with itself. We saw a huge freshwater lake (food and water), energy (sun and rivers) and numerous, flowing rivers (irrigation), yet witnessed no pending famine. What farming we saw was subsistence based, with little organised growing. The pristine road network would permit fast distribution and access to markets on the assumption that there were excess crops. As for that 'smile of Africa,' we could not comment. No one had been rude or threatening (quite the opposite), although the incessant haggling and pestering was irritating at best and symptomatic of a deeper malaise or hardship. We understood that such behaviour was only likely to get worse the further north we went; time would tell.

Chapter 14
In the footsteps of Burton and Speke

Mbeya is the southern district, provincial town with a reputation for lawlessness; we were advised to give it a wide berth. The border crossing at Songwe was smooth enough, despite the most vicious stamping of passports thus far. Despite Tanzania's reputation for corruption, we knew we'd get visas (US$50 each) on the spot, and half an hour later, we were heading north. We were unsure whether to head direct to Dar es Salaam or explore a more scenic route along Lake Tanganyika's eastern edge via Kigoma, with options to swing across to the Serengeti or rotate through Burundi, Rwanda and Uganda, back to Kenya. This would satisfy an earlier ambition to visit Mahale Mountains National Park, only accessed by boat or on foot. Here, chimpanzees and lions coexist, similar to Gombe Stream National Park (just to the north, close to the Burundi border) where researcher Jane Goodall reported her observations on chimpanzee behaviours.

Despite the allure of the more rugged, less trodden route, we knew we wouldn't make Kenya in time. We had an administrative commitment during August in the UK, so we were targeting flights from Nairobi. Plus, the Northern Safari Serengeti circuit is a magnificent wildlife arena and the option to travel under our own steam was seductive. We sought to explore the Tanzanian coast, not only Zanzibar, but the more remote, wonderful islands of Pemba. Friends had dived there, extolling its wonders, although recent pirate activity and rAIDS were disrupting tourist activity.

Passing through well-maintained tea plantations in the Kipengere Mountains in the south, immediately we noticed people just going about their business, not standing and staring as we passed or looking for handouts. Tanzania is a relatively poor country, but the mountain soil here appeared well irrigated, rich and cultivated. The potholes had returned, but nothing like Zambia, plus more heavily-laden cyclists wobbled down the roads. We headed for a campsite gem at Kisolanza, whose farm shop sold us a kilo of beef fillet and various large bags of vegetables for less than US$12, which included our camping fees! Tanzania appeared significantly more affluent, especially when seeing the plentiful and colourful markets of Iringa. It was

July, their winter months, where parts of the Udzungwa Mountains around Iringa are at 5,000 feet and temperatures can dip to freezing. For us, it was like a warm, pleasant UK summer's day.

We joined the main Tanzam Highway, a single carriage road that divides two major reserves either side. These huge parks are lesser known, as access is challenging and scant facilities exist, yet the same could be said about the Serengeti in the early days, or the Kalahari. For the true enthusiast, they are proper reserves and an area we'd explore, should we ever return. Now called Ruaha National Park, this area has amalgamated smaller reserves; the largest protected area in Tanzania and East Africa. The Ruaha River, flowing along the south-eastern margin of most of the park, maintains the focus for optimal game viewing. The South African naturalists, Tilde and Chris Stuart, wrote in their Africa's Great Wild Places book a very detailed chapter on many of these southern parks.

Although Tanzanian national park authorities mandate no 'natural resource harvesting', this is ignored; logging, hunting, poaching and a myriad of other offences occur. Again, the Tsetse fly that thrives in the south remains the best protection for wildlife. This region - initially 'opened' to Western eyes by slave traders and explorers, around the time of Burton, Speak, Livingstone and Stanley - was mostly focused on Lake Tanganyika and beyond. Within the miombo thickets (miombo, known as a tropical and subtropical grassland, savanna, and shrubland biome) thrives a diverse variety of all animals, like roan, topi, kudu, Grant's gazelles and many other ungulate species, notably Lichtenstein's hartebeest. Massive elephant and buffalo herds that previously roamed here have been severely depleted.

If the Ruaha National Park was a potential revelation, then the Selous Game Reserve to the east would be even greater. Covering an area the size of Wales (four times the size of the Serengeti), the Selous Game Reserve is significantly more inaccessible. It is (was) a pristine, raw reserve with the Rufiji River slicing through as the core feature for almost 50 kilometres, breathing life into the area. Ultimately flowing into the Indian Ocean, the river culminates as a maze of mangroves, riverine forests and swamps at the coast. All pristine wilderness areas are threatened by modernity, and Selous was no different. Mismanagement, official corruption and poaching has devastated wildlife numbers already, but this would be negligible when compared to the proposed hydro-electric dam at Stiegler Gorge that resurfaced at the time of our trip. Whilst not a new concept, nothing has emerged over the intervening 50 years as access is challenging, as are geological and environmental impact. The World Bank was looking to finance the project in the 1960s and 1980s, but corruption and poor financial planning thwarted the programme. In 2018, construction began and, at the time of writing, the Julius Nyerere Hydropower Dam is 78% complete. A huge scar and major environmental damage has been inflicted, yet still no power has been delivered.

The game reserve got its name from Frederick Courteney Selous, a white African hunter, British Army officer, author and conservationist. He was the son of the chair of the British Stock Exchange, with expectations to follow suit. But at 19, Frederick travelled to Matabeleland to shoot game, where he stayed for 20 years. Eventually, in the employ of Cecil Rhodes, he was awarded a Royal Geographical Society Founder's Medal for his insight and reports. Frederick fought in the first and second Matabele Wars, alongside Robert Baden-Powell. Then in 1916, aged 64, he, like many colonialists, he rejoined the British Army for active service in East Africa, to be awarded a DSO. When fighting on the banks of the Rufiji River in 1917, his camouflage and concealment skills let him down; he raised his head and binoculars to locate the enemy when he was shot through the head by a German sniper and died instantly. A modest stone marks the grave near where he fell, under a tamarind tree near Chokawali, just downriver of the Stiegler Gorge.

In the same conflict, the Battle of Rufiji Delta saw a major naval engagement conducted within the mangroves and coastal waters of the Delta. The powerful German battleship, SMS Konigsberg, was damaged and blockaded by smaller, British battleships. With superior range of her guns, the SMS Konigsberg protected and camouflaged herself within the Delta for nine months whilst she affected repairs, but with dwindling supplies, ammunition and sickness (malaria), she eventually succumbed. This does raise many issues around war memories being biased toward European losses, despite the devastating impact wrought upon the colonies. As with the Forgotten Armies in Burma and Asia 25 years later, East Africa was the battleground of four empires, each possessing territories in Kenya, Uganda, Tanzania and Mozambique. Millions of lives were lost in East Africa, yet it's one of the least known theatres of war. If the fighting was not sufficiently appalling in itself, with extreme conditions and wild animals also taking a toll, sickness and pestilence carried the greatest danger to life and caused misery at best.

During our tenure in Tanzania, most of the Rufiji sector was designated a photographic and tourist area for high-end, fly-in lodges and camps. The rest was set aside for lucrative big game hunting under privately leased concessions. The magic and fascination of the Rufiji River and Selous were captured by the pre-eminent travel writer, Peter Matthiessen, in his book, Sand Rivers. I later read his African Trilogy (The Tree where Man was Born, African Silences and Sand Rivers) that evoked strong and visceral imagery of our trip, rekindled by insight and powerful description. Matthiessen was a native New Yorker, a writer of both fiction and non-fiction, but his naturalism and travel writing stirred curiosity around the world. Sand Rivers describes a 1979 walking safari in the Selous with Richard Bonham, the late Hugo Van Lawick and a young Zambian, Robin Pope. We had experienced the Robin Pope-style walks at South Luangwa, and Richard Bonham (whom we were scheduled to meet later) was instrumental in setting up photographic safaris from his permanent lodge at Sand Rivers, a few bends downriver from the Stiegler Gorge. We never explored the Selous; it remains unfinished business.

One factor was Eddy the Eagle. I am not referring to the fearless Olympic ski jump legend, but an eccentric officer from the regiment. Young David was posted to 2 PARA and joined us in D Company just before we went to Canada. I was a newly promoted captain and was made temporary 2IC of the company for the trip, before taking over the Patrols Platoon, so I tried to look after David and show him the ropes. He was fit, very active and obsessed by wildlife, specifically anything he could shoot. So far so good - yet conforming to acceptable behavioural norms appeared beyond him. His girlfriend worked at Whipsnade Zoo where he'd disappear (understandably) at the drop of a hat. It was not uncommon for him to reappear with the odd raptor under his arm to look after. During one memorable mess night, David foolishly let his prize owl loose. Suffice to say, his subsequent mess bill and fine to repair the colours and the priceless, Arnhem painting was sizable, plus provides sufficient insight into his derived nickname. He served a few years before leaving to run a golf course; a euphemism for his passion to shoot things. Curtailing the story, Dave ended up in Tanzania as a big game hunter, reportedly in the Selous area whilst we were there, although we failed to get comms with him. A meeting would have been wonderful, although we'd probably skip the shooting party. By chance, in 2020, Dave and I spoke, although he was working in Libya at the time. He spent several years in the Selous, making good money with big clients, when he and his wife (the same girlfriend) moved to South Africa. Their kids attended Grahamstown University; his lad became a commercial pilot and his daughter had ambitions to join the army. Dave and his wife completed a similar journey to ours, riding motorbikes south some years after us - it's a small world.

Iringa is the southern district capital of Tanzania, situated on the edge of a steep escarpment and plateau in the Udzungwa Mountains. The indigenous Hehe people inflicted a significant defeat upon the occupying Germans in the late 1890s before they were subjugated. The Germans built a military station at Iringa to avenge the death of their commander, Emil Von Zelewski, enforcing Hehe respect for German authority. Iringa's strategic position compelled the German East African administration to make Iringa their southern capital, explaining the guidebook description of Iringa as possessing 'the air of a dilapidated Bavarian market town'. It was a fair assessment, yet it retained a distinctly African flavour; the markets were a riot of colour, plentiful and well presented. Just south is Isimila, one of the most significant archaeological sites within Africa, where stone tools of early human habitation (hand axes, cleavers and hammers) had been found, dating back 60,000+ years. After Iringa, we stopped at the delightful Baobab Campsite in Mikumi, an area covered with ancient baobab trees. The landscape here was similar to the Serengeti, although dotted with more acacia, baobabs, tamarinds clumps and rare palms. The guidebook suggests a chance of seeing tree-climbing lions, more commonly observed in Uganda's Queen Elisabeth National Park.

Unsurprisingly, the nearer to Dar es Salaam we drove, the more the Tanzam Highway deteriorated. Combining the worst vestiges of African driving from large lorries and matatus, with increasing police roadblocks, it was not a relaxing drive. Dar was an African melting pot and best avoided. Austin and Una advised us to try the Silver Sands Hotel, a campsite to the north on the Bagamoyo Road. They had used it several times and it offered safe, cheap camping near the beach and was a secure option whilst visiting Zanzibar. We never explored Bagamoyo itself, despite it being the capital of German East Africa and one of the most important trading ports of its day along the East African coast. In Swahili, Bagamoyo means 'lay down your heart'; an interesting translation, considering it was the main port for slaves, as well as ivory and coconuts. It was also the start point for most of the renowned European explorers in the 19th century, such as Burton, Speke, Stanley and Grant.

Secluded behind a quiet, affluent and sprawling coastal suburb, the Silver Sands campsite was distributed under the palms. There was a central attap and bar with a lovely veranda, above a modern, lounge-style swimming pool. Views stretched out over endless, sandy beaches. Relaxing on the veranda, we ordered a fish and chip lunch, which became a battle with the baboons who knew the score. Once we were served, a baboon decided that he also fancied our lunch. He hopped onto the table and brazenly helped himself. Foolishly, I batted him away with a sweep of my arm, immediately realising the error of my ways. The baboon thought there was competition for 'his' chips. This sort of human interaction with wild animals is bad; I didn't want to risk an infected cut or scratch, or worse injury, so we retreated, leaving the waiters to deal with the problem, which they showed little sign of rectifying. It explains why the baboons ran the joint, which was our sole criticism of an otherwise delightful spot.

Dar es Salaam means 'haven for peace' in Swahili, the predominant culture along this coastline. Dar only became the capital once the Germans recognised the value of the deepwater harbour at the end of the 19th century. In 1974, then-president Julius Nyerere decreed that Dodoma would become the new capital as it's in the centre of the country. As with all things in Tanzania, full transfer of bureaucracy was decreed 'officially' completed in 1996, yet most would say the process is yet to start. Dar was an eclectic mix of old and new; it was hot, dirty, crowded and exasperating, yet exciting too. We only had a short explore on our way to the ferry to the island of Unguja, or Zanzibar, as Europeans know it.

Zanzibar has held great significance, disproportionate to its size. The reach and influence of the Omani Sultans stretched far inland to the Great Lakes, controlling the supply of ivory and slaves. Slavery was nothing new in Africa, yet the Arabs elevated the trade to new heights, either trading or using slaves, trading around 60,000 a year, thus depopulating huge areas. Arabs arrived on the monsoon winds and took safe harbour in the natural port of Stone Town. The first Europeans to arrive were the Portuguese, initially Vasco da Gama in 1499, who negotiated a trading peace treaty for two centuries. In 1698, the Omanis eventually regained control, yet all parties leveraged the provision of slaves to manage the fertile lands and trade the spices, notably cloves, back to India, Persia and Arabia, sailing back and forth on the trade winds.

We tried to prearrange accommodation on the island, but this became too difficult. There was a lack of information and unreliable comms, yet we were told we could sort it on arrival. We took the risk and headed for the faster hydrofoil to Stone Town. True to form, we ended up on the three-hour ferry boat because of a mechanical issue on the hydrofoil. The boat was a tub and its image was not enhanced by the captain's gallows humour at playing reel to reel boat disaster movies piped to the TVs.

Sometimes the slow road is nice; the weather was delightful and the waters calm, deep and blue. As we approached the island, the palms along the golden beaches gave way to the terracotta roof tiles over old, white walls; it was evident that Stone Town was a defended place. The natural harbour was quaint and obviously there had been no development of the quayside since Nelson. Old dhows vied for position with a few newer boats. With a simple immigration stamp in our passports, we joined the taxi throng to find our proposed hotel. We had been trying to find and book the Emerson House, quoted in the guidebooks as being 'one of the top hundred best small hotels in the world' by the Daily Telegraph, yet reasonably priced. It was described as a wonderfully restored, 19th century Swahili sultan's palace; a multi-storeyed, small town house with an inner courtyard, with one of Zanzibar's best restaurants and a rooftop tearoom and terrace. What could go wrong?

There were warnings about guides and taxi drivers extorting tourists' money after taking them on a fool's errand around the island, racking up a bill and then leaving them in dodgy accommodation, so we agreed a price with Rashid. After 15 minutes of twists and turns around Stone Town, and feeling relieved that we'd not tried to walk it, we arrived outside our intended hotel. Apparently, it had been closed for almost a year, which would explain why we couldn't book it. We then trailed around a few full hotels with waning patience, for Stone Town was packed with tourists. To Rashid's credit, he was trying hard. Whilst we were looking for an alternative, we came across a wedding party, dancing down the streets. There was a band, followed by the bride, groom and guests, all resplendent in colourful dresses and shirts and garlands; it appeared that everyone was invited, for we too were ushered out of our taxi into the melee to tag along. Whilst I was doing my David Bailey bit, a small boy tugged at my arm. Bless him, he was concerned for my safety as I was standing in the road and a car was approaching; never mind ruining my prize-winning photograph! Finally, Rashid took us to Emerson and Green Hotel, a more up-market hotel than our original intended location, where we found a room at an inflated price. Poor Rashid was somewhat crestfallen at not being able to provide us with our original request yet did not demand any more than the agreed amount, for which we were very surprised, for he certainly had earned his tip.

Not unlike Emerson House, the Emerson and Green Hotel had been restored in a similar manner to a rich Swahili owner. Each of the 10 rooms were different, but on a similar theme. They were spacious and ornate, with huge, carved, wooden doors and marbled floors. Nearly all the rooms had the most amazing stone baths, the size of a modern jacuzzi. Some had verandas, depending on their aspect and most had four-poster beds with silken mosquito nets stylishly draped around them. Shutters and drapes, vivid colours of purple, blues and green with dark woods were the delightful colour palate. There was no aircon, but the old, traditional, colonial build-style meant it was not required.

Once ensconced and refreshed by our stone bath, we ventured out into the street. On our first evening, we enjoyed sundowners on the veranda of Africa House, on the edge of Stone Town. Africa House is a stylish renovation of the old British club and it was due to reopen as a hotel, having been the British Council building. Walking through the streets at night is both exciting and safe. Near the harbour, at the Jamituri Gardens, were numerous food stalls selling local delicacies and 'African fast food'.

We were rewarded with a magnificent rooftop breakfast and stunning views across the roofs of Stone Town and beyond. We overlooked the Palace of Wonders and the Portuguese Fort next door. Under the sunshade, we sipped local coffee, freshly squeezed orange juice and ate fresh, baked breads and delicacies, while being washed in the warm, scented air. Regrettably, we could only stay a single night, so they arranged our second at their sister hotel, Baghani Hotel, which was similar, but not a patch on the Emerson and Green. Navigating the backstreets was easy, safe and laidback; the locals were relaxed, apart from the few hawkers.

On our way to the ferry back to Dar, we came across the fabled, genuine, local tourist guides who casually show people around without undue pressure. I was trying to photograph St Joseph's Cathedral with a view that incorporated the tower of the Bohora Mosque in the same shot, when a voice suggested a better photographic angle. Mohammed was a quiet, mature gentleman, very keen to discuss cricket and to show us around the spots we had been for the last two days. But in his short time with us, he indicated the major sights and suggested as we parted that the ornate, carved, blue door belonged to the parents of a certain Freddie Mercury, the global phenomenon and singer of the rock group, Queen.

Built by Sultan Barghash in 1883, the Palace of Wonders was a white, colonial, veranda-ed building with an eclectic mix of exhibits pertaining to the history of the island, the power and reach of the Omani empire and early life on Zanzibar. Juxtaposed was the Arab Fort next door from the 1700s, originally built by the Omanis to defend themselves from the Portuguese. Ironically, the fort sat upon the site of an early Portuguese church. Later, after more twists and turns through the maze of back streets, dodging hand carts and overloaded bicycles, we found the Anglican Church of Christ, built on the site of the old slave market. The church was erected to commemorate the end of slave trading by the British. The altar is positioned over the original whipping post. Outside was a memorial stone pit, containing four shackled figures within, kneeling and chained via their necks.

Slaves were a valuable commodity for Zanzibar, delivered by dhows, jammed in with no regard for safety. Many did not survive. On arrival, slaves were stripped naked, cleaned and their bodies were covered with coconut oil, then a gold bracelet was attached to denote the name of their trader. The slaves were subsequently marketed by marching them down the streets in front of potential buyers. When a purchase was indicated, the buyer conducted a full and invasive inspection, including the mouth and teeth. Then they were made to run, to ensure there were no foot defects, after which a price was settled. Slavery was a global market, including USA, who by 1837 had a consulate on Zanzibar. The British were also here, but now with a view to stop slave trading in the face of overwhelming opposition. Britain could not achieve an end until 1876, although slavery openly existed for a further 20 years. Even today, there are those who wish to enslave others, thankfully being addressed under modern slavery laws. Under the neighbouring church, we saw small slave cells with wall chains. Interestingly, Zanzibar's religious tolerance from those days still pervades today, with all denominations practising in harmony. Inside the church was a small, wooden crucifix, apparently carved from the tree under which David Livingstone died in Zambia, where his heart is buried, in Chitambo.

We caught the hydrofoil back to Dar and grabbed a waiting taxi back to Daph, ready to revisit the Northern Safari Circuit. I mentioned our previous trip being the potential spark for this journey, yet the mention could have occurred anyway – if you want to do something badly enough, you will always find a way! For us, it was here that Catherine and I recognised we were on the same page. We were wrapped up within the trip and its daily events, yet in the back of my mind I was still cogitating about a career change and what I would end up doing next....

In 1999, we flew to Arusha to find our driver and guide, Winston, for our 'personalised,' two-week rotation of the Northern Safari Circuit, in our own Land Rover. It was one of those 'no effort required' safaris; the real Out of Africa deal with large, canvas walk-in tents, a separate shower/toilet and dining tent. Winston and Aga were a silent team in sync, and obviously had been doing it for a while. Aga's English was OK; he thought nothing of being left alone to guard a wild bush camp in the middle of the Serengeti whilst we drove around madly with Winston.

Winston was an experienced guide. His ability to impart knowledge and translate what he was observing was outstanding, but he was less enamoured by the safari hordes. As witnessed at the first three parks, where he deliberately avoided the massed vehicle ranks around a kill or sighting, he was always correct that there would be something special nearby. It was a conundrum for him; guiding was his livelihood as it made him money to provide for his family, yet he was a passionate conservationist. He could read the bush and ensured we reached the best spots first. His encyclopaedic knowledge of flora and fauna was faultless. He worried about the footprint of Man, damaging the delicate ecosystem. We appreciated his willingness to 'bend the rules' (safely) to ensure we had a better experience, or at best, he'd make us think that. It calls to mind the early morning balloon trip, floating over the savannah at dawn, watching the wildlife from above. We made it just in time, although Winston's short-cut may not have been totally legit!

We were crammed into a 12-person balloon basket with Narmy, our American balloon pilot, who was just too cool for school, posing at every juncture, with his shades and leather flying jacket. The flight was amazing until Narmy decided at the last minute that he'd misjudged the landing. His demeanour instantly deserted him and he started spilling air as fast as he could. Not fast enough; we all had to brace as the basket thudded into the ground, tipped and we were dragged a hundred yards or so. Narmy was lucky; we stopped metres short of a huge ditch. Had we crashed into that, we'd have had casualties for sure. No matter, as everyone climbed out to enjoy the excessive champagne breakfast laid out beside the 'crash site', worries dissipated. Except for Narmy, left wondering how he could extract his precious balloon that was impaled across a large acacia tree.

Travelling in Daph towards Arusha, we explored the Pare Mountains and Lushoto, an old, German mountain retreat. The German administrators once considered this town a contender for their East African capital. Thinking akin to Shimla in the Indian Raj, a hill station set high, Lushoto had fresh, clear mountain air for the administration to de-camp during the summer heat. Set among beautiful, fertile mountains, the slopes of the Pare Mountains were terraced and heavily cultivated, a testament to the early European settlers. The road up from the main highway was poorly tarred, twisting through narrow sections. Daph was performing well, but our slow progress meant that we were running out of daylight; yet it would be a further three hours or so to Lushoto. Examining David Else's alternative advice within his Lonely Planet Trekking in East Africa, we stopped to walk to Soni Falls. Time certainly marches on, but that could not be said for the nearby Soni Falls Hotel; it was closed. We couldn't find a camping option, so stopped at Kimbute 'guesthouse' where the helpful owner was unprepared for white guests. We trekked to the Falls, to gaze over a commanding view of the plains below. Looking up to the basalt rock formations above, it was understandable why this might have been an option for a capital, access aside.

The Arusha road had fine tarmac all the way. We were expecting to see Kilimanjaro rise in front of us at every bend or hill crest. We knew the mountain is frequently covered by low cloud and difficult to see if approaching from the south, but when it emerged just short of Moshi, the outline was breathtaking. I first saw Kili in 1986, during the 2 PARA Kenya tour from the other side; other young officers and I hired a car to 'tour' Amboseli National Park. The northern view from Amboseli offers the classic image: elephants and giraffes strolling underneath the towering slopes above, with the white snow cap gleaming. This northern side is unencumbered by relatively clear foothills, unlike Kili's farmed, southern slopes. These slopes are very fertile, supporting two crops a year, benefiting from two rainy seasons. It shares an ecosystem with Tarangire National Park, each furnishing the other with water at alternate times of the year. The local Chagga people are great agriculturalists and vary their crops, depending on plot elevation. A bewildering variety of bananas are grown here: red, sweet ones, a savoury one and some are used to brew local beer or as cattle feed. Arabica coffee is the main cash crop, being able to flourish on the upper slopes. Kili displayed its classic snow-covered dome in 2002, but today, the loss has made it a poster boy for the effects of global warming.

Possibly named from a Kiswahili derivation (there is great debate), Kilima-Njaro is understood to mean 'Mountain of Greatness' or possibly 'White Mountain'. Either way, Kili stands at 19,340 feet, making it the highest, free-standing mountain in the world. It is Africa's highest mountain, the fourth highest in the world and its base footprint is larger than Greater London. Kili is dormant, as opposed to an extinct volcano, and is relatively 'youthful' in geological terms. Formed around 750,000 years ago, it has three volcanic cones (Kibo, Mawenzi and Shira), with Kibo being considered dormant. Uhuru Peak is the highest summit on the Kibo crater rim. It is a mountain that looms large in history; Ptolemy refers to 'Moon Mountains', Herodotus implies 'Egypt is nurtured by the snows' and Portuguese sailors fed back 15th century native caravans tales of a very high, Ethiopian Mount Olympus beyond the Mountains of the Moon and the source of the Nile.

Commercialism has descended upon the world's extreme features, at Everest and Kili alike. Charity challenges and worthy endeavours rotate climbers and walkers up Kili in increasing numbers, commensurate with the environmental and ecological debate. In 2012, the Kilimanjaro Park Authority reported US$51 million revenue from just over half a million tourists, yet the management plan expected half the number of visitors. Being 'just a walk', there are tales of people from all walks of life reaching the top, both fit and unfit, young and old. For anyone reaching the summit, it's a fine achievement. Today, the trek numbers are presenting a serious environmental impact; for every tourist, there are also numerous porters, guides and assistant porters, the ratio being more than one to five for each tourist. This in turn drives up park fees to discourage visitors; in 2021, fees were between \$600-1,000, depending on the reputation of the company and the level of tips one wishes to pay on descent. Sadly, money presents no barrier, yet one travesty remains the low pay and conditions for the poor locals.

At the end of our 1999 Serengeti safari, we flew from the Seronera airstrip in a light plane back to Kilmanjaro airport, before a flight home. Among the half dozen other passengers were a couple of very mature, spritely Americans, sporting T-shirts that read, 'I climbed Kili' and, 'So did I'. They were a fantastic double act, clearly ebullient in their achievement, but made it clear that if you pay enough, you could be carried to the top, with every need catered for. These guys were living the dream; as young men, they were drafted to the Vietnam War. One of them flew helicopters, Hueys, for the Air Cav and the other flew spotter planes. Both are extremely dangerous and short-lived flying career choices, especially for the unarmed spotters (not unlike the 20-minuters for First World War pilots), but these gentlemen were game for anything. The spotter pilot still flew and persuaded our pilot to allow him to sit up front and fly us, which he did - and we survived to tell the tale. Just as well, for frequent cloud and poor weather around Kili lead to a high number of incidents and air accidents. There had been a recent air crash with a disorientated plane flying into Kili in cloud; welcome to 'White Knuckle Airways'.

Although we carried our gear with a plan to summit each high feature along our journey, the accident had revised our ambition. Of the seven potential routes up Kili, the majority approach was from the south, with the most popular being the Machame or Marangu routes. In recent years, a few elite, ultramarathon runners have completed the round trip (all via southern routes) in around five hours, but this is extreme. It takes on average six to seven days, should one be allowed to successfully summit. The locals are fond of saying, 'pole, pole' or 'slowly, slowly', for altitude sickness (or AMS, Acute Mountain Sickness) can be a killer. The longer, southern routes offer the greatest opportunity to ascend high, then loose height, to minimise the effects of AMS as teams ascend. Speed and fitness are not necessarily helpful at altitude. The faster you ascend, the greater the potential for AMS, the only real treatment being a descent.

I am reminded of an impromptu Parachute Regiment attempt when such sage advice was ignored. Working in Kenya, they followed the northern Rongai route from Amboseli, allocating five days. Failure was never an option. Park fees and requisite border authority fees were paid, but no guides or facilities were required as this was 'just another TAB for the regiment'. The Rongai route is an open, gradual and consistent ascent. With only light packs and boots, the team gamely set off, at their usual pace, ignoring the suggested resting spots. Unsurprisingly, altitude casualties started; sickness and vomiting, severe headaches, the only cure being to descend. This fostered a leadership challenge for those seeking to summit; most reached Mawenzi peak on day four, before recovering the whole team down safely.

Omitting our Kili plans, we pressed on to Arusha on good, tarred roads. Back in 1999, these roads resembled something recently struck by an artillery barrage, they were so appallingly potholed. Whether these road improvements were routine, the outcome from a generous donation or assistance to the burgeoning tourist trade was unknown, but the presence of the UN at the Arusha International Conference Centre to examine the 1994 Rwanda genocide and war crimes might be pure speculation. In Arusha, we picked up supplies, fuel and critically, an internet connection. Our journey was in those pre-blog, or vlog days; Catherine had written our website in very basic HTML that we could update on the laptop as we travelled. Invariably, we could not upload our work as the mobile revolution was yet to occur, and getting a (reliable) connection in Africa was becoming a real mission. Dar was hopeless, as was Zanzibar. In fact, we had not achieved a viable connection since Botswana. The terrestrial telephone landline in Africa was broken and unreliable, but now a few internet cafes were popping up with wireless satellite connections, which made good sense. Our need to upload was becoming a distracting diversion from the value and pleasure of travelling, but once you start such a project, it needs feeding. Once resupplied and connected, it was time for the big one – back to the Serengeti.

It takes time to understand and observe the magnificence of the Serengeti ecosystem for it transcends the artificial or country boundaries. The rift geology generates the rain cycle that crucially supports fresh growth across the grasslands. In turn, this triggers a clockwise migration of ungulates seeking fresh grass across the Maasai Mara and Serengeti plains. Millions of years earlier, the pre-active Ngorongoro volcano would have dwarfed Kilimanjaro. Around 20 million years ago, the shifting tectonic plates and volcanic eruptions found a weakness in the earth's crust; essentially, the African Plate was splitting into the Somali and Nubian Plates. Volcanic activity (a pressure release) along this line released vast quantities of molten materials, reshaping the landscape. Today, the majority of these volcanoes are dormant, including Kilimanjaro, Mount Kenya, Longonot, Meru and Elgon. A few remain active around Lake Natron, such as Kerimasi and Ol Doinyo Lengai or, as the local Maasai call Lengai, 'Mountain of God'; it is often depicted with a tall plume of ash arising from its chute. The eruption left fertile, volcanic soils that were fed by moisture-laden weather from the Indian Ocean, fostering one of the most productive biomasses ever. Today's endless cycle of rejuvenating grass gives life to the multitude of herbivores, who in turn, are followed by the predators.

The symbiotic behaviour between herbivores, coexisting on a single grass, has led to a unique feeding strategy to avoid unhealthy competition. Zebras engage first as they can digest long, coarse, relatively unpalatable grass stems. Behind them come the broad-mouthed wildebeest, eating the protein-rich grass blades. This exposes the new growth shoots and small, herbaceous plants sought by the Thompson gazelles. The long-muzzled ungulates, like the topi and the small-mouthed feeders, can pick at the most nutritious grasses. As the poor grasses are mown down, the smaller rodents, birds and insects can now dine. Roughly three million ungulates trample and strip this grassland, migrating towards new, fresh growth, driven by and being dependent upon the rains. Although rain can fall all year in the Mara, the heaviest rains occur in December through to January and in April. The arrival of fresh rain in the south initiates the rotation. Not all groups move at the same time, dependent on their feeding strategy. Aligned to the February rains and the expected, plentiful supply of new grass, the wildebeest (locally known as gnu) gather to calve on the short grass plains of the southeastern areas. Around half a million calves are born within a two to three-week period. Calves stand and suckle within a few minutes of birth and are able to run with their mothers straightaway, yet most kills occur within the first week of birth. Later rains at the end of May drive the animals northwest towards the Western Corridor and Grumeti River, where they typically remain until late June. By July, they are migrating north to the Mara, where they cross the Grumeti and Mara rivers. Once in the Mara, they'll remain for the duration of the dry season, then at the start of the short rains in early November, the migration moves south, back to the short grass plains of the southeast. They arrive here by December in time for February's calving season.

Migrating numbers crossing the Mara and Sand rivers, where they are predated upon in huge numbers, has increased since the 1970s, due to improved cattle and rinderpest controls. Rinderpest used to inflict mass deaths on wildebeest and other species, given their symbiotic feeding strategies, yet ironically, the higher ungulate numbers have not benefited the dwindling apex predators. Insight was offered by David Read's book, Beating Around the Bush, regaling life as a Tanzanian vet treating cattle and wildlife. Interestingly, there was a professional link between David and Catherine's Uncle Ernie, who worked on similar east African farming initiatives in the 1950s.

En route to the Serengeti, there are smaller, linked parks to visit, the first being Tarangire National Park, that we'd visited previously with Winston. Now, seeking different camping options with Daph, our first was Meserani Snake Farm. On arrival from Arusha, we discovered that it was closed. The mere mention of snakes sends shivers up my spine, something not helped by the dilapidated state of the farm; we can only hope they found suitable, alternative accommodation for the liberated snakes. We had little option but to camp at the public Tarangire site. It was cramped, fly-bitten and uninspiring, yet the following day, the park showed that it was part of the lush, fertile valley floor running down the East Rift from Lake Natron. Tarangire has a bimodal rainfall like Kilimanjaro, enjoying almost consistent water, making it a good place to visit. Here, as elsewhere, there is conflict between the conservationists, pastoralists and farmers. As larger farms and populations grow, so does competition for land. Controlling rinderpest regionally has increased both cattle and wildlife numbers too, and for the last 20 years, there have been discussions on how and where best to create wildlife migration corridors between Tarangire and the Gelai Plains.

The bush in Tarangire is thick acacia, with scattered baobab trees, forming a distinctive topography. This Maasai Steppe park hosts the second largest (and little known) migration of ungulates in East Africa, the largest concentration of elephants in northern Tanzania and approximately 500 different species of birds. We expected to see the Tarangire River flowing, but it was worryingly low for the time of year, with some sand tributaries. Of the large elephant herds, there were mostly young bulls in bachelor herds. Concentrated around the rivers, they were frisky, offering warnings and displays to safari vehicles in their path. We kept our distance, but with Winston, he was a tad too cheeky and liked to get close, probably to scare his passengers. We were very privileged to see an exhibitionist couple of leopards mating in a baobab tree. Poor things had an audience, with a dozen or more parked up safari vehicles watching, yet the chap was not put off at all. Apparently, once leopards have found their mate, they copulate every 15 minutes, for five days. It's not uncommon for the male to bite the female at the nape of her neck, which often gets a snarling response with bared teeth. The theory and justification being that it's supposed to increase ovulation, but I guess no one has asked a leopard. Top tip; don't try this at home, even if you can't manage five days!

We saw the usual herds of zebras, wildebeest and buffalos and other assorted ungulates. Parked on a high bluff, watching grazing elephants below, we were plagued by more horse flies. These pesky, nasty insects certainly brought me out in huge wheals, being 'sweet meat' for any biting insect. It was the same when we were with Winston, who detested them; he always had to stop the Land Rover to fight them out the door. Catherine had been researching bites and treatments before the trip and came prepared with a clicker or zapper, a small, plastic applicator that applies a piezoelectric charge to the bite area, supposedly relieving the urge to scratch. Five to 10 clicks should reduce the itch as it's the scratching that does the damage. However, the zapper will not remove any toxins or associated infections from any bite, so it's best to avoid getting bitten in the first place. We applied the usual sprays and wore long trousers but these horse flies were particularly notorious in Tarangire. We gave a zapper to Winston who thought was it gold dust, as did I. We still use them today, although I quadruple the recommended click number, and then add some! Pausing to watch the elephants attracted numerous birds, including a hoopoe bouncing around in front of us and a flight of carmine bee-eaters with their iridescent plumage.

The Great Rift Valley runs down to Mozambique, splitting around Lake

Turkana in Northern Kenya. The eastern rift follows the classic line through Kenya and Tanzania, whilst the western branch runs down the Uganda-Congo side of Lakes Victoria and Tanganyika to the Zambezi. Both offer impressive escarpments, and to get to the Serengeti, you must climb the eastern escarpment, which we did at Mto-Wa-Mbu, near the entrance to Lake Manyara National Park. Mto-Wa-Mbu, translated to mean 'Mosquito Creek', has an excellent, local market as the valley floor is very fertile. Here, transient villages spread across the plain in the dry season to capture the irrigated valley floor, despite the constant risk of flooding and high incidence of malaria. Unsurprisingly, the tar road ends here too.

We avoided Lake Manyara National Park, for we had visited it with Winston. It's a good, little park and well worth a look around, but we pressed on to the top of the rift to look out over the valley and plains stretching away below. Once up the escarpment, we continued to climb. The temperature dropped, we had light rain and the vegetation became almost tropical. We camped at Karatu, the last village before entering the Ngorongoro-Serengeti Game Conservancy. Karatu village is a small ribbon development along the main road, where we camped at Safari Junction. This was a pleasant campsite, which offered clean water and great showers, but it had seen better days. We wondered if it had been an old hill station, for it was like camping in someone's garden and considerably cheaper to reserve prices.

The next day, we drove up through heavy clouds to the outer slopes of the crater rim. These slopes are cultivated up to an altitude, after which the dense rainforest clads the crater rim. The Ngorongoro Crater is the world's largest inactive, intact and unfilled caldera. The crater floor has a unique, mini ecosystem all of its own. Thought to have erupted 2.5 million years ago, it spread its volcanic ash and deposits west, across the Serengeti. The rim is around 8,000 feet elevation and there is a 2,000 feet descent on to the crater floor. Inside is a 14 square mile circular area, with its own fresh salt lake, bush, scrub and forest. At the park HQ, we were obliged to pick up a guide, compulsory for all vehicles descending into the crater. We squeezed a rather large Daniel into the cleared rear spare seat and descended. Daniel's English was poor by comparison to most guides and his knowledge was little better than ours, which rather spoilt our expectation. Vehicles are strictly controlled on the valley floor and all visitors must leave by 6.30pm. There is one track down and another track up.

Estimates suggest there are up to 25,000 large animals, mostly ungulates, living on the crater floor. The crater rim is a scant barrier to free animal movement (in or out), but the abundance of food on the basin floor offers little reason to leave. It's thought that around 20% of wildebeest and half the zebras migrate during the wet season, but the buffalos remain. Eland and Thomson's gazelle numbers are falling, possibly due to the changing nature of the grass, brought about by fire prevention management. A lack of fire means the grasses do not regenerate, but stay long and tall. This is suitable for the buffalo, but for the short grass eaters like eland and gazelle, they can 'dine' better elsewhere. Only solitary bull elephants roam the crater, as the matriarchal herds remain on the rim. Equally scant are top grazers such as giraffes, topi and impala who are discouraged by the rim's slope. Predators have a relatively easy time hunting. However, as elsewhere with isolated prides, the lions here becoming increasingly inbred. The side effect of the natural enclosure protects the existing males, leading to unusually high sperm abnormalities and disease within the feline population. Hence, numbers of lions in the crater are plummeting, partly caused by drought, carrying associated blood-sucking flies with tick-borne diseases and canine distemper.

The Ngorongoro Conservation Area and surround is Maasai land. A common sight is herd boys tending their 'god given' cattle, dressed in the traditional, red blankets and carrying spears. There is growing tension and conflict between traditional village ways and modernity, particularly with tourism. Conflict is not just with tourists, but with the authorities, who exclude the Maasai from their traditional grazing lands. The authorities argue that tourists do not want to see local tribes people herding cattle in areas of pristine wild beauty. This erroneous justification is used to prevent the Maasai grazing their cattle on the crater floor. Nothing would please me more than observing the natural balance of life, with local endeavour thriving alongside wildlife, provided the locals benefit from the tourist income by way of health and education. This is not a zoo. We witnessed Maasai cattle herds on this trip and previously with Winston on the crater floor. The steeply eroded paths to the crater rim bear testament to this regular activity. That the Maasai do not share in the profits from tourism is another matter. As a proud Nilo-Hamatic tribe, they steadfastly refuse to adopt modern ways, yet they are not slow to stop each and every safari vehicle to demand a handout for a picture. Winston, being a Maasai, was very keen to look to new ways. He was blessed by a good education but recognised the contradiction. His education shifted him from a traditional life to one escorting tourists for more money to support to his family, who now live in Arusha.

The Lerai Forest was an eerie, damp place and generally home to elephants, leopards and rhinos. 'Lerai' is Maasai for 'Fever Tree', an alternative name for the yellow-barked acacia tree. The evening light offered a yellow hue to the bark of the acacia. The bull elephants continue to trash and destroy these few trees on the crater floor, pushing them over to access the highest, tender leaves and to scratch their backs. There are very few rhinos remaining; we understood there were only seven or eight individuals of both black and white rhinos. We were fortunate to see a black rhino with Winston, but saw none on our second visit.

The larger soda lake on the crater floor was ringed with thousands of pink flamingos feeding off the algae within the water. Other animals desire the salt too, and we watched a couple of hyaenas amble up to the lake, eyeing the flamingos and water alike. They licked the water, taking the salts, and one hyena even proceeded to lie down and nap at the water's edge, confident of his security and domain. Interestingly, there are two freshwater pools nearby, hidden within a natural fold in the ground and fed by natural springs. They were large enough to have a few hippos wallowing and yawning under the reeds and aquatic plants that part-camouflaged them. Witnessing the second Ngoitoktok Pool was a shock; it is partially hidden by tall reeds, but inside, it was jammed full of safari vehicles and tourists on the banks enjoying lavish picnics - a veritable African Hyde Park.

Tour operators had blankets and deck chairs out, champagne on ice and crustless cucumber sandwiches. Nature was taking advantage as a few black kites occasionally swooped to poach food from the tourists' hands, beckoned or not. There is a paradox here with tourists paying for a wildlife exposure, whilst altering the dynamic and ambiance. It's the same in the Mara and elsewhere, with hordes of safari vehicles crammed around kills and resting predators, perpetuating a zoo mentality. Safari operators jostle to get their clients the best view, with little or no regard for the flora they are revving over. Such behaviour used to drive Winston mad; he was always reporting bad and errant people. Yet, the offending driver would always argue that they were trying to position their client to provide the most authentic experience. It questions the added value of the guide; certainly finding one's way here was child's play. We spotted a family of cheetahs in the near distance that were unobserved by others. We had a real challenge to get Daniel to see them; it seemed such a shame to spoil his nap.

Accommodation around the crater rim is at a premium. The Simba Campsite is a cheap, basic, damp site on the chilly crater rim, so shame on us that we booked into a lodge. Both the Serena and the Ngorongoro Crater Lodges were seriously luxurious and riotously expensive, but the wildlife lodge was both available and affordable, being government run. It was also a trip down memory lane as we had stayed there last time. The view down to the crater floor was as amazing as ever, location being everything. Irritatingly though, we might have been better off camping; the lodge had neither power to charge our devices, nor hot water to wash ourselves or our clothes. Part of our justification 'to lodge' was to conduct some crafty administration, but with a bath half full of wet washing, we continued in the cold darkness. Whilst our safari gear is designed to dry fast, there was no real option to string a line in our room; we should have camped! The sun was on the crater side of the room, which was beaming through the glass wall, so crazily (as I shudder to recall), I was out of the window, hanging out the clothes on a makeshift washing line, clinging on like Spider-Man, when the maid knocked to clean our room. Long story short, the room was cleaned, the clothes dried and I lived to tell the tale, although I had no clue what the view was like from the outside…I was clinging on for dear life.

Later, we got chatting to other guests, equally enjoying a sundowner out on the deck, drinking in the crater views. We got talking to an American lawyer who was enjoying some quality father-son bonding. We initially sought to avoid them as the poor lad stood out a mile, not because he was a square-jawed, six-foot and a fine athletic sort of chap, but because you couldn't miss the 'high and tight' severe Marine haircut. Actually, he was a lovely lad, a young captain in the US Marines, learning to fly Apache helicopters. We had quite a laugh, partially at his expense, as we got the full military West Point credentials; I may have led him on a tad, for I didn't have the heart to tell him I was just retiring.

The viewpoint from Naabi Hill, just beyond the East Gate to Serengeti

National Park, affords all-round views across the plains and back to the crater. Interestingly, the unfenced area enables the animals to roam freely, yet the humans are herded by artificial boundaries. Between Naabi and Ngorongoro lies Olduvai Gorge, a steep-sided ravine. Olduvai had been a research site for many years, notably when in 1959, Dr Louis Leakey and his wife, Mary, discovered early humanoid remains of 'Nutcracker Man' (Australopithecus) and 'Handy Man' (Homo habilis). These humanoids pre-date Man walking on earth by 1.8 million years. This key find was surpassed later, again by Mary Leakey, just to the north at Laetoli, with the discovery of footprints preserved in the volcanic ash. Evidence of three humanoids (possibly a man, woman and child) walking upright were dated to 3.5 million years ago. The Leakey's son, Richard (who also made his own name in Kenyan environmental circles), continued his parents' work by unearthing significant discoveries in the Turkana region of northern Kenya, placing early Man in the region around four million years ago.

We toured the southern reaches of the Serengeti, stopping at the kopjes to gaze out. Elevation is needed to see over the grasses; it's the same for the predators. It's not uncommon to see cheetahs or topi halfway up a termite mound to see out. The Serengeti is so extensive, both the animals and those humans looking for them are widely dispersed across the park. We headed to Dik Dik Campsite to set up, using the Oztent and awning for shade, something we rarely did. There was no premonition, but within half an hour, the mother of all thunderstorms arrived; thunder and lightning arced across the sky, which was all very dramatic, and warm. The hard rain washed the dust away and after a bit, we started to collect the freshest, sweetest rainwater off the awning to replenish our stock. The muggy air was refreshed; this was one of the few occasions of rain we endured on our trip. Rain can turn the black, cotton soil here quickly into a soup-like morass, impeding meaningful transport. Not this time - it was not the rainy reason, so it dried hard rapidly.

We expected the majority of animals to be around the Western Corridor and Grumeti River at this time of the year, our target for the following day. Predators, usually territorial animals, tend to follow the migration. The rivers, dry or otherwise, around the Grumeti were stocked with massive crocodiles, lying in wait for the annual feeding frenzy. Given their size, we guessed many animals had recently passed already. We saw a lot of diverse animals here, including the elusive Colobus monkeys screeching from the treetops around the rivers. But we didn't see the hordes of migrating gnu that we'd expected. 'Top spotter' Catherine saw a lioness quite content in her tree, until she decided to get down. Lions are climbers, but not natural tree climbers, apart from those adapted Kalahari lions or in Uganda (at Queen Elizabeth Park). We watched the descending lioness over-balance and collapse into the fork of the tree before tumbling out. Elephants and giraffes were grazing around the river, feeding on the treetops. Dead carcasses littered the plains from kills that had been disturbed or abandoned - more evidence of excess. Nothing here is wasted; hyenas and vultures will clear away the debris. We came across a dead topi, surrounded by vultures and other birds crowding around a kill. The 'boss' vulture had its head up the bottom of the ex-topi, enjoying a good meal; nature is brutal.

At park HQ near Seronera, we enquired about entry into Kenya, crossing via the closed Sand River Gate direct into the Maasai Mara. Such a privilege is usually reserved for East Africa residents, but as we could prove we were staying with a Kenyan resident, the customs official granted us authority. This was great news as we then headed to the northern Lobo area. It didn't take long to find and follow the huge herds of gnu massing northward. The huge volume and endless lines of migrating ungulates was an awesome sight, driven to move onwards by the quest for fresh grasses from the rains. It's not just the grass-feeding strategy that conjoins these animals; the zebras associate with the wildebeest and waterbuck, relying on their superior smell to sniff out water over huge distances, whilst the gnu and waterbuck tolerate the zebras for their superior eyesight, able to provide predator early warning calls. The predators were in tow, organising their hunts and sighting prey. Lions were easy to see, although the more silent hunters were not seen; I expect we were being 'lined up' as we advanced too.

The river crossing spectacle is quite amazing. Seeing is one thing, but to hear and feel the tension and noise, and to experience the ground tremble all around, is palpable. The massing herds and the ensuing confusion fosters an air of tension. The primeval urge to cross, and the few crossing points, concentrates and compresses the animals, kicking up dust melees. Uncertainty builds, each waiting for the first brave soul to plunge across. When one goes, they all go, in a surging mass. Stay in the middle and risk drowning or get separated on the edge for the waiting crocodile. At the bank, there is much scrambling and gouging as they panic to get out on the far side. This is where groups panic and get it wrong; too steep a bank forces the exhausted animals back across or to take alternative downstream options. Sometimes, young are separated and call for their mothers, some fatefully plunging back in a desperate search for their offspring. It's ferocious and nothing is wasted.

Part 4

EAST AFRICA

Blue Nile Falls

"*I never knew of a morning in Africa when I woke up that I was not happy.*"

Ernest Hemingway

Camping in the Serengeti

St Georges Chapel Ethiopia

Oli Polis School, Kenya

Great Migration, Serengeti

Digby Tatham Warter

David and Sonja

Chalbi Desert, Northern Kenya

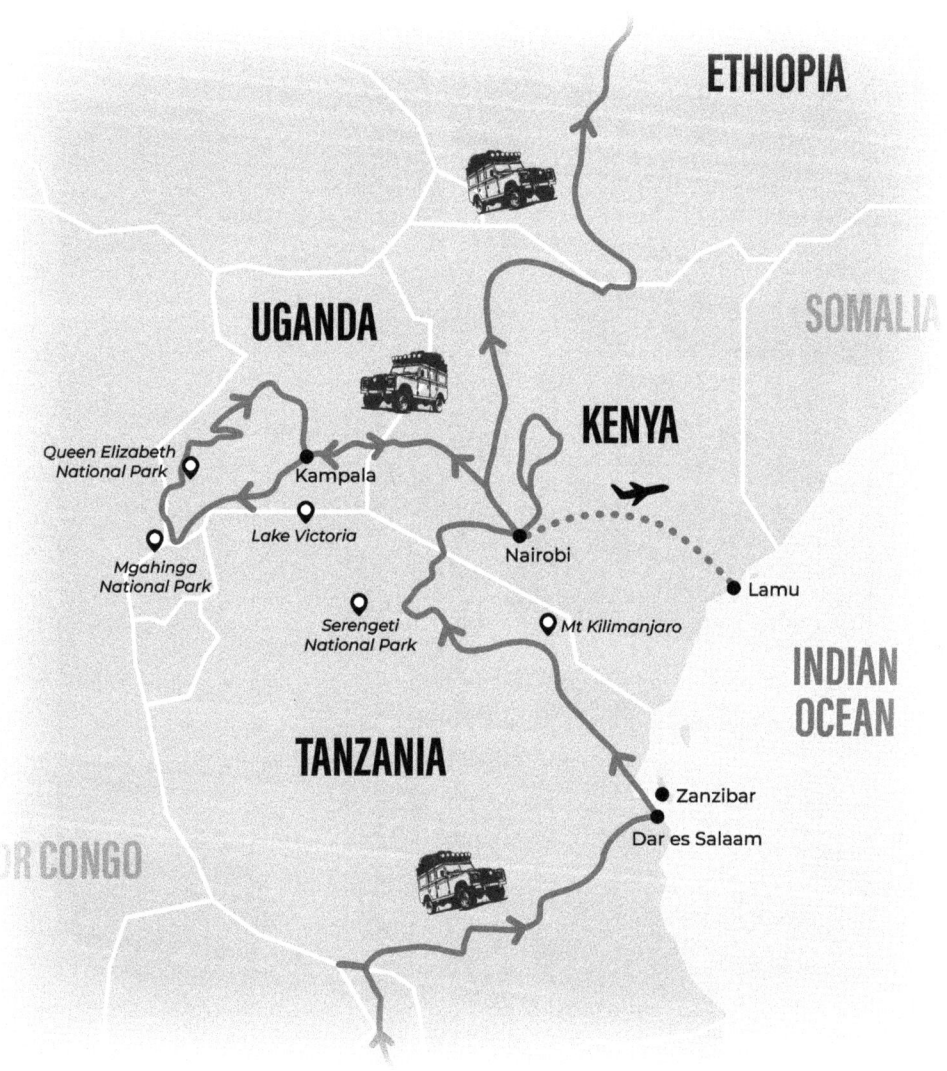

ETHIOPIA

SOMALIA

UGANDA

KENYA

Queen Elizabeth
National Park

Kampala

Lake Victoria

Mgahinga
National Park

Nairobi

Lamu

Serengeti
National Park

Mt Kilimanjaro

INDIAN
OCEAN

TANZANIA

DR CONGO

Zanzibar

Dar es Salaam

Chapter 15
Crossing the equator

The fidelity of modern television provides indelible images of wildebeests and zebras plunging across rivers in such close-up detail that we feel we are crossing too. To tug on our heartstrings, they like to focus on the plight of the little ones. Driven by the primal search for fresh grass, the ungulates strive on. There is always synergy in nature; the predators, like crocodiles, lions and others, lurk on either bank. The TV images convey the melee fantastically, but until we have smell-a-vision or visceral-feelings-a-vision, it cannot quite convey the full enormity of the drama; the build-up, the noise and smell, the press of animals surging with primal need.

Being present during the Mara migration was an unplanned bonus. We were aware that our schedule may place us in the vicinity, but this was a delightful outcome. The huge columns coursing across the Lobo area were endless, explaining the earlier reduced animal sightings. The ungulates were massing in their hundreds of thousands, ploughing north, all without visas. We, on the other hand, had spoken to the park authorities at Seronera, to be told that there was no 'official crossing' between Tanzania and Kenya, but a crossing was possible with the correct paperwork, which we understood we had. The Tanzanian authorities didn't bat an eyelid at our documentation and Carnet, and waved us on, with the throwaway comment, 'See you later.' Ominous, had we thought about it. Now, 12 kilometres on and having waded through the Sand River, we arrived at the Kenyan authorities. We had no Kenyan visa and the wily guards knew it. They were angling for a bribe, or should I say, 'duty' on items that we didn't have.

Thus far, we had not really experienced 'issues with officialdom' that we couldn't talk or blag our way around. The idea of paying a bribe was abhorrent - not an option - but our hosts could play the long game. Their intransigence and arrogance was startling, so whilst indefatigable, they knew it would take two or three days backtracking via Arusha or west about via Lake Victoria and Tarime, which was closer, but reportedly less safe. The inherent 'opportunity cost' of our standoff was more poignant. All I had to do was flash my military ID card and we'd have been across, but I was reluctant to draw unwarranted attention or create 'awkward questions' for our (potential) host. I say potential, for we had failed so far to communicate with a dear friend from the regiment, David Parkinson, in Nairobi, who commanded all UK troops in Kenya. We wanted to avoid him (and ourselves) any unnecessary embarrassment or inconvenience. After an hour or so of banter and stalemate, all without a cup of tea (one has to manage each situation as it occurs), a backhander of a few dollars was a very easy decision, given the alternative. Irritating yes, but we were technically in the wrong and were not unduly inconvenienced.

Besides, there were thousands of other (four-legged) beasts that were far more interesting and challenging to catch up with. Who said lions never climbed trees; 'top spotter' Catherine again saw a male lion climb some branches, only to have them collapse under his weight. We pressed on north through the Mara valley with the migrating herds to the oldest and most colonial of all the lodges in the area, Keetorok Lodge, for some refreshments. On their manicured front lawn was Lamb Chop, their mature warthog behaving like a friendly, oversized dog. It was a bustling place with a relaxed, unpretentious air. We enjoyed a post-safari light lunch; 'mad dogs and Englishmen in the midday sun' and all that.

The vegetation in the Mara was immediately different from the grass plains of the Serengeti; here, we saw more green, rolling hills and short grasslands, evidence of rainfall on a higher elevation. Heading west through the southern half of the Masai Mara, via the hippo pools and the Mara River, we came across two dozen or more safari vehicles crammed around a small bank, squashed in to see a few hapless wildebeest cross the river, complete with poised crocs and hippos. Compared to the Serengeti, the mass of tourists in zebra-painted Kombi vans, jammed around a sighting, was a shock. It jarred against the beauty and tranquillity of the environment. The animals were not daft; they were playing their usual, extended waiting game, so we didn't stop. Instead, we headed up onto the rolling grassland escarpment to overlook the Mara area with an early sundowner at Serena Lodge. The sundeck has the most amazing viewing platform across the plains. Here was mass tourism in all its glory; hordes of combi vans with fretting guests anxious to extract value from five bucks. We weren't staying, for we knew we had to be out of the park boundaries before dark. As in the Serengeti, the Mara roads can be quite tricky, especially after rain, and we found a few damp spots of sticky gun-cotton, black soil near the rivers as we made our way to Oloololo Gate, the most western park access. We spotted a notoriously shy serval, a sleek, small cat with a beautiful, distinctive coat. As soon as the camera was out, it slipped into the long grasses, conducting its distinctive pounce on its prey. Oloololo Gate House had a new structure and the park staff were happy to let us camp beside the building. The toilet block facilities were welcome, but the endless passing safari traffic was inevitable; not for the first time, we found ourselves the novelty and photographed just as much as the park animals.

At last, that evening we spoke to David on the Sat phone and explain our situation. He was good as gold, delighted to hear from us and invited us to stay. He instructed us to come to his barracks and he promised to sort the visa issue. The park rangers advised us that it was better to transit back through the park towards Narok (on the same ticket; thanks chaps) to access Nairobi. So once the 'morning train' of dawn safari vehicles had trooped past and back for their hearty, luxury lodge breakfast, we set off across the Mara. It was beautiful; classic Out of Africa. The tracks out from the park were fine and eventually became a reasonable, tarmac road. But this was Africa; near Narok, the tar disintegrated and the potholes were worse than no tar. Approaching the Great Rift escarpment on the Lake Naivasha road, the traffic volumes increased significantly. Ascending the escarpment with the Nairobi-bound traffic, it was chocked full of laden lorries, long past any viable MOT. All the traffic was engaged in battle with the overcrowded minibus taxis, with locals randomly jumping on and off. These Matatus are a nightmare; we saw more than one on their roof, following an accident. It seemed we had swapped the animal migration for the human version. We had caught up with the press ofhumanity and population explosion of Nairobi. This was shocking and jarring against the majestic, stunning scenery looking over the Rift Valley behind us.

Our immediate challenge was to find David, lodged within the larger Kenyan Army barracks of Kahawa, on the Thika Road. It was 15 years since I was last there, when new to both the military and Kenya. The Nairobi rush-hour was a scrum, but again, our safari bull bars afforded a marginal moral edge. Most of the bewildering configurations of safari vehicles were Land Rovers, although they seemed in poor repair. But this was nothing when compared to the dilapidated state of the 100,000 odd Matutus offering essential local transport. It never ceased to amaze us, here, as across Africa, how the locals emerge from these vehicles so smart and pristine, clean for work in the city, from less salubrious areas and shanty towns. More power to them; Westerners certainly cannot achieve half such standards.

In 1987, the night we arrived at Kahawa Barracks with 2 PARA, we lost a soldier who was run over whilst crossing the Thika Road at night. The offending vehicle only had one headlight. In 2002, we were ushered into David's office, where we found him in his element, managing a team of experts and enablers to prepare, receive and assist UK battlegroup training. Today, all visiting troops are kept clear of Nairobi, being flown directly into Lakipia to a purpose-built facility. Delightfully, Sonja, David's wife, had come across to lead us to their home. Being July, David had an endless round of visitors and friends staying, many being regimental friends and families who had flown down to enjoy a personalised safari and holiday with David. It was wonderful to catch up with them over a sundowner and barbecue.

Their Nairobi residence came with the job; it was a large, colonial, planter-type residence with a secure fence and a few outbuildings. It was excellent for hosting, with the setup reminiscent of our home in South Africa. The house was deliberately low-key, unlike the obvious American Embassy house that drew attention to itself. I'm guessing their armed guards, armoured patrol vehicles, high razor wire fences and hi-tech security may have had something to do with it. David had a night askari (local soldier) to keep watch, plus a gardener, a butler and Rose, the cook. These locals were a great team; they clearly enjoyed being there and had worked for many of David's predecessors. Rose was especially genial; her English was proficient. We were quite taken aback on meeting Rose, for at the same time, we greeted Sonja's cat that had just strolled in (we remembered her from the UK). We said hello to Rose and bent down in the usual manner to stroke the cat, when Rose said, 'Ahh, the cat knows you are white.' I'll let you draw your own conclusion, but our faces must have been a picture; Rose just chuckled. The cat survived the heat and conditions yet must have been towards the end of her nine lives. Only the previous day, she had killed a baby green mamba snake in the garden, trotting in to present Sonja her latest scalp.

Nairobi has received significant investment. Major corporations and UN bodies have moved in, bringing wealth and corruption. David lived in

Westlands, but even during their time there, they've noticed heavier traffic and bigger, more expensive vehicles, indicating wealth. The houses around them were being developed. Down the road and towards Karen, there were bigger houses in a largely white suburb, attracting more robberies, muggings, rapes and worse, yet they have less protection. The security needs to change; gangs of 20 plus were targeting houses. The police cannot cope and most are being bribed to look the other way. Money talks. Most whites believe they are secure as they have an askari, so it's the askari who gets it first, although this may not be a given. The Maasai still rule, for one Maasai askari is believed to have killed two with his bow, one with his spear and chased the remaining predators off a neighbouring property. It is common in Africa; should violence occur, it's fast, very violent and suddenly over. Still, we had faith in Rose; she would brook no nonsense.

We went past some of the shanty towns when driving in and out of Nairobi, but just like Soweto or elsewhere, we wouldn't dare venture in unless invited or escorted. These areas are rapidly spreading with the population. Increasing wealth is bringing rural people into the capital and they are struggling to cope. Poor health conditions prevail, aside from malaria and AIDS. Poor water, sanitation and air quality feature; the smog and pollution from wood fires is appalling. Transportation is bad too; most of the road vehicles are largely unroadworthy by Western standards and the Matatu minibuses are death traps. Resolving these issues is stretching the humanitarian agencies and government. Yet Kenya, being the third most corrupt world country during our travels, saw the West flooding inward investment. Increasing lawlessness, violence and crime was inevitable.

David and I returned to the barracks in the morning to make us legal and sort our return flight to the UK. Little wonder that David had a good team around him; half the seniors I recognised from my time in the Airborne Brigade. ASM Young offered to check Daph over; he was delighted we were 'parking her' with him. He also offered to have a look at our water filtration system too. Just as we were leaving, the pay staff sergeant caught up with me - blimey, it was Corporal Miles from 2 PARA! Catherine and Sonja had been to Westgate, shopping and lunching, before we all reconvened at the Muthaiga Club. The Westgate Mall was the new, upscale shopping centre, the same place that was attacked in 2013 by the al-Shabaab terrorists, killing and capturing hostages. That said, little had changed at the Muthaiga Club, a bastion of its colonial past. We stayed long enough to arrange a few up-country trips; David suggested that on our return from the UK, he could arrange a trip to Richard Bonham's lodge in the Chuylu Hills, just off the Amboseli National Park. They had been recently and thoroughly enjoyed their stay. This was the same Richard Bonham who was one of the three guides who accompanied the travel writer, Peter Matthiessen, through the Selous Game Reserve, recorded in his book, Sand Rivers. We did not need to be asked twice as it was a fabulous offer.

Sonja invited us to see Oli Polis School, located in the beautiful Ngong Hills. The British Embassy, military and others built and support the 320 children here, aged between four and sixteen. Many of these children ran the daily two-hour gauntlet each way to school, to attend from 7am to 5pm. The kids loved these visits and gathered to sing a welcome. Providing a daily meal is a key factor in retaining these children in education. We appreciate this may be controversial, but it was often the main meal for many. Education is invaluable, yet paradoxically runs counter to the family requirement to tend the goats, cattle or farm; kids are integral subsistence labour. Education should be a given right, yet too often, those with an education rightly expect a better job and life, which in some cases are not available or accessible; it is extremely hard. For many, a poor situation is made worse when family sickness and illness occurs. AIDS and malaria are still devastating parts of the continent; too many kids are being fostered by infirm grandparents.

The school was a delight; a beacon of hope. All the kids were clean and bright, dressed in their smart, green uniform and shoes. Food was part provided by a UN food aid programme and some British military engineers were finishing a borehole to provide clean water. The local teachers were brilliant, being part-parent and part-teacher. We were staggered to hear they were learning the 1950's English Cambridge education syllabus, studying the medieval kings and queens of England. The teachers knew it was bizarre, but it was a system, and I'm sure in time, their own history will be taught. The head teacher, a Maasai, explained that the community had raised some funds and it was clear he was leading from the front to organise their support and education. It was a real tonic to see these kids and it struck us how happy the pupils were and how enthusiastically they took to their lessons, even maths.

Catherine was delighted when Sonja later took us to Daphne Sheldrick's elephant orphanage in Nairobi National Park. When David Sheldrake, a founding warden and naturalist at Tsavo National Park, started rehabilitating wild animals, his wife, Daphne, became an authority on rearing fostered animals. She perfected elephant milk formula, discovering that coconut oil was the nearest fat substitute. The orphanage had five baby elephants when we visited and a couple of rhino orphans. The keepers were rotated to prevent any calf becoming dependent on a single person, for the keepers sleep with the calves to provide comfort. Baby elephants need emotional support just as much as physical support; like humans, without emotional support, calves will not survive. These elephants were happily playing and enjoying themselves, being cheeky to their keepers. The trust was restarting a rehabilitation programme at Tsavo, which we now know was successful and continues to thrive.

We are eternally grateful and hugely indebted to David and Sonja for their assistance whilst in Nairobi, not just with our requirement to get back to the UK in August, but for their wider support. They embraced our challenge and readily offered onward advice and connections. Whilst it was lovely to get home to the UK for two weeks for essential activity, we were itching to return, refreshed and focused on our journey. Sonja picked us up from the airport and took me to Kahawa to collect Daph. The work on Daph was not quite finished (usual story) so I went to wait at the mess facilities, only to bump into my old B Company sergeant major - what were the chances? Spike was now a captain, supporting the helicopter force, and was about to head up-country to recce a planned exercise. Of all the places in the world that we should bump into each other! Like all good things, we had to move on, and Daph was ready. It felt good to be driving Daph again. She was performing well, without her customary weight, as I headed back to David's to repack our gear that had been stored in David's garage.

Still being the UK summer holidays, David's house was full and they were taking a group of friends to the bush and northern lodges. David had secured our invite from Richard Bonham, so we'd leave the following morning. As we were driving out of David's gate, he stopped us, as clutch fluid started to pour out from under Daph. Suddenly I had no clutch. After a quick examination, we agreed that I would go back into Kahawa for a repair and he would carry on with his safari. ASM Young was in the UK but his deputy booked us into CMC Motors downtown, the main dealer that managed such issues. Sadly, this forced us to miss our slot with Richard Bonham... maybe another time? CMC Motors collected Daph, informing us that clutch fluid was leaking into the bell housing, causing the clutch plate to slip, so a new clutch was fitted. Whilst there, we also replaced the rear half shafts as they were suffering from years of 'backlash', a damaging, torsional twist to the shafts leading to eventual failure. We had not noticed any diminution of performance, but the new shafts provided a positive enhancement.

David returned at the same time as CMC finished their repair and we sought to reconnect with Richard Bonham. David had an alternative solution; another couple had pulled out from their Lamu Island trip, and he wondered if we'd fancy it. Fantastic, yes please! We joined Ian and Libby at Wilson's Airport to fly to Manda aerodrome. David and Ian were young officers together in the regiment before Ian (now a colonel) transferred to the Army Air Corps. David too was planning to get his pilot's licence in South Africa, so you can guess what the chat was about as we flew to Lamu. Since the 12th century, Lamu has held Swahili predominance here.

Manda airfield, on the northern side of the estuary, meant we required a local dhow to reach Lamu Town, the principal, inhabited part of the island. A human settlement grew when Arab traders created a port in the 14th century, trading slaves, grains, ivory, cowrie and tortoise shells for oriental silks, spices and porcelain from Arabia and India. Lamu was administratively aligned with Zanzibar until Kenyan independence in 1963, when Lamu reverted to Kenyan rule. Lamu's authority declined once the British forced the end of slavery in 1873. There are no cars on Lamu, leaving the island unspoilt by tourism.

We were staying in Shela, just up the coast, where the dhow dropped us beside the Kijani House Hotel. The rooms were delightfully and traditionally appointed, and the food was superb. Shela overlooks the harbour entrance to the Indian Ocean. A relaxed and gentle pace is an essential difference between Zanzibar. As we walked, people greeted us and did not push their services upon us. The atmosphere was pleasant and safe for walking in the evening. Although August is mid-winter, it was still hot and relatively busy, for crowds were gathering for the annual dhow race - a major island event. The neighbouring Peponi Hotel was sponsoring the race, which was just as well as their boat won the big race and the regatta. We went dhow sailing the following day; it was beautifully relaxing, yet these large vessels were not that easy to manoeuvre and attain speed.

Common to Zanzibar, many houses had large ornate, carved doors. Interestingly, the mosques here did not have minarets, so it was not immediately obvious what was a mosque or what was a private house, although the traditional Muslim 'call to prayer' still rang out. Many buildings were constructed with coral, extracted from the protective reefs beyond the island. Coral may be porous, but once set, it becomes very hard. In Lamu, we were invited inside a Muslim traditional house. Outside the front door, there were two bench seats for people to meet without entering the house, allowing men to chat without entering the predominantly female household. Mixing between the sexes was frowned upon. Beyond the carved, wooden door was a courtyard with a large tree providing shade. The accommodation was on four levels, the fourth being the rooftop. There was a well in the courtyard that fed a secluded bath, a separate plunge pool and a flushing, sit-down toilet. After the age of seven, brothers and sisters are separated. Carved niches in the walls held their possessions. There was an interesting, early anti-malarial protection system, where catfish were in their water to eat the mosquito larvae - perhaps more environmentally friendly than today's DDT alternative.

The most amazing, sandy beach stretched all down the coastline when one walked beyond Shela to the Indian Ocean. On the edge of Shela village, an Italian count had built a striking, yet incongruous mock castle. Aligned to the old Omani style, it was built from local mud and coral, yet we understood it had been unoccupied since construction years earlier. It must have cost an astonishing sum to construct and there was little benefit back to the community, as promised. Today, the fort is now run as an outstanding, luxury spa and yoga retreat. A delightful and serene setting, providing the Somali pirates or AQ raiders don't come calling as they have done before, and they have continued to threaten this coastal area over the last few years. Pirates aside, the pace of life in Lamu was extremely gentle and we had a relaxing time. Our last meal was at the house of 'Ali Samosa', run by Abdullah. We had a traditional Swahili lunch, in his airy, whitewashed, rooftop restaurant, of samosas, seafood chapatis, fish curry and coconut rice, all washed down with tamarind, lime, orange and watermelon juice. It was a delightful interlude - thank you, both.

During an evening barbecue in Nairobi, to say goodbye to Ian and Libby, we met (among others) Charles and Francois Thom; Charles had been the former Defence Attaché in Uganda. It was a delight to have met him, but he also extended an introduction to his daughter, Vanessa, who was working with her husband at the UK Embassy in Addis Ababa; another invaluable contact. David and Sonja's passion for Kenya meant that they were staying in-country, despite being offered promotion. David left the military to become the deputy at Lewa Downs Wildlife Conservancy in Meru County, north of Mount Kenya. We had discussed some up-country options and he insisted we visit Lewa and some of the other landowners, as we planned to explore northern Kenya.

David had arranged access for us to stay at the Rhino Retreat for a few days in Aberdare's national park. Driving north up the Thika Road, the road cut through the highlands, where the steep road sides were bedecked with overflowing foliage, fostering a picture-postcard, jungle image. Aberdare is said to be 'the most exciting of Kenya's parks' due to the intrinsic beauty and diversity of flora and fauna. The western slope is astride the Rift Valley, with steep sides and limited big game viewing, unlike the moorlands that offer stunning waterfalls and distant views. The lower and warmer 'treetops salient' retains the steep slopes and forest ridges, with fast-flowing trout streams. Much of the wildlife here is specific to the Aberdare. The private Rhino Retreat, a three-bedroom cottage, was built by British Royal Engineers as an aid project in 1993. It is secluded in the hills above the Ark Lodge and controlled by the Rhino Ark charity. Rhino Ark is a fundraising initiative to benefit the local communities around the Aberdare and to foster wildlife sanctuaries, notably for the rhino. The retreat has its own waterhole, attracting a constant stream of animals. Three bull elephants dominated the waterhole during our time there, despite a small herd of buffalo and bushbuck sniffing and sneaking a drink. Inevitably, one bull elephant charged the drinking buffalo, but at the last minute, the bull raised his head so as not to gore the buffalo. It could have been nasty, but the buffalo did not run far and was unperturbed, returning to drink.

The nearby Ark Lodge resembled a ship, with decks and cabins. We enjoyed a sundowner on B deck, overlooking a large, illuminated waterhole. We drove past Treetops, as much as to pay homage to Her Majesty, Queen Elizabeth, although it was quite hidden, not easy to find and not as grand as we perceived; we did not explore inside. Low cloud and mist shrouded most of the Aberdare, so we did not spot any rhinos, the elusive bongo or sitatunga; maybe another time. But it was a peaceful couple of days and special to watch the elephants play at the waterhole. As we travelled north, we passed the iconic Aberdare Country Club that affords the most wonderful view over the Laikipia plain. We stopped for tea and a nose around. I remembered the principal lecturer on my MBA showing us a film clip of the 'New Year's celebration' scene from the film, Out of Africa. The courtyard of the Aberdare Country Club was the set, dressed as a Nairobi main street; stars Meryl Streep and Robert Redford were dancing, and unrecognisably, beside them, was a couple waltzing, which was our lecturer, Ron, and his wife.

We took the obligatory equator photograph at the signpost, just short of Nanyuki, suggesting we were halfway home. Thanks to David's connections and a locals' rate, we treated ourselves to some serious indulgence at the Mount Kenya Safari Club (MKSC), an exclusive country club, managed by the Lonrho chain, on the lower slopes of Mount Kenya. Reportedly established between a Texan oil baron, a Swiss millionaire and the film star, William Holden, there was a colonial feel to the place and stunning views. Manicured lawns and gardens were maintained, complete with the 'Millennium Maze' and ornamental ponds. There are tennis courts, bowling, a golf course, heated swimming pool and horse-riding for those inclined, plus guided trips up the mountain. The William Holden Wildlife Foundation Animal Orphanage seeks to educate young Kenyans about their indigenous wildlife. Our guide, James, introduced us to the elusive bongo, more colobus monkeys, the white (wide-mouthed, square-lipped) rhino and the Liberian pigmy hippo. We also met a 140-year-old giant tortoise, halfway through his lifespan and a Suni, a fairly rare antelope that was the size of a hare. After a lazy start and a fabulous breakfast, we came across Neil, the Scottish head chef, checking out Daph; he was enthralled and asked for our website details.

We bypassed Nanyuki, although it brought back memories from 1987. All battle groups are based at the showground, in the foothills of Mount Kenya, at 6,000 feet. When we arrived with 2 PARA, we went straight out for a run. We may have been young and fit back then, but the altitude was noticeable; no wonder Kenya and Ethiopia generate such excellent runners. Since Oman, 2 PARA enjoyed a constant round of 'hot weather' equipment issues; the most prized being the lightweight doss-bag (sleeping bag) of parachute silk. They were excellent, especially with the new Gortex bivvy bags, invaluable for airborne troops, for whom reducing carried weight was an obsession. The conversation with my experienced platoon sergeant went like this: 'You won't need your maggot (issue sleeping bag) Sir, as we are on the equator; it will be blazing hot at night. I am using the lightweight doss bag.' Stupidly, I believed Brummie, only to freeze each night at Nanyuki, the coldest place in NATO. I dressed in every item of clothing to keep warm and still froze; my sole consolation being that Brummie was equally freezing his arse off.

The Nanyuki showground was used during the Second World War to detain Italian POWs. It's possibly not changed, for interestingly, the cold and privations that the Italians endured were recorded in Felice Benuzzi's classic book, No Picnic on Mount Kenya. Benuzzi was a pre-war, Alpine mountaineer, whose response to the depressing tedium of camp life was to climb Mount Kenya (17,000 feet). He and two other like-minded internees cobbled together some improvised equipment and squirrelled rations for their attempt. Using a hand-drawn map (secured in an Oxo tin), the weak, sick and ill-prepared men escaped to ascend the mountain. After 18 days, they broke back into camp to face their punishment of solitary confinement, which seemed preferable to their climbing exploits. The camp commandant, however, commuted their punishment in recognition of their sporting endeavour. I had some mates who later climbed Mount Kenya with 3 PARA a few years after our trip, only to fail their Batian summit; their ropes were too short!

Aside from the excellent training, we enjoyed six days' R&R to see the wonderful country. In 1987, many activities were restricted because AIDS was big news across Africa, and in Kenya it was particularly rife. We were banned from the standard coastal trips, so with my fellow company officers, we hired a car to drive around Amboseli National Park. Not every company was so lucky; poor B Company arrived under a cloud, following some misbehaviour in Cyprus, so had to endure collective punishment of litter-picking on Mount Kenya. They described it as 'walking around the snowline for a week with a headache and a black bin bag like Wombles'. One group came across some well-equipped, European hikers conducting their long-planned ascent of Mount Kenya. When asked by a clearly less than prepared paratrooper for their rubbish, they were utterly dumbfounded; in shock, they recoiled back down to Base Camp. Bryan, a friend within the attached PARA Engineers, grew up on a tea farm in Kenya; they never had a guard dog, just a hippo roaming around their grounds at night; they slept well, with few (known) visitors. Bryan told me that his father recently climbed Mount Kenya with some friends, wearing normal shoes and carrying a plastic bag with some sandwiches; hard boys, these locals!

In 1987, the AIDS epidemic meant extensive lectures and awareness training for the boys. I was the Camp Duty Officer the evening Support Company arrived. For many of these experienced soldiers who operated the heavy support weapons, the last time they were in Kenya was just before the Falklands War and they remembered the local hostelry, the Sportsman's Bar. Late in the evening, a dishevelled, local lass was hassling the guard at the main gate. One of my own reliable corporals was commanding the guard, yet he couldn't quieten the complaining young lady. She was claiming compensation because one of the soldiers in the Sportsman's had ripped her T-shirt. She was drunk, emaciated and was not in a good frame of mind. There is no real rulebook for such events; she sought compensation for a new T-shirt, which was a big deal for her. If true, it was not unreasonable, but finding the miscreant would be another matter. We were not in-country to take advantage of the locals; quite the opposite. I asked her if she could point out her assailant; she reluctantly agreed, so I told Corporal Godfrey to take me to the Sportsman's. He sensibly pointed out that it might not be such a good idea for an armed bunch to walk into the Sportsman's with Support Company enjoying an evening of revelry (or words to that effect). Without an alternative, we drove the young lady to the Sportsman's. On arrival, a big, beery cheer went up; oh God, Corporal Godfrey was right.

Walking in, predictably, the complainant made herself scarce. One problem sorted, replaced with another! I was mobbed and groped by a whole load of 'similar young, emaciated ladies', questioning why the lads didn't want to purchase their dubious charms. Apart from the obvious, it was a nightmare, although I spotted one worse-for-wear chap emerging from the back, doing up his trousers; he was grabbed for the doc's attention in the morning. To be fair, the Support Company chaps were in a jovial mood, enjoying banter and a chat. One of the senior corporals I knew pulled me to one side and said, 'Sir, can you get rid of these women, clearly they are making a nuisance of themselves.' Easier said than done. I collared the barman and asked if he ran the place; he did, but he was not responsible for the girls. I told him that as he was accountable, if the girls were not removed rapidly, for good, I would have the place put 'Out of Bounds' and asked him to reflect on the loss of potential revenue. As if by magic, the girls were instantly gone and I was able to extract myself without loss of uniform, dignity or anything else. Thankfully, the boys enjoyed their evening; I could go back to freeze in my doss bag and Support Company could look forward to the sobering, hard run the following morning. I read latterly about a 2010 incident that resulted in death rather that a ripped T-shirt; quite another matter. Naturally, I have no insight or judgement on these events. The use and frequency of Kenyan training facilities increased with a higher operational tempo; where there is more military, there are those seeking to support and make money, legitimately and otherwise.

Lewa Downs was our next invitation, again courtesy of David; Lewa is a private game ranch that has become a leading light within ecotourism. The Lewa Wildlife Conservancy (LWC) covers 62,000 acres, established in 1995 by the Craig family, to protect their wildlife, especially rhino. By the early 1980s, it was doubtful if the black rhino would survive. At Lewa, formerly a cattle ranch, the Craigs were protecting rhinos from banditry and poaching with high security sanctuaries. Today, Lewa has a beautiful setup and flourishes as a not-for-profit organisation. The extensive range of international donors, programmes and support needs management, something David will adopt. We drove in, crossing the airstrip, which explained David's enthusiasm to acquire his licence. The Big Five are here, plus (in 2002 when we were there) more than 25% of the world population of Grevy's zebra, 32 black rhino and 34 white rhino, which were monitored daily. There are various animal research projects and local community support initiatives, where profits are recycled back to them. Working alongside the Kenya Wildlife Service, LWC is encouraging communities to support tourism from wildlife. The Il Ngwesi and Ol Pejeta communities are the thriving early adopters, with LWC's assistance.

Parking Daph outside 'Hogwarts' (one of the main houses), we bumped into an old friend we met at David's; he was project managing the build of a statement property on the estate for a wealthy VVIP American donor. David's chum was quite a character, who first visited Lewa as part of the protection team for the young royal princes who stayed at Lewa following the death of their mother, Princess Diana. The stay fostered a long-lasting bond that the princes have for wildlife, Kenya and Africa. It was at Lewa in 2010 that Prince William proposed to the future Queen of England, Kate Middleton, although at the time of our visit, William was pursuing another suitor, a certain Jecca Craig, a fellow St Andrews' student and daughter of the Craigs. We were to enjoy a large supper with the Craigs and others, where the chat was about Rory Bremner; his article was published in the Daily Telegraph travel supplement extolling the virtues of the Lewa community projects. We can only echo Rory's fine words, for within the first 10 minutes of our game drive, we had seen both black and white rhinos, elephants, scores of ungulates, including the Grevy's zebra and Masai giraffe. Within the swamp area, we saw our first sitatunga. I remember reading an email from Sonja years later, recording her joy and excitement of being able to watch an elephant giving birth there.

The following day, I was shown around the security detail and their preparations for a night patrol. Organised like an army battalion, they were a well-equipped, armed force, with good communications, night viewing devices and mobility. They had air support and tracker dogs; they looked efficient, skilled and able to react to events across the northern county, not just LWC. If you are up for it, one of the most exciting ways to view Lewa is to sign up for the annual Lewa Safaricom marathon to run on local tracks, which predictably favours the locals. The last time I glimpsed David was on the telly in 2007, whilst watching the actors, Ewan McGregor and Charlie Boorman, filming their second series of Long Way Down, riding to Cape Town. The two soaked riders and entourage arrived after dark at Lewa Downs, cold, wet, tired and hungry, into the waiting and enabling arms of David. These actors rode their BMW motorbikes on a similar route south as ours; we hoped to follow their route up the Nile and across Libya. Time would tell.

David had pulled further favours for us to stay with Kuki Gallmann, just across the Laikipia Plains. The few landowners and white farmers on Laikipia are linked and support one another. The Ol Ari Nyiro Conservancy is at the northern edge of the rift, overlooking Lake Boringo. Born of Italian aristocracy, the Gallmanns arrived in Kenya from Venice in 1972, seeking land. Slotting into white Kenyan society, Kuki fell in love with Ol Ari Nyiro, where her early life and passion for the continent are captured within her memoir, I Dreamed of Africa. The book became a Hollywood movie with Kim Basinger in the lead role, playing Kuki. Kuki's story of love for Kenya had equal tragedy; her husband, Paolo, was killed in a driving accident when she was pregnant with Sveva in 1980. Emanuele, her 17-year-old son, fascinated by nature and an enthusiastic collector of snakes, died when he was bitten by a puff adder only a few years after the loss of Paolo. Their graves are marked by a pair of yellow-barked, fever trees on the estate.

Kuki was busy arranging uber-glam, walk-in safari tents and facilities for the forthcoming wedding of her daughter, Sveva, yet she dropped everything to meet us. She declared that we must stay and wanted to give us a tour of the estate. We were quite astonished and unaware what David had said, yet it didn't take long to realise that we were on an impromptu job interview. She had a security issue with encroaching local pastoralists and felt she needed a permanent security detail, akin to Lewa, beyond her few askaris at the lodge. Her estate was fenced, but not maintained; it was breached six months or more earlier when local townsfolk drove a bulldozer through the wire. Her security man fled, yet Kuki apparently leapt up onto the bulldozer and talked the tribal leader down. She was an amazing and fearless lady, full of big ideas and plans, yet it was immediately clear that she needed someone to bring them to fruition. We understood that she sought to emulate Lewa's environmental programme, but her terrain was considerably denser and more overgrown, so precluded easy game viewing. Linking the Laikipia estates and programmes was an obvious solution, but the locals need to engaged with it.

Kuki had more projects; she gave us the estate tour. She wanted to formalise some ancient, archaeological finds, catalogue Emanuele's untouched research and, piquing Catherine's interest, Kuki implied she had a big pharma interest to commercialise a local weed. Whether she knew of Catherine's work to test the efficacy of new drugs to market or not, it led to some insightful and probing questions that become rather taxing for Kuki. It emerged that the pharma's response was pending. Oh, and she had decided where we could build our own house on the estate too!

Returning to the lodge for high tea, we were requested to join Kuki for supper. We were gobsmacked and retreated to a delightful, walk-in luxury tent; an egg-shaped, igloo design, with sliding glass doors and an amazing vista across the sundeck. These Arabian walk-ins were specially commissioned for her daughter's wedding, for which we came to appreciate nothing but the best would suffice. Supper was delightful and Kuki was ebullient over some paying guests. The following day, we shared a delightful, late breakfast, discussing her plans and then we were asked to feed back about her ideas. It was evident that she was not looking for options or proposals; it was her way, or no way. Wanting and needing to drive things herself was ingrained behaviour. With regard to her priorities, the pressing security concerns and the aspirational wealth from the weed were paramount. To organise and manage all her activities, especially security, would demand a fluent Swahili speaker. For her plant programme, Catherine suggested it would need investment before any return. Kuki was delighted, and asked us to think about it. We said we were travelling around Uganda and would be back in Nairobi in a week or so, which suited her. We were still taken aback by this unexpected, potential job offer.

Kuki suggested that we take the old, little used, northern access off the property to Lake Boringo, as it would take hours off our journey time. On departure, there was a small ceremony performed by the locals who washed Daph; all part of the fantastic and personal service at Ol Ari Nyiro. I didn't have the heart to say how horrified I was; we had hoped to convey some Kalahari dust to London. More importantly, we wanted to blend in and not stand out in a shiny, white Land Rover. No matter, five minutes down the road, we were grubby again. The northern route was not really a route; it certainly was not used and probably took longer than the alternative. We bumped and bounced down a dry riverbed and saw no game, only a couple of fish eagles circling us all day, an ominous sign as we descended off the plateau. Daph lapped up the disused track and we spun round to Roberts' Camp on Lake Boringo as dusk settled in.

We planned to follow the Soda Lakes south under the rift escarpment, which runs from Lake Baringo, down to Lake Magadi and Natron, although we'd stop at Nairobi. Baringo is the northernmost, freshwater lake. The small camp had toilets, a hot shower and a restaurant, and it was stiflingly hot, having descended off the plateau. The next lake south was Lake Bogoria (previously called Lake Hannington) where thousands of flamingos flock. This lake has a very high soda content which would scald or tear the flesh off everything bar the flamingo, which feeds off the primordial soup. We watched fish eagles hunt flamingos here, by making dive-bombing runs that caused the panicked flamingos to fly away, where they were then plucked in flight for eagle supper. There were many hot springs and streams around Lake Bogoria, with a pungent, sulphurous odour; in fact, it stank. The spring water boiled as it emerged from the ground, so much so that it was difficult to photograph because of the heat and steam.

Formed in 1961, Nakuru National Park has a wide variety of game, notably protected black and white rhinos. Interestingly, we read that the number of lions here need to be culled due to overpopulation. Lions had started to attack the rangers. Nakuru is renowned for the two million flamingos at its water's edge and when observed on high on Baboon Cliffs, the birds form the classic pink tinge around the lake. I remembered this image from my platoon's week of erecting rhino fencing back in 1987. The military offer the community support, so we provided some labour. That said, each afternoon we used our lorry for wonderful evening game drives; the same could not be said for the quality of Corporal Hogan's Beetles' singalongs in the dark as we travelled back. The pink colouration in flamingos' plumage is derived from the carotenoid pigments in their food, being converted into absorbable pigments via enzyme action in the bird's liver. It's thought that this bright colouration is essential to stimulate breeding, being one of the few species that practise mass breeding activities. Being able to withstand the soda lake conditions means that few predators can interrupt their breeding (unless you are an eagle), leading to higher survival. Despite the sheer number of flamingos, they are unable to make a dent in the amount of blue-green algae generated; estimates suggest that between five and eight tonnes of algae are cropped each year.

We were allocated a camping spot at the southernmost site, beside Makalia Falls. The facilities were basic but in a lovely location, with impala grazing nearby. Sharing the site was a tour guide camping near us, who had a magnificently maintained Classic Range Rover. He was escorting a group on a night drive, but whilst we were all out, the baboons got into their tents, seeking food and absolutely trashed the place; their gear was everywhere. I had to laugh, although it was no laughing matter; it was quite a rookie error. Nakuru was only 85 miles northwest of Nairobi, but the journey took over three hours given the road conditions and heavy traffic. We gave Lake Elementeita and Lake Naivasha a miss but stopped near Gilgil at Delamere Farm to pick up an offering for David and Sonja. As we climbed back up the rift escarpment, it was like someone had flicked a switch from rural to urban. David was amazed to hear about Kuki's offer; he had not seen that coming. He thought the potential synergies and opportunities with him at Lewa would be fantastic, but acknowledged the challenge. It would be a real heart versus head matter, especially as the pressures from local pastoralists and communities were increasing. He was unaware of any related discussions at Lewa. Neither had he heard of the commercialisation of Kuki's weeds, potentially exciting, yet a complete unknown.

A distressing after-story from 2017 reported attacks on Kuki's conservancy, wounding Kuki in her home. Herders invaded the farm in search of water because of drought conditions across Laikipia Plains. The police ejected the farmers and shot around 100 cattle. The attack on Kuki's lodge may have been retribution, and whilst no guests were staying, Kuki had her daughter, Sveve, with her nine-month-old baby with her. Kuki suffered two gunshot wounds to the stomach during the attack that also burnt her home down. She was helicoptered to the British military base at Nanyuki before being transferred to a Nairobi hospital. Although Kuki describes herself as a veteran of such setbacks and appears determined to carry on, this was the latest of a series of attacks on her and her land. A few months earlier, British military veteran and long-time rancher, Tristan Voorspuy, was beaten and killed on his ranch. In 2021, Kuki was again ambushed on the property and suffered gunshot wounds to her legs. The pressure on land, ownership and increasing water stress is only going to get worse. Lawlessness, reckless political aims, coupled with diminished tourism and a wider preponderance of available weapons, is advancing towards a crisis point.

For us, the worst and most devastating news came. In December 2013, there was an exceptionally sombre gathering at Hurstpierpoint village in Sussex for David Parkinson's memorial service. We didn't know this at the time but as children, David and I grew up on the edge of the neighbouring Sussex village, about a mile apart. David's father had been in the regiment and now, as friends and officers came from far and wide to celebrate and mark David's life, you could hear a pin drop in the chapel. It had been a huge shock to read in the news that summer of a house invasion, although, typical of David, he tackled the invader to allow Sonja time to reach their safe room. But simply awful for Sonja, to have to witness such mindless brutality - the shattering of their hopes and dreams in a fleeting moment. Even now, I can feel a lump in my throat. At the memorial service, Sonja and the girls were marvellous, obviously still distraught, but able to face the moment.

Hurstpierpoint held the usual wake; it was lovely to catch up with people I hadn't seen for many years, despite the sadness of the occasion. The first person we bumped into in the car park was Spike, and unsurprisingly, he was now a colonel. He found his niche and was thriving. There were a bunch of past and serving officers present in Kenya at the time of the attack; it would appear that since David left the forces, his post was filled by a succession of regimental officers. David and Sonja had moved on from Lewa, down the road to run another conservancy at Lollodaiga, on the slopes of Mount Kenya. Years later, I was speaking with Brigadier Mark, who at the time of the attack was fulfilling David's old appointment. He had been sharing a sundowner with David literally hours before he returned home on that fateful evening, along with Neil, with whom I was a fellow company commander in 2 PARA. Neil and Mark were amongst the first responders to the attack. The strength of David and Sonja's security, aside from physical measures, was their support to the local community, but the attack was conducted by bandits from Somalia; the community was not able to protect them. Of all the mindless attacks, David scared the invaders away only to die from his wounds that evening. Despite everything, Sonja loves Kenya and wants to continue her work and passion, helping and supporting her group of craft ladies. We are confident that whatever she turns her hand to, she will make a success of things. All the best Sonja and stay well.

It was a bad month, for two weeks later, a car was shot at containing two previous officers from the regiment. Jamie Lodden retired after company command in the regiment to assume a Barclays security role in Kenya. His father, also a retired colonel from the regiment, was out visiting Jamie. As the family were returning home, after supper out, thugs were waiting to ambush them. Their house was in the wealthy area of Nairobi, near Langata; in the crossfire, Jamie's father, Colonel Ted Lodden, was shot and died. Only a month later, the Westgate attack at the shopping mall by the Al Shabab terrorists occurred. The 2013 pre-election year was a violent one.

Chapter 16
The 'Pearl of Africa'

The Naivasha Road out of Nairobi was the usual jam. Matatus were battling for road space with the over-laden haulage trucks, ploughing the main arterial road to Uganda. The safari companies use this road to access the western parks. The drive was hot and dusty, but alertness was essential as animals and people do odd things and wander on the road. Descending towards Nakuru, the road conditions deteriorated, but as we ascended to Eldoret and the tea plantations, the road improved. Ironically, the better the tarred road became, it was matched with a deterioration in weather. What should have been a straightforward transit took far longer, resulting in our arrival at the Malaba border crossing at dusk - never ideal. The border crossing was closed. The transit town of Malaba was not an inspiring place as HGVs and trucks clogged the roadside stops.

For ease and security, we checked into a dodgy B&B. Our primary concern was securing Daph behind a wall and wire. It was a depressing place and evident why AIDS and other diseases were spiralling out of control. Young girls were providing a brisk trade amongst the waiting drivers held at the border crossing, despite the omnipresent health warnings. Our early start only inserted us into the mega jam of trucks and cars. The hawkers were rife, but thankfully not persistent. The processing was confused and the Kenyan administration was annoying. We had to pay extra road tax (a legacy of our unofficial Sand River arrival) but the Ugandan administration was unfathomable. Inside a half-built administration building, the immigration was simple, but customs were a total pain. We shuffled back and forth between customs and the bank to get the Carnet stamped. If we suffered, the lorry drivers were queuing for hours longer, although I noticed more than a number of white Land Cruisers barging through with scant checks. Africa's two-tier system was working well.

An hour later, we were free and driving down a smooth road towards Jinja, passing what appeared to be vibrant farmland. On the shores of Lake Victoria, we arrived at Jinja. This is the epicentre for adventure tourism, capitalising upon the white-water rapids of the Victoria Nile River that flows north from Lake Victoria. It was here, on the edge of Lake Victoria, that John Hanning Speke claimed 'the source of the Nile', marked by a memorial statue. We didn't stop to investigate and carried on to Kampala. Passing over the top of the Owen Falls power plant and dam at Jinja was impressive, although the dam was showing its age, yet still retaining the immense pressure of Lake Victoria.

The roads and traffic in Kampala were oppressive and appalling. It was a rainy Saturday evening. The potholes were symptomatic of the fading decay of what once must have been an impressive capital. A place Winston Churchill described as the 'Pearl of Africa', there was evidence of inward investment. Modern, glass edifices and half-erected buildings were both abandoned and the road signs unfathomable. Getting to Backpackers to camp was a mission, but it was a tranquil, safe haven among the city mayhem, given the heavy rains and uncomfortable humidity. We had a week or so before Kuki might respond, so a loop around Uganda filled the gap perfectly; we weren't expecting a positive response. We sought to explore the Great Lakes and the disputed border between Congo, Rwanda and Burundi. This habitat is the epicentre of the mountain gorillas' range, supposedly the closest mammal to us humans, and we knew 'close' experiences would be both rare and expensive. The infamous footage of David Attenborough lying eye-to-eye with his silverback was inspiring and often marketed, yet such ecotourism and conservation comes with challenges and cost.

The central African region fascinated the Victorians and fuelled their obsession with defining the origin of the River Nile. We initially thought to trek the Rwenzori Mountains, the fabled 'Mountains of the Moon', as mentioned by Homer and Herodotus. This region also had a deeper meaning for me; it was an area of missed military deployment at one stage, notably the refugee crisis around Goma. The 1994 Rwandan genocide sparked regional conflict around the Congo; it consumed the nine neighbouring countries around the DRC/Zaire, such are tribal connections and Victorian boundaries. The 'African World War' theoretically finished around 2003, but more likely it's 2023 as tragedies still rage. An estimated 5.4 million deaths have been recorded, the highest death toll arising from conflict since the Second World War. The significant refugee numbers are double those killed, with many wounded, displaced, raped and traumatised. It was these refugees massing around Goma that came to the attention of the MoD, and potentially, me. Yet this was in stark contrast to the diaries of Dr Christopher Everett and their rotation around the Congo in 1958. Reading their diary in 2013 highlighted the last vestiges of colonial rule; they visited and aided many hospitals and outposts, where today these services would be utterly swamped, or destroyed!

King Philippe of Belgium wrote to the DRC president in 2020 to express regret for Belgium's colonial past, 60 years on from independence. Delivered during the nascent Black Lives Matter era, the King wrote of shared 'painful episodes', referring to the brutal and violent suppression of the colony. Critically, he stopped short of an apology. King Leopold II brutally suppressed the Congo, treating the country like his personal fiefdom for 30 odd years. By 1960, Belgium ceded control to the characteristic Patrice Lumumba, Congo's first Prime Minister. Predictably, a year on, Lumumba was assassinated by Congolese rebels and Belgian army officers (probably under CIA orders), and the looting of the Congo never really ended. Its resources remain stolen and the masses brutalised. Alec Russell's excellent book, Big Men Little People, documents the many and varied African chiefs, or 'Big Men of Africa', who effectively lined their own pocket at the expense of their people. The gold standard was set by Mobutu Sese Seko's ravages that crippled Zaire, and similar from Idi Amin in Uganda, where we were now driving.

My regimental service was within the UK's 'ready for anything' Airborne Brigade, whose operational doctrine was to deliver an 'Out of Area' (OOA) capability, including 'Services Protected Evacuation' (SPE) operations. Armed forces were used to rescue stricken nationals, with the benchmark SPE being Operation Dragon Rouge in 1964. Questions were asked at the time in parliament whether the UK could conduct a similar operation; the Belgique Paracommando Regiment parachuted 350 men onto Stanleyville to rescue nuns and hostages being brutalised by Simba (communist supported) rebels. Negotiations failed, so rapid force was projected by Belgium and helped by 'Mad Mike' Hoare and his band of merry men. Britain's 5 Airborne Brigade and 3 Commando Brigade (and today's unit derivations) prepare for similar eventualities, as conducted in Kabul in 2021 and Khartoum in 2023. Today, these are called Non-Combatant Evacuation Operations (NEO) to align with American nomenclature.

Ethnic tensions between the Hutus and Tutsis festered throughout the 1970s and 1980s, dislocating thousands around the Great Lakes. The

Hutus dominated Rwanda, although the Rwandan Patriotic Front (RPF) languished in Uganda and aligned themselves with the Ugandan National Resistance Army rebels (NRA) under Yoweri Museveni. Tensions increased when leaders were assassinated, culminating in the Arusha Accord, in 1993. This toothless accord failed dramatically, with Rwandan violence by the Interahamwe (Hutu militants), slaughtering several hundred thousand Tutsi friends or neighbours in 1994. The RPF invaded and captured Kigali. The French reacted quickly and launched a limited (parachute) force to secure southwest Rwanda and halt the RPF movement south. But the genocide fizzled immediately; Western communities responded with humanitarian relief. The UK sent support elements (engineers, medics and logistical support) from 5 Airborne Brigade, whom I helped prepare and train, but frustratingly, could not go. I had to make do with reports and 'stories' from friends; one pal managed to take his engineer troop to Virunga to climb the volcano. Sensibly, the gorillas moved away.

The Rwandan genocide left thousands of displaced people streaming across the border to Goma and other areas in Zaire and Tanzania. UNHCR struggled to contain the crisis of 2.1 million refugees, whose spiralling health concern of cholera, diarrhoea or other epidemics were widespread. But the presence of irregular military and Interahamwe among the refugees threatened (and questioned) the safety of the UNHCR and the displaced people. President Bill Clinton fanned the media with statements like 'the worst humanitarian crisis in a generation'. It led to an existential crisis for UNHCR; the camps were becoming militarised and worse, aid was being targeted; the militias were hiving off aid for themselves. Soon, a viral 'feed the killers' crisis spread among the aid community, causing the departure of IRC, Oxfam, CARE and Save the Children. The British military, with the UN, were asked for more support in the face of such flagrant violation of refugee law. By 1996, the irregular forces were sufficiently powerful to launch the First Congo Wars to overthrow Mobutu. Violent clashes toppled Mobutu by Kabila, which, in 2008, the International Rescue Committee estimated to be the 'deadliest conflict since the Second World War'. Ironically, the Western world was looking to the former Yugoslavia, as the Balkan Wars took Western attention from Central Africa.

Human conflict impacts wildlife, especially the mountain gorilla. An attempt to preserve their habitat in 1991 came from the creation of the

Bwindi Impenetrable National Park, which bestrode three borders, over 130 square miles. Thought to be a positive move, sadly it excluded the indigenous Batwa pygmy people from the park. Those people with the closest understanding and ability to co-exist with native species were removed from the ecosystem. However, today's community-based approach is better news for the Batwa. Indigenous people are encouraged to be active within biodiversity, to protect their heritage and become involved in the wildlife decision-making process. Controlling the harvest, filtering tourist funds back to local people and fostering trust funds for indigenous communities has had a regenerative effect. In 2008, Rwanda generated around $8 million income from around 20,000 gorilla tourists and now, Uganda is starting to recognise similar contributions to their Ugandan wildlife budget.

Community engagement and goodwill can evaporate quickly. Fresh in our minds was the kidnap of 14 western mountain gorilla tourists and their guide, three years earlier, in Bwindi Forest, by more than 100 former Interahamwe rebels from across the DRC border. Borders have scant impact on lawlessness. The Interahamwe sought to destabilise Uganda and scare away tourists, depriving Uganda of their tourist dollar. Six victims survived their kidnap ordeal, whilst the remainder were tortured, raped and/or hacked to death. The local guide was doused with petrol and set on fire. The Interahamwe temporarily achieved their aim to horrify and disrupt tourism, which meant that armed guards now accompany most tour groups.

We headed to Mgahinga National Park in the southwest, on the Rwandan border. A permit from the Ugandan Wildlife Authority (UWA) in Kampala is needed to trek with the gorillas. Such permits need to be booked months in advance, costing around $175-250 per person. The permit was only the start of an open-ended cheque; operators added travel, accommodation and guide costs. Only six people are permitted to visit each gorilla family per day. Inevitably, the big tour operators overbooked, allowing scant opportunity for independent travellers to gain a place. We were told that the UWA office at Kabale could issue permits (and will only do so if there is a real chance of trekking, thus preventing a fruitless journey into each park), but we cannot substantiate this, or the fact that if you pay enough at the park, you'll get to see gorillas.

We declined the permit and, being independent, headed to Mgahinga. The road south was reasonable tar towards Kabale but the road signs were poor or non-existent. It took some five to six hours of hard driving and progress was slow, winding through stepped terracing and cultivated lands. The land and soil were a vivid, red colour and cash crops of rice, tea and coffee were evident, on what appeared to be a commercial basis. Getting these crops to market is the constant African challenge. I later read the Economist's Economics of the Guinness Truck, which benchmarked the capability and logistical calculations of the Guinness truck around Cameroon - 'if that can get through, anything can'.

We arrived at Mgahinga National Park late, as dusk settled. We found a camping spot under the darkening, imposing, conical shape of a towering volcano. The national park had three active volcanoes within the Virunga Mountain range; the highest peak of Mount Muhavura (4,127 metres) was open to be climbed. This was new terrain for our trip; we no longer traversed plains or savannah, and now had dense rain forest. I had spent many months deep in far eastern, central and southern American jungles with the military and recognised the hallmarks of secondary thickening (re-growth) from logging. Whilst the higher slopes were considered primary terrain for the gorillas, the forest hosts many other fauna, both black-and-white and possibly red colobus monkeys, and maybe even the rare blue and golden monkeys. Other fauna such as elephants, buffalos and bush pigs may be seen, partially justifying why we ventured here without a permit. We sought the local ranger to assess our limited options; interestingly, we were offered a gorilla trek, despite admitting to no permit. I'm sure that money would have been sought at some point. Catherine's shoulder was OK, but not really up to a full day's trek in the hills, so we chose the nature trail. We anticipated the potential for an anti-climax and were not surprised; this would be a typical African escapade. But, as with so many things in Africa, you never know.

We had our obligatory Ugandan army patrol with us. Lessons from the Bwindi incident demanded patrols with tourists. Whilst no real deterrent to the militia, it only depletes scarce military resources, leaving the border unprotected and porous. Perhaps it might have been better to allow the army to do their job, to concentrate on and around the border (in depth), providing an effective deterrent by patrolling crossing points, with an aggressive follow-up with each and every breach. Then there would be no need to patrol with every nature ramble that a tourist might embark upon.

But this was Africa and not a military mind at work. By walking amongst the upper slopes of Mgahinga, we 'might' glimpse a roaming gorilla troop. Our scheduled ramble was due to start at 7.50am.

Theory seldom matches practice. It was past 8am before the 30-man military unit trudged off into the hills to sweep away the hordes of rebels and human guerrillas; they were escorting the lucky six paying tourists. We had to wait for the military to clank and rumble off, armed with welly boots and RPG rocket launchers, machine guns and AK47s; my heart sank. First, the poor Westerners were going to be disappointed; the gorillas would hear and smell this lot and bugger off, and second, so would the rebels. Further, the rebels would then have the upper hand, for they knew where the military were, so they could circumvent them and 'attack' the remaining unprotected tourist facilities at will.

Meanwhile, we had to wait a further half an hour for Fred Kano and his army to get ahead, before we set off with our boy scout. We left at 10am, in the heat with around eight in our group, of varying abilities. We required height, to rise above the logging and secondary thickening, so we slogged up the volcano. It was very hot, sweaty work, threading ourselves through dense thickening. With elevation, we reached the primary canopy and the cooler half-light of creepers, yet the first Westerner had had enough. Our guide was great, enthusiastic about the bugs, poo and signs he observed, yet our strung-out group could hear little or nothing of these undoubted pearls of wisdom. I was at the back, helping the older chap in the group, who was practically having a heart attack trying to keep up. During our four-hour trek, predictably, we saw nothing other than evidence of the marvels that might have been. Later, the gorilla trackers returned, tired and deflated. They'd had a 'good day' considering they glimpsed a silverback and troop at a distance, disappearing rapidly across the border into the Congo.

Interestingly, the young captain in charge of the army troop sought us out for a chat, for he was fascinated by our trip. He was clearly a bright, university-educated lad who really wanted to move on into commerce and business. He was doing his time in the military and was irritated by the directives from his superiors, which he thought were unfeasible. At least he too questioned the logic of carrying an RPG anti-tank weapon up a volcano. I later learned from two of the gorilla trekkers, both VSO doctors working in Kampala, that they would get a 75% cash rebate due to the distant sighting of gorillas; apparently, it was not their purchased up-close viewing experience. So trekking was not quite the sunk cost we initially understood and, whilst being happy for the trekkers' rebate, it further questioned the viability of the whole business model, given the vagaries of the disappearing gorillas. Yet the authorities needed to be seen to act and regulate market forces, controlling access to gorillas and protecting these endangered animals, which we applaud. The two doctors were well prepared, possessing better maps, from which I was able to make a sketch map for our onward journey to Queen Elizabeth National Park (QENP).

In 1952, Kazinga National Park (the Pearl of Africa) was renamed to commemorate Her Majesty the Queen's visit. Henceforth, Queen Elizabeth National Park was known for its diverse wildlife, tree-climbing lions and abundant birdlife. Situated on the western side of Uganda, under the Mountains of the Moon (the Rwenzori Mountains) to the north and west, we needed to skirt around Bwindi Forest to reach the park. We had to transit mountainous terrain, terraced farmland and forest, with no straight road or obvious track, only twisting, local, logging tracks and an absence of road signs. There were no towns to head towards either. At the first settlement of note, Kisoro, we found fuel. This terrain meant we were consuming more fuel, so we grabbed the opportunity whilst we could. However, we also needed to change money and strangely, we also found a bank. The exchange rate was appalling but the fuel was so cheap, it evened itself out. The weirdest thing occurred on entering the bank; I was happy to wait my turn, yet the locals insisted we were ushered to the head of the queue. Whether they got a rake from the Muzungu rates charged, I was not aware, but it was a strange, yet an honest and genuine gesture by ordinary folk. I was suitably humbled.

We tried to follow my VSO-derived sketch map but were struggling; their actual map would have added little value. We passed through parts of Bwindi National Park, observing evidence of logging, altering the landscape and roads. This area was more subsistent farms of red soil, being leached by the rain and mud rivers. Near Kambuga, we came across a settlement with a general store, so poked our heads in. It was very quaint; clearly they did not get many visitors here. We bought some local pasteurised milk (which wasn't too bad), local bread (very crispy) and eggs, before joining the main track leading to the southern QENP Gate at Ishasha. The track was probably a logging track, certainly wide enough for two logging vehicles to pass, but it was rough and unmade.

We were progressing slowly up a gentle slope when we saw a 4x4 racing towards us, kicking up a huge dust plume. It was weaving all across the road, possibly avoiding the worst of the potholes; it was hard to tell, it was travelling so fast. It showed no sign of slowing down as the gap closed between us. I was concerned that the vehicle had a steering issue and was out of control, so I pulled over to hug my roadside to avoid contact and minimise my presence. I had almost stopped and my lights were on so I could be seen. There was ample room for a lorry to pass. The 4x4 shot past at an alarming speed, clearly out of control. There was a screech of brakes and tyres as the driver wrestled for control. I glimpsed a local driver with what I thought were a couple of white passengers inside, and assumed they were tourists or local aid workers, but as it flashed passed, I recognised the company (tobacco) logo. The posh Toyota 4x4 continued to weave past us and down the track, where it clipped the side of the bank. From what I saw in my side rear-view mirror, the rear two wheels of the Toyota were flipped in the air before the truck came to an untidy sideways halt off the track. How it did not roll, I have no clue. What was the hurry? Was the driver on drugs, overly tired or asleep, or all of the above? Our natural instinct was to rush and help as we empathised with their plight.

Being concerned for the safety of the crash victims (although in their case, it was at their own hand by speeding), I reversed back down the track to see if they needed any help, recovery gear, medical assistance or to use our comms. I could see people walking outside the vehicle and one white chap walking towards me up the track. I stopped short, told Catherine to wait in Daph, but she was already getting the first aid kit out. I walked down to assess what was going on and proffered a greeting to ask if they were OK. The response stopped me dead; I got a curt reply along the lines of yes, no thanks to me. 'What did I think I was doing stopping in the middle of the road?' or words to that effect, just significantly less polite. The bloke's English was good, but clearly not his native language. To say I was taken aback by the response is an understatement; my jaw gaped open. I assumed he was in shock so I let it pass initially, but the guy started to become aggressive and was shouting. Well, that was it. I saw red and gave him both barrels, verbally. I really wanted to knock his block off! Their mess was of their own accord, so let them stew in the problem of their own making (I told him so). I said I recognised their logo and would report him, his attitude and the event to the park authorities. I didn't listen to any of his diminishing, hollow rhetoric as I walked back to Daph as I was seething at the injustice. Catherine was out the vehicle with the first aid kit, walking towards me, but her mouth opened as she heard the exchange. I had to wrestle her back into Daph, for she was also outraged. So much for us helping them! Any thoughts of tending to the wounded were abandoned by the small-minded idiot trying to blame others for his own stupidity and recklessness. You reap what you sow. Besides, I saw four men walking around their steaming, stricken vehicle, so they were not badly incapacitated.

I was still irritated when we arrived half an hour later at the park entrance. The south gate was unmanned. It was like driving into an English country estate with the white picket pavilion guard hut, cattle grid and fenced entrance. Shortly beyond the entrance, we came to Ishasha Sector Park HQ. We paid our fees and were allocated a campsite. I reported the incident, still angry, but equally concerned that there might have been injuries or stranded people. I wrote a short statement as I didn't want any adverse false report to bounce back our way. It transpired that there was no need for concern; the rangers were already on the lookout for that vehicle. We learnt that a farming rep was touring local growers with Europeans and they were simultaneously helping themselves to a freebie safari around the park, without paying. The rangers knew the local driver, so they were grateful for my statement. Still, to go on the offensive for their own idiocy remains contemptable. As I write and recall this event, I still wish I had knocked the fella out. All the same, and the idiot aside, I hope no one was hurt from their stupidity. Rebounding from events is all about how one reacts; clearly, they reacted appallingly (a sign of guilt), so they will have to deal with the outcome.

Queen Elizabeth National Park straddles the equator in southwest Uganda. The park soils differs here, being derived from relatively young volcanic deposits. Situated east of the Bwindi monopane mountains and forest, the park flora is semi-deciduous forests, savannah, small swamps and thickets. The grasses support numerous herbivores, some unique to the park, such as the Ugandan kob. Being similar to, yet larger than an impala, the kob has longer horns and is golden-brown all over; it does not have the impala's distinctive, black markings on the hind quarters. The kob once roamed all of East Africa, but now is only found here. Another relatively unique adaptation occurring in the Ishasha area is the predominant tree-climbing lions. Why the lions behave like this is not generally understood; lions are not great climbers. It is thought to be a mechanism for them to cool down, whilst others suggest it's to reduce tsetse fly bites. Whatever the cause, we had also seen this in the Grumeti area of the Serengeti, yet it is rare. I guess no one told the lion not to climb trees.

A ranger called Silver guided us to a small campsite overlooking the Ishasha River, which formed the border with the Congo, for our first night in the park. There was a stone pagoda in the clearing, stocked with firewood. The adjacent Ishasha River had five or six pods of huge hippos wallowing, but Silver assured us that they would not be able to climb the steep bank on our side to graze the grass during the night. Thankfully, he was correct; we could hear the hippos noisily munching through the grasses on what we hoped was the opposite bank. Hippos kill more humans than any other animal in Africa; never get between them and their water source. This was the Congo - the Heart of Darkness - what Tim Butcher calls 'Africa's broken heart.' In the early 1900s, the Europeans led a civilised and cultured life on and around Lake Tanganyika, if a tad oppressive (to say the least). It was here that Dr Christopher and his crew toured the lakes in 1958, from Lake Kivu to the Rwenzori and the Semliki River.

Today, the evolving insurgent and humanitarian crisis, centred around Goma, is a totally opposed existence. One of the most evocative books relating to the risks and rewards of travelling in Africa is by Tim Butcher, in his 2007 book, Blood River, a Journey to Africa's Broken Heart. Like Alec Russell, Tim was also the Telegraph's 'man' in Africa in the late 1990s, and his book is a bestseller. Previously a war reporter, Tim spent a harrowing six weeks travelling the length of the second longest river in Africa, from its headwaters near the base of Lake Tanganyika, caging lifts on charity aid motorbikes, to barges floating the 2,900-odd miles to the Atlantic. During Tim's somewhat grim trek, he asks, 'Why are the Africans so bad at running Africa?' He sheds light on the Congo-fatigued international community, a thoroughly humane story of continued suffering, with little to no end in sight.

Just as dusk approached, we had a fire going, to minimise the mozzies, and the roof tent open, when a 4x4 came crashing through the bush and thundered across to us, lights ablaze. It was all very aggressive, unnecessary and highly alarming. As Andy in his trashed Landcruiser pulled up and shouted 'Kapstad' enthusiastically to us, I realised I was gripping our machete. I wasn't sure if this was the same crowd that we'd encountered on the road earlier. Bless Andy, he was like a bull in a china shop and thankfully had not noticed that I was chopping wood. He was very friendly and looking for fellow South Africans to rap with and speak Afrikaans, hence his Kapstad reference. We shared a beer and swapped stories, for he gathered from the rangers that we were from Cape Town, given Daph's registration plate. He really couldn't hide his disappointment; clearly, he was lonely and was reaching out for his kin. He had been an IT worker in the UK for years and was returning to Durban in his over-priced, flashy Landcruiser that was suffering. He had struck a ditch in Kenya or somewhere and ripped out most of his front suspension; his repair was a jury-rigged solution using his hi-lift jack. It was a clever fix because he was still moving, although we wondered for how much longer, given his heavy right boot. After a beer, he chose to speed off to his campsite. Once he was gone, we were left in the eerie stillness of the night, snuggled by our campfire on the riverbank, looking through the blackness and gazing up at the glistening array of the African night sky. The clarity of the African night's sky is a marvel and one of which we never tire. With the Milky Way spread above us, we listened to the grunting hippos; it was quite surreal.

We rose before dawn to meet Silver at the park HQ to guide us around Ishasha for a few hours. It was still dark as we departed our campsite, leaving our embers still (safely) glowing. Silver was bubbling with enthusiasm as we saw ungulates (kob, topi and impala), bull elephants, buffalo herds and numerous birds, although the famous, tree-climbing lions remained elusive. Silver was crestfallen, yet his bird knowledge was encyclopaedic; just as well, for the variety and diversity of birdlife was supreme. It was evident that wildlife numbers were down, for later we found evidence of poaching and exploitation (logging). Given the burgeoning humanitarian crisis, it was unsurprising. We were careful not to say we found the park experience disappointing; we headed towards Lake Edward. Almost immediately, top-spotter Catherine saw a lion in the tree, then another; they do exist! The park road to the Kazinga Channel took a couple of hours. Apart from glimpses of the amazing Rwenzori Mountains in the cloud breaks, it was uneventful. The clouds were rumbling as we arrived at the campsite, which was bare and exposed, so we slunk back to Mweya Safari Lodge for a beer.

The East African Rift created the linked lakes, running south-to-north from Lake Tanganyika (the longest, freshwater lake in the world), Lake Kivu in Rwanda, to Lakes Edward, George and Albert that lie south and east under the Rwenzori Mountains and which denote the DRC border with Uganda. Ultimately, these lakes flow into the Nile, more precisely, the White Nile that flows from Lake Albert. Lake Albert is fed from Lake Victoria by the Victoria Nile River that flows from the eponymous lake, starting at Jinja and running north, via Murchison Falls. During the great era of Victorian exploration (for around 20 years from the 1850s), overseen by the Royal Geographic Society, the renowned explorers of Livingstone, Stanley, Burton, Grant, Speke and the Bakers each lay claim to having found the source of the Nile. Without the benefit of technology and modern imagery, they trudged around and made assumptions about the geology and water flow. They were remarkably accurate, each seeking the 'scoop of the age'. Speke corrected Burton, each closely trumped by the Bakers. Stanley, in 1876, having met Livingstone, finally defined the Mountains of the Moon (the Rwenzoris) as a major water source. Documented in his 1890 book, In Darkest Africa, Stanley demonstrated that the Rwenzori caught the prevailing westerly wet weather, which then drained south and east, via the Semliki River and swamps to feed Lake Albert, as an alternative source of the Nile.

Founded in the 1930s, the Royal Geographical Society (RGS) sent explorers out to 'unlock the mysteries of this planet'. By the 1850s, the Victorians became as obsessed with Africa – in particular, the source of the Nile - and Sir John Franklin and his NW Passage or the Polar feats of Scott and his brethren. Their Kensington residence at Lowther Lodge (since 1911) bears testament to this thirst for the truth and the Victorian fascination for the source of the Nile. Sir Christopher Ondaatje, sponsored by the RGS for his 1998 book, Journey to the Source of the Nile, believes it is the Victorian zeal that led the Africans to coin the phrase 'mzungu', meaning 'he who walks around in circles'. Ondaatje was obsessed with Burton and his fellow explorers, so journeyed to retrace their paths. In the early 1990s, he travelled across East Africa, walked around Lake Victoria and managed (despite the poor security situation in 1996) to walk the foothills of the Mountains of the Moon to confirm the importance of the Rwenzori Mountains for the flow of the Nile. Being guided by a local Batwa pigmy guide, he recognised the importance of the Semliki River as an equal source. The tectonic movements and volcanoes along the great rift effectively meant the Nile headwaters were in Zambia, until the flow became blocked. Ironically, we carried Ondaatje's book with us, but only read it once home; it may have altered some of our route decisions or actions. Ondaatje returned to his start point on Zanzibar and travelled across the Serengeti and Olduvai Gorge, acknowledging this as the cradle of the human race. Leakey's find of 'Upright Man' (conferring the associated expansion for the brain) left Ondaatje to observe that the search of the Nile and Man did not 'discover' this area of Africa, but the European explorers merely 'returned to their ancestors'.

Gazing out over Lake Edward from the comfort of Mweya Safari Lodge, we watched the dark clouds rumbling across the lake towards us. It swayed our decision; we took a ridiculously cheap room at the practically empty lodge. Satisfied with our choice, we enjoyed a beer and saw the empty pleasure steamer on the Kazinga Channel becoming swallowed by the heavy rain clouds. The Kazinga Channel region is supposedly rich in elephants and leopards, yet we saw little game. According to a 1990 census, 8,000 hippos inhabit the channel alone, excluding the huge herds of hippos in the lakes. As the storm subsided, the abundant bird life came alive. We used our time at the lodge for administration. The southern and eastern volcanic lava plains from the Rwenzoris left numerous cones and craters. At Lake Bogoria, the air was rank with a sulphurous stench, as we observed large salt pans being commercially harvested for salt, via evaporation. It was very hot, yet the elusive Rwenzori Mountains rarely appeared from their cloud veil.

The Rwenzoris are a UNESCO World Heritage Site and sustain a unique and 'un-African' flora; many plants are related to the protea family, akin to those found on Table Mountain. Higher than the Alps, the seven summit peaks are named after the great Victorian explorers (including Stanley, Speke and Baker, although none of them climbed them), with the highest peak being Margherita at 5,109 metres. The Rwenzoris are the third highest mountain range in Africa, featuring glaciers, snowfields, waterfalls and lakes. Had we wanted to, the prevailing security situation prevented us ascending these mountains, where rebel militia were reportedly hiding. Kasese was the trekking base camp for the area, which we drove through the following morning. It was here I read that Christopher Ondaatje ended his Rwenzori trek; a dilapidated town, with numerous Ugandan military units and soldiers guarding the bridge over the Kazinga Channel.

Kasene used to have a railhead that transported copper and cobalt to Kampala, but we didn't stop, and carried on to Fort Portal. In 2020, I read reports of unchecked violence and brutality since 1996, despite UN monitors in place. A 2014 UN Security Council report accused the Congolese army commander of financing and supplying the militia, but no preventative action ever occurred. Killings continued, like at Beni in July 2019; here, a DRC village just the other side of the Rwenzori Mountains from Fort Portal, close to a Congolese army base, is where the militia reportedly murdered up to 800 men, women and children. A similar number were said to be abducted and 200 wounded, abandoned to forage for food. Aside from persistent and endemic famine and disease, now mortars and machetes commit fratricide upon unprotected people, not to mention rape. Rape endures as a weapon to punish, humiliate and destroy communities. The UN assess that 1,200 women are raped every day in DRC since 1996. Despite such an alarming statistic, nothing happens to prevent it.

Fort Portal is the district headquarters with a bustling market that retained some old, colonial charm. We thought to stop but the B&Bs and camp spots were closed, or non-existent. We stopped at an internet café to check for a response from Kuki Gallmann, but there was none. Whilst there, it transpired that the café owner was born and educated in Lewisham, South London. He turned out to be the town's legal officer, although we were not really clear what that entailed. His advice was to check out Kibale National Park further east. Kibale is one of the last remaining parks to contain both lowland and montane forests, yet as elsewhere, human pressures were evident. Fertile land is sought by farmers and loggers, who were active, yet Kibale remains one of the pre-eminent locations for primate study. We followed the advice to Lake Nkurubu, where we stumbled upon a delightful, tranquil camping spot by a crater lake. It appeared to be abandoned, although the shower and toilet block were maintained. There were signposts all around indicating walks; one implied it was safe to swim or camp down by the lake. Walking round the edge of the crater and peering down, the water looked like a huge, black hole some 200 metres or so down. We eventually found a footpath down.

The 'Top of the World' trail was a delight. Warm, spring light dappled through the tranquil canopy, when all of a sudden, a cacophony of colobus monkeys kicked off. The park is known to habituate chimpanzees and the rare Ugandan red colobus among others, but this troop were definitely black-and-white colobus and they were warning us off. Their noise transported me straight back to the Belizean jungle, when many years earlier, as a young officer on my first jungle patrol, we deplaned from the Puma helicopter that had squeezed down through a jungle hole. Once alone, on the Guatemalan border, the jungle erupted with a troop of howler monkeys, shaking the trees and screeching. It was amusing, yet pretty scary. We had no clue what we had landed in, miles from anywhere, but I imagine the same was the case for the monkeys when a big helicopter descended on their patch of jungle just half an hour earlier. Kibale was a real bonus stop en route to Murchison Falls National Park and back to Kenya.

Murchison Falls is the largest park in northern Uganda, covering around 4,000 square kilometres. It is bisected by the Victoria Nile, running from Jinja to Lake Albert; the Victoria Nile thunders through a narrow gorge only seven metres wide, plunging 43 metres. Referenced by both John Speke and James Grant, it was Samuel and Florence Baker who named the Falls in 1864, after the then president of the RGS, the geologist, Roderick Murchison. The campsite above the Falls was infested with insects and tsetse flies, so we chose the excellent Rest Camp nearby that had just been acquired by Debbie and Steve a few days earlier. It was a lovely spot, not least due to their tame, hand-reared bushbuck, a pair of marabou storks and a family of warthogs. It transpired that Steve knew Charles Thom, further evidence of our shrinking world. We took Steve's advice and headed along the recently regraded escarpment, along the coastline of Lake Albert, providing stunning views across the lake, back to the border and Congo.

It was still raining and chaotic in Kampala, so we pushed on to the more bucolic Jinja and a delightful campsite at Bujugali Falls. Jinja is the epicentre for the white-water adrenaline junkies down the Nile. I subsequently heard that a past sergeant major, Budge from 2 PARA, relocated to a wonderful, self-built house above Jinja, having worked in security for many years; shame our paths couldn't cross. The following morning, we steeled ourselves for more chaotic shenanigans crossing the border, but as 'returning Kenyans', we passed through with minimal hassle. We drove to Nukuru to stay at Kembu campsite and farm. It was delightful; aside from the heat and insects, if one closed your eyes, the place could almost resemble a warm summer's

English evening. We climbed the Rift Escapement again, bearing steaks and other gifts from the farms for David and Sonja. It was a couple more days before we heard from Kuki and her negative response to our offer. Her PA told us on the phone that she was in Nairobi but wouldn't be seeing us; we were not surprised - actually, we were relieved.

After our long goodbyes and gratitude to David and Sonja, it was time to push north. We headed back up the Rift Valley near Nyahururu (previously known as Thompson Falls), which offered a wonderful view of the eponymous Falls at the top of the Aberdare National Park and views down the rift valley to Maralal, via Rumuruti. Rumuruti denotes the start of barren, northern Kenya and for us, a long, gravel road. In order to avoid the notorious Marsabit-Moyale road, we thought to cross into Ethiopia via Banya Fort, near Ileret on the northeastern side of Lake Turkana. But local advice was discouraging, due to continued insurgence activity from Southern Sudan; Banya Fort was no longer a recognised crossing. All options pulled us back to Moyale. Aside from being the most atrocious, corrugated road, one needed to be escorted, something we wanted to avoid. The Marsabit-Moyale road suffers frequent Somali militia attacks; Paul Theroux experienced one during his Dark Star Safari journey, getting ambushed despite his military escort. Evidently, it was no safer with an escort; in fact, we thought the opposite, for a collective escort presents a concentrated target. First, we wanted to explore the northwest, to visit Sibiloi National Park and where Richard Leakey found a wealth of archaeological evidence; I was reading Leakey's book, Wildlife Wars in Uganda. Whilst the Omo River and National Park of Ethiopia endured extreme starvation and malnutrition in the mid-1980s, this region also drains into Lake Turkana, making it geologically and archaeologically rich for hominid fossils and finds.

We needed a plan. Ethiopia was a difficult country to enter. As we headed north, the Rumuruti road was dusty, all the better for not being tar. We arrived at Maralal and the Yare Safari Campsite just before dark. Renowned for camel safaris and the annual camel derby, the year we visited, there was no sponsor. We were led to believe that the campsite and bar was a lively place, but no. The only other souls around were a pleasant French couple in a hired Gametrackers vehicle, doing the Northern Circuit. The only thing missing in Maralal was the tumbleweed rolling down the street! This is the capital of Samburu County, yet the town was a small, ramshackle market town. The locals wore their bright red colours, with shaven heads, and hordes of necklaces to elongate the necks of Samburu women. Maralal is also home to Kenyatta House, where Jomo Kenyatta was detained prior to his release. However, the rather unassuming, modern house has another significance; we were led to understand that Wilfred Thesiger, the British military officer, explorer and writer (he of the Arabian Sands), made his home here.

The following day, we climbed a steep, pine forest cliff, heading north for Loyangalani on the eastern shore of Lake Turkana. Shortly before Baragoi, the scenery dramatically changed as we dropped off a pine-clad, mountainous ridge down to a lunar landscape of solidified lava rocks on the desert floor. The track to Loyangalani is poor; very rocky and requiring care. South Horr is a thriving Samburu community, where the warriors proudly still wear their traditional dress. The village also represents the theoretical dividing line between Samburu and Turkana grazing areas; theoretical, for even today, there are physical, tribal clashes over land and grazing. This terrain is arid, hot desert and scrub. We also saw numerous wild camel herds, a number of dik diks and gerenuk, which hitherto had just been a mythical creature in the safari guidebooks. The gerenuk is an ungulate, with a distinctive, long neck and pointy ears; the Spock of the 'grazer' world. It has a higher grazing reach than a giraffe when raised on its hind legs. We were led to believe that Grevy's zebra were here too, but we saw none.

We bashed our way north on rocky, desert tracks. As we crested a ridgeline, suddenly Lake Turkana appeared. The lake is in a trough, left from shifting tectonic plates (one mantle pushing over the other) when the rift was created. An apt European reference to it being the 'Jade Sea' arises from the turquoise colour when observing the lake from a distance. This is due to algae rising to the surface in calm weather. I say European reference, for the lake was formerly known as Lake Rudolf, named in honour of Crown Prince Rudolf of Austria by a Hungarian from an Austrian expedition in 1888.

Lake Turkana is the world's largest, permanent desert and alkaline lake. It remains volcanic, for the central, uninhabited island can still erupt. Counter intuitively, the area endures frequent and violent storms propagated by the lake warming and cooling slower than the surrounding land. This fosters violent windblasts akin to artillery fire swamping boats and fishermen. Scott Griffin describes the effects of such weather in his book, Medair: My

Heart is Africa, documenting his 1996 adventures as a pilot with the Flying Doctors Service. The Canadian flew his small prop plane across the Atlantic (and back) to offer medical support. He also narrates his misadventure of an ill-advised landing on Turkana's South Island, also known for its Nile crocodiles. Struggling with light, space and time, he caught a wind draft at the last moment that got him airborne, which seconds later could have enforced a swim home.

The Turkana people are a small, hardy bunch, scratching an existence as semi-nomadic cattle, goat and camel herders, yet remaining chronically vulnerable to starvation. The lives and culture of the Turkana is centred around their livestock, with a direct connotation between cattle and wealth for each herder. Their livestock sees them through harsh times and drought. Three rivers (primarily the Omo) feed the lake, which has no outflow; it is an endorheic lake, where the only water loss is through evaporation. The brackish water can be drunk, but as it has excessive fluoride and is diseased from wildlife and excessive cattle grazing; the locals rely on underground springs for drinking water. The variation of lake water volume was described in Blaine Harden's book, Africa - Despatches from a Fragile Continent. As the Washington Post bureau chief in the late 1980s, he was both a hard, fearless reporter in a unique position to observe the banal incidents and interventions from well-meaning (big-spending) donors/organisations at first hand.

The Norwegian government (Norad) sought to help the people of Lake Turkana, to alleviate their severe water stress. Norad could not appreciate the over-reliance on livestock, given their proximity to the lake. The Norwegians understood fishing; why were the locals not sustaining themselves with fish? The lake was vast and well-stocked. The locals were not fishermen; they were suspicious of the water and believed the lake could not be trusted. The Norwegians could teach the locals to love fish and they would build a fish processing (freeze-drying) factory on the water's edge and migrate them towards a piscatorial future. The factory would provide jobs and wealth to an area in need. The locals were encouraged to sell their goats for boats and support was provided to the reluctant fishermen. A factory was built and produced quality products from the initial fish catches. A year is a long time in Africa and the rains failed. The fishermen struggled without their goats; the lake waters receded until it was too far to carry the day's catch to the factory. To chill the fish to freezing point (due to the high daytime temperatures) would have consumed all of Kenya's electricity, so the excessive energy costs made the fish far too expensive. Inevitably, the inland $2bn factory closed. The Omo River in the north was experiencing a once-in-a-30-year drought, so the lake shrank and disappeared, along with the majority of the fish. Many of the 20,000 Turkana encouraged to fish were destitute without their livestock; many died.

We pressed on towards Loyangalani (meaning 'a place of many trees'), our target for the day, but progress was slow. The Jade Sea looked impressive, but the flat light and heat shimmer prevented us from capturing a quality photograph. As we approached the village, we noticed the low, oval rondavels had an air gap near ground level that lent a makeshift impression. Our vehicle was mobbed by the locals and it turned out they wanted to know the location of the supply ship. Err, what supply ship, and from where? We never really found out the truth. We understood that there were two camping options; a posh oasis lodge, which had long fallen into disrepair, and El Molo, which we used. Also staying there were researchers from the Nairobi Museum, examining the local diet, tracking nutrition and disease. We didn't see a dilapidated fish processing plant, nor the thriving village community depicted as the setting for John le Carré's novel, The Constant Gardener, that was also filmed here.

The researchers were travelling to North Horr and were happy for us to tag along. Their driver had driven up from Maralal too, in a Land Rover. It turned out that he was one of Wilfred Thesiger's personal drivers - small world. We were glad of the guide to North Horr, for the route was less than obvious and our map was poor. David had told us of an ecolodge gem at Kalacha which, despite the GPS reference he provided, was cleverly hidden. At North Horr, the researchers stopped at the Catholic mission to stay with Father Graham, the priest here, formerly from Germany. The church was rather incongruous; it was a massive, stone building with a plastic, sail-like fascia over its steeple, with little else all around. Father Graham was very hospitable and took in the lost sheep. He gave us water and allowed us to make a sketch of his excellent wall map. He recommended that we cross the Chalbi Desert to Kalacha, in preference to the stony track on the map. He also recommended the desert route on to Marsabit, from where we could tackle the dreaded corrugations of the infamous Marsabit-Moyale road the following day, if we wanted to go to Ethiopia; but he did imply a more direct route to Moyale was possible.

Father Graham's advice was spot on and we loved the Chalbi Desert. The sand crust was firm and the track clearly defined. It was reminiscent of a salt pan with a straight track through an endless, flat, desert landscape. The heat haze and camels in the distance leant an air of space and enormity. We found Kalacha oasis easily, but the ecolodge was well camouflaged. The locals were oblivious to its existence; so much for ecotourism engaging the locals! We were considering switching on the GPS when we stumbled across it. What a haven amid the harsh surroundings. Lying low within an oasis of palm trees, it was obvious from a southerly direction. They had us booked for the previous week, so when we arrived, the face of the staff lit up; they were relieved to know we were not lost in the desert. There was a steady stream of visitors and we spoke to a couple who were just leaving to tour northern Kenya on a KTM motorcycle. Despite looking like something from Mad Max, they were charming and very helpful. They appeared to have little gear and certainly the scratched leathers, shorts and flip-flops would not help should they tumble, but best of luck to them. Having the place to ourselves was so peaceful and relaxing for the few hours under a cooling atap, before a young male and female walked out from the edge of the oasis and requested rooms. They turned out to be postgraduate researchers returning to Ethiopia, also avoiding the Marsabit-Moyale road. They were travelling cross-country via the Huri Mountains, on Father Graham's northern route, leaving only a 70 kilometre dash on the dreaded main road to Moyale. Good - they wanted company. Stuart, who turned up with a battered Toyota truck, had some GPS coordinates. He was running an NGO project in the Bale Mountains, studying the Ethiopian wolf. It sounded really interesting and we thought to accept his invitation to visit the project, although we had a sort of time commitment to meet Vanessa in Addis. Alistair hailed from Durban but had previously studied the wildlife here in northern Kenya, looking at the domestic and wild grazing competition. He was delighted to note the increased number of gerenuk. Nat, a Mexican student who had lived, studied and travelled extensively, was joining them both in Bale. We understood that her wealthy father owned a significant Pepsi franchise in Mexico, but she was focused on women's rights groups in Ethiopia.

They were a friendly crew, but were inconsistent in the things they said; they didn't really know each other at all, but they asked us to join them to Moyale. The following morning, we drove through thick scrub and arid, dry bush, on a very twisty, turning route. Their truck had seen better days and it wasn't long before they had a puncture. We fixed it (thanks to our air compressor) and pressed on, stopping 20 kilometres short of the main road to bush camp, hidden behind a major rock and cliff, so we lit a fire and chatted. The heat of the day soon left; it was a chilly night. Up at dawn, they were ready for the off. Again, it was strange, for Stuart was very jittery. He explained that his truck wouldn't go fast, so once on the road, I should press on. Whilst this made sense (for I could minimise the corrugations through speed that he couldn't sustain), if there was trouble or an ambush, we would be hit first, so clearly he was playing a double game? To my mind, if there was trouble, going slowly, we'd both cop it. Speed would be our friend to drive through if possible and we'd be compromised if they couldn't. That road was a gamble and we didn't want to wait for the military convoy either. The die was cast; come on, road – do your worst.

Chapter 17
High expectations for the 'Roof of Africa'

We were really looking forward to Ethiopia, believing it to be a highlight of our trip; a unique country, having forged their own independence. Ethiopia radiates potential, yet so few visit. It remains the only African country not to have been colonised, despite Italy's partial five-year attempt in 1936. Ethiopia evolved as a modern country from 2,000 years or more of isolation. The Axumites, around 4-6AD, evolved a language and commercial farming using the plough and terracing still recognisable today. They maintain their own Julian calendar, celebrate New Year on 11th September and Christmas on 7th January.

Just as unique is Ethiopia's flora and fauna, arising from their geographical isolation and high plateau. Much of the northern area is Christian, maintaining unique Orthodox churches, hewn from solid rock, such as Lalibella. Many claim they hold significant religious artefacts, like the fabled 'Ark of the Covenant' at Axum. The headwaters for the Blue Nile rise within the Ethiopian Highlands; around 40% of their land is above 2,000 metres and 85% of that above 3,000 metres. The plateau is well-watered, fertile and cultivated, although this land needs to feed an excessive and expanding population. Even in a good year, the country struggles to feed itself. Little wonder that years of extended drought, following a brutal civil war in the 1970s, presented the world with unprecedented starvation and suffering that existing charities and world aid groups were incapable of supporting. Most would be aware of the world's outcry and response, in part championed by Bob Geldof and his Band Aid campaign - a clarion call to alleviate deprivation and human misery. So how could any country live up to such expectation? We were about to find out.

We arrived at the Moyale border crossing so much earlier than the scheduled military escort was expected, so unsurprisingly, the Kenyan authorities were not around. After a couple of hours on the bone-shaking corrugations, we thankfully arrived at the Moyale escarpment without drama. At one point along the road, a loose-hanging chain across the route sent the heart rate up a few notches. Was this an ambush? If so, it was a pretty crap one! I had time to slow down and drive around the edge of the unmanned checkpoint. Just as well I was awake (never an issue on corrugations) and not drawn into the soporific nature of the long, hot rumble along the pancake-flat plain.

Once up the ridgeline, the small town at the top sat astride the border. Administration huts were on either side of a shabby, fenced gate – the border crossing. The Kenyan wooden huts were functional but dated. The offices were open but there were no staff to process us, despite a bunch of locals waiting. They told us that 'the man with the stamp' would be back soon. Interestingly, the 'man' reappeared within 10 minutes of our arrival and stamped our Carnet, apologising profusely for not being there when we arrived. We were not used to such behaviour; apparently he had been to the post office. Then the immigration officer arrived and we had our passports stamped too…it was all too easy.

The Ethiopian side was predictably chaotic. We had to present various documents to separate brick buildings, whilst dodging the incessant clamour from the Kenyan shilling change boys. At immigration, we were given an exit card to complete (bells started to ring), but assuming this was the only form, we completed it and moved on to get our passports stamped. We didn't realise at the time (their stamps were impossible to read) that the officer gave us an exit stamp, ignoring the absence of an entry stamp. Customs were on the opposite side of the road, where we spent a hot and airless hour waiting for the clerk to meticulously copy all the details from our Carnet on to another form. They did not stamp the Carnet (Ethiopia did not officially recognise the form) but handed back a copy of their form, for which we were asked to pay one US dollar.

For the first time, Daph was searched; we had been warned that this could be a long and thorough process, but it turned out to be a cursory affair. We were supposed to declare things like the laptop and digital camera, but despite the rumours, they were not bothered. We had a little argument about our copy of the Carnet, stamped by the Ethiopian Embassy in Nairobi. The officer wanted the original copy, yet we had been told very firmly in Nairobi not to give this up to anyone. Fortunately, it was lunchtime, and everyone was trying to get out of the building as quickly as possible, so he settled for a copy and we departed.

That was easy…but as we left town, we fell directly into their trap, a police roadblock. The same passport official who had stamped the passports had changed and was now demanding our passports. I recognised him and greeted him so, but now we were challenged by 'his exit stamp' error. We had to go back to immigration, which was more irritating than a pathetic scam (no money changed hands), exacerbated by everyone out at lunch. By chance, we collared a different immigration officer as he was leaving, who understood the issue and sorted it. Following leisurely behind, Stuart obviously knew the score. They were processed along with us but parked in town for lunch, avoiding the roadblock (he could have said?). They were unsurprised at our return, although they double-checked their entry stamps. Whilst we pressed on for Addis, they planned their two-day trip to Bale. Yet again, we wondered whether we should have taken their offer to see wolves.

The road outside Moyale was tar that ran all the way to Addis. The potholes were not too bad and the countryside was low, flat African scrub. Scattered litter was everywhere around Moyale - not a very appealing invitation to the country. As we climbed imperceptibly towards Yebello National Park, the land became more undulating; we had obviously risen in altitude, for the temperature was dropping and it started raining. The main challenge was trying to avoid the cattle and animals strolling on the roads, as well as the odd wandering local. We weren't going to make Addis in one day as the guide suggested. We broke our journey at Fiseha Genet. There were no camping options - a recurring theme - so we checked into a hotel on the main road at dusk. We chose the Lacewon Hotel as it offered secure parking. It was a strange, cultural mish-mash, being Ethiopian, with a Chinese restaurant. We were unaware when checking in, but enjoyed a fabulous (if spicy) Chinese meal. However, the coffee was outstanding - Ethiopian black gold.

The sheer number of animals wandering on the road was crazy; travel was punctuated by slowing down for people and animals. The following day's progress was slower than expected. The terrain became progressively hilly, but the closer we got to Addis, the roads improved, unlike the standard of driving! We reached the capital just after lunch and headed straight for the British Embassy. Addis Ababa is striving to be the 'political capital of Africa'. It hosts the African Union (formed in 2002, superseding the Organisation of African Unity, OAU) and United Nations Economic Commission for Africa (ECA), bundled with numerous other continental and international organisations. Addis Ababa was founded in 1886 by

Emperor Menelik II, King of the Shewa province, before anointing himself as Emperor of Ethiopia. Successfully avoiding all colonialisation until 1936, when the Italian army invaded from Eritrea and Djibouti, the Italians sought to unify their Italian East African colony with Libya. Their partial occupation remained until 1941, when Addis was liberated by Major Orde Wingate and a returning Haile Selassie. In 1963, Haile Selassie formed the Organisation of African Unity.

The British Embassy lies within the grounds of the original emperor's palace, a large, sprawling parkland with its own golf course. It is a tranquil, walled oasis within the centre of Addis. Vanessa worked in the visa section and, under her guidance, we were able to initiate our Sudanese visas. Vanessa was the soul of efficiency and ensured that we had a letter of introduction for the Sudanese that afternoon. She had also done some research to support our up-country travel and had earmarked some onward destinations and hotels for us. It transpired that camping was not common in Ethiopia - frowned upon, even - but hotel accommodation was relatively cheap, so we secured some bookings for our northern cultural tour.

Addis Ababa was no different from any bustling mega-city; people walked in the road everywhere, plus the vagrant animal problem did not improve. We saw cattle grazing on the grassy, middle section of a dual carriageway and stray dogs and cats everywhere. Vanessa booked us into the Hotel Axum, being cheap and one of the few hotels with secure parking, but in all honesty, it was a dump. Yet it was so much better than camping in the Bel Air Hotel grounds, an unpleasant dust bowl. Vanessa also arranged for Daph to get a service with the embassy fleet manager, which would have made camping a challenge without the roof tent, so the Axum worked.

The next morning, we took the hotel transport to the Sudanese Embassy, presented our letter, two photos, a copy of the Carnet, our passports and our proposed route through Sudan. We had to pay US$61 each and were told to come back the following day after 2pm. So quick? We were not hopeful, yet they were - well done, Vanessa. After the embassy drop off, we strolled up the main street in Addis and around some back streets. Addis is famous for its strong, flavourful coffee and pastries, a delightful legacy from their Italian period. There is a café on most street corners. In parts of the older city, the streets have wide boulevards and gardened, central parks, plus wrought iron balustrades fixed around upper balconies, common in Mediterranean towns and cities. The Addis shanty towns are jammed between the smarter, bourgeoning, hi-tech areas; it was like the city was at war with itself. Being at altitude (around 7,500 feet) and very hilly, walking is easy but taxing. We calculated that we could cut through a township to the Hilton Hotel, then grab a taxi back to our hotel. The Hilton is on a wide boulevard, near the president's palace. Addis is a safe place to walk, providing one is careful, even after dark. Apart from the usual beggars, the general populace is very friendly. That said, we became unwitting victims of a pick-pocket scam. It had to happen at some point, but we were fine walking through the township area. Maybe it was because we were not as vigilant once in the (safer?) boulevard near the Hilton.

We both had an inkling about something, but were not quick enough to take preventative action; events occurred very suddenly. We were following a couple of Rastafarian lads. The Rasta cultural following is big in Ethiopia, for the Jamaicans identified Hailie Selassie as their cultural leader. The Rasta lads were 'jamming' down the street like most boisterous youths. I'm ashamed to admit that I was wary about any threat emanating from them, so we were taking it slow. Just then, a lad pretending to sell a newspaper came up from behind me and shoved a newspaper around me and under my nose. As I started to wave him away, somewhat surprised, I felt his hand go inside my trouser pocket, at the same time I felt a nudge to the back of my knee, causing me to fall. I don't recall shouting, but I must have, because I was acutely aware that my perceived threat - the two Rastafarian lads - were starting to run towards us. I assumed this was the real threat. As I was falling, I slammed my hand down and half-grasped the thief's invading hand within my pocket, which he was now tugging to get free. Partly because the thief was trying to pull his hand free and part instinct, I swung my free leg around in a pirouctte to trip up the newspaper thief as I fell. It sort of worked; the thief only half-tripped, causing him to drop what he had in his hand as he ran off. Moments later, the two Rasta lads ran past me, shouting at my assailant as they gave chase after the thief. I bounced to my feet as I was worried and unaware what had happened to Catherine, on my blind side. Thankfully, she was unharmed; shocked yes, but unharmed. I picked up the cheap watch and a few notes. I was slightly disorientated, but no material loss was apparent; we were OK.

I don't know how common this is, especially on a main tourist street with an armed guard outside the Hilton Hotel, for it was either a very desperate, elaborate scam or just plain bloody stupid. I started to feel really silly. The Rastas had chased the thief up the road; one broke off the chase and ran to get police help. The locals on the street gathered around us and were very shocked. One man told us that this was a rare occurrence and asked us not to become insecure. The irony being that we had just been walking down some dodgy side street where nothing happened. I guess this is where the criminals find the rich tourist pickings. Of greatest concern, Catherine had our valuables and the camera across her chest in a flat body bag, but thankfully she was not targeted. The Rasta lads came back all sweaty and very apologetic that they'd failed to catch the thief. Indeed, they were most indignant that such things should occur on their streets. Who knows if this was part of a larger scam or genuine; no one was caught and the locals and police were apologetic, yet not really bothered. Nor were we bothered, as crucially, we were fine and nothing was lost.

We stayed in Addis for a couple more days. Vanessa and Glyn taking us to their favourite restaurants. For the imminent weekend, they were heading south for a break at Shala National Park lake, so we planned to set off on the northern circuit. I spent the morning checking the oils and filters, tightening parts that needed it, and ensuring the right lubricants and oils were changed with Marko at the Embassy. Daph's front axle bushes were worn so we replaced them. Given Ethiopia's roads north, I am so glad we did.

We visited the National Museum to see 'Lucy'; the common name being AL 288-1. Lucy is several hundred pieces of fossilised bone representing 40% of a female skeleton of the hominin species, Australopithecus afarensis. Her nickname 'Lucy' was reputedly acquired from the Beatles song 'Lucy in the Sky with Diamonds' that was repeatedly playing in the expedition camp by her founder, the American paleoanthropologist, Donald Johanson, in 1974. Thought to date back around 3.2 million years ago, the skeleton has a small skull, not unlike non-hominin apes, but critically, there was evidence of an upright walking gait. Lucy was found on the eastern Ethiopian border with Djibouti in the Awash River valley; this area was thought to have endured significant water run-off from the Rift Valley formation.

Near the Hilton and the (new) African Union Headquarters was a premium hotel for Africa, the new, five-star Sheraton hotel. Whilst it was opulent and impressive, it proclaimed to be the 'best hotel in Africa'. It was good, especially given African standards, but it felt somewhat lame to us, more like a pushy four-star in the UK. We felt we had enjoyed better in Cape Town or Lamu, but I suppose location and expectation was everything in Addis, as it sought to find its place of prominence within Africa. With all the important politicians passing through the city, its success was assured.

Most tourists fly between the spaced out, northern, historic circuit tourist highlights, for the road system was awful, clogged with dilapidated HGVs and overladen coaches fighting for every inch. The internal road system here was poor, although significant improvements had been made by the NGO/ aid community. The Coptic Orthodox churches around Lalibela can be reached in one hard day's driving, but effectively it took us two. Using the Debre Birhan road, we broke our journey at Kembolcha, after seven hours. From what we witnessed, Kembolcha was little more than a truck stop and it's fair to say, we had a poor night in a shabby hotel and rubbish food. Unbeknown to us at the time, Kembolcha was the base for the UN effort in 1984, centred around the local airport. There were roadworks, numerous herds of cattle/goats/donkeys on the road, not to mention loads of people. Our drive north was anything but relaxing, although the countryside became increasingly dramatic the further north we travelled. There are precipitous mountain roads, sheer cliffs and very green, fertile valleys. The hillsides are often terraced and cultivated and, on what little lowland there was, there were large, state-owned farms.

Ethiopian driving is poor, hampered by atrocious roads and poor-quality vehicles; but when stimulants and drugs are added (by drivers struggling to stay alert), concern increases. Catherine had been reading about Khat. In Kevin Rushby's book, Eating the Flowers of Paradise, he travels around the Horn of Africa where psychoactive leaves are legal and chewed openly. Whilst Yemen appears to be the main locus, the Highland Road to Addis is a popular trading route. Interestingly, it can be bought openly on London's streets, mainly in the East End, where it's legal, although the drug, whose effects are described on a scale from 'mild as tea to as addictive as cocaine', has been banned by the US. Khat, sometimes spelt Qat, is native to eastern Ethiopia, with a social history akin to chewing coca leaves of South America or betel nuts from Asia. The WHO classifies the alkaloid cathinone as a stimulant that causes euphoria and excitement. Whilst suppressing appetite, critically WHO believe the addictive, psychological dependence is not a serious problem. We started to observe the large bundles of leaves being transported as we drove north.

The Ethiopian Highlands are the largest, continuous highlands on the continent, frequently referred to as the 'Roof of Africa'. These fertile uplands manage three harvests a year. The coffee plant was exported to the Arabian peninsula and it's believed this is where the name coffee is derived; from Arabic gahwah, or kaffa. The highlands were once The Kingdom of Kaffa, an early modern state. The spread and press of humanity has over-farmed these lands and the natural, wild vegetation has largely been removed.

Our second day in the highlands found the road splitting at Weldiya, denoting the start of the new road to Werota, near Lake Tana, made from a hard gravel/maram, built by NGOs to enable aid distribution and crossing of the high plateau. This new road meant that our maps were out-of-date; we were on the point of turning round when we asked advice from one of the local farmers who approached us. We were told that we should carry on to a small village and then turn right. Taking this advice, we dropped down off the escarpment and came across a magnificent, tarred road just short of Lalibella. This tar road links the local airport and town, justifying the fly-in tourist money. We made the mistake of stopping halfway down the escarpment for lunch; within minutes, we were surrounded by extremely persistent and annoying children, so we had to move on, leaving them our food. We obviously recognised their need; had we been in their position, we probably would have been just as insistent.

Modern Lalibella was little more than a dusty, undeveloped town, yet delightfully free of the usual tourist panphilia that generally surrounds a site or place of significance. We arrived at the Jerusalem Guest House at approximately 3pm and arranged for a guide to take us around that afternoon. The eponymous, rock-hewn churches of Lalibela are named after the 13th century Zagwe Dynasty's King Lalibella. He built eleven, rock-hewn churches to recreate the holy city of Jerusalem in his own kingdom. The first Christian church was commissioned here by Aksumite King Kaleb after he founded his city of Roha in the 6th century AD. Today, these churches are protected by UNESCO. Held in importance by Ethiopian Orthodox Christians for their spiritual and symbolic pilgrimage, the churches are used for daily worship and prayer. Each monolithic and semi-monolithic church, along with their inter-connecting tunnels and passages, was excavated using basic hand tools.

On our first evening, we saw the Church of Saint George, which was quite memorable. Near sundown, standing over a small, partially hidden hole, emerged a stone cross tomb at rock level. They do not impose or claim huge hero status, but they are utterly remarkable. The Saint George's Cross is exact; amazing, considering they were hewn from the monolithic rock by hand. The hollowed interior contains a simple shrine to Saint George and, behind a curtain, forbidden to anyone other than the priest, lies an apparent replica of the Ark of the Covenant. You need three or four hours to see all the churches. We split our tour over two days, which made it all the more important to agree a written tour price upfront. One needed to be careful as the guides were inflating their prices by the hour, ignoring verbal agreements. Without a written price, which they disliked, by the end of the tour, they were asking for eight times the agreed value, which excluded tips and extras. Most of the guides sub-contract a boy to 'look after your shoes' and things, for these need to be left at each church entrance and the boy requires his tip. On the first evening, we toured the western group of six churches and the following morning, we completed the rest. Half the churches are linked by tunnels and alleyways carved from the rock, but during our visit, most of the free-standing churches had scaffolding and some form of overhead protection, erected under an NGO environmental programme.

Most of the churches are very cramped; enough space for a priest, a few singers and a limited congregation. There was also gender segregation; men and women had to enter by separate doors and sit in different parts of the church. Each church has its own set of treasures and processional crosses that the priest will display for your photos, providing you make the necessary (US dollars only) donation. Visiting all the churches was not cheap. During dinner, guests from the posh Roha hotel joined us in our alfresco restaurant hut for an elaborate coffee ceremony after the meal. All these tourists were being flown around and were simply unaware of the wider Ethiopia around them. It may sound harsh but they were kept in their tourist bubble, inured from the realities around them, in a privileged world of tips and 'petit cadeau'. I dare say none really were aware of anything different - why should they be? We endured a similar experience in China in 1994, just after the country opened up. It was the only way to travel between the sights, unless you had independent means or extended time. We endured an escorted tour, similarly inured within our isolated, Western bubble. It is true that we saw all the amazing sights and fantastic features. I distinctly recall being allocated a 'generous and extended' 45 minutes to view the Terracotta Warriors at Xian, to then be forced to spend two hours in the expensive, tatty gift shop at the end. Being free-thinking and enquiring Westerners, I guess we have become too used to evaluating everything upon its merit and not having it imposed upon us. I'm ashamed to say, we found the Lalibela experience a glorified tourist trap; an immense shame, given the magnitude of the original structures and their intricate story.

We were considering the full northern circuit to Axum and the Danakil Depression, although FCO security advised against travel in northern Ethiopia, especially the Danakil Depression. This is the hottest place on the earth, physically and due to security. Ethiopia's highest point is the Semien Mountains, home to the gelada baboon (those monkeys that run up and down the vertiginous cliffs), the Ethiopian wolf and the Walia ibex, to name but a few. However, we believed it insufficiently compelling to make the full journey on what were already trying roads, especially as we would have to backtrack at some point, assuming we got as far as Axum. Axum had obvious attractions, not least the fabled home of the Ark of the Covenant. The Old Testament implies that the Ark was to be held in the Temple of Solomon in Jerusalem forever, yet it vanished when Jerusalem was sacked around 586 BC. The Orthodox Christians in Ethiopia believe that the Ark was taken to Axum by Menelik, the son of the Queen of Sheba and King Solomon in around 10 BC. The Book of Exodus states that God commanded Moses to make an Ark of acacia wood, a glided chest created by the Israelites, having been freed from Egyptian slavery by Moses. Within the Ark, Moses placed the two stone tablets with the Ten Commandments. It is believed for the last 50 years that the Ark is retained within the Chapel of the Tablet in Axum by Emperor Haile Selassie, where no one is allowed to enter, except a single holy monk. A great tale - yet one we would be unable to confirm or deny if we even made it that far.

The region of Tigray, bordering with Eritrea, had all sorts of banditry and mishaps for the uninitiated. The border security situation has never been good, but peace collapsed in 2020, when the Eritrean forces invaded, superficially to kill and capture the Tigray People's Liberation Front. Artillery bombardments and organised attacks left 800 people killed in and around the Church of St Mary of Zion in Axum. Wild animals were dragging and eating the cadavers. Widespread looting, rape and murder was reported, with humanitarian organisations warning of a looming crisis, similar to the scale of the mid-eighties, with six million people cut off from help. In addition, heritage experts were alarmed at the looting and cultural annihilation being waged across Tigray.

We never made it to Tigray. To reach Bahar Dar, we needed to retrace our steps to the Weldiya-Werota road and then travel a further six hours. The countryside was dramatic, although we were struck by the large number of aid vehicles, most of which were either broken down by the roadside or were travelling empty in the equal and opposite directions. It was all very strange. What did they know that we didn't? The countryside was littered with old, military wrecks and broken or destroyed tanks (old Soviet era T62 and T72's) from their civil war. Vanessa had booked us into the Tana Hotel, but by the time we found it, we had booked a camping spot at the Ghion Hotel. It was cheap and we had a quiet, grassy site. The Ghion was on the edge of town, with a series of low-lying chalets on the southern shore of Lake Tana. Our camping seemed to be attracting a fair number of visitors who gathered (at a distance) to watch us and look at Daph. It appeared at first glance that they were 'courting couples'; how sweet. We later found out they were not courting; it was a simple, financial transaction for the deed. The local shagging point was under the small cliff below us but thankfully, we were blissfully ignorant!

The following morning, we set off to visit the Tisissat Falls on the Blue Nile, sometimes called 'the Smoke of the Nile' or 'Tis Abay Falls'. The locals were maddening, trying extremely hard to persuade us that we needed to hire a guide to show us the way. It was quite unnecessary as there was only one track and it was obvious which way to go. We had to be quite firm in declining all offers, which by now were becoming annoying and utterly disrespectful. From the car park, the route dropped down to the 17th century stone bridge over the Blue Nile gorge and takes you over the hill above the Falls. As you crest the hill, the Falls are spread out, almost half a kilometre below. It was a breathtaking sight. It was possible to walk all the way down to the base of the Falls to swim and, as delightful as that would be, we thought the better view and ambiance was to drink in the full majesty of the Falls from a distance.

Walking back to Daph, we witnessed the full horror of the local guides, who had leached themselves upon a poor, young, Asian couple. One look at the scene was laughable and simultaneously lamentable. Centre stage was the besieged, young couple, clinging to each other, frightened and struggling to find their way down the path. All around them were the court jesters, one with a parasol, another couple as guides, another to carry her bag, another to sing them a song, whilst another played the lyre. God knows how many were dancing around these poor, well-meaning tourists. Our hearts went out to them; clearly, their culture is not to insult or disappoint, but they were being abused to the point of destroying any pleasure. The poor girl had a haunted, besieged, pleading expression as we passed.

Extra vigilance is required at all times. Not only was this a clear example of the haves and the have-nots; it was a sad indictment of what we observed to be a pervading, aid-dependent culture. Statistically, Addis Ababa has the worst accident rate in Africa, but I guess of only those recorded accidents? It's not difficult to know why it is so bad here; no driving tests or training, poor or failing cars, lack of awareness and road rules not being enforced, not to mention the shocking state of the roads, but this is by no means exclusive to Ethiopia. A key factor has to be the livestock constantly roaming across and along the road. Many stories abound of Western drivers being financially fleeced should they have the misfortune to hit an animal, let alone a person. Livestock appeared to spend more time on what might be described as the road than grazing, so no wonder they are not as healthy as they should be. On more than one occasion, we witnessed goats, cattle and donkeys being actively driven into the road in front of our vehicle. The multitude of reasons are all designed to extort money in compensation. Were it a veiled attempt to slow us down and foster goodwill to derive a tip or handout, there were some serious miscalculations going on. The ultimate is for a person to walk in front of a vehicle, the poor driver having little chance to avoid the pedestrian. Given that contact is inevitable, the driver then stops to check on the casualty, being human by nature. A fatal mistake, for the inevitable crowd develops and surrounds the vehicle and the driver is then 'caught'. If the casualty is dead, injured or otherwise, the driver is guilty and then has to pay compensation as extorted by the growing crowd, who are meanwhile stripping anything and everything from the vehicle. We had a few close calls, but thankfully escaped without any experience of the above.

After the Falls, we went to Gondar to see the walled Fasil Ghebbi Fortress and palace compound, once the seat of Ethiopian emperors and the capital during the reign of the Fasilides in the 17th century. Situated in the foothills of the Semien Mountains, the town possesses many spectacular churches and castles. Dominating these is the immense 17th century castle of Emperor Fasilides, which combines Portuguese, Indian and local architectural styles. This royal enclosure covers 7.6 hectares, in which there are five castles, interconnected by tunnels and raised walkways. Outside the complex is Debre Berhan Selassie Church, with an interior of elaborate murals, including a ceiling of faces. Our hotel, the Goha, was at the top of the city in a mock crusader castle. The view from the hotel's gardens was fantastic, although we were in for a storm; the heat haze and approaching cloud obscured what would have made some outstanding photographs right across the city. Interestingly, the hotel was government-run, with reasonable food, although hot water was only available between certain times, and rationed. Although the room rate was set at US$50 , they would only take local currency, so we had to go to a bank the next morning to pay.

Once I had found a bank willing to exchange dollars, I was provided with what could only be described as the worst customer service I have ever experienced (globally), way beyond the shoddy service throughout Ethiopia. In the bank, I handed over dollars (in good condition) but received local birr that were so worn and illegible that I couldn't even read what I was getting, let alone determine if I had the correct amount. When I questioned it, I had the door slammed in my face. Trying to remain calm, I asked to see the manager, who was reluctant to appear, but to his credit, he eventually did. I asked him to count the birr I had just been given; he couldn't. When I asked him if it was fair that I should accept such an exchange, again he reluctantly had to agree with my point and changed the money to vaguely more readable notes. Despite the manager's contrition, that event was too much; get me out of Ethiopia! It was just too bloody annoying and insufficiently interesting to stay any longer. Trip highlight? You're kidding, we'd had enough, in more ways than we excepted. As we were at the jumping off point to get to Sudan, we were ready to use it.

Dire accounts circulated about the stretch of road to the border at Metema and, given what we had experienced hitherto, we steeled ourselves. It should take around four hours, although we read stories of it taking people several days, especially in the rains which were brewing, but we were also pleased to find a new road. Some parts remained unmade and it was here that we caught up with a couple of Toyota Land Cruisers containing seven French people, heading for Egypt. Intriguingly, they were part of a consortium of owners for the Land Cruisers, which they had used for the last two to three years to travel throughout Africa. They had Carnets issued by the French AA that covered Egypt, although they had to pay more for these than the standard Carnet. What an excellent concept - a consortia to maximise the vehicles and the group experience.

Since we passed through this green and latterly arid valley, today it represents something like the Somme, due to the Grand Ethiopian Renaissance Dam project. Constructed over the last 10 - 15 years, this will be one of the world's largest hydroelectric gravity dams. Built to address Ethiopia's acute electricity shortage, it is designed to offer surplus to neighbours. It does raise the interesting debate about 'ownership' of rivers. Egypt, unsurprisingly, is objecting, concerned about critical irrigation downstream and an implication of a 25% reduction of Blue Nile flow downstream. It remains a controversial programme that demands cooperation across all affected countries, something that has been limited since inception.

The distance between the Ethiopian and Sudanese side of the Gallabat border was around 40 metres, but there was a marked difference between the two. The Ethiopian side was relatively efficient in stamping the exit visas and customs declaration. Their building was a green Nissan hut, surrounded in verdant green foliage, with a small storm ditch in front. There were any number of people milling around, either waiting for processing or transport; it was not clear. From where we had parked Daph, I hopped over the storm ditch, taking a more direct path. I thought Catherine had waited with Daph, but it transpired that she had followed me. This only became obvious by the commotion behind me, causing me to turn around. There was Catherine, who had not quite made the storm ditch hop, with one foot well and truly stuck in the muddy ditch. The amusing sight was the three local women standing together around five metres away. Each was dressed in their colourful, calico dresses, baskets at their feet, looking identical. They were standing in a row, all half bent at the waist, leaning forward, with the same arm extended in front of them, with their wrists flapping up and down, calling 'Mister, Mister'. I was agog; Catherine was stuck and getting more frustrated, yet these ladies were rooted to the spot. I guess they helped by drawing my attention to Catherine's plight, but I was astonished that they had not tried to help her. I guess culturally, Catherine 'belonged' to me, although I know Catherine would, rightly, bridle at any such suggestion. I had to help her, not them. I was aware that my humour at her plight wasn't helping, so naturally I ran and extricated Catherine, without her (now extremely smelly) shoe, which had to be recovered separately. Meanwhile, the hand wavers continued to provide the Disney commentary in song, with appropriate oohs and aahs. So, whenever there is a mishap, even to this day, the 'Mister, Mister' phrase is trotted out.

Chapter 18
Changing our religion

The formalities of the Ethiopian side were not replicated on the Sudanese side. The official building was smothered by a village, quite unlike anywhere we'd seen. There was no pushing and shoving, no hawkers or beggars. At customs, we appeared to jump the queue by accident, although people were sitting around doing nothing. We were swiftly processed for one US dollar. Immigration was content with our visa but we were asked to pay a further 4,000 dinar ($16) each to register; clearly a fudge, but we were not in the mood to argue. Interestingly, they wanted this in local currency, and now, of all the ironies, this crossing was the only one we'd experienced with no currency hawkers harassing us. We were directed to the market to find a money changer and whilst haggling, we met the local Gadaref Minister for Education. He was extremely helpful and interested to know more about us. He summoned someone to change our money, which we noted was a good rate.

Immigration complete, we set off to Gadaref on a reasonable gravel road. Care was necessary as there were occasional dongas (dry riverbeds) across the road, where full brakes stopped us crashing through them. We immediately hit a wall of heat. We descended from the mountains at a balmy high 20°C to an oppressive, dry 40°C. Our water consumption increased dramatically, and the landscape flattened. It would be fair to admit we entered Sudan with some trepidation. We had expected Ethiopia to be a highlight, but sadly this was not our experience. Hitherto, all the countries in southern and eastern Africa were relatively similar, not unlike an extended wildlife safari. But north of Kenya, everything changed; the infrastructure was nascent. Europeans or Western travellers were infrequent. Life was more basic on a subsistence level and significantly, the religion had changed. We were prepared, but not for how the people looked back at us.

Ethiopia was difficult to summarise. It has always been an independent 'outlier' within the continent. It struggles to feed itself, even in a good year. I dare say there will be outrage if we suggest that Ethiopia appeared to be dependent upon aid, but I guess it questions how aid is applied. The early

1980s famine galvanised the world's attention to the plight that killed almost one million people. The real question now was how to support, sustain and enable a country; with real help and without sticking plaster? The continent is plagued by corruption, wars and famine to this day. I guess our views weren't helped by my reading Graham Hancock's book, Lords of Poverty. It is a shocking exposé of the corruption, ineptitude and delusion surrounding the aid industry. As a sociologist and journalist with much experience of the developing world, Hancock reports the crass stupidity and impact that well-meant donations have on inequality. He opens with funding and delivery of high-quality refrigerators to Somalia, necessary to preserve key medicines and food products, only to find thousands of them stacked and unused in warehouses, simply because there is no electricity to power them. It goes downhill from there.

Ethiopia was not doing well. Flies were everywhere and assuming flies were an 'indicator' for health and hygiene, Ethiopia was struggling. It was the first time we had really been bothered by insects throughout our travels. Few huts appeared to have toilet facilities, unlike most other countries we had passed. Many people were just defecating at the roadside. Most locals, especially children, were covered by flies, even at the high altitudes, as well as in Addis. For such an advanced culture and heritage, Ethiopia appeared stuck and lagging. The countryside looked like a picture postcard image of Anglo-Saxon, feudal England, especially the Gondar Royal Enclosure. As a large country, Ethiopia now had an all-weather road system, of sorts. The distances, like elsewhere in the continent, were long and arduous. Driving here was frustrating, dangerous and attritional, exacerbated by the local attitudes and the loose animals on the road, unique to Ethiopia. Was it 'learnt' behaviour that Westerners were seen as a 'meal ticket'? We accept that we had privilege and money, but we hadn't encountered adverse behaviour elsewhere. This experience coloured our thoughts as we left the relatively known part of our journey, heading to countries with potentially less. In our experience, we found that those with the least offered the most.

We were told to register at Gadaref police station for an onward travel permit. We needed to wait as the station also doubled as an immigration centre. Ironically, once seen, it transpired that no such registration was necessary. By now, it was getting dark and we had no overnight plan, but the police offered their compound for the night. We hoped that when the sun went down, the temperature might drop, but no, it remained just as hot - so much for desert temperatures plummeting at night! Though secure, the compound was a rubbish dump; we were grateful for the elevated roof tent, capturing what breeze we could. Five minutes after leaving the following morning, we heard a horrendous, squealing sound from a front wheel. Seized bearings? I assumed the worst. Stopping in a deserted back street, I removed the front wheel. Interestingly, an old boy kept the children away from pestering us, as if they were goats or sheep, and he too kept his distance. Hitherto, we'd be mobbed. Once the wheel was off, a couple of men, from what we discovered to be a nearby garage, wandered over to help remove the offending stone lodged between the brake disc and guard. I was grateful that it was nothing more serious and we were soon on our way.

On the main Port Sudan/ Khartoum Highway, we were stopped at a toll booth and charged 600 dinar, with the all-important receipt, conveying us to Khartoum. It was 411 kilometres which took six hours of very hot driving. If we ever had a justification to switch on Daph's aircon, it was now, but we ignored it. The sooner we acclimatised, the better. Daph's front air vents provided an invaluable breeze whilst driving. The tarred highway was manic; there were huge, hard to spot potholes and a strange variety of speeding trucks and coaches of questionable roadworthiness. The worst offenders were the brand-new, super coaches that appear from behind and overtake at speeds above 160 kilometres per hour, regardless of what is approaching.

The best view of Khartoum is on the bridge over the confluence of the White and Blue Nile, but if one took a photo, you would end up in jail, for it would include the Presidential Palace, a big no-no. The river divides Khartoum into three: central Khartoum, Khartoum North and Omdurman to the west. The origin of the name Khartoum is contested. Some argue that the translation is from Arabic 'khurtum', meaning 'trunk or hose'. The early Dinka settlers and their scholars believe the name is derived from a Dinka word 'khar-tuom' meaning 'place where rivers meet'. The Nubian word 'agartum' (or the 'abode of Atum') implies the Nubian reference to 'God of creation'. Other Beja scholars suggest Khartoum is derived from the Beja word 'hartoom', which means 'meeting'. Either way, a settlement has existed here for millennia. In 1821, on the incorporation of Sudan into his realm, Ibrahim Pasha, the son of Egypt's ruler, Muhammad Ali Pasha, established Khartoum 15 miles north of the ancient city of Soba. Initially only an outpost for the Egyptian Army, Khartoum grew quickly, initially from slave trading. Captain James Grant arrived in Khartoum in 1863 as part of Captain Speke's expedition. By 1884, troops loyal to the Mahdi, Muhammad Ahmad, lay siege to Khartoum (defended by General Gordon), culminating in the infamous massacre of the Anglo-Egyptian garrison by the Mahdists. In 1898, retribution came in the bloody Battle of Omdurman, when Mahdist forces defending the city were defeated by British forces under General (later Lord) Kitchener.

The shiny, modern Hilton hotel in the centre of Khartoum was frequented by business travellers and the more affluent. Apparently, you could get a beer here, in a Muslim country. Whilst true, it was a non-alcoholic version of Heineken, doing its best to reach parts not tasted before. As we arrived at the Hilton, so too did the French; sweeping in like a motorcade and dumping their Land Cruisers to be valeted, they checked in to their pre-booked suites.

The Hilton could not provide the information we sought, with no maps of local information nor the ability to change money. A nearby hotel was more established (old) and very colonial (faded glory), but Holiday Villa was built for the heat; it was cool even without aircon - bliss. We could change money and communicate online. We were trying to get hold of an old university and army pal who was working here for the Foreign Office, but Ed was not responding. The Holiday Villa was on the Nile, next to the Presidential Palace. Nearby was the Blue Nile Sailing Club that had General Kitchener's sailing barge as an office. According to Africa on a Shoestring (our sole guide by now), we could camp here for US$11, but the facilities looked dreadful. The toilets were a health hazard, there was no hot water and you had to use the dusty car park.

We heard about a campsite on the southern edge of town - the National Camping Ground (a repurposed army camp), approximately 10 kilometres south of the centre. It had basic facilities but for a dollar, it was both clean and safe. It was temporarily housing Ethiopian refugees and other dispossessed souls awaiting onward processing. Also, a bunch of Sudanese athletes were training at the camp. Finding shade was challenging but we were allowed to park under the few trees on their grassy beds. We became a source of interest for the encamped spectators who were intrigued by our roof tent. Most just sat a few yards away and watched, but the kids came up closer. Young Attack, a local lad and camp cleaner, told us that they get bikers and other vehicles here, but not today. We walked around the camp and watched the local lads play soccer (mostly bare-footed) until the light faded; actually, their skill levels were high. We both felt the atmosphere, eyes watching us all the time, not unlike the Tim Robbins character in Shawshank Redemption, walking around the State Penitentiary waiting for a hit. Clearly our minds were racing five steps ahead for we had nothing to hide and were not 'locked in'.

The heat by day was as oppressive as it was by night. Unlike most major, hot desert cities, Khartoum's temperature stays above 30°C all year round. The climate seasons are divided into hot, hotter and very hot, so it was ironic to know we were experiencing the cooler season. It didn't feel like it; daytime temperatures were 40+°C and not much less at night. A hot Harmattan (dry, continental trade wind) sweeps in from the desert with dry, stable air. Nights brought no relief and left us sweating in the roof tent with all the flaps and doors open. One night, we rigged up a fan to stir the air; frankly, this made it worse. Then the fridge alarm was triggered in the middle of the night, from the lack of vehicle running. We stressed the auxiliary battery and starting our engine to stop the alarm was an equally unpopular move.

Ten years or so later, whilst working in Riyadh, rescuing a start-up, regional airline, the temperature rose to 50+°C in the shade. One could feel the moisture being wicked off your eyeballs. It was a very dry heat and because aircon was everywhere, one never acclimatised. The street coffee shops used to spray water over the verandas and people sat underneath because of the refreshing evaporation, leaving a refreshing, cool mist. Humidity is so much harder to manage. Operating in various jungles around the world (when both fitter and acclimatised) I found the humidity debilitating. At higher elevations on the Kalimantan/Borneo border under the canopy, it was cleaner and more shaded, thus easier to manage. It never ceases to amaze me the reach of modern brands and global TV; in Iban longhouses at isolated villages on the Borneo border, we struggled to make ourselves understood, but through their satellite TV, they knew all the players of Manchester United better than me!

One evening at the camping ground, a Land Rover arrived, headlights ablaze. Will and Justin were directed to camp beside us. These two post-grads were driving from London to Cape Town and recording their trip on www.2farbyfarby4by4.co.uk as part of a fundraiser for the St Philip's Clinic in a remote part of Tanzania. The clinic was run by a friend of theirs and they intended to stop and assist en route. They had driven south from the Egyptian border that morning and had blown a shock hitting a pothole at speed. They struggled to get their troublesome half shafts fixed at Wadi Halfa and couldn't find a suitable mechanic. They were informed of a local, Sudanese 'fixer' called Midhat, who had become an online legend for overlanders at Wadi Halfa. Midhat had relocated to Khartoum and the lads were looking for him. Will and Justin were not quite alone, but let's not call it a race. Fellow grads in another vehicle, the Cambridge to Cape Town (CTC) crew, had taken the coastal route from Morocco around West Africa and were thought to be partying somewhere in Niger or Chad, leaving Will and Justin ahead.

Route selection and vehicles always dominate such conversations and clearly their Carnet included Egyptian cover, as it originated in London. The boys had a 110 Single Cab Land Rover, retaining a jump seat across the front, should they need to take a passenger. Their cheaper copy roof tent leaked in heavy rain in Europe (note to self; don't skimp on kit). On the Aswan ferry, they attempted to fix their half shaft, but it remained a work in progress that Will wanted to repair on arrival. Catherine cooked us all supper and I assisted Will, armed with our trusty Haynes Manual and tools. Three hours of wrestling later and we still had a stuck half shaft and a sheared hub bolt. We need a reliable mechanic; we needed to find Midhat.

Leaving Will tinkering, we took Justin to find Midhat the next day, finding him in an office in the Central Bazaar. Over the weeks, we got to know Midhat well, as we wrestled officialdom and visa requirements. Midhat was everything, and more than the hype around him. First, he got us travel passes and photo permits. He got us to the Libyan Embassy to enquire about visas; during this first cordial meeting, they told us to provide a letter from the British Embassy and come back early Sunday morning. No problem; a further justification to get hold of the 'missing' Ed. Midhat's knowledge was invaluable, and he was desperate to share his knowledge and culture. His influence may have originated in Waldi Halfa, but here, he was invaluable in sorting out visas, local suppliers and parts for Land Rovers; we cannot thank him enough.

Midhat directed us to Papa John who owned a general engineering works just down the road from the camping ground. His side gig was repairing vehicles, for Papa John provided heavy plant and in-country engineering to water borehole NGOs and construction companies (including the nascent petroleum pipeline industry). He had a couple of vehicle ramps and was happy to help, provided we sourced the spare parts. Midhat directed us to the new Land Rover retailer in North Khartoum, where the staff were helpful, but also very expensive. They tried to sell Will a very small pot of sealant for US$100 - he was not impressed.

Khartoum was burgeoning and becoming a real cultural melting pot; Westerners were able to move around freely without being hassled. Catherine was not expected to cover her head whilst outside, although she respectfully wore long trousers and shirt sleeves. The 1970s and 1980s saw an influx of refugees from neighbouring conflicts such as Chad, Eritrea, Ethiopia, CAR and Uganda. These immigrants were assimilated into society or settled at the city edge. Now, refugees from South Sudan and Darfur were arriving.

We bumped into Jahid, a Sudanese chap who lived in the UK (Sheffield) but was back training the athletes at the camp. He was fascinated by our trip, so he invited us to his athletics' meet. We later discovered that it was not just any athletics' meet, but a AAA meeting, adjudicated by a UK colleague, William, from UK Athletics. The four of us were entertained alongside all the other invited VIPs at the National Athletics stadium. We were astonished to be seated on the front row, reserved for the VVIPs, ambassadors and senior government appointees. A regular supply of cold drinks and snacks was passed around to make us comfortable. Will ended up sitting next to the secretary of Sudanese Athletics, who was also a colonel in their police force; useful to know. He was a mine of detail and gave us all the inside information as to which athlete was the favourite for each race. Athletics aside, Catherine was treated as an honouree male, addressed as such and seated alongside me. I mention this, for there was very strict segregation in place; all the other ladies were duly covered and seated on the back row. It was they who were nudging and shaking their heads at Catherine's 'high status', wondering who she was and why she was sitting at the front.

The standard of running was quite good. The majority of visiting female athletes were dressed in the usual athletic, Lycra regalia, notably those from Kenya, Tanzania and Ethiopia. However, the three local Sudanese runners were running in their headscarves and veil, with baggy trousers. Sadly, and unsurprisingly, given the drag factor alone, the local runners were way behind the Lycra winners. But fair play to the local ladies, they never gave up and committed their all. We were proudly informed that Sudan was a country that allowed women to participate, in contrast to say Saudi Arabia, where this would have been forbidden. The ladies were running out of dignity and pride. I was sitting next to Paul Ereng (Kenya's Olympic gold medallist 800-metre runner, running his own coaching academy in Eldoret) who assisted William in presenting the medals.

The next morning, we were back at Midhat's offices near the Meridian hotel; I had just parked Daph when an extremely battered car crashed into the back of us. There was no visible damage to Daph, although the front light of the other car was impaled on our exhaust. The driver just walked off. Apparently, this was normal, but Midhat, who was standing next to me, saw red. Midhat 'marched' the driver into his office for a stiff talking to, at the end of which the man was crestfallen. An apology was all we were going to get, for the man had no money, even if there had been some damage. Culturally, we felt that Midhat was embarrassed, so he arranged for some traditional Sudanese coffee to be served. We were given a small cupful of sugar with a ginger lump on top, before coffee was poured from a great height onto the sugar. Wow, this was the strongest coffee I had ever drunk, but this would imply one could sip it; it was more like taking a spoonful at a time as it was so sweet. The ginger gave the coffee a real kick and our tongues were alive for the rest of the day.

With both Land Rovers back on the road, we set off to Meroë, some 300 kilometres north of Khartoum. It was a three-hour drive to Meroë and, despite some hassle at a checkpoint, we arrived and found Mustapha. He was the caretaker at Meroë, who showed us around the pyramids. We took pictures and captured the sunset; it was obvious that nobody had visited that day for the sand blowing over the pyramids was pristine. Meroë was an ancient city on the east bank of the Nile; it had been the capital of the Kingdom of Kush, in one of the many early states within the Middle Nile. Meroë has more than 200 pyramids in three groups, although many are now in ruins. During the fifth millennium BC, migrations from the drying Sahara brought a neolithic people into the Nile Valley, and with them, agriculture. The fusion emanating from this cultural and genetic mixing formed a social hierarchy that ruled for the next few centuries. In 1700 BC, the Kingdom of Kush had its capital at Kerma. In the eighth century BC, after the Bronze Age collapse of the New Kingdom of Egypt, King Kashta (the Kushite) invaded Egypt. His success meant Kushite kings ruled as pharaohs over the 25th Dynasty of Egypt for a century, before being driven out by the Assyrians. At the height of Kushite glory, their empire stretched from modern South Kordofan to the Sinai. The Kush were first to smelt iron; they were mentioned in the Bible as having saved the Israelites from the wrath of the Assyrians, although disease among the besiegers may have been a key factor. During the Classical Antiquity period, the Nubian capital remained at Meroë. In ancient Greek geography, the Meroitic Kingdom was known as Ethiopia, a term also used earlier by the Assyrians when encountering the Nubians.

Back at the parking area, an entire village had respectfully spread out their wares around the vehicles for us, although who knew from where they came. Recalling Midhat's advice, we thanked them and skirted round the enclosure to a hidden camping spot on the back side of the enclosure. In this half-light, Daph got stuck in soft sand. At one point, both vehicles were stuck, but Will was just about able to drive theirs out. We got stuck because Daph's clutch kept slipping, generating no torque, only a terrible, burning smell. A straight tow line to Will quickly extracted us, but having only replaced the clutch at CMC in Nairobi, this was very frustrating. No power was being transferred to the wheels; the engine was still ticking over but the clutch was spinning, therefore burning fluid.

Once freed, we could drive around to our intended camp spot. Mechanical issues aside, it was wonderful to be camping in the open desert again. The air was clear, the skies so open; we slept soundly thanks to a cooler breeze. The boys left to go back through Khartoum and on to Gadaref and Ethiopia the next day, leaving us to return at a leisurely pace to sort out the clutch and hopefully secure our Libyan visas. This little exercise, if nothing else, really emphasised the value of a second vehicle.

We called Papa John to discuss the clutch. Our timing was poor as we'd hit another public holiday, but aside from a delay in getting parts, Papa John offered his facilities for us to stay in during the repair. Just as well, for the camping ground was becoming frustrating. We always strove to be kind and approachable, but having possessions inevitably made us a target. A few young boys threw stones at the tent which I witnessed, then quickly dashed to grab one. Clearly there was a language barrier; he was scared and I was cross; the boy understood that. I let him go without a fuss but went to complain at the camp office, but as no one was there, I dropped the matter. In the morning, a chap who I assumed to be the boy's father dragged the miscreant over to us and tried to apologise, admonishing his son in front of me; now I felt bad. But mutual honour was restored when I thanked him, so smiles all around.

We shifted to Papa John's. Papa John was Dutch. After a business life in engineering, earth moving and land reclamation, he helped build roads in Dutch Guyana. The prospect of retiring was so abhorrent 18 years earlier, he came to organise aid distribution in Africa, Sudan in particular. Now he ran his own company, sinking boreholes. His own borehole drew the cleanest, sweetest and delightfully cool water we had ever tasted. Behind the workshop and hoists was a small compound with two little rooms and basic ablutions. Perfect; we could lock our gear in one room, leaving Daph 'clean' on the ramps, and sleep in the Oztent. Papa John's mechanics announced that our clutch repair was a two-day job to get the correct parts. This dovetailed with our visa efforts; our UK Embassy letter (US$61) and Libyan visa application were still pending. It seemed to have fallen into an administrative, Libyan black hole. We were unable to get past the front door at the Libyan Embassy, even with Midhat's diplomacy and translation skills. It had become a joke (at best) if not downright rude. On one occasion at the embassy, we were directed to a side window/shutter; we'd knock, and someone would open the shutter, shout abuse and slam it shut straight away. It was like the Monty Python sketch in the Holy Grail, where King Arthur seeks entry to the French castle, only to be told to F-off! During this time, other travellers from the north were easily accessing the coastline, experiencing a welcoming country.

Khartoum became a stumbling block. Our original intent was to follow the Nile, but without the relevant official documents, we ran the risk of Daph being impounded or incurring a huge fine. Despite his efforts, Colonel Peter (a previous commander and then the DA in Cairo) could not get around the need for us to place a bond (the equivalent sum of £20,000) to assure Daph would not be sold on the Egyptian black market. Hindsight being that wonderful thing, we should have just flown to Cairo and played tourist from Khartoum, however sub-optimal. The Libyan dream was also fading. We'd read that Libya has so many unfettered Roman remains that one could still walk to view them. We had a mad concept to access the Libyan southeastern border at Al Jawf involved a 1,000+ mile unsupported desert crossing from Dongola. It would be a major undertaking in an inhospitable, mined and unmarked desert with no support vehicle. Even if we trusted our new clutch, Daph had sand history! Without a visa and assuming we could not bluff our way in, we would be stuck at the border, without fuel for the return 1,000 miles. Whilst we love a challenge, this one was not happening.

In the southwestern corner of Egypt is the Gilf Kebir. It also remains unexplored for both Colonel Peter and us. It is a mined and protected border with Libya and controlled to preserve the prehistoric, Neolithic petroglyphs (rock art) of the area. One example was the Cave of Swimmers, uncovered during the Count Laszlo Almasy, Colonel R Bagnold and Patrick Clayton explorations during the early 1930s. Their collective mapping and knowledge gave rise to the Long Range Desert Group operations during the Second World War and as dramatised within Michael Ondaatje's film of the book, The English Patient.

Three days later, we took Daph off the ramps to test the new clutch. She was drivable, but there was an annoying rattle emanating from the release bearing. It was not right and there was a distinctive clutch delay. It emerged that Papa John's team had sourced the clutchplate from the local market. The Land Rover's Achilles' heel was its extensive and varied supply chain. Of the numerous manufacturers making, for example, oil filters, each one had different threads or tolerances; no wonder Land Rovers leak. The clutch suffered in the same way. The original Borg & Beck part from Land Rover was different to that replaced at CMC Nairobi (and again, probably a market knock-off). Before the trip, I snuck myself on to the Special Forces Army Vehicle Repair course with a team from the Pathfinder Platoon. I enjoyed a week learning bush repairs, including a clutch replacement, which involved jacking a Landy up a tree and dropping the clutch down. My subsequent learning was that you don't do this in a desert (no trees) and ensure you have an army of blokes to manhandle the vehicle. We ordered the 'correct part' direct from Land Rover, conferring a further delay. I supervised the replacement and this time the clutch plate slotted in easily first time. Fair play to the mechanics; they were a patient and resourceful bunch. One evening, the lads were working late on another vehicle when they asked us to join them for supper. It was very touching when they insisted that Catherine joined too, for they wanted the event on camera. Their sem-sem (similar to sesame seed) meal was seed ground to a paste and eaten with unleavened bread. It was very tasty, yet very sweet, like most of the Sudanese diet, and washed down with some delightful hibiscus tea. We had been at Papa John's for nine days; our Sudanese visa was nearly up - we needed to get moving.

Catherine was enjoying Khartoum, a freedom to move around without hassle on bus trips to the Meridian to update the website and communicate with friends and family. We also visited Omdurman, for two key events happen every Friday. First, the world-renowned camel market was not that dramatic, but was exceptionally smelly, and second, we sought to observe the followers of the Sufi Qadiriyah order whirl. These dervishes gather at the Hamed al-Nil Tomb in Omdurman to dance and pray. Supposedly quite a sight, their long, green and red robes flow as they chant to the clash of cymbals and drums and the dancers spin in a spiritual trance to commune with God. But not for us; irritatingly they were a no-show. Omdurman was a maze of old world, ramshackle, traditional markets, bazaars and craft souks. Midhat had said that the traffic was always bad in Khartoum, but we had the added weapon of our bull bars. According to Midhat, 'he whose bonnet is marginally in front has the right of way'. It was true; we could nudge our way through traffic and the bars appeared to be respected, but here in Omdurman, nothing moves (or so we thought, as we queued).

We were static and behaving ourselves when a wreck of a car suddenly slammed into the back of Daph. So much for bull bars! This was annoying to say the least and I wasn't sure if the driver behind was incompetent or if it was deliberate. Catherine remained secure in Daph while I got out to remonstrate and check the damage. The driver spoke no English and clearly had no money, but I think he was trying to apologise; it was all noise and gesticulation. I was ignoring the ensuing traffic jam as I checked the functionality of the rear door. The Land Rover rear door is a known weak point, as we'd found out in Botswana. If the rear door seal was buckled or broken, aside from the security concern, dust would be drawn into the cab. However, a quick look revealed that the impact had been absorbed by the spare wheel swing-arm, leaving a tasty dent in the battered Arab driver's bonnet; we were OK. As the hapless driver was apologising, a bus crawled level in the next lane and a wealthy-looking, elderly Arab standing in the open doorway shouted across in English, 'If you bring a strong car to Africa, you must expect things like this; he cannot pay you.' Oh, that's fine then; just because we have a strong car, then it's acceptable for everyone to drive into us? There was no point arguing and as no damage had been done, I simply laughed and continued to queue in our 'strong vehicle'.

Our visa was running out, but should we turn left or right? One option was to explore Europe, coming up from Turkey, having skirted the Middle East (Israel, Jordan and through the crusader history of Syria on up). Theoretically, one could drive from Cape Town to London without using anything more than a ferry, assuming Egypt was passable. But now it was not, we had to cross the Red Sea via Port Sudan. Getting to Port Sudan was a challenge. Eritrean rebels were attacking the oil pipeline at Kassala on a daily basis and the alternative railway route was closed. We would cross to Jedda in Saudi, itself being loaded with challenges and legalities; infidels could only get a three-day Saudi transit visa to Jordan, and woe betide any female behind the wheel. Thankfully, today such attitudes are changing.

By turning right (west) we would maintain our African theme, but at some point, we would have to cross or circumvent the Sahara, currently an unknown. Ultimately, we could follow the West African coastline, but we were not sure if we could access Morocco from the south, given the Polisario dispute in Western Sahara. Then, you could only drive north to south. We had bailout ports in Ghana or Senegal should things become too difficult, but we needed to get going; our Sudanese transit visa left us less than a week to reach a border. Having visas for Chad swayed matters, yet any western direction meant passing through Darfur.

Part 5

THE UNKNOWN AND THE AMAZING SAHARA

Agadez Mosque - built from mud

AAA athletics meet, Khartum

"No man can emerge from the desert unchanged."

Wilfred Thesinger

Swiss Team - Peter, Barbara and Kasper

Meroe temples

Essential repairs on the piste

The road to Djanet

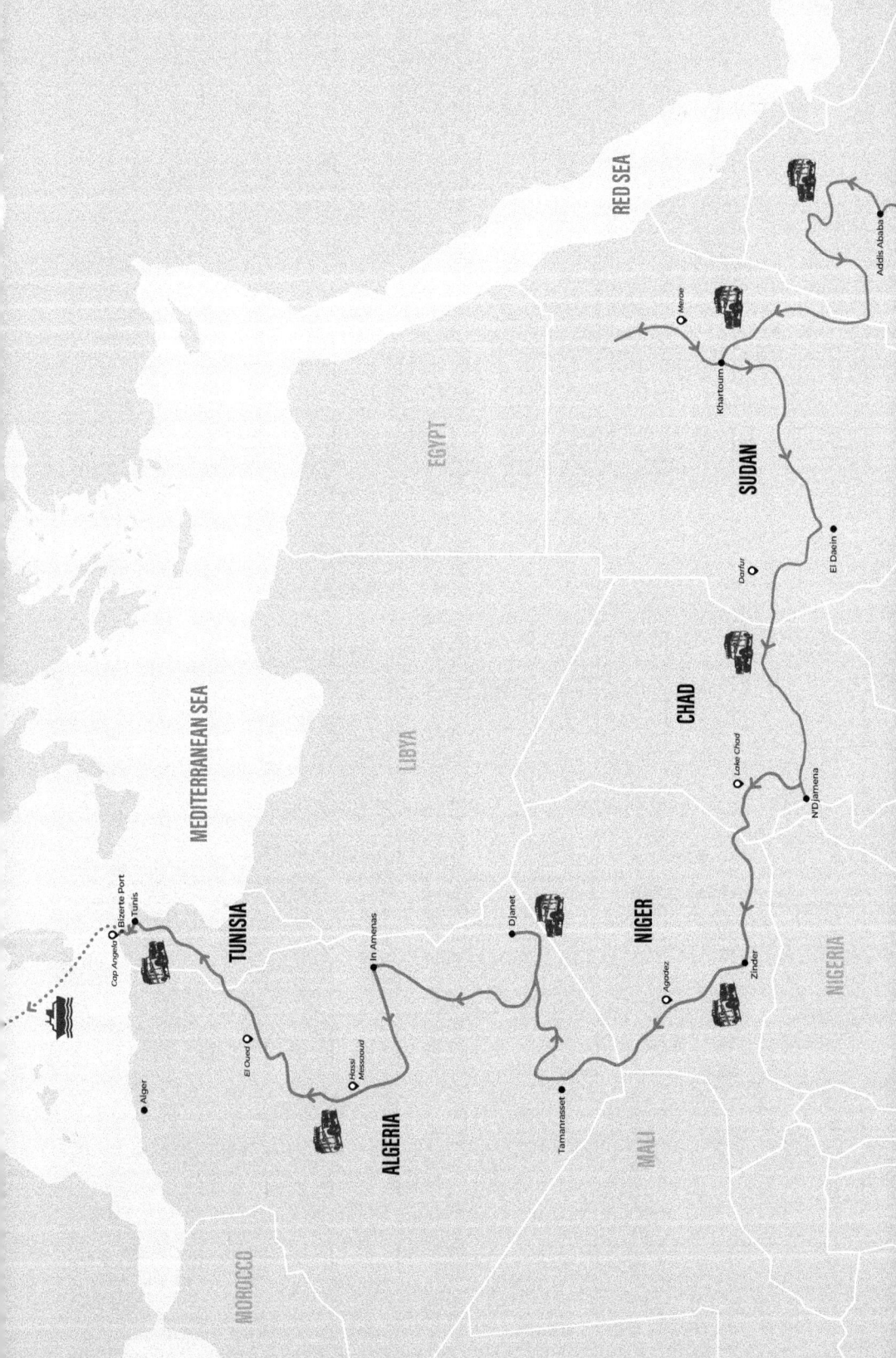

Chapter 19
The kindness of strangers
(You are pointing that gun at me, aren't you?)

We needed to move. Papa John and his team had been great. It was quite an emotional departure for the boys, who seemed to have grown accustomed and protective towards their rather strange guests. Driving south from Khartoum, we passed many checkpoints on the tar road to El Obeid, monitoring the numerous oil tankers plying the north-south route. Turning west beyond El Obeid, the tar road ended abruptly, replaced by deep, sandy, hard-baked and rutted tracks. This was hurting us. The central sand hump was so high and solid that we were effectively ploughing Daph through baked sand on her unprotected sump and under bodywork. Tall grasses, reeds and what appeared to be crops grew either side, with evidence that some vehicles had previously driven through. Aside from not wanting to damage crops, I hadn't fitted our seed net as we wanted maximum airflow over the radiator and engine. But if grasses and seeds jammed in the radiator, it would soon clog up and stop us, so I quickly fixed the seed net.

The Darfur region straddles Sudan's western border, populated predominantly by traditional, non-Arabic people. Of the original native Sudanese cultures, the 'Fur' refers to the native Sudanese assimilated around the 1880s, prior to the British re-colonialising in 1916. Darfur in Arabic translates as 'home of the Fur'. Disputes here are constant, over land and water access; NGOs were reporting instability back in the 1990s, but by the 2000s, this conflict escalated to be known as the 'Land Cruiser War'. By 2003, the war in Darfur was a full-scale, armed conflict between the Arab-dominated government (known as the Janjaweed, or mounted gunman) and the Christian and animist black southerners (the rebels), claiming half a million lives by 2005. Local NGOs were warning about ethnic cleansing before 2001, manifested in brutal village rAIDS with killings, beatings, rapes and crop destruction. We were unaware; it was a confused picture. In the pre-internet and smartphone era, we were getting updates from passing NGOs at Papa John's. We understood that there was a safe corridor via Nyala, which avoided the main Al Fashir route and Gol (more conflict on the CAR border) to the south, but to get there in a week would be tight.

Not long after El Obied, we bumped into a Red Crescent (Red Cross equivalent) team looking to camp, who flagged us down in the dusk. We were looking to wild camp in the bushes, so strength in numbers worked. Their team leader, Ismail, said they were heading back to Khartoum, and provided excellent route information and a situation update. We never really worked out if he thought we were NGOs, but our white (-ish) Land Rover may have given that impression, even though we never intimated anything about ourselves. They were fascinated by the roof tent but we, on the other hand, were not too impressed by their night watchman who was asleep before we were.

Thankfully, the temperatures were dropping to a more manageable thirties by day and cooler by night. Ismail and his boys were off sharpish in the morning to Khartoum. We pushed west on more hard-baked, sand tracks. We tried all sorts; having one wheel in the ruts and the other on the central hump. but none were really sustainable. These conditions were forged by heavy lorries, yet we saw none. Occasionally, there was a side-track, running parallel to the main route that always offered easier going until we were using it. Once, we found ourselves totally off-track, bashing through head-high grasses where we couldn't see beyond the bonnet. At one point, we ended up in a corn field, then one of watermelons. We felt bad, but at least they had crops, which was better than in sub-Saharan Africa. Back tracking wouldn't have helped; it was similar to flying in cloud, totally disorientating and discombobulating.

Ismail said keep heading west, and we had little choice. Once I had to climb onto the roof rack to see where to go. Hours later, we emerged onto a dry riverbed with a clear track heading west. We glimpsed a town ahead that we hoped was En Nahud. We were exhausted, having covered 242 kilometres over rough terrain and we were grateful that Daph just soldiered on. The town was largely deserted and when we stopped to get our bearings, a Care International Cruiser pulled up beside us and asked what we were doing. Amazingly, they immediately offered their guest house facilities nearby, although disconcertingly, they kept repeating that it was safe. Language barrier aside, they went out of their way to make us comfortable. They offered us a room, but we used the roof tent; it was easier. The seed net had done its job, but was on its last legs, so I spent an hour refitting a new one. My initial scepticism at the need for a seed net was wrong; same for the air-compressor. Aside from being invaluable for tyre inflation and cleaning out the seeds, we helped the Care International boys with a slow puncture. After an hour, I had quite a pile of debris extracted, sufficient kindling to light all the fires in town.

The following day, we were shown where to get fuel and obtain a 'vu en passe' stamp from the gendarmes, required at each major town. This was a head-scratcher - why, in a largely ex-British, colonial country were there gendarmes and a French pass system? We were directed through the town maze on to the 'light vehicle' route to El Daein. This donkey track was more of the same, especially when weaving in and out through villages. These were poor villages, mostly reed rondavels and subsistence living. Worryingly, people hid from our vehicle, except the young who just gawped or giggled at the 'whities'. The adolescents were shy and evasive. Ironically, the old men were better at English; whether it was a colonial thing or that they were better at bullshitting, who knows.

As we weaved between the huts, we came across an old man. 'Hi, Jambo, which way is El Daein?' I asked, along with a massive smile and gentle but exaggerated gesticulation. Pointing left and right, the poor chap was petrified. I was doing my friendly best, but flipping a coin may have been better, so we crawled on. We saw and asked another old man, who effectively saluted Daph. What was going on? He pointed back the way we had come...we may as well have been asking the way to Nelson's Column. Clearly, the pronunciation of El Daein was incorrect - mea culpa. 'Where is El Daein?' 'I don't know but El Daein is that way.' 'Oh, El Daein is that way?' - pointing in the opposite direction. Eventually, we found El Daein astride a dried river and dilapidated bridge. Whether it was jungle drums or what, we bumped into a Save the Children vehicle, who insisted we followed them. Their compound was well set up with flushing loos and satellite CNN. Again, presenting ourselves to the police for our stamp, they were eating, so they told us to come back later with copies of our travel permits. Catherine wasn't falling for that one and produced copies there and then. Stamped, we were on our way.

Daph's steering was getting worse, juddering and vibrating through the steering column. I was still conducting my daily vehicle checks, but nothing led me to understand the steering vibrations, other than a bent steering rod.

I worried about the sump; it has the drain nut at its base that was taking a pounding, yet it was fine, unlike a weeping, rear-differential seal. The Haynes Manual implied that a bent steering rod should not be removed without clean conditions and a replacement damper and split pin; I had neither. I was starting to re-evaluate the validity of heavy, under-body protection, yet I still believed the standard Land Rover should be able to cope. The Save the Children boys were all in Toyotas. Our biggest concern was the increasing air of nervousness pervading all activity. We observed the hustle and bustle of village life becoming more furtive; people started to avoid our gaze, yet the aid agencies were overly helpful, for which we were grateful. We started to wonder if it was us that they were nervous about; who were these white people?

The Save the Children boys again showed us the Nyala road, telling us to stay within half a mile from the railway line: easier said than done. More than once, we were back-tracking through grasses and scrub to find a path. The railway line was built up on a significant three metre-high embankment with marshes, ponds and ravines either side. We crossed over the tracks to test both sides; neither was better. We read that some vehicles drive along the train tracks themselves. This seemed very risky, as getting off quickly might not be a given, but we could see why. Route finding was hard enough. We tried to drive along the edge of the tracks, but frequently, the embankment was either too steep or there were major ravines that suddenly appeared without warning, which would be terminal. It nearly was, for braking hard forced me to swerve and descend the bank, plunging the front of Daph into a swampy, pond edge. I started to imagine gravity was pulling Daph down like a Hollywood quicksand nightmare; either way, we needed to extricate her quickly.

I had the recovery kit ready and prepared by the rear door this time, but the door lock had become temporarily jammed by some Wolf Pack boxes, bouncing up against the lock when we hit something violent. Typical! This day was turning unpleasant as I scrambled through from the front to open and extricate the winch gear. Stress levels were rising. I quickly set up a recovery with the only solid anchor structure being the railway line. Not ideal; thankfully no train was in sight. Wrapping a tree strap around the rail, the tirfir winch pulled steadily and straight, but Daph was not shifting. I re-rigged a shorter pull and achieved more success, but Daph was still stuck.

Just then, Catherine pointed to three lads who were standing and watching us. Just what we needed, not a soul for miles and now we were going to get turned over! Yet these lads were as friendly as could be. Despite no common language, they came and pushed; I winched and Daph popped out like a cork. There was palpable relief, when Catherine shouted, 'Train!' Flipping heck; I had a steel cable across the tracks and an anchor point stuck fast around the rail. I kicked and shouted at the steel cable as the lads suddenly realised they needed to pull it to one side, whilst I tackled the anchor. Thankfully, no train was derailed; we cleared the hazard in time to wave to the train driver as he leaned out of his window and waved back. Our three Samaritans were strong lads, despite their skinny demeanour. They asked for cigarettes; we had none, but they were more than satisfied with the few dollars and were gone in a flash. We still had to get to Nyala.

Sod it. We decided to try driving along the tracks – surely there wouldn't be another train now? Our wheels slotted in between the rails and crashed through the bigger gaps in the sleepers, which was mad; we would end up doing serious damage at some point. One theory might have been to glide along at speed over the bumps, akin to harmonising one's speed over corrugations, but like many theories, this would have taken a brave man. Following a couple of very uncomfortable miles, at varying speeds, we saw a viable route to the side and extricated Daph down from the rails. I was sweating as I checked Daph over. She was still running fine, although the rear diff leak was now more than a weep, and the steering shudder was bad. It took us seven hours to get to Nyala, almost twice as long as expected.

Nyala was a major town where we filled up with fuel. There was an air of hostility and remoteness here, quite unlike the vibe from our three 'railway' Samaritans. We tried unsuccessfully to contact Henri at the border where he worked with the UN World Food Programme (UNWFP). using both the Sat phone and mobile. He previously told us of a guest house four hours beyond Nyala in the Jebel Maram Mountains near Zalinger, but we wouldn't make that now. As we assessed our options at Nyala, we needed another immigration stamp, which took more time, so we were thinking of bush camping that night out of town.

At an open area on the edge of town, we stopped to try Henri one last time on the Sat phone, but got no response. As I paced around the vehicle, I noticed two local lads striding towards us out of the heat haze. They were not light-skinned, but very dark, striding purposefully and directly towards us. There was no other logical explanation for their demeanour; this was something not within the natural order of things, alerting a sixth sense. The military refer to this as a combat indicator. Both chaps wore big, dark shades and were confidently striding in our direction; locals don't stride, they amble. The hackles on my neck rose and I said to Catherine, as casually as I could muster, 'Get in the car' as I turned and led them around the back of Daph and jumped in my side. You could have knocked me down with a feather as Catherine got in and locked her door without question. We had previously discussed such 'actions on' in the case of an event like this, but I never imagined it would come to pass that she was even listening, nor more significantly, that she'd do it. Being one who likes to make her own decisions, she said later there was something in the tone of my voice that made her react in such a way. I was eternally grateful, for whatever it was, minutes later, the tall, skinny guy with outsized shades and a black beret was shouting out of control and waving a 9mm automatic pistol in my face on the other side of the windscreen.

What the f***! This was getting serious. I was stunned and a crowd started to gather, from nowhere. The other henchman stood by Catherine's door, waiting for instructions, while 'Pistol Boy' was getting quite animated. I'm ashamed to say, I inadvertently escalated the situation by starting to laugh. It was not bravery or anything other than fear, for after everything, was this really it? The more I laughed, the more animated Pistol Boy became. He was shaking and wobbling the pistol all over the place; he was so close to the vehicle, yet I reckon he still would have missed Daph completely had he pulled the trigger. This was a farce, but any armed robbery would be violent and we'd clearly not fair too well. I was wondering if I could start Daph and plough through the crowd before shots disabled us; it would be both unpleasant, unwarranted and Daph was not really a nimble weapon for such activities. This was not Hollywood.

It was at this point that a man in semi-combat uniform said at Catherine's window, 'Don't worry, you have not done anything wrong.' What? I sat bolt upright in my seat looking for Uniform Man and started to point and gesticulate in an exaggerated manner at him to come around to my window, something he was reluctant to do. Thankfully, he did comply and after a fashion, he said that Pistol Boy wanted to search the vehicle. No way, not here or anywhere. The crowd would have us for breakfast like a plague of locusts. Pistol Boy was losing a lot of confidence by now and his mate was totally subservient. This was crazy. I asked to go to a police station, but Uniform Man was not happy; Pistol Boy didn't understand. I should not have held any cards or power in this stand-off, yet I was calling the shots. Why not the police? I figured it might be better to get done over by the police than here on open waste ground. The Mexican stand-off endured when Pistol Boy agreed to the police station and wanted to get in. Haha – nice try. They could hang on to the outside of Daph if they wanted? Pistol Boy was losing face, panicking, so I started the engine and stared at him. He folded like a pack of cards. With the three protagonists hanging off the running boards, I drove under Uniform Man's direction to the police HQ, or its equivalent.

Crazy thoughts of shaking off our passengers and legging it entered by head, such as driving close to a wall, but such antics were best left to the movies. This was a laden, diesel Land Rover. On arrival at the HQ, Pistol Boy was behaving like a conquering hero. Catherine had the key documents in her cross-body bag, and we made sure that Daph was locked and alarmed, whatever good that might do, as we were escorted inside. It was painfully obvious that this was not a police station, but a military HQ, where a Monty Python-esque charade began. By now, we had attracted an entourage. We were ushered into a room, where I wasn't letting Uniform Man escape by grabbing his jacket firmly. The three of us sat opposite a grinning Pistol Boy and his lame accomplice. Someone, I guess Pistol Boy's boss, came in and started shouting in a local dialect, demanding to see our papers. Catherine handed over our stamped passports. Uniform Man sat implacable as the boss walked out and ushered in another boss who started shouting. This was starting to amuse me; Pistol Boy was visibly swelling with pride. Then another boss of the boss took his turn to harangue us, after which I nudged Uniform Man, who hadn't stopped staring at his boot laces. How many bosses could there be? After the fifth escalation of boss, I again nudged Uniform Man, who nodded this time. When the sixth authoritarian figure emerged, Uniform Man said a few words, I don't know what. The balloon was popped, with the de-escalation of haranguing back down the hierarchy to the man who handed us back our passports. Pistol Boy deflated like a rag doll, but we walked directly out to Daph and quickly buggered off, having thanked Uniform Man. I have no idea what he said or what authority he had - who cared? We were gone. Later, we surmised that Pistol Boy thought he had captured a couple of spies using a radio device in a military area. Maybe it was the sight of the whites in a white Land Rover? What shocked me was Catherine reacting correctly to my suggestion, which (to this day) remains a first!

By now, dusk was descending and we had no immediate plan. Heading west out of town, mulling over our options, we passed a hospital and some Red Crescent vehicles. We stopped for a chat and asked after Ismal, explained our journey and the recent debacle. They took us to a SCF guest house where they discussed the growing security situation. We had seen many migrating camel herds and families that they considered unusual. Talk eventually came around to Daph and her growing list of ailments, but these SCF lads used Land Rovers. They had a mechanic in the market who we visited first thing. An old chap appeared, in his flip-flops, to drive Daph and I around the block, immediately diagnosing the steering rod. Back at the market road/dirt track, he was straight under Daph, whipping off the steering rod and hammering it straight, with one flip-flop foot holding it like a vice, the other hand hammering like a blacksmith. He clearly knew what he was doing and knew Land Rovers. The guy was ferreting through my tools until his trained eye pronounced the rod straight and replaced, with the Haynes Manual ignored; this was a 'bush style' repair. Maybe there would be an inherent weakness in the steering rod's strength, but I had no spare and the old boy test drove his handiwork around the block. I handed him my spare rear hub seal and that too was fixed in a jiffy, along with some replacement rear brake pads that I passed him. I paid him more than he requested, but it was still cheap, timely and a real find; Daph was rejuvenated. The mechanic started checking other aspects, like I did on my morning checks; a real Land Rover enthusiast. He was satisfied, pronouncing Land Rover a 'strong vehicle' and handed back my tools. Mohamed told me that the old boy lamented the loss of Land Rover in Africa to Toyota; seemingly, he was not a fan.

Meanwhile, Catherine, with another SCF chap, was in the market buying some staples at local prices: flat bread, hibiscus tea, tomatoes, onions and bananas, items we found throughout Africa. Mohamed was still expressing his concern about the declining security situation and their ability to function. He described the route to El Genena and also told us about the safe house halfway in the Jebel Marra near Zalangei, should we get delayed. We had survived a rollercoaster thus far; we needed to make the border. We passed some foothills and thankfully, there were no more deep sand tracks, just rolling terrain. There were many criss-cross tracks, each of equal size and importance, for the route was never obvious. This was the case when we crested a rise and below us was a maze of potential routes, but ominously, there was a dominant 'Block House' with a bunch of soldiers guarding and administering themselves. But which track did we need? I was very conscious that pausing to decide which route to take was drawing unwanted attention. Avoiding them might be even more suspicious and we did not want a repeat carjacking experience.

Confidence was key here. We boldly descended directly to their position, although Catherine shrunk low in the vehicle, pulling her cap down. I jumped out, shouting Arabic greetings with a few Jambos and English thrown in, as if I owned and commanded the place. 'Where is your commander?' I demanded as I strode about, looking around at an array of automatic weapons, machine guns and mortars. Oh blimey; I hoped we had done the right thing. Some chap appeared and I vaguely saluted him, smiling and thrusting a map under his nose, asking about the border and which direction we should take. He never looked at the map, only at me and Daph, clearly very unsure of the situation. Someone behind him started indicating the Zalingei Road, to which the commander sort of nodded. I said thanks, turned on my heel with a friendly wave, jumped back into Daph and drove (as calmly as I could muster) away before any more questions could be raised, with my heart thumping. I was just thankful that Catherine stayed low and unseen.

We climbed the gentle, rolling hills, where pines trees appeared on the skyline. On the edge of the Marra Mountains (Sudan's highpoint), we were making good time and felt confident that the challenging route-finding was history. Zalingei appeared, nestled in a valley, with a long, low bridge over a dried riverbed. The area was very green and a mist was over the hills; we pressed on. Later, we discovered that Zalingei was the capital of the Central State for Darfur, yet it appeared to be a small and unassuming town. The tracks descended towards El Genena, in the familiar, sandy scrubland, causing our pace to decrease.

Daph was performing well; the agility of the springs and chassis absorbed the jarring and bounce. El Genena was a dusty, low-lying town of small huts, a few brick houses and some central official buildings. There were a few people milling about, but we didn't see a market or a centre. Again, amazingly, we bumped into an SCF vehicle. We regaled the last few days and said we had left Mohamed at Nyala. This appeared to be of some relief as they were unaware of their colleagues' travails. They introduced us to Medair, a local fixer and three European nurses; Mariella from Holland, Karen from Germany and Susan from England. The girls were great, although tired and worried about the declining, regional security. Susan was an 'old hand'; as a young nurse, she first volunteered during the 1984 Ethiopian famine crisis and had been supporting similar initiatives ever since. It was a Friday, so nothing would happen at the border and they insisted we stay with them. They had been given a sheep to slaughter as part-payment for some work and the good Henri was due that evening. Walking around was free and easy and we didn't feel the need to take any special precautions. It was optional for ladies to cover their heads; Catherine was always polite in public, yet it was not expected here. As usual, I was taking pictures and snapping away with a long lens at some boys playing football. Suddenly, a man hit me on the head from behind with his slipper. What the hell? This was new! After the initial shock, I angrily turned to smack the assailant back, but the Medair fixer already had the scrawny chap. Though angry, I didn't want any fuss or insult, but it transpired that the scrawny chap believed I was photographing some young Muslim girls who had just walked past us, in their full head scarves. I had stopped to let them pass so they would not block my shot of the footballers. Crazily, it transpired he thought that my picture would 'steal the girls' souls'. A key feature of digital SLR cameras was the ability to scroll back and view each picture on the screen, common now, but a new innovation then. Via the fixer, I showed him the football pictures; the guy was amazed yet crestfallen and started to overly apologise. I said he had to help Medair as recompense, which I later found out he did. So, some good may arise out of an unfortunate event.

At last, the mythical Henri appeared that evening to take tea with the girls and join the feast. All the chat was about the deteriorating security situation and whether to extract the girls and staff by air if the border closed. We had a day left on our month-long visa and didn't fancy a return trip to Khartoum. Clearly, the deteriorating unrest was a worry; stories of distant villages being raided was not uncommon and the speed and violence of events was escalating. It sounded so indiscriminate, but who was co-ordinating the action? Given our experience of the police and military presence, these attacks could not have been random.

The following morning, we said our goodbyes and wished the Medair team well; we headed for the border with Henri. He introduced us to Sudanese Border Security, where the WFP frequently transit and where he was known. He confirmed that the border was open, so departed, leaving us to deal with immigration, which he implied would just be a matter of routine. At immigration, we were invited to start the documentation but the 'man with the stamp' for the Carnet was not there. It turned out he was having breakfast. 'OK, how long will this take?' 'He will be here soon; would we like to join him?' 'Thank you, but no, we are happy to wait.' Two hours later, we hoped breakfast was worth it, but we got our stamp, which included a US$10 dollar scam. We were past caring and it was clearly being 'trousered' by the officials. We smiled; after all, 'Westerners may have watches', but we learnt that 'Africans have time'.

Chapter 20
Parlez-vous francais?

It was around midday when we escaped and we knew it was around four hours to Abache, the first major town in Chad. But we had not factored in the extended distance between border posts or the two-hour time shift that thankfully compensated for the distance. After an hour on good tracks, the border post came into view. Immediately though, we noticed a few significant changes.

Firstly, the man, or to be more accurate, the caricature, was unmistakably French. The dark-skinned soldier was a classic double-take for the French 'Lucky Luke' image: tall, lean, beret (not Stetson) tilted forward on his head and cowboy boots (well, army boots), leaning back laconically against a wall. Critically, his cigarette was lounging out of the corner of his mouth. Eventually, he mooched towards us, with his AK47 over his shoulder. Oh blimey, we thought we had left all that behind. Secondly, it seemed bizarre to hear a local speaking French; we expected it, but it sounded completely out of context. At least we were able to communicate as he told us his chef had gone for lunch but would be back shortly. Here we go again... but no, the chef appeared within five minutes to stamp and complete the Carnet and documents quickly and accurately. Within ten minutes, we were nearly through, when the chef implied that we had to give half a dozen locals a lift. We looked at the extended Arabian family, in their white jellaba and caps, plus luggage, patiently expectant. Catherine and I looked at each other, confused; we had a single jump seat, but Daph was full. Catherine said out of the window, 'Etaient pleins'; the chef and the Arabs looked at our comparatively empty vehicle aghast; we did not look full to them. We sort of felt bad, but with the gradual depression of the accelerator, we set off for Abache.

The route was obvious. Being French, there were the classic, white stone mile-markers, common across rural France. We transited relatively flat terrain, dry riverbeds and ravines on sandy roads. We passed a few wrecked lorries, on their sides and rusting away; this was a new development. There was no immediate clue for the demise of these lorries, except age, no maintenance, over-use and quite probably, severe overloading. No wonder the chef and the family at the border were aghast at our 'empty' vehicle as we witnessed most lorries and vehicles heavily overloaded. We passed a low-loader laden with grain, a tractor on top, plus dozens of people hanging on. We felt bad that we were not the Samaritans we could have been, but for the sake of security and progress, it was the right decision.

A couple of hours towards Abache, we saw a Land Rover approaching us; it was the CambridgeToCapeTown (CTC) crew, casing down Will and Justin. They recognised us too as they flashed their lights and flagged us down. It was quite surreal to meet people we hadn't actually met before, yet we all knew about each other. Philip, Ben and Luke had spent an enjoyable few days getting their Sudanese visa in N'Djamena and knew we were heading in their direction. Yet, what were the chances for us to meet? We quickly swapped stories, briefed them about the deteriorating security in Sudan and gave them the usual pointers on where, with whom and how to get information and help. In turn, they told us where to stay in N'Djamena and about their recent experiences. They had driven through Spain to Morocco and partied their way around the West African coast. Clearly, they were enjoying their time-off after exams, but they were big lads, each over six feet tall, so folding themselves into the Land Rover must have been a mission. They had a similar Land Rover to Will and Justin, so in rotation, one had to sit either on the jump seat or in the back. Oh, to be youthful again! Their intent was to dig boreholes for a charity in the Masai Mara, before spinning down to party in Cape Town. It was great to meet them and to mark the occasion, like the classic Stanley-Livingstone image, we took a picture in front of our vehicles, shaking hands, before pressing on in the fading light.

Dusk was descending as we entered Abache, when we came across a policeman on a scooter, who insisted on escorting us to security. At the police post, our passports were efficiently stamped before we were directed to the UN WFP Guest House (known here by the French as Programme Alimentaire Mondial, PAM). Whatever the assumption, this was a good option, but it appeared to be closed on arrival. Eventually, the night watchman wandered to the gate to allow us to camp in the relative security. It appeared he knew of Henri, for PAM used an old military camp that had the classic hangars and 'spider' barrack blocks and central washrooms. We camped in the roof tent, near a wash block, enjoying a peaceful evening.

The C2C boys suggested that the route via Mongo was safer, despite being a southerly detour, for the main N'Djamena road was threatened by bandits. They themselves had run the gauntlet along the main road and rough camped along the way, but regretted taking the risk. We understood northern Chad was off limits. It was an academic desire to go north through the Tibesti Mountains, but they were politically, geologically and culturally blocked. In many ways therefore, it makes them a perfect place to explore; you just can't expect help if you get into trouble. Apparently, the amazing geography and vivid colours of the rocks still show signs from early Man. Discovered rock art offers an insight to a way of life that has not changed. Volcanic eruptions formed the Tibesti Mountains, leaving the highest peak for both Chad and the Sahara region to be Emi Koussi, at 3,445 metres. These volcanic peaks have been eroded, leaving spires and dramatic warrens of carved canyons from ephemeral rivers which, when they do run, are immediately swallowed by the desert.

I had heard about the Tibesti Mountains before. As a captain in the British Airborne Brigade HQ, I arranged the hosting of a French airborne battalion (2e REP Régiment Etranger Parachutistes) in the UK. They were recovering directly from the Chad-Libyan border, where they had been discouraging rebel incursions; hot and dusty work. The cunning plan was to parachute them into Otterburn, a UK training area in Northumberland, to conduct live firing alongside a similar PARA battalion, utilising on all-arms live firing brigade assets and aircraft. Being springtime, Otterburn can experience all four seasons in one day (i.e., it rains) - what could go wrong?

First in, 1 PARA Battlegroup jumped, to go-live from the drop zone, conducting exacting battle drills. On the following day however, the weather closed in, preventing the French drop, so instead, they were inserted by helicopter, enabling them to conduct similar manoeuvres. To be fair to the French parachutists, neither they, nor their kit, were prepared for the Otterburn conditions. Normally based in Corsica, a warm, Mediterranean climate, and having just returned from northern Chad, their light vehicles and equipment rusted in minutes, became bogged and were a liability. Most of the battalion suffered with exposure and cold-related illness; the relatively modest objectives became the 'retreat from Moscow'. We hunkered both battalions into the forestry blocks and made our visitors welcome, in true airborne style. They were good lads, for I dare say if

British PARAs were ripped out of Chad into Otterburn in such conditions, it would have been unpleasant.

We managed an early start from Abache. The night watchman was helpful and also implied we should use the Mongo route, which was well signposted by white route markers, on the 'wrong side' of the road. Some stretches were well graded, but mostly it was winding, sandy tracks through thick scrub and bushes. Occasionally, there was a stout, white post with a French road sign, saying 'bendy road' – quelle surprise. Winston, our Tanzanian safari guide, taught us that, should we need a bush pee, we should tuck in behind the vehicle, looking away from the vehicle, because this area had been driven over and the snakes or whatever would have buggered off. Reasonable or not, we had been exercising such protocols - or so I thought. We stopped by a bend, checking there was no one around, to allow Catherine to go behind the vehicle. I stood at the front, looking forward and around, thinking we had all-round observation. I heard an engine noise behind me, so I turned around to see Catherine mid-flow, but looking back to me 10 yards or so away from Daph and not facing out. Unbeknown to her, a lorry packed with maize bags, with the customary dozen or more turban-headed passengers stacked upon it, was coming slowly around the corner. All the passengers were looking at a pasty, white arse in front of them, eyes out on stalks. The lorry then slowly reversed back around the corner, at which point the gig was up. Catherine was unaware but was concerned that I was facing her and not the other way around. 'What?' she cried. 'Nothing,' I said, stepping slowly in her direction - fatal. I was roundly castigated for not rushing the 20 yards to protect her modesty, yet had I done so, that in itself would have panicked her. Either way, she would have ended up a tangled heap on the ground, trying to pull up her trousers mid-flow. Whatever I had done would have been wrong! She had finished, the lorry had backed away, so off we went, one of us red-faced.

We came across a wide, shallow, flowing river that we needed to ford. Bravely, we allowed a following vehicle to show us the way before we plunged in. It was fine, although far wider than anything previously encountered. Other parts of the road had huge potholes, large enough to rip off the whole wheel assembly, but thankfully, we arrived in Mongo just after midday. We had been unable to trade any dollars for local currency as the customary hawkers were absent at the border. We needed fuel, therefore local currency, but the Mongo banks were closed. We registered with the police, who were both helpful and polite; indeed, one officer even showed us to the market where we could obtain fuel. There were no fuel stations in the traditional Western sense; here, the fuel was hand-pumped from gallon drums into smaller containers, to then be poured into our fuel tank. Most discussions were in French and we had a reasonable chance of communicating, despite a strange dialect. There was some competition between traders to attract our business, but we followed the police suggestion. He left, and we started negotiating. I was concerned about the quality of the fuel and contamination; thankfully, we had a fuel filter on Daph for the large particulates, but not for watered-down diesel. It also smelt strange, but we had little option.

We struck a deal for 100 litres for US$60; so I told them to fill Daph. I say them, for we started to draw quite a crowd and many willing helpers. Catherine stayed within Daph, doors locked, as per our security drill, and soon we were topped up with what I hoped was 100 litres. I had no way to check, but handed over the US$60. Now the argument started; this was not enough. First, they argued amongst themselves and then demanded more than double. One chap spoke pidgin English and tried to explain (frankly, it made matters worse); this was getting out of hand. I was all for driving off, although this was not really viable, so I called for the police, which caused further discourse. The garage owner (I guess it was him) toddled off on his moped and flip-flops to fetch the police. We waited whilst the haggling and argument continued. He was gone for quite a while, but he returned with a large, black chap in a white UN vehicle; clearly not the police.

Dr Jonathan introduced himself in English. He was working with the UN WFP here, although he hailed from Cameroon. It was clear that he commanded some respect, as he too got his fuel here. Initially, he couldn't understand the problem, wondering if we didn't have enough money. I explained the agreement and said I'd handed over the US$60, but they wanted to double it. It was all quite theatrical and strange; he started shouting and raging in both French and local dialects and just as with children, the squabbling stopped. We paid an extra US$20 (not the requested US$130), everyone had saved face and he asked us to follow him back to his UN compound. There was only a few hours of daylight left and we were keen to move on. Dr Jonathan lived in a typical suburban close of houses (albeit wooden prefabs) around a shaded garden and tree enclosure within a protected camp, with

UN guards on a gate.

We parked Daph on his driveway, for he said N'Djamena was a 10-hour drive, manageable in a day. He invited us to stay and asked us out for a beer. Dr Jonathan was a gynaecologist by training but was providing basic, medical support with the UN programme; clearly a man of talents and intellect, yet he was bored. We hadn't really had a drink since Kenya, so we got into his jeep and set off for Mongo. Frankly, we could have been anywhere and this was a risk; our Samaritan was unknown, although making all the right noises. In the bar, he ordered Gula (a Dutch, dark beer brewed in Chad) that kept flowing; Dr Jonathan had quite an appetite. He loved the crowd and invited his mates (anyone in the bar) to join the throng.

It was a good night, but the beer went straight to our heads on an empty stomach and general depletion; it didn't take long before I wasn't keeping up. Dr Jonathan benefitted from a good English education, still based upon the British colonial system, of which he was demonstrably proud. Cameroon was split into an English and French half, of which he was proudly English. Whilst we were delighted to know this, I was left wondering what he'd have said had we been French. He had been working away from home for the last eight years, leaving his wife and children, taking the UN dollar in Bhutan, Niger and now Chad. Learning of Catherine's medical background was music to his ears; he wanted to show off his new, honoured guests. We tried to discuss the plight of women's health issues and the NEPAD initiatives in southern Africa not achieving any effect in Nigeria and the local region, as intended.

All of a sudden, he announced he was off home to get food and ushered us out of the bar. I wasn't sure if this was because I was almost asleep on my feet or becoming incapable of logical responses; I was past being able to tell. Back at his home, his chicken and rice meal was excellent, if a tad spicy (flipping hot!) but frankly, I was not making much sense; no change from normal. How I didn't break my neck unfolding the roof tent on top of Daph was a miracle for a drunk person; we crashed out.

I woke at dawn to see the watchman sitting quietly at the end of the drive on guard. What had happened? God, I felt rough and inwardly castigated myself for placing us at risk, but all appeared well. The world was still swirling and I wanted to get off. Jonathan was up, fresh as a daisy, still buzzing from his unexpected guests, and having us to stay. He was more than happy to change US$100 for local currency; I wanted to pay him more for the hospitality, but he was having none of it. He left at 6.30am for his clinic, so we too packed up, ate some restorative porridge, fed the watchman (who was delighted) and moved on.

The initial 200 kilometres to N'Djamena were on good, freshly-graded roads and we made good time. There were a few traps to be wary of: deep, concrete ravines and drifts that appeared out of nowhere. With full anchors applied and a lot of praying, we managed to slow each time; it was a sobering drive. As expected, such a road couldn't last; we then hit the old road and realised why it needed improvement. As bad roads went, this was really bad. It was so dry that the clay and salt tracks had severe ruts and potholes, hardened like concrete. Poor Daph took a hammering, but her suspension and flexibility ate it up; the OME shocks were working overtime. We did hit a bone-jarring crash and I thought our chips were up; I think we were actually airborne, at 50 kilometres per hour. Two jerry cans had flipped out of their cage and hung down the back of Daph, held only by the flexi-lock. Full marks to the lock, for the cage was only aluminium. Luckily, the cans were empty; had they not been, they would have smashed the rear window, or worse. Although if full, I suspect the weight would have kept them in place. The rear work lamp was a casualty in the process, but I had never really used it, so I yanked it off. I was able to bend the cage back straight with the cans back in place and, in extremis, I could have secured them with a rachet strap but I didn't need to; we pressed on. Daph was performing well; the diesel appeared OK and the steering and suspension were all fine.

With 80 kilometres to run before N'Djamena, we hit main roads, villages and markets. Colour started to appear all around; red bougainvillaea, ladies in vivid red, yellow and green dresses, and coloured fruit displayed at market stalls on the roadside. There were still potholes and cracks in the tar, but this was nothing significant and easily avoided. We noticed a distinct French feel; wide boulevards with foliage in between and buildings with wrought-iron balconies. N'Djamena was a bustling capital, with traffic to match. Without pressing too hard, we had arrived in seven hours; admittedly we hadn't stopped, but the new, graded road made a difference. As advised by the C2C boys, we headed to the Novotel and camped at the rear of the hotel beside some paused construction work. Here we had security, lights, water and access to the pool area (a shower and flushing porcelain) and a café bar where we chilled, assessing our options.

N'Djamena rests on the confluence of the Logone and Chari Rivers, which forms the border with Cameroon whose most northerly Koursseri was on the opposite bank. N'Djamena was originally founded by the French and named Fort Lamy in 1900, after their general who gave his life defending it. It is a very poor country, dependent on agriculture and livestock, which is in turn dependent on unreliable rains. The World Bank and other embassies are represented here, which was ironic; we totally failed to acquire any money from any bank or elsewhere. Indeed, we spent a frustrating day bouncing between Niger and Algerian embassies seeking visas and paying in US dollars as we had no local currency. We got our Niger visa directly, but unsurprisingly, the Algerian Embassy resembled the Libyan Embassy in Khartoum.

We returned late afternoon to our campsite to find the pool crowded with relaxing French and UN soldiers, and prostitutes clearly doing a vibrant trade; we left them to it. Taking advantage of our security and washing facilities, I removed each of Daph's wheel and serviced all the moving parts, brakes and de-gunged everything I could find. This led to pulling everything out of the back of Daph and cleaning everything down. Dust was everywhere, but it was good to know that the packing system was working. Inside the Wolf Pack boxes and containers, everything was clean and our equipment was working. As dusk approached, we were hot, filthy and in need of a drink. The soldiers and girls had played themselves out, so we had the pool facilities to ourselves for a swim and sundowner, before heading out into the crazy N'Djamena evening traffic. Daph was driving well, but the French roundabout system was not so good. Having priority from the right meant that each large roundabout became a car park for the hawkers and street sellers to ply their trade. We headed to the new Carrefour hypermarket to find largely empty shelves. We treated ourselves to some expensive French cheese and pastries that had seen better days and shopped for better quality and far cheaper fruit and veg on the street stalls.

Our plan was to circumvent Lake Chad as the C2C boys had done. We were aware of the challenge and understood that the military patrols and bandits avoided the other. It meant soft sand, terrain we feared most, but it was passable and we could avoid longer detours in more vulnerable countries. We were still unsure where and how to cross the Sahara, if at all. We thought we might have to ship Daph home, which would be a disappointing outcome, having come this far.

The following day, we left N'Djamena and headed to Ngouri and then Bol. Once off the main road, the tracks had a fine, white powder that settled everywhere. These roads were passable (graded and dilapidated tracks) and Bol was manageable by non-4x4 pick-up trucks, most of whom were overladen with a dozen extra passengers and baggage, if not more. Plus, they sped past us. We reached Bol at around 4pm to find a collection of mud huts and a few wooden buildings under trees. The immigration hut was actually well-marked, but the chef was not there. After a wait and some haggling, we were taken on foot to the chef's hut where, sprawled out on carpets and rugs, he was sharing tea with his friends, but he was genial and stamped the passports. Back at customs, they tried to force a price hike for overtime and a 'petit cadeau' if they were to stamp the documents that evening. Or they could do it for free tomorrow! Fine, I said we'd come back tomorrow and got up to leave, when they promptly stamped and returned the documents.

We were shown the official camping facilities at Bol; an awful, unsafe disgrace by the market area. The place was infested with flies and God knows what. To cap this, it was five times the price of the expensive Novotel and with no facilities. No, thank you; we'd be safer and better off bush camping, which was what we left to do. Later, we came across an experimental farm that was closing for the night; we waved at the farmer and asked if we could camp out of sight from the road inside his perimeter. He was very interested in our journey, embraced us within his secure area and showed us around the farm. He said he'd be back the following morning and that his night watchman (aka Sleeping Beauty) was walking about if we needed anything.

The following morning, we tried to pay the farmer but he refused, however we did buy some of his produce and some excellent, fresh bread. The route up to RigRig was very soft and sandy going. On more than one occasion, I thought we'd had it. I had my tyre pressures as low as I dared and we tried to keep a low range momentum going. Then it happened. All of a sudden, a loss of power and we sank, stuck fast. Naturally, I did the wrong thing, but it was an instinctive reaction to power ourselves out. We were stuck fast in the middle of nowhere amid a sandy morass. But we knew what to do, so after some judicious shovelling and getting our handy track mats out and under the wheels, we popped out. Phew! This was going to be a long and arduous leg. Direction finding around RigRig was a drama and we became discombobulated. We should have remained on the western track to avoid the village, but we thought we had to get the police stamp before we could exit the border, so we blundered around. Eventually we found the police hut, with a very old, drunken and blind man to scribe his initials and stamp our papers, pay and critically get the US$1 receipt as evidence we were stamped. A young boy showed us the way out and thankfully, we slipped and slithered our way out of RigRig. We were trying to play by the rules, as you never know what's down the road, yet I was struggling to see the point. I think most just drove through without stopping.

We crossed the dunes and the pan; Daph soldiered on, despite the soft sand. Getting the rev range balanced was key; too little and you get nowhere and dig in, too much and you lose control and dig in, yet just right and you can glide over the surface delicately. At the far side of the pan was a police post and border. It was manned, but they said they had to wait for the chef - here we go again. We showed our papers and they let us pass, so clearly if there was a system, we never sussed it out. I'm sure the locals did their own thing, paying bribes.

Now out of Chad, we had a 60 kilometre stretch of No Man's Land before Niger. It was academic of course, as these were straight lines where once there was a lake and shifting sands. It was getting late, so we broke track and stuffed ourselves into a thick bush and rough camped, with Daph well-hidden in a slight hollow. Rather than raise our profile, we comfortably used the Oztent. We cooked a Spanish omelette from the Carrefour's eggs and cheese, then settled down on the warm sand for a quiet night. But sadly, it was not to be; poor Catherine had a bad reaction. For the first time on the trip, we had gippy tummies and Catherine was up and down like a Jack in the box, with me following behind with a shovel to ensure we were not contaminating our camp site; it was all very Laurel and Hardy. By morning, we were exhausted and Catherine was very dehydrated; I was getting salts and water down her as best I could, but clearly the exertions that day had been too much. Evidently, her shoulder was stiff and painful, but she never said so. On reflection, it was just as well we were on the ground and not up in the roof tent; that really would have been exhausting.

Chapter 21
Following a hunch

We woke to hear lorries trundling past some distance away. How did they navigate the soft sand and officialdom? No matter, we were shattered. Catherine was taking on liquids, which was good. She felt better, but travelling would only exacerbate any symptoms and feelings of grottiness. She popped a paracetamol and declared herself off solids for the day to see how she felt. We had previously discussed holing up under such circumstances and, whilst we could last several days in our little hollow, we both wanted to move on.

We swiftly covered the last 40-odd miles to N'guigmi, the first principle town of Niger. Like most towns of the Sahel, it basically formed a grid pattern, with six-foot high mud wall enclosures and scattered scrub and bushes. It was common in North Africa to be unable to see into these compounds, conferring a soulless air to the place. N'guigmi used to be on Lake Chad's shoreline until the lake retreated, for the town has always been a crossroads for the traditional camel caravans crossing the Sahara.

Entering N'guigmi was like entering Fort Zanderneuf of the Beau Geste tales. We reported to the obvious gendarmerie for our entry stamp, where they directed us to Murdo; the local Mr Fix It. This was an interesting development and we wondered if this was another ruse to obtain a 'petite cadeau', which was becoming all too frequent, but Murdo found us in the customs compound. He took it upon himself to get our Carnet stamped, as he clearly knew what he was doing and commanded the place. Although a large, imposing fellow, dressed in his white jilbab and hat, he was very helpful and spoke passable English. If there was a catch, it was the absence of local currency facilities; there were no banks in the town. Murdo guided us through the market to enable us to change our CFA and some dollars into BCEAO (the equivalent of West African francs). It appeared that food supplies were plentiful here, so we topped up and Murdo also directed us to fuel. The administration was swift and accurate, plus we acquired a péage ticket all the way through to Agadez. Initially unsure on the value of this yet, it proved to be a real help at subsequent checkpoints. Murdo advised us on routes and places to stay and interestingly, he implied it was possible to get an Algerian visa at the consulate in Agadez. Our ears pricked up. He insisted that his services were free, although we realised there was a healthy percentage within the exchange rates that we negotiated; nothing here was free.

The first thing I did was inflate Daph's tyres. She was driving well and the steering rod repair remained solid. We were told that the 670 kilometres to Zinder was all tar, which became true, although the road between N'guigmi and Diffa was appallingly potholed with broken tar. We transited what appeared to be a plain; the Sahel has vast, open spaces with light scrub scattered across the horizon. Making good progress, it was likely we would reach Zinder in a day; it was a long slog, but we arrived at Zinder just before sunset. Without messing about, we took Murdo's advice and stayed at the Hotel Damagaram in the centre of town. Zinder was a large town, where the BIA-Niger Bank advertised the use of credit cards. However, as we arrived on a Friday evening and they observed a Muslim calendar, we were not able to take advantage, which was irritating. All was not lost for whilst the Damagaram was more than we wanted to pay (and was still not particularly comfortable), we were able to exchange dollars to pay our bill at the bank rate. Our main worry was for Daph as we had to park her outside the hotel perimeter; not ideal, but we were assured that we were just down the road from the police station (not that this was a comfort) and the hotel employed a guard to look after the vehicles.

After an anxious night, the night watchman was as good as his word and Daph was fine. Since this was a Muslim country, I guess any petty thief wanted to retain the use of his hands, and the watchman wanted to keep his job. It did call to mind an Italian experience, where no matter who you are or what security you have, if a robber wants something, they generally get it. I was thinking of a particular week in Italy, working alongside the Director SAS and his staff, when we had driven down from Pisa to Naples for a key meeting in the NATO HQ. We, or rather the SAS lads, parked their hire car as directed, outside the main NATO HQ gate, 20 yards away from the armed guards. As we passed through the gate, they told the guards where the car was and asked them to keep an eye on it. In addition to the inherent car security, they fitted a provided 'steering and clutch' lock for good measure. Well, no surprises, on returning to the car a few hours later, it was gone. The gate guard had seen nothing. Mind you, if we thought

Khartoum or Nairobi's traffic was bad, it was nothing compared to Naples, where driving was definitely a combat and contact sport.

Being Ramadan, the hotel restaurant was closed. We decided to cook a snack in the room using one of our multi-fuel camping stoves. We had not used these since testing them in Pretoria. It was a new version of Primus, a hiking Spider and multi-fuel gas bottle. Well, I nearly set myself on fire as the flash and flare on ignition was tremendous. The gas had been shaken so much, there was obviously some leak. Thankfully, it was not serious, and no curtains or eyebrows were damaged. Later, we enjoyed a coffee at the bar, when a white South African came up to us and said, 'You must be the chap from KaapStad.' The guy was working with CellTech, establishing mobile phones in the country. He was excited to speak with other Westerners, but clearly disappointed not to meet a fellow South African! Still, we enjoyed a very amicable evening.

We had covered quite a distance relatively quickly; notable, given that Niger is one of the larger West African countries and over 80% is covered by the Sahara. Despite its size and the uranium ore extracted at Arlit, the country suffers a subsistence economy, being one of the world's poorest. It is landlocked, although the mighty Niger River runs through the western side. Niger remains a natural transit and trading country for the caravans passing across the Sahara; humans have inhabited the territory for millennia, as stone tools and rock art has been found, dating back to around 280,000 BC. Early hunter-gatherers here enjoyed a much wetter and more fertile Sahara than today, a phenomenon archaeologists refer to as the 'Green Sahara'.

In 2019, scientists used nascent technology to re-count tree density; they assessed that there were three trillion trees in 2015, compared to the last count of 400 billion in 2009. First, who knew they counted trees? And second, this is not an individual wandering around with a clicker. On both occasions, they used satellite imagery for the audit, but fidelity in 2009 was only able to detect large clumps of trees or crown size. By 2015, they applied AI and supercomputers, discovering 1.8 billion trees. The blank areas of their maps were not blank. Measuring the planet's arboreal count is a vital step towards assessing the planet's health. The more accurate a tree count would, by implication, determine stored carbon levels. Deforestation is key to appreciating weather patterns and global warming events. Well, a drive through the scrub and arid areas could have indicated a greater number; it reminded me of WWF-UK, who produced a report announcing an increase in panda numbers over what was expected because they had looked in a wider area than before.

We had read about the Aïr Mountains being green and offering a fascinating, geological destination. Indeed, we understood that the Tuareg-led dominance of the north (mixing with the Hausa tribes) had created the Sultanate of Aïr exerting control over the trade routes, based around Agadez, until their eventual dilution from the spread of Islam and Arabs mixing with the southern tribes. The Mali (desert) Empire dominated the region, until the rise and takeover by the Songhai Empire, exerting their trade and influence of the Niger River. The southern tribes constantly fought for control, yet the tribes based around Lake Chad grew in dominance. Around the 1700s, rule was exercised by the Sayfawa Dynasty and the Sultanate of Damagaram, whose regional power was centred on Zinder.

By the 19th century, Europeans started to take a greater interest in Africa, initially exploiting the Niger River, first led by Mungo Park. Europe triggered their unseemly 'Scramble for Africa', carving territories with straight lines without heed or credence to populations or tribes. France gained control of the upper Niger River and administered its territory from Zinder, until around 1900, when the Military Territory of Niger was subsequently created and the capital formed at Niamey, then little more than a village.

Zinder was another crossroads for us; which route to take home was becoming an overriding quest. Travel for the sake of adventure was becoming secondary to completing our journey home. Despite the bailout and shipping options, we really wanted to get to Morocco to explore the Atlas Mountains. Now, we were almost at the point of making things up as we went along, or rather, taking opportunities as they presented themselves. Not being the internet age, we were relying on a few source materials, principally (or rather solely) our Africa on a Shoestring guide, which was a little dated by emergent events. Libya was starting to open (for north-to-south travellers only) and Algeria's borders were closed. The border with Morocco and Algeria was closed and the disputed lands to the south were being contested by the Polisario Front.

Yet Murdo had been correct on most things thus far, so why should we doubt him now? He suggested that we could get an Algerian visa in Agadez and we wanted to see the Grand Mosque. The most reliable location to acquire a visa would be the capital, Niamey, which was at least two days' driving each way plus the time to obtain the visa. If that was not possible, at least we'd be further down the road for the alternative southern options under consideration. All of this was likely to preclude a trip north to Agadez; we knew that the chances of getting an Algerian visa there were slim. Ironically, the more we realised that Algeria was closed for tourism, the more we wanted to get there. The real kicker was the Lonely Planet's Shoestring book that only had a few pages, most of which were focused on the south and west of the country. Agadez warranted a page and a town diagram, on which was an arrow pointing out of town to an Algerian consulate. That was good enough for us so we decided to head there. It would remove a week or more between Niamey and back if we were successful in obtaining our visas, and if not, at least we would see the desert north.

The following morning, we went to register with the police but 'the man with the stamp' was not there and we were told we had to wait until 10am for him to arrive. Usual story. This time we didn't wait, but pressed on, for our stamp was supposed to give us passage to Agadez already. The first half of the 450 kilometre drive to Agadez was on reasonable tar, the remainder being light, graded, sandy tracks. Although slightly corrugated, these sandy tracks were maintained and nothing like what we had already experienced, so we whizzed along. The scenery was sand and scrub, mostly flat, until we hit the Falaise de Tiguidit, a rock escarpment that broke the monotony. We completed the journey to Agadez in an uneventful four hours.

The first sight of Agadez was the airport, usually a reliable source of information, but this 1920s-style relic was small, deserted and closed. Aside from a graded strip, the terminal building was a stone, single-storey building with a green, corrugated, tin roof, with a second floor on the side for the control tower. Agadez appeared a confusing town, a grid pattern but on a slant that defied logic; the main road north bypassed the town. We expected to see the Grand Mosque standing tall and proud above the skyline, but no. We found the Main Square by accident, only then finding the unimposing mosque feature. We tried to go inside the Grand Mosque, but due to our infidel status, we were barred. It certainly was impressive, built in 1515 and rebuilt in the same style in 1844. An imposing, mud-built tower, it was reputed to be the tallest, mud-brick structure in the world with distinctive, wooden poles jutting out horizontally at intervals throughout its cone steeple. On the Main Square was Pension Tellit that we knew to be the posh accommodation in Agadez, again a classical mud-built construction. But we also learn of another B&B (Pension Tellit de Vittorio) on the edge of town and close to the Algerian consulate.

The Pension Tellit de Vittorio staff were extremely friendly, although initially quite unsure and shy about our unscheduled request to stay. The owner was an Italian (Vittorio) and was at home in Italy at the time. It turned out that Vittorio also owned the other Tellit and the principle restaurant on the square, the Restaurant Pilier opposite. Moustapha appeared to be left in charge; he was very efficient and allowed us to eat at the restaurant on our hotel bill, so we had a magical dinner there that evening. From the outside, the mud-constructed, fort-like building was distinctive; tables and chairs were arranged in the open central square under the stars. We sat warming our feet in the hot sand, gazing up at the sky. There was no roof nor light pollution so the full gamut of night stars opened up before our eyes. The food was a fascinating fusion of French, Moroccan and local cuisine. For the first time since Ethiopia/East Africa, we came across tourists; the only others we had met were aid workers or business people, and a few travellers like us. Here though, within our Beau Geste Fort, we met a group of French tourists on a package holiday to Niger, destined for a short trip into the Aïr and Ténéré desert; we were not aware such packages were possible.

The following morning, whilst queuing to register with the police, we met three Swiss travellers, Peter, Barbara and Kasper. They had travelled down through Algeria, the way we thought to go, so we hastily arranged to meet later that day, after we had registered. Whilst registration was free, the policeman suggested a 'petit cadeau', but when challenged, he backed down and told us we could go. We scuttled out before he could change his mind and ventured into one of the travel agents nearby, Caravane Voyages. We asked their advice regarding Algerian visas. After much sucking of teeth and hesitation, they suggested we speak to their representative at the consulate the following day, which we successfully arranged.

The historic centre of Agadez is a UNESCO World Heritage site; the market was flourishing, selling silver and leather handiwork, as well as fresh fruit and vegetables, and camels. Agadez is a focus for camel caravans, mostly bringing salt from Bilma. Caravans traded in all directions, between the West African cities of Kano, down to Timbuktu, to the North African oases of Ghat, Ghadames and Tripoli. Today, the core transportation by trucks is the uranium, mined at Arlit.

That afternoon, we met the Swiss and shared travel tips; they were proof that travel in Algeria was possible. They had been planning their trip for a while, for Peter had prior experience of adventure in Algeria. They weren't sure if it was possible to enter Algeria from the south, but critically, they gave us their GPS waypoints and maps to download onto our computer, should we get our visa. They in turn were heading down through Nigeria and on to the southwestern African coast to Angola, itself only just opening, so our advice was generic. Route experience is invaluable, especially names of contacts. Hitherto we had not really used our GPS; there's a first time for everything. It didn't take long to start discussing each other's vehicles. They loved Daph, especially the roof tent. Their Toyota FJ62 was desert-adapted and Peter was concerned about jungle and mud, which would feature prominently for their remaining journey.

Travel is never smooth; there can be highs and lows, even within a day. When incidents occur, they are sudden, frequently violent and always shocking. We thought about venturing into the Ténéré, as we understood it's a uniquely fabulous expanse of uninterrupted desert. There is something quite wonderful, clean and honest about a desert. The nights are pure and clear, if somewhat cold. The absence of light pollution provides a terrific view of the night's sky, whilst the days are hot and bright. Obviously, travel can be inhospitable and challenging, but most deserts are not rolling sand dunes, but rock and shale. The Ténéré is a vast sand sheet; a featureless wilderness of desert covering almost 150,000 square miles of hyper-arid, extremely hot and a year-round, bone-dry desert, devoid of plant life. Described by NASA as one of the sunniest points in the world, it's also among the most extreme environments on earth. Water is notoriously difficult to find, even underground. The wells may be hundreds of miles apart, yet ironically, back in the Carboniferous period, the region was beneath the sea. Later it became a tropical forest before it dried out.

The Ténéré bestrides northern Chad, Niger and part of Algeria and Libya, flanked by the Aïr Mountains to the west, Hoggar Mountains to the north and the Tibesti and Lake Chad in the east and south. There were numerous travel agents in Agadez happy to charge for guide services into the Ténéré, for a price, for a single vehicle off the beaten track would be unwise. The bandits know the authorised guides and avoid them, but an unrecognised vehicle is catnip. Peter knew of another Swiss couple who had ventured into the Ténéré, who sadly fell prey to bandits. It's all too easy to blame the Tuareg, hence I use the term 'bandits' who were rife in this area, ready to hold up any unsuspecting traveller. This poor Swiss couple were robbed, the man beaten half to death, the poor wife raped and their 4x4 taken; the robbers' ultimate prize. We were sad to learn that the wife died, but the man was found on the edge of death trying to walk out of the Ténéré. He was reportedly found by chance when a Taureg guide came across him and recovered him back to a hospital in Agadez.

The following morning, we kept our appointment with Caravane Voyages, the travel agent presenting our visa case. We were told that their representative would speak to the consulate before we met again at 11am. We made sure that he understood we were unable to apply whilst in the UK as we had been travelling for the past seven months, having previously been residing in South Africa. We were not keen to repeat our Khartoum experience with the Libyan visa. At the appointed time, we arrived at the Algerian consulate with the representative from the agency and together, we waited for an hour or so outside the consul's office. Just as the place was closing, Catherine and I were ushered into an office. The consul was suited, very formal and business-like. I guess it was a cultural thing, but the conversation was all in French. We tried to look as presentable as possible and throughout the formal exchange, the consul never took his eyes off me. He understood we were travelling and had tried to get visas in London previously but asked why we wanted to travel to Algeria. Catherine's French is far superior to my rather clunky, schoolboy translations, so watching the consul carefully, I introduced Catherine to explain. I could feel Catherine's hackles rising from across the room as she set off like a machine-gun, explaining our journey, hopes and aspirations, and why Algeria would be a highlight of our trip. She said later that it all came tumbling out. After five minutes, she came up for air and the consul, still looking at me enquiringly, said, 'Sorry, can you say that again please, but more slowly.' 'Yes, of course,' I said, and asked Catherine to repeat our position. I was sure steam was still rising from Catherine, but I chose not to look. She repeated the tale and the consul, still looking at me, said fine, please come back tomorrow morning.

The travel agent was delighted to have helped, confident that we would get the visas and refused to charge for their services. We went to celebrate with a second visit to Pilier restaurant that evening, where we met a Danish and Australian couple. They had spent the last year or more running the container port at Benin for Maersk and had flown in to experience the desert before they swapped Benin for their next appointment in the US. They were great fun, amazed by the clear sky at night and for us, a useful backup contact if our plans needed to change. Well, with every advance, there is an equal and opposite, something like one of Newton's laws, for as we arrived at the embassy, the staff were evasive and started to ask basic, administrative information. Here we go - our morale took a slump. We were told to return at 5pm.

We prepared to move, checking Daph over, refreshing the water jerry cans and cleaning; staying positive. The well water at Agadez is worthy of a mention, for it was both crystal clear and had a sweetness and freshness to it. Strangely, we had never really 'tasted' water in the same way, other than to note bad or stale water, having resided in plastic or metal for too long. We steeled ourselves for the 5pm consulate meeting and again we were kept waiting for almost an hour. Then, a new set of large, ornate doors were opened and we were ushered into another, more plush room where the consul presented us with our visas. Blimey, you could have knocked us down with a feather! He was beaming and wished us a bon voyage and, with a flourish in English, said as a parting shot, 'I don't think you could get visas that quickly from London.' Too damn right; well done sir, and thank you. After handshakes and a photo with the consul, an administrator ushered us out and caught us to pay. It was the going rate and, whilst he was filling out a form (always the endless forms), he kept asking me about my job. I had always put down 'economist' as it covered a multitude of sins, yet he remained flummoxed, so I simply beamed at him.

The next morning, we were up early and hit the road at 5.30am. Agadez was a peaceful and welcoming place, although there was a definite 'undercurrent' of people skulking and hanging about; we supposed it didn't help that they all wore blue turbans and covered their weather-beaten faces. The journey to Arlit took less than two hours on good tar, across a barren and featureless road. We were ready and expecting the various officials to wave us down to see our passports as we'd been warned about their expectation.

There was nothing at Arlit to stop for; it was a typical village with mud walls around compounds and sandy streets, yet the uranium mines and factories on the edge of town were huge. We almost drove into one, for the route took us straight into it. Created by the French in the late 1960s and early 1970s, two large, open strip mines have gouged the ore from the earth and the uranium is shipped to France by road and sea through Benin's ports. Interestingly, we never saw any trucks moving north or south in our time there. NGOs and other organisations have been highly critical of the environmental impacts and poor health and safety standards at the mines. The early boom years slumped by the 1980s, although we understood a resurgence in the early 21st century has occurred. What was evident was that little to no traffic went north past Arlit. One persistent officer at a road barrier on exiting Arlit was desperate for a 'petit cadeau' and asked us for our car insurance; a first for us in this part of the world and a little too late as we were leaving Niger. The hand of friendship was alive and well for the poor, confused policeman.

Given what we'd heard about the unfortunate Swiss couple in the Ténéré, we didn't venture into either the Ténéré or Aïr Mountains. We didn't want to place ourselves in a compromised position; crossing the Sahara as a single vehicle was sufficiently dodgy. Yet this was a shame, for as we passed the Aïr, we could see the triangular mountain range rising out of the sand expanse. As we got closer, it revealed part of the nine circular, granite massifs that form the Aïr Plateau. These are remnants of an extinct caldera, leaving the high plateau of today, criss-crossed by the seasonal wadis where rivers once flowed. Known as a green region, the Aïr are largely bare of vegetation, and the dry wadi valleys (known locally as 'Kori' by the Hausa) channel and hold rainwater in gueltas (stone pools), creating the picturesque oases within the sharp, slab-sided valleys. Underground watercourses continue to provide year-round water and seasonal vegetation to the subsistence farmers in the area. The Aïr contain ancient rock art, some of which dates back to 6,000 BC. A particular discovery from 1999 depicts a five metre giraffe carving at Dabours, indicating hunting or conflict using what appears to be horses pulling chariots.

The sandy piste out of Arlit was reducing our speed to between 60 and 80 kilometres per hour. Soon, we had the classic dilemma over directions across a featureless, endless expanse. It certainly led to a meaningful discussion in the vehicle. As a first, we had the Swiss' GPS up and running; its information was contrary to all the other information and data we saw. Classic navigation (by day, without a sun compass) is to move between known points. But if you cannot see such known points, move between key route markers, those denoted either by oil drums or substantial, existing tracks. In the books by Chris Scott (Desert Travels) and Tom Sheppard (Vehicle-dependent Expedition Guide), both include great detail on navigation, waypoints, direction AIDS and the dos and don'ts. It's all very logical and simple, until you're faced with the tracks disappearing right, the oil drums marking left and the GPS pointing straight on.

The first step was to reduce the tyre pressure; you'd be amazed at the impact this has on traction and going in soft sand. And this was soft sand. Secondly, if the GPS said central but we went left or right, we'd know how to correct any error. Finally, the tracks must be recent, as there were loads, and whilst the wind would cover them eventually, these were fresh. So logically, we chose the drums. Whilst they too can shift on the moving sands, they also had tracks and the drums had been placed there for a reason. We pressed on and gradually the routes coalesced and intertwined. After all, there was only really one destination, Assamakam, on the border. Apart from the occasional patches of very soft sand, we easily managed to maintain momentum and progress.

This was our first real test of the Garmin. I bought it initially for flying, as a back-up tool for the topographically embarrassed student pilot, but although I programmed it and carried it as a support tool, visual flying was more fun and very manageable. We had used the Garmin as a speedo when the speedometer cable broke in Botswana, but we were never really dependent upon it for wayfinding, so never had to trust it. Neither had I experienced one in the military; the mark one eyeball, map and compass, bearing and pacing was always sufficient. Today, people use the function every day to navigate around the streets or shops via their smartphone, but in 2002, this was nascent technology. And we were crossing the Sahara. Our first-generation Garmin was a hand-held, battery-powered (albeit chargeable on Daph) device with a simple compass direction pointer, which indicated both speed and altitude, as well as latitude and longitude. There was a map function on a simplistic, black-and-white, grainy screen, showing only major roads, towns or known waypoints. We could plug in waypoints; indeed, we loaded the waypoints from the Swiss so we could backtrack their route, which we were picking up. This last piece of knowledge was a huge relief, offering some surety as we ventured into the unknown. It really brought to mind early travellers stepping into the unknown; the 16th century sailors navigating to the edge of the flat earth or the caravan routes across the Sahara, let alone space travel. Well, one step at a time.

As we reached Assamakam, we nearly didn't stop. The ramshackle, white, flat-topped, mud or brick buildings were being gradually swallowed up by sand. The place was deserted and most buildings had sand up to the top floor levels. Few buildings had windows of any sort and the setting did not inspire confidence that this was Niger's northern border. It was a totally non-descript, deserted village, with empty buildings half-buried with sand and rubbish blowing all around. The customs and immigration buildings were not immediately obvious. Walking between the buildings was a major effort, as the sand was so soft; it was a classic case of one step forward, three back. In the event, the customs process was easy, but immigration were irritating and wanted to see our driving licences. We weren't sure why, as we were exiting Niger, but we didn't argue. The immigration office was akin to all the others, a room consisting of a couple of beds, one of which was occupied by an officer who was woken up to log our driving licences and a desk at which two other officers sat. There was graffiti all over the walls. Outside, a money changer kept hassling us to change our dollars (we eventually found out he was offering a better rate than in Algeria), but we only exchanged our remaining West African CFA for Algerian dinar. A hawker tried to sell us diesel by telling us we could not get any at the next village, which we knew was not true, as fuel in Algeria was much cheaper and we already carried sufficient. We crossed the border, thus opening a hitherto closed country, the People's Democratic Republic of Algeria.

Chapter 22
Joy from an unexpected bonus

Once officially out of Niger, we continued to follow the oil drums and tracks, reassured we were on track with the GPS, for a further 12 kilometres. The soft, endless sand gradually gave way to more gravel and a firmer surface. Rock features started to appear to the flanks. The weather was hot, dry and bright. Eventually, the Algerian customs post came into view, a brand-new facility which was a fenced, concrete, prefab building that jarred against the environment. We presented ourselves to the customs official in my halting French, who promptly replied in fluent (condescending) English, 'Speak either English or French.' Efficiently, our passports were stamped, before sending us on to customs; it was like a drive-through processing system, a first on our journey. Customs took a while longer as we were behind two waiting trucks. We had seen no other vehicles en route and supposedly the border was not open. Yet we followed fresh tracks, despite the border being 'officially' closed to northern bound travel.

We'd read and heard that customs could be harsh, confiscating items like cameras and binoculars (now secreted) but we experienced quite the opposite. After about 20 minutes, we were called in, where an officer compiled his report, stamped the Carnet and completed a currency declaration sheet. He was meticulous, transcribing detail across eight different books, making a point of explaining each one in good English. Another officer came out to search the vehicle, but in the event, he only checked the chassis and VIN number, before stating we were free to go. For the most unlikely border crossing of all, it was unexpectedly smooth, efficient and all too easy; we were in Algeria.

We drove on an open piste for around 12 kilometres before arriving at the border town of In Guezzam. Arranged in the familiar grid layout of mud-brick compounds, we felt there was a quiet, almost deserted feel to the town. Admittedly, it was close to 4pm during Ramadan and we needed to find the gendarmerie to check in. In a compound on the edge of town, we sat whilst the policeman laboriously translated our passport details into Arabic. We were keen to zip off and hide in the desert for the night, preferably after refuelling. Fatal - by asking where we could obtain fuel, it just prompted more questions. Eventually, the Chef de Brigade came out to meet us and said there was no fuel in In Guezzam. As it was Ramadan, he insisted we pitched our tent outside the walls of the gendarmerie, on the street for the night. This all sounded a bit strange, but on reflection, he was clearly concerned about regional security and didn't want foreigners wandering around his patch. I asked if we could camp inside the compound, to afford Catherine some privacy, but the chef stressed that safety was not an issue; during Ramadan, nothing would happen to us. Eventually, it was agreed that should we need anything, we had to ring the bell. Catherine was offered the bathroom facilities if required and he would find fuel in the morning.

If felt strange to be camped on the street outside a compound, but to call it a street would be a misnomer. There was no road demarcation or pavement, just a sandy expanse on the edge of town. One might have thought we presented a greater risk being there, where people might hassle us at best, or worse, someone drive into us, but we were assured such things did not happen in Algeria. No one stopped and the few people who passed just hustled by, heads down. The chef turned up after dark to ask for two empty jerry cans, just at the point when a three-vehicle patrol roared out of the compound. Observing their religious rules, we were cooking, so offered the chef some food, which he gracefully declined. He promptly returned our full cans of diesel and insisted we did not have to pay; it was his gift to us. Naturally, we were very grateful and appreciate that Muslims support fellow travellers, but we rather felt that he wanted the infidels off his patch. We packed everything away and huddled into the roof tent, snug and secure. Despite the plummeting temperature, we crashed out.

The 2011 division of Sudan, recognising South Sudan, meant that Algeria became the largest African country. The majority of Algeria's population and the country's primary economic activity is aligned along the coast, except for the country's oilfields locked under the central desert ergs. The northern Tell Atlas and Saharan Atlas have large plains for agriculture. The southern ergs are primarily large, extensive sand dunes. Further south is the Hoggar Mountain range, covering almost 200,000 square miles, containing the country's only natural World Heritage Site, the Tassili n'Ajjer National Park. This UNESCO site contains ancient and unique rock formations with evidence of early civilisation and associated rock art. Desert temperatures remain hot year-round, and classically, after sunset, temperatures plummet. The clear, dry air allows rapid heat loss leading to cool, chilly nights, conferring extreme daily temperature ranges.

We were definitely feeling the cold mornings now, so we didn't hang about. I needed to wear a warm jacket to make the morning cuppa until the sun did its thing. Catherine sensibly stayed in the roof tent until her tea was passed up before she stirred so we were noticeably slower in packing up and moving off in the mornings. The initial piste after In Guezzam was a mix of potholed tar and sandy tracks, both frequently covered by sand drifts. Overnight, I had reinflated Daph's tyres, as the terrain was changing, no longer being just soft sand. Maybe we were being overly cautious; we'd heard many stories of people (legally or otherwise) using any standard car to reach West Africa to sell on at an inflated price. How they struggled through the Sahara was not always a mystery, for we saw many abandoned vehicles and all kinds of wrecks littering the piste. The considered classic desert vehicle was the Peugeot 504 and we saw a few of these abandoned. Others imply the Citroen 2CV was more adapted, being light, agile and when stuck, easily lifted out. Thankfully, we saw no abandoned Land Rovers.

The Second World War and resultant post-colonial revolt against French rule culminated in 1962 with independence, after a brutal civil war. Travellers and adventurers transited Algeria to explore further south. Algeria was akin (although second fiddle) to the 1960's 'Hippie Trail' through Turkey, Iran, Afghanistan to Thailand, but such freedoms ended with oil exploitation, civil unrest and the economic recession hit in the 1980s. The country became closed and isolated during a further civil war from 1991 and it only opened (for us?) in 2002. The piste and Swiss GPS waypoints were relatively easy to follow. The conditions varied from open and sandy, occasionally corrugated gravel track, or dry riverbeds, paralleling few escarpments. At one point, the GPS implied we were way off course, but we were following the oil drum marker posts, signed Tamanrasset. We were climbing as the Hoggar Mountains revealed themselves. All routes led to Tamanrasset, the capital of southern Algeria.

Reading the 1958 teams diary, they endured an eight-day epic to get from Tamanrasset to Agadez, compared to our easy couple of days. Despite our more modern equipment and GPS (a huge assurance), fundamentally the area, tracks and route markers were similar to those that Chris and the team traversed. They received advice from Mr Sorrel, the Counsel General in Algiers, who connected them to Saharan veteran, Freddy Fox, who briefed them. Their movement between Algiers south through the ergs was slow and radio-controlled, given the high French presence in Algeria; there were nearly 450,000 French troops and police in-country. By the time they reached Tamanrasset, recent flash floods had washed away much of the piste and markers, forcing the local chef to halt all southern bound traffic for a few days. Lorries were dragging old tyres behind them to smooth out key routes and remark the piste. The boys' luck held, for as they waited at Tam, they connected with a Frenchman (Andre) who was intent on delivering an excessively heavy load of stores to Agades in an ancient UMIC lorry. He had a team of Arabs, his mistress and a local Toureg guide, but as a packet, they were permitted to depart. The going was tough and the truck endured constant mechanical issues. There was much digging and sand-channelling to keep them moving; they travelled mostly in the cool of the night. The fech fech around In Guezzam was extremely challenging; at one stage, they were tugging the recalcitrant lorry out with both straining Land Rovers. More than once, they considered abandoning the lorry to its own devices. Their route was not direct, instead, they were navigating between water wells. One has to wonder the true load on that truck! They eventually emerged near Agadez at a Toureg nomad camp, where a goat was killed for a collective feast. This was fine, until the doctors were presented with the traditional camels' milk and goats' blood cocktail!

They just avoided the first atmospheric atomic test at Reggane on their return up the western Algerian border, but the later underground tests in the mid-1960s at In Ekker, south of Tamanrasset, were after they passed. Just as well the local inhabitants were evacuated, for these later tests did not go as planned; the underground site was insufficiently sealed and black smoke and debris radiated around the detonation. Unsurprisingly, there is no public health data or records regarding radiation effects or local impact, but activists have been pressing France to clean up such sites, both here and in French Polynesia, since 2008. Thus far, little has happened, despite the pressing factor of potential natural gas 'fracking' from under the Sahara being considered. We were oblivious to these issues as we travelled through and so far, we do not glow in the dark, but who knows about long-term health risks?

Since the 2002 opening of the southern border, the Maghreb Insurgency spread south and was supported by militant groups aligned to al-Qaeda. They initially called themselves the Salafist Group for Preaching and Combat (GSPC) before they became known as 'al-Qaeda in the Islamic Maghreb', or AQIM. By 2007, Algeria and other affected Maghreb states were offered assistance from the US, Europe (mainly France) and the UK, under Operation Enduring Freedom-Trans Sahara. The Sahel security situation had deteriorated; Tamanrasset had become 'Route One' for Sahel immigrants, refugees and insurgents seeking passage to Europe. By 2020, President Macron was looking for an exit strategy from their eight-year military involvement, like all Western countries struggling to maintain and fund operations. Some commentators were implying AQIM operations were 'France's Afghanistan'. President Hollande sent parachute forces into Mali in 2013, where they initially halted AQIM activity. The ensuing Sahel-wide Barkhane Operation sought to quell regional lawlessness; operations that President Macron suggested costs France around €1 billion a year and the lives of 55 soldiers, to monitor the loss of 10,000 dead West Africans and a further two million being forced to flee their homes. As with Afghanistan, it appears that the Sahel has no enduring solution.

Ten years or so after our trip, I was walking the dogs in our Hampshire village when a car drew up and a head popped out. 'Hello Tristan, what are you doing here?' I asked. What were the chances of a young chap from the regiment set to marry the daughter from one of the large, local farms? We both did a double take! I recalled two young, Kenyan schoolboys visiting 2 PARA in Kenya in 1987 for an insight to the regiment. Tristan and his brother were great lads; both joined the regiment and performed well. Tristan had a fantastic wedding, secure in the knowledge that they were off to Paris for his studies and to work with the French for a few years, on promotion to lieutenant colonel. He was deployed to Mali and the Sahel; being a fluent Swahili speaker, I'm sure this helped on many occasions. In 2023, Tristan addressed our annual village remembrance service, just before he hung up his boots.

Tamanrasset developed as a core node within the network of Saharan camel caravans. Naturally, the French established a military outpost here, to guard trade. The Swiss recommended the Caravanserai campsite that we found easily. The owner was happy for us to register with him (saving us the bother of the gendarmerie) and even exchanged some US dollars; we still had no local money because of Ramadan. Caravanserai was true to its name; it had a large, open courtyard of white, mud walls with smaller rooms leading off for those that wanted them. The courtyard was fine for us. We flipped open the roof tent, cooked some food and made use of the excellent showers. The literal meaning for Caravanserai refers to the trans-Saharan trade, where weary travellers or caravanners could rest. The side courtyard rooms offered security for the traders to store their wares, and sometimes their camels, whilst they recovered. Already present were some very chatty Austrian and German bikers, clearly desert experienced and crucially, they had beer! They had travelled down from northern Algeria and were delighted to share route information. They were well kitted out with ATM and BMW bikes and possessed a very detailed, German guidebook offering GPS routes and useful information. It made our Africa on a Shoestring look woeful, however, their GPS data chimed with the Swiss points. They were amazed by our journey and implied that they were unaware of life below Tamanrasset.

Waking to a very chilly morning at Caravanserai, we heard that there was a fuel shortage in Tamanrasset as the truck had not arrived. We drove around a few stations in hope, to see many European 'desert adventurers' queuing, mostly French and Germans, in 4x4 groups. We met a hopeful bunch of French heading south, a couple of blokes, a girl and an excitable, small dog travelling with their two standard Peugeot 405 cars, both massively overloaded. We had read that the gendarmerie are the people to ask for help, so when I saw the Chef du Brigade, he similarly explained they too were waiting for the fuel truck that was due after lunch. This could be any time, so we retired to Caravanserai. Eventually, late afternoon, the truck arrived with predictable chaos. The huge crowds and locals descended upon the pumps; it was impossible for the poor, local lad to dispense any fuel. We paused, clearly at the back of any queue, so I asked the watching gendarmerie how we should proceed. In their defence, they were unwilling to be drawn into the melee. Catherine decided to remonstrate about the chaos with the Chef du Brigade, who appeared goaded to take action. He dispatched three officers into the crowd with sticks to push back the demanding locals and gained control of the fuel pump. He then whistled up a young boy to fill our four jerry cans, dispensing 80 litres. The queuing locals watched us European, 'Johnny come lately'-types being allocated the first dibs; clearly, we felt bad and wouldn't blame any local for being pissed off. The jerry cans were almost as big as the plucky lad who carried each can to us, where I hastily stashed them on the roof. We were effusive and grateful and the lad earned his few shackles, but any and all attempts to pay for the fuel were refused; the officers waved us off. We couldn't believe it and thought it was some form of game, but boldly buggered off before we were mobbed. Whilst massively grateful, this gesture was again so unexpected and characterised the country, a place juxtaposed with itself. Mind you, I have never won an argument once Catherine gets going, so I guess the chef was saving himself.

It was getting late and once the sun goes, as in all Mediterranean and desert countries, it gets very dark and cools rapidly. We considered climbing Assekrem, a highpoint, renowned for an amazing sunrise over the Hoggar Mountains. Assekrem is where Charles de Foucauld built his hermitage in 1911. Born Viscount Foucauld in 1858 in France, he was assassinated (hence considered a martyr) in this hermitage near Tamanrasset in 1916. Like most French noblemen, he was initially a bon viveur, a cavalry officer, then explorer and geographer. Finally, he became a Catholic priest and ultimately a hermit who lived among the Tuareg. His inspiration and writings led to the founding of the Little Brothers of Jesus among other religious congregations, that in turn led to his beatification in 2005 by Pope Benedict XVI.

Despite his holiness and our recent fuel excitement, we decided against the harsh trek to the top and a cold wait for the sunrise. We heard mixed views on the sunrise; it could often get clouded out, as was forecast for us. I also read that the descent was difficult at best. I was sure Daph was up for the task, but at this stage in our adventure, I was unwilling to risk damage to Daph; we were nursing her (and us) home. The deciding factor for us being more sensible was Catherine's call home to her parents while waiting at Tamanrasset. Her mother burst into tears at the sound of Catherine's voice. We hadn't phoned for a few weeks as we had no signal; they had read adverse reports on the news, only to draw immediate and negative conclusions. That was a surprise and shock to us.

Overlooking the delights of ascending the highest track down from the Hoggar, we took the direct route towards Djanet, following the Swiss GPS, heading initially for Hirhafok. The dirt road was totally open; a straight, soft, sandy piste stretching into the distance across a wide, featureless, open plain. The going was fine, although there were mild corrugations in parts.

After 50 kilometres, we pulled off into a river course and bush camped for the night behind some rocks. This was a lovely campsite, although we were both suffering with headaches. Whether this was due to the increased heat and getting more exposure as we travelled north where hitherto we had been unaffected, we were unsure, even though we were adequately hydrated. Catherine wondered whether it was the effects of stopping our malarone tablets. The malarial threat was reduced past Kenya as it was too cold. The cold, early morning reinforced our decision not to climb Asserkrem, for unusually that morning, the Hoggar Mountains were shrouded in cloud. The cold mornings were having a noticeable effect; everything was just more reluctant to function, including me!

We pressed on down the piste, through Hirhafok and on to Idles. The scattered, mud huts and collection of people were so unnoticeable, it was hard to justify a town or village name. In Idles, similarly appearing deserted, we noted a fuel pump, but it was locked up. The road out of Idles was confusing, requiring us to drive over volcanic scree before we hit the piste beyond, but we trusted the hitherto faultless Swiss GPS. Back on the piste, the motoring was rewarding. For 50 kilometres, we drove along a sandy riverbed before reaching the village of Serouenout, as indistinguishable as the previous villages. At this point, the tracks all swung abruptly south, as did the oil drums and markers, but our GPS still pointed east. By now, we trusted the GPS, yet all my instinct and navigational experience suggested we should turn south - or north. By continuing east, we were going to slam into the oncoming rock wall. This led to a 'meaningful discussion' in the cab; surely the GPS will pick up the waypoint soon and turn? But no; by now, we had transited almost half a mile of north-south tracks. This was getting crazy, but the GPS resolutely pointed east. As we approached the rock wall, the route we were on led up to the unseen gap in the rock wall, slicing through at an angle which, after a left and a right, threading through the cliff face, we emerged at the head of a verdant valley. This was a magnificent scene - top marks to the Swiss. Just as we started down the valley, a troop of French-guided 4x4s roared past, waving. Who would have realised this valley was the direct route to Serouenout? The water source obviously ran from the cliff face, for as the valley opened out, it dried up.

We stopped early for the day in a narrow, sheltered valley. I wanted to check Daph's rear differential and Catherine wanted to take some photographs.

Hitherto the wind had been blowing the sand up that obscured clear desert pictures, but now the wind was abating, so Catherine wandered off. This was unusual, but she obviously felt safe. This gave me a chance to inspect underneath Daph. The ground was both flat and firm gravel, although I still chocked the wheels with rocks. As I had done many times previously, I used the hi-lift jack at the rear to lift Daph, prior to placing a second axel-stand for safety. My solid plank of wood baseplate for the hi-lift had good purchase on the gravel. I removed the rear wheel to ease my access under Daph and to get a better look at the rear diff. I was on my back and positioning the axle-stand under the rear axle when I heard a crack. I rolled out like a startled rabbit, all my hairs on edge. The plank of wood under the hi-lift had split, causing Daph to lurch sideways and drop in height, leaving the hi-lift bent, taking the full weight of Daph's rear. Had it slipped completely, I might not have been around to tell the tale; Catherine would have returned to Daph with her idyllic pictures only to find a disabled vehicle on top of me. I was still shaking as I looked at the situation. The rear wheel carrier had caught the bending hi-lift and was now jammed. I frantically repositioned the bottle jack to lift and ease the pressure off the hi-lift and put the jack stand in place. I then dug out the hi-lift; it was slightly bent, but still functional. Hi-lifts are notoriously fickle bits of kit and real care is needed. I believed I had been careful, although I admit I should have left the wheel on until a second support was in place.

I didn't have the nerve to tell Catherine of my incompetence until later. The 30-minute task to repair the rear diff took 90 minutes; further justification why I was never keen to embark on repair jobs. I managed to get the repair gunk on the rear diff seal, partially solving the issue. But in the process, we appeared to have another problem; the alarm started to malfunction, after the vehicle lurched. Every time one of the side panels was knocked or a door closed, it emitted a beep. Attempts to re-set the alarm with the emergency (EKK) code were unsuccessful, so to avoid the continuous noise driving us nuts, I unplugged the main battery for the night.

It was a beautiful, serene night, alone under the stars. Connecting the battery the following morning, the alarm seemed to be fine, for now. Eventually, the village of Serouenout appeared with a hilltop fort, occupied by gendarmes who drove out to meet us. They were very friendly and after taking our details, wished us well. The piste to Borne was wide, open and relatively free driving. Again at Borne, all we found was a simple, brick arch in the middle of nowhere, yet the village appeared prominently marked on the map; we never found the village. The GPS advised us to turn right to Borges el Haoues along a well-marked, corrugated piste. Borges el Haoues sat astride a pristine, tar, main road, with ribbon development along the road to Djanet. Around five kilometres south of Borges el Haoues, we came across an isolated fuel station, with no one around. Back on tarmac, I checked Daph and inflated the tyres; the rear diff repair was holding and the irritating alarm problem seemed to have abated. We searched for someone at the fuel station, but it appeared to be abandoned, yet I was able to fill up. I searched for a means to pay yet found none; fuel here was a head-scratcher. Why was Tam so short, yet here it was freely abundant?

Our final 120 kilometres to Djanet was like being on a French motorway, albeit with some glorious, desert vistas and rock formations along the way. Dust clouds still blew and created a haze. We pulled over under a lone tree for a shady lunch spot, just in time for Daph's alarm issue to annoyingly resurface. Just as we stopped, a convoy of European 4x4 adventurers passed, with three Land Rovers flashing their headlamps. Daph's engine was wheezing somewhat too, so naturally I assumed the worst, but I hoped it was just the dry air.

Djanet is an oasis city at the bottom of the Tassili n'Ajjer plateau. The intermittent Oued Idjeriou River (or wadi) has carved out the valley, where the bourgeoning town grew. Hidden, were rock pools within deep canyons, lined with sandy carpets and local oases. Well-maintained houses hung to the hillside, the streets bustled and the markets appeared plentiful. The locals were friendly and fuel was available, without queues. We were directed to La Belle Etoile, a campsite on the southern edge of town, where the campsite owner was amazed by our trip. Once settled, I addressed the recalcitrant alarm, but again defeated, I disconnected the battery. The owner knew an electrical engineer who agreed to come in the morning.

Shortly after dark, a few other 4x4s started arriving, including a French couple who stopped near us. They planned to travel south for four months in a clockwise circuit, south from Algeria, through Burkina Faso, Mali, Mauritania and home through Morocco. They also were uncertain about southern access into Morocco but were not worried; a Gallic shrug implied there were always ways around such challenges. They had also heard about the poor Swiss couple robbed in the Ténéré; evidently bad news spreads fast. It didn't take long before we started discussing each other's vehicles. They thought their Toyota had a harsh ride, although it was well adapted for the desert. They loved our roof tent and unsurprisingly, one of their lilos had already punctured. The chap offered to look at Daph's electrics, but he had not seen a second battery/fridge set-up before and, like the mechanic the following morning, neither were any the wiser. We managed to disconnect the horn, so the symptoms were no longer audible.

The Tassili n'Ajjer National Park covers a vast area and contains some of the most exceptional groupings of rock paintings and engravings of prehistoric cave art. We understood the Berber translation of the name means 'plateau of rivers', referencing the extensive, subterranean water system draining towards Djanet. One of the main access points to the park was through Iherir, an oasis village located centrally on the plateau. We headed to Iherir the next morning, backtracking on the highway to Borjes el Haoues and on towards Illizi. Taking the gravel track to Iherir was like descending into a giant, open-cast quarry. The dark, sandstone rock has been stained by a thin, outer layer of metallic oxide deposits, revealing a near-black and dull, red-coloured rock. It was like a lunar landscape; the deserted and pockmarked rock fostered a very eerie atmosphere. Wind erosion has formed around 300 natural rock arches and other strange rock shapes across the park, many of which we observed during the drive in.

Advice from Djanet was mixed; some focused on the amazing rock art in the park, whereas others insisted that a guide was essential. We wondered if this was a commercial yarn, although we acknowledged similar advice related to the Ténéré. The park was said to suffer from insurgents and bandit activity. Hitherto, we had seen and experienced very friendly and overt people and police patrols, so why should the park be any different? But as we approached Iherir, we did experience a very different, eerie atmosphere as we descended down the meandering track to the valley floor. We observed furtive glances as the 'locals' fixed their headscarves and scurried away. One gets a sixth sense that was shouting, 'You're not welcome here.' The community at the bottom appeared shut for business as there was nobody around. There was no birdsong or any ambient noise. The place gave off a dead, spine-tingling atmosphere; the only thing missing was tumbleweed rolling down the street. Were our minds playing tricks on us? Eventually, someone appeared at the national park checkpoint; they demanded an entrance fee, for which a guide was compulsory. The chap asked, 'Naturally, you will want to trek to see the rock carvings, how many days will you be staying?' He spoke very little French, the guides only spoke Arabic and the price was outrageous. It just did not feel right; we were also told we could not camp here at Iherir. Having made the initial effort, sadly we turned around and drove back the way we came, disappointed at the reception and sinister overtones. Interestingly, this was totally at odds with everything else we had experienced so far in Algeria.

We climbed back out of Ihere and continued north towards Illizi and re-joined the Swiss GPS coordinates that led us to a delightful campsite just to the south of Illizi town. Shade was available under palm trees, along with excellent facilities and fresh water. There was a small restaurant onsite that we couldn't resist. Whilst there, three German vehicles rolled in. These adventurers came over to chat and one was carrying some cans of German beer, implying we needed one; he was not wrong. They were quite surprised about our journey and inspected Daph with a critical eye. They were touring Algeria and hoped to get into Libya from Tunisia. They had a VW Combi, a Toyota truck and an excellent, sliver Range Rover Classic. The Rangy was a clear labour of love and I reckon the owner made a note about our roof tent, his next acquisition.

The following morning, we had a slow start; I had to pump up the two rear tyres and we topped up with cheap fuel at Illizi. Our next leg towards Dep Dep brought us close to the Libyan border, but again, this was largely on tarred roads. Interestingly, the Swiss GPS advised against the main highway, guiding us instead across the Grand Erg Oriental, after Dep Dep. By now, we totally trusted the GPS but the terrain across the Grand Erg Oriental turned out to be an extensive expanse of flat desert. Immediately, we noticed the tighter security around the oil fields, especially close to the Libyan border. Dep Dep itself was a 'one horse town', so after refuelling, we drove on.

Just before last light, we swung off into the desert and pitched camp. It was surreal, quiet and totally isolated, all the more surprising given the security patrolling. Daph was still wheezing in the dry conditions and we had a slow puncture on one rear wheel. Given the distance and terrain travelled, the tyres had stood up pretty well. The front tyres had fared better than the rear, which was odd, considering the power was fairly evenly distributed, yet the weight balance was heavier to the rear. I rotated the two rear tyres with the spares and used our plug device to repair the puncture, to be a spare. I was impressed, it repaired easily.

We ascended a major escarpment the next morning before we swung west to Hassi Messasout. Crossing the Grand Erg Oriental sounds better than the reality. It was a tar road for much of the way, although huge, 30 metre-high sand dunes had blown across sections of road, in areas completely obliterating it. Beside the tar road was a sand track, which was perfectly drivable in normal or high range and was a constant feature, without sand dunes. Oil and gas operations dominate the In Amenas area and present an attractive target for insurgent activity. One of the most audacious terrorist events occurred in January 2013, when al-Qaeda-aligned terrorists took expat hostages at the Tigantourine gas facility, near In Amenas. Four days into the crisis, the Algerian forces raided the gas facility to free the hostages. Sadly, at least 39 foreign hostages were killed, along with an Algerian security guard, although the true figure is not known. A total of 685 Algerian workers and 107 foreigners were freed, whilst 29 terrorists were killed and three captured. Not long after the event, I received an email from an old sergeant major of mine; it turned out that young Jimmy M was working locally with BP and was one of the 'first responders', putting his medical skills into practice. He was polite enough to say he had read and enjoyed our website whilst out there and passed it around a couple of other regiment lads.

We reached Hassi Messasout late in the day and whilst refuelling, we attempted to find accommodation. Thoughts of camping in the desert were fruitless as the terrain was flat and featureless; this was 'oil town'. We found no accommodation in Hassi Messasout, indeed the town was quite unwelcoming and the place was totally focused on supporting the oil fields to its south. We pressed on in fading light to Tougourt, in the hope of finding either accommodation, a campsite or a desert camp spot. On arrival at Tougourt, we had the sinking feeling that this town was like Hassi Messasout, but we were proved wrong. We asked the way to a hotel at a cafe/truck stop, whereupon a smart chap offered to show us the way to the 'Wassim' Hotel. Initially suspicious, we followed the chap on his moped around the back streets of what was a grand, French-inspired town, to the

Oasis Hotel. It was quite a smart place, if faded from its former grandeur. Our guide was quite insistent that a 'cadeau' was unnecessary; indeed, he offered to loan us money for the hotel should we have insufficient funds until the banks opened in the morning.

The Oasis Hotel had obviously been one of many hotels on the tourist circuit (generations ago) around the oasis towns, but was now a trucker's stop. The key advantage was the secure parking for Daph, in a locked and guarded compound. That said, we were not expecting a problem in Tougourt, especially during Ramadan. The hotel restaurant had closed, so again we cooked some food in our room, this time avoiding setting ourselves on fire. Breakfast was from 6am but at 6.30am, all the lights were still off and the receptionist was asleep - Ramadan. We decided to hit the road. We had read that kids were a problem close to the border near El Oued, their sport being to catapult stones at tourist vehicles, but being so early, we experienced no problems and reached the border at 9am.

Part 6
HOME...
WHAT'S NEXT?

HIGHEST PUB IN AFRICA

Cape Agulhas (Southern tip of Africa)

290

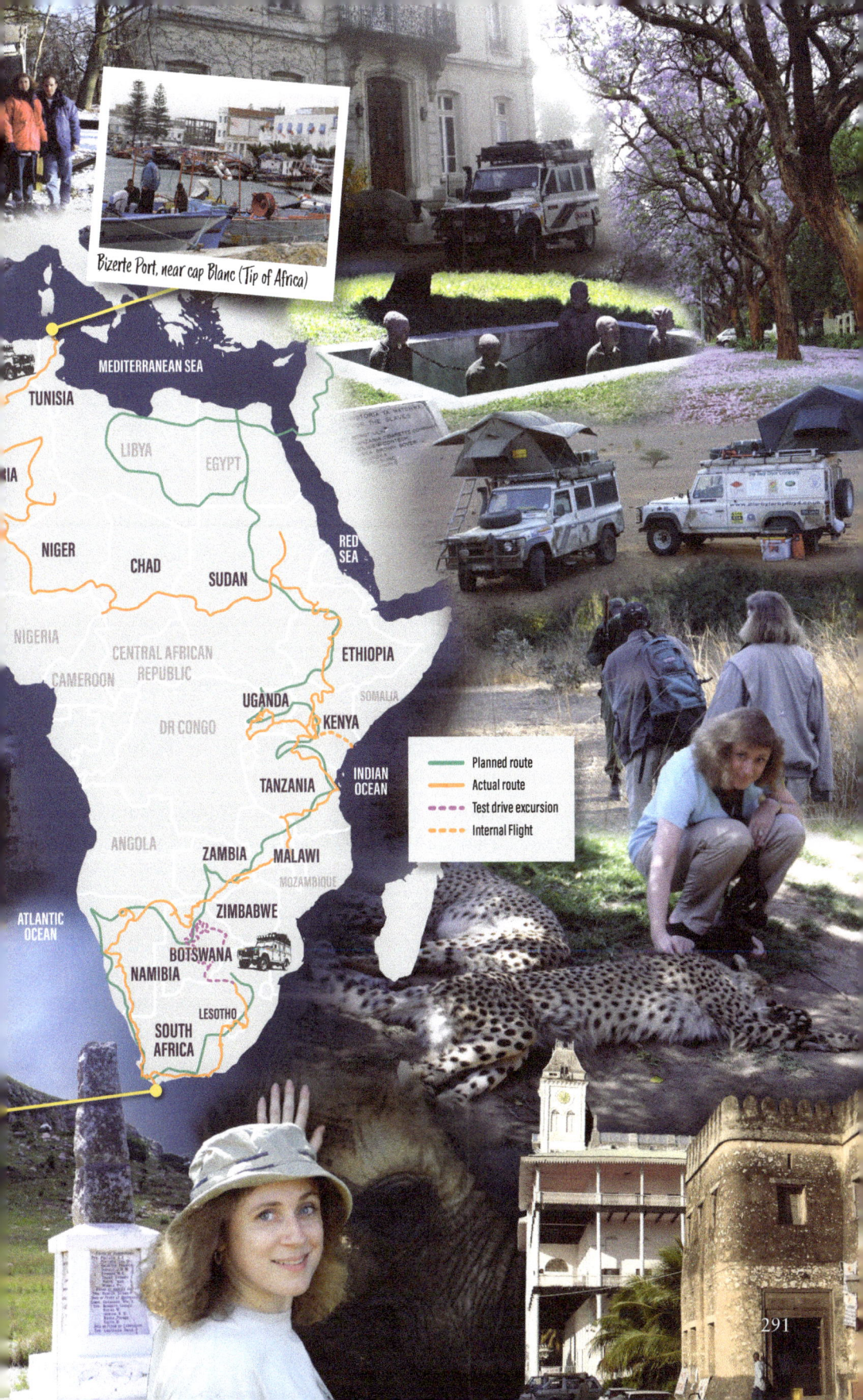

Bizerte Port, near cap Blanc (Tip of Africa)

MEDITERRANEAN SEA

TUNISIA

LIBYA

EGYPT

NIGER

CHAD

SUDAN

RED SEA

NIGERIA

CENTRAL AFRICAN REPUBLIC

CAMEROON

ETHIOPIA

UGANDA

DR CONGO

KENYA

SOMALIA

TANZANIA

INDIAN OCEAN

ANGOLA

ZAMBIA

MALAWI

MOZAMBIQUE

ZIMBABWE

ATLANTIC OCEAN

BOTSWANA

NAMIBIA

LESOTHO

SOUTH AFRICA

	Planned route
	Actual route
	Test drive excursion
	Internal Flight

Chapter 23
After Cap Blanc, we must change continents

As we followed three Austrian Land Cruisers into the Algerian customs, we noticed one had their back window taped up. They had fallen foul of some locals, but not stone throwing. They stopped to shop at a small village, when kids tried to hammer their way into their 'luxury' Toyota that morning. The border facilities here were ramshackle and not the shiny, new facility we'd experienced at the southern border. The immigration officer was getting confused filling in the forms; he had not experienced travellers entering their country from the south. We noticed the locals getting more hassle than the few tourists. Customs were not so happy; we had not officially changed any money in Algeria. Outside Visa payments, we had no official currency exchange receipts, thus implying we had used some elaborate, sinister black-market deal. He was also unclear about what to do with the Carnet; indeed, he stamped two pages in error, but we moved on. We endured a cursory search of Daph, which ended abruptly when the officer got his hand filthy on the sooty end of the storm kettle, deliberately positioned by the rear door, just to see what would happen; it had the desired effect!

At the Tunisian border, we met a charming, Swiss couple, Jacques and Chantal, with an extremely elegant Land Rover TD5 conversion. They had spent a lot of money on a marine-quality conversion within the rear of their Land Rover, with full cooking, fridge and lounge facilities built in. Their sleeping quarters were a marvel: a wooden-based, double bed accessed from inside their vehicle once the roof was raised, again from inside. They were frequent desert travellers; old hands at border crossings and able to point us in the right direction. They were intending to catch the Genoa boat on Friday (the following day) and were planning to stay in Hammamet overnight. Apparently, this was much more pleasant than Tunis and only meant a 50 kilometre drive to the boat the following day on excellent roads.

The Tunisian immigration officials were efficient but customs had more Carnet problems; they seemed to understand what needed to be done but nobody was interested in stamping it. When we were asked for 1,000 Tunisian dinar for a road tax/stamp, we were initially shocked and we had none. Like many of the previous French administrations, the decimal point requires adjustment, so we were grateful to Jacques who resolved the problem by offering us one dinar; around 50p. The inference being we needed to move the decimal point three places. Again the physical customs inspection of Daph was curtailed by the grubby storm kettle. The final coup de gras occurred when one of the customs men tried to swap his pistol for my Leatherman multi-tool. He drew it from its holster to proudly show off his new Sig Sauer. The two were incomparable and the suggestion completely bizarre! Europe must be a dangerous place in his mind…or was it a trap? Whatever, it was utterly ludicrous, and time to escape.

The first major town towards Tunis was Tozeur, north of Chott el Djerid, the largest salt pan of the Sahara Desert. The Arabic translation means 'lagoon of the land of palms'. Like so many, it is an endorheic salt lake, having no in or out flow. The pan covers over 7,000 square kilometres and the heat haze shimmered classically over it, evoking that romantic desert view into the distance. The reality was shattered by the stink; a pungent, sulphuric smell was all-pervasive.

Tozour was a tourist destination, replete with numerous, smart 'tourist' hotels ringing the southern edge of town. Waiting outside these hotels were fleets of modern, smart tourist coaches. Tozeur has a hot desert climate, super-heated by the sirocco wind pushing temperatures above 50°C. Cultivating hundreds of thousands of palm trees, dates are a major export. Today, in the ancient market, it's the tourists who provide the income, along with the movie industry. Huge blockbuster films such as Star Wars, Raiders of the Lost Ark and The English Patient were partially filmed outside Tozeur.

We stopped in the old town to get some currency from an ATM and local provisions. The old mosque dominated the skyline and was surrounded by market traders. One stall owner shouted across the road, enquiring if we were German. Once he found out we were English, he broke out the full-on rendition of Del Boy; 'Ahh, lovely jubbly', seeking to sell us his goods. The more we laughed, the more we got the full Trotter repartee. He was excellent; it just shows the power of the international media…and we thought we were there to get a Tunisian flavour. No camels or carpets were exchanged.

We drove from the border to Tunis in a day (some 550 kilometres) along excellent motorways that had a stretch of péage (2.4TD). Apparently, most desert travellers stay at the Hotel Amilcar in Carthage, which is easy to find from the motorway and takes you past the thriving port and town of La Goulette. The Amilcar was suffused with faded 1960's glory, although perhaps we are being unfair, as that was the quite season. There was ample safe parking, it had its own private beach and it was cheap, with reasonable facilities, but no other travellers were staying.

Tunisia lies centrally within the Maghreb region, also known as the Barbary Coast during its history. The northern-most point of the African continent is Cap Blanc (or Cape Angela), our target to complete our Toe to Tip transit. Much of Tunisia's land is fertile and they have seaports on the Mediterranean Basin offering access to Europe. Inhabited initially by Berbers, the Phoenician immigration began in the 12th century BC, building Carthage. Carthage was a major, mercantile power and military rival to the Roman Republic. In 146 BC, the Romans defeated and occupied Carthage, where they stayed for the next 800 years.

The Romans introduced Christianity and left architectural legacies like the El Djem amphitheatre and Dougga. During the Roman period, the area enjoyed prosperity. It was known as the granary of the Roman Empire, yet by the second century BC, olive oil exceeded cereal exports, along with trade in exotic, wild animals. Other exports included textiles, marble, wine, timber, livestock, pottery and wool. The Muslims eventually conquered and occupied Tunisia in 1574, after which the Ottoman Empire held sway, ruling for over 300 years. The French colonised in 1881 until independence in 1957.

Tunis was a town of two halves: the very smart, French uber-upmarket 'ville nouvelle' area with wide boulevards, paved pedestrian areas, trendy shops, trams and traffic jams. Juxtaposed was the old medina, with its narrow streets and Grande Mosque. Both had equal charm and were easy to explore, reflecting a French influence. We bought a ferry ticket for the Marseille boat on Sunday, in preference to the Friday Genoa boat, to give us more time in Tunisia. We also felt that it would be easier to travel north on the N7 or A7 through France. That said, the Genoa boat was marginally cheaper and faster. We witnessed the arrival of a vast array of desert vehicles and bikes queuing for this boat, the majority of which appeared to be German. We were surprised by the popularity of desert exploration and the range of specialist vehicles, considering it was November and the reported high-risk levels throughout North Africa. So many European travellers, yet so few using Hotel Amilcar; we should have gone to Hammamet.

Wanting to complete our Toe to Tip Continental transit, we took the péage from Tunis to Bizerte. Being Africa's northern-most city, Bizerte was a thriving, upmarket retreat and port. Founded by Phoenician settlers around 1100 BC, it's one of the oldest known settlements in Tunisia. The weather was poor as we drove around the Cape Blanc peninsular and failed to find a marker post or anything to indicate its significance. It was not especially picturesque, the light was poor and it was wet and very windy, so we retreated to the town for a celebratory lunch. Regrettably, the town was not much to comment upon either, so with the bad weather and Ramadan effect, Cape Blanc was a washout. We cut our losses and returned to Tunis for an excellent fish supper in La Goulette within the port area. The ruins of Carthage have been subsumed by modern Tunis. The Amilcar lies close to the Presidential Palace and is within the modern diplomatic, as we discovered when strolling around the old sites. Carthage still has the most 'complete' Roman bathhouse in the Western world. We knew Daph was safely parked because of all the large, suited 'gentlemen' on street corners, with covert ears pieces and bulges under their armpits.

We had not planned to travel this area, so had not researched North Africa before the trip. We had (still have) a strong desire to experience Morocco, but we never imagined that Algeria would open up. Both countries either side of Tunisia had closed borders, so we excluded the easy ferry crossings to Europe from Tunisia. As customary, we were winging it, and Tunisia has much to explore. I had a vague notion that I might visit some of the Second World War battlefields, not least because it was here that my regiment earned their nickname: 'The Red Devils'. This was a reference to the hard and aggressive manner in which they fought, inflicting an 80% casualty rate on their opponents; little wonder that the Germans referred to them as 'Die Rote Teufel'. When planning Operation Torch (the allied invasion of North Africa in 1942), the nascent 1st Parachute Brigade was attached to the allied force. In November 1942, units from the Para Brigade dropped near Bône, Souk el-Arba and Béja, and later at Pont Du Fahs. They were to seize airfields, holding them before linking up with the allied armoured advance. The subsequent inability of the British First Army to advance as expected meant that 2 PARA, the Pont Du Fahs force, under Lieutenant Colonel John Frost (he of Arnhem fame), were forced to fight a 50-mile withdrawal back to allied units. Such was the hard nature of the fighting and subsequent demise of the German Africa Corps, that the British Airborne proved their fighting tenacity.

It reminded me of a time back at Aldershot when my company had the honour of hosting the PARA 2 Club; the existing 'old and bold' regimental veterans from the Second World War. It was evident that these independently-minded chaps only wanted to be paraded and shouted at by my sergeant major, meet their mates, share their stories and enjoy a few jars in the officers' mess. We lined up a few lads to talk about their experiences in the Falklands. Whilst one of my lads, Corporal Taylor, was talking about being under fire when it felt like he had been shot; he had felt down to find his waist and trousers totally soaked. 'That's it,' he thought, 'I've been shot.' To his ultimate relief, he discovered that the bullet had passed through his water bottle and he was unscathed. Whilst Taylor was recounting this story, one of the old boys was rolling around on the floor with laughter. We thought he was having a fit, but apparently the same thing happened to him at Arnhem. It was a great event and a real honour to share their stories and experiences. These guys had endured six years of war, surviving Normandy, Arnhem and the Rhine Crossing. That did not deter a few chaps, who sidled up to me and my sergeant major later in the evening to proclaim that the majority of these Arnhem chaps were lightweights. Naturally, I cannot repeat their actual words here, but these chaps had been in North Africa at the start of the war when there had been real hard fighting; they were the real Red Devils.

We attempted to get some Roman culture by visiting Dougga, some 100 kilometres southwest of Tunis. The site, on a plateau, commands an uninhibited view of the surrounding area. As a UNESCO World Heritage Site, it proclaims to be 'the best-preserved Roman small town in North Africa', despite the encroaching modernity. The stand-out monuments are the theatre, the Temples of Saturn and those of Juno Caelestis, apparently, for sadly we never got there. We were caught in a Tunisian mega traffic jam. Events conspired further when Daph decide to play up. Her universal joints on the propeller shafts were so worn that they clonked every time power was engaged and it was getting worse, especially in traffic. The unnerving, whizzing sound from under her bonnet (a bearing on one of the pulleys on the serpentine belt may have been seizing) made quite a sound out on the road. We compounded her ailments with an ill-advised U-turn. All we did was to bump over a central reservation to get out of the jam; technically not an issue with a 4x4, yet we got mildly stuck. The brick kerbs were excessively high and there was nothing in the centre, making the obstacle harder, but use of the low range diff-lock shifted us off the kerbs. We should not have needed to use such extreme measures to free ourselves, but now the real issue was our inability to disengage the diff-lock. No matter what we tried, it was stuck! Driving on roads in low-ratio induces 'wind-up', creating unacceptable torsion pressure within the half-axels until something breaks, usually the axel. Low ratio driving is slow over bumpy terrain, so wind-up cannot occur because the torsional pressure is dissipated by the uneven surface. But at speed on a smooth road - ping. We never made Dougga; we limped to the hotel car park for some tinkering and finally managed to release the low ratio; Daph was fine, but she needed some TLC. Instead we 'marked' our finial African meal in the medina in the Del el-Jeld, a traditional, Tunisian restaurant that served excellent food within the main, covered courtyard, reminiscent of the Emmerson House in Zanzibar.

After squeezing the last drop of cheap, Tunisian fuel into Daph, we headed for the ferry port at around 9am, in time for our midday sailing. By comparison to Friday's swarm of 4x4s, our boatload was considerably more restrained. We were the first in the queue and were held for around two hours before any processing. To say this made us anxious was an understatement; Africa was having its last laugh. With less than an hour before sailing, we knew they were not going to be that efficient and, as if by magic, we learned that the boat was delayed for around four hours before docking. Just as well there was a delay as it took over an hour to resolve the Carnet. We were entering Europe and no one wanted to stamp it! Most passengers were French, desert travellers, in groups of six or more. Everyone was wandering around and comparing and admiring each other's vehicles. The majority were Toyotas; people were discussing suspension bushes and extended fuel tanks. Daph was different and probably the only Land Rover, overland vehicle thus more robust than most desert vehicles. Plus, she had the roof tent. Most interested parties could not believe the journey we had just completed. However, Daph was not the biggest draw; the honours for the 'impromptu 4x4 appreciation award' went to our friends and border crossing saviours, Jacques and Chantal, with their pristine Land Rover. They arrived at the back of the ferry queue and came to find us. Apparently, the Genoa boat was overbooked. Plus, the Friday crossing experienced appalling weather. We left them to their guided tours but arranged to meet for an aperitif on the boat. We got our table and chairs out for a picnic by Daph and waited for boarding.

Unsurprisingly, boarding - when it occurred - was as organised as the Le Mans start. Despite being first in the queue, loading was a free for all, not that it mattered as the boat was only half full. The unseemly surge for the four loading lanes was a scrum, but not a patch on Khartoum's traffic, and Daph was afforded some respect, probably because of her bull bars. Our ticket allocated us a spacious cabin, within which we enjoyed maximum sleeping hours during our reasonably smooth crossing. We joined Jacques and Chantal in the restaurant for a very pleasant dinner. It transpired that they owned a vineyard in Montreux and invited us to stay; that was very seductive, but we thought we'd better get back to Blighty for Christmas.

The reason for the ferry's late arrival was the loss of one of their four engines, and although disconcerting, they managed to claw back an hour on their return trip to Marseille. Whilst France considers itself as being on the edge of the EU and combatting the flood of illegal immigrants, few, if any of the 4x4 vehicles, were searched on arrival. Equally, at immigration, a cursory search of passports occurred, but most were just waved through customs; all very French. I'm sure there are procedures in place like in every port, for we had to stop for our Carnet EU entry stamp and, despite the customs officer recognising the Carnet immediately, it still took some 20 minutes to get a stamp. We erroneously thought we had left African administration behind.

European soil was damp and by the time we departed Marseille, it was raining as we drove north on the main A7. We pulled off just north of Avignon and stayed at a charming, typically French logis in Bédarrides. Bougainvillea was trained around the pale blue shutters as we crammed Daph into the off-street parking. Though still unseasonably warm, we could have camped, but it was December so the roof tent would stay shut. Shame, for during our trip, the roof tent had been a game-changer. So much had changed in Europe, yet things were still familiar. The Euro currency had replaced the French franc and we were paying European prices. By now, we were focused on getting home. Although being so close, we had to make a detour for a few cases of Gigondas from the chateau's vendor direct.

We pressed on north and stopped near Macon at an opportune chateau for a cheap B&B. It was a classic, faded chateau with Napoleonic furniture and object d'art inside each room. The outbuildings had a two-storey stable block and surrounded by its own moat was a keep, complete with its own drawbridge. The chateau had just been acquired by an English couple, who were absent, but the French caretaker was fascinated by Daph and our trip. Francois was a great help in finding a mechanic, for he was not just any mechanic. We hoped to limp home, despite the tyres being close to slicks, at the bare legal minimum (not ideal on the slippery, French, sodden motorways). The engine was wheezing less, thanks to the damp air lubricating the pulleys, but the universal joints were not; they needed looking at. The following morning, we arrived early at a rural garage that was jammed full of broken Land and Range Rovers. The guy was dying to see Daph; I'm sure we would still be there today, for this Landy fan wanted to repair everything. He thought that Daph was running well, but replaced the UJs there and then, followed by some tinkering under the bonnet – pulley squeak solved. He only charged me for the parts, labour was 'gratuit', although we shared lunch and a bottle from the back of Daph.

We had to press on, for the following evening, we were booked into Cercle National des Armées, a French officers' club in the heart of Paris, on Boulevard Haussmann. It was a bit of an homage as we had stayed in the classic building with ornate décor a few times. The new UJs were fantastic and once power was applied, it was no longer a lottery when the surge of momentum was going to be delivered. Unusually for the French, the crazy, Parisian drivers were giving us a wide berth as we cut through the rainy evening's heavy traffic. All Parisian roads head to the centre and soon we were driving around the Place de Concorde and up the Avenue des Champs-Elysees. The Cercle National had private parking, but their underground facility nearby was too low for Daph to get under; yet the door guard/night watchman was so taken and proud of his new charge that he told us to park Daph by the main entrance on the pavement. Apparently, he had a steady stream of visitors asking about her all night long! We went Christmas shopping in Galleries Lafayette and enjoyed supper in Montmartre before crashing out; thankfully, we had just enough clothes for a freezing, Parisian evening.

The following morning, we had a somewhat slower start than usual, before heading to Calais. We had a ferry booked the following day; Daph was still attracting admirers and even the gendarmerie came for a look around. Thankfully, they were more taken by the spirit of adventure than examining our tyre tread. At Calais, we stayed in a cheap motel, with Daph parked outside our window within a fenced compound. Frankly, it was our worst night's sleep in the whole journey and with hindsight, we'd have been better off camping, so the following morning, we caught the ferry and were swiftly processed through customs and immigration. The familiar white cliffs of Dover soon loomed and we were disembarking.

35,248 kilometres later, we arrived at Dover, but British customs had the last laugh. They refused to acknowledge Daph's arrival at Dover, stating that we had entered the EU at Marseille (although technically, she exited France by virtue of the Calais stamp, so no UK stamp was necessary). It took an hour or more to make Daph's arrival in the UK legitimate. That was not quite the end; we phoned our respective parents from the ferry, who were relieved and delighted that we were fine.

Bless him though, my brother was not so pleased; I subsequently understood that he had a big 'surprise welcome home' banner and party planned for the weekend, with a reception on Dover Cliffs - the lot! So he was not happy that we'd slipped quietly home under the radar on Friday. Oops, prior planning and preparation…no one told us?

Chapter 24
Making sense of it all

Once home, it took a week or so to decompress from our travel routine; the endless repacking, sourcing food and the quest for a secure place to stay each night. Such behaviours had become ingrained and lingered for a while. My military experience made this transition easier, although even now, Catherine chides me for not having truly left the army over 20 years on. Undoubtedly, the journey was a watershed moment for us both, a test of our confidence and resilience. We had realised our dream and tasted a sense of freedom, even though we knew it was not unique. Gone was the safety net and camaraderie of the services 'wrapper' which we found freeing. Stepping away from the military framework can be daunting, especially for those with long service. The services seek to cover all the 'home bases' of family support, individual training, wellbeing and administration, to enable the service folk to concentrate and deliver themselves fully to their vocation. We were somewhat cushioned; Catherine had her career, we had our own home and we had never lived on the 'patch'. Initially, I found the release from the forces liberating, excited by the challenge of 'what's next', although I needed to find work.

We slotted right back into village life. That Christmas, we enjoyed the usual round of family and friends, welcoming new family additions. Of course we missed the thrill of travel, the daily focus and curiosity. Eventually for Catherine, it was back to what she had been doing, so in essence, nothing superficially had changed. But the reality was that everything had changed. We had bonded, become closer, refined our new internal frame of reference from a shared experience. Catherine felt a greater sense of confidence and robustness. Then, after Christmas, that niggle I'd had all throughout our journey hit me - what were we going to do now?

All too quickly, Catherine was headhunted for a big pharma role in Kent at their European HQ. After Christmas, I drove her down for the interview. Catherine was not sure if she wanted the role, so felt she was only going through the motions to maintain her profile. Whilst she was being entertained, I looked around the area. I picked her up and enquired about the interview.

'Good,' she said, 'I think I have a job at a higher level.' 'Great,' I replied, 'as I have a flat for you to look at.' Cutting a long story short, she got the job and flat, commuting weekly, initially in Daph. She wanted her time with Daph before saying goodbye. So much for me leaving the forces to spend more time together; ironically, we spent as much time apart, still travelling for work. Admittedly, this time, my working circumstances were considerably more comfortable, civilised and enabled with modern communications.

The journey opened our eyes and made us more accepting of alternative situations and circumstances. It was frustrating that we could foresee issues, yet remained just as unempowered to act, as before. The itch to travel had been scratched, but not extinguished, although my proposal to sail across the Pacific was flatly refuted by Catherine: she did not 'do boats'. We have travelled since for holidays and I have worked in the Middle East and US. Catherine and I lived in Seattle for 18 months, but we have not overlanded again - yet. Would we? In a heartbeat. But we know it would be very different every time. You make your own luck as you travel, managing 'events', although experience helps. A different trip and justification would be required to drag us out again, for we are commercially engaged in driving businesses, which is motivating and challenging.

More interesting was how people viewed us. Most were keen to know how the trip went, yet they did not want to dig too deep. Most people were too embroiled in their own daily lives and immediacy of their events to comprehend or appreciate our nuances. Common questions were around the basics: finding food, camping and security, route finding and related aspects. The most frequent question asked was, 'How did your holiday go?' Holiday? To be fair, if people have no insight, it's hard for them to comprehend or appreciate such a trip. One response that irritated Catherine more than she let on was comments such as, 'Oh, we'd love to do that, but my wife won't camp.' Rationalising this years later, it just shows how far modern society has evolved, that camping is seen as a luxury (glamping); only to be done if there is plumbed, running water, a Wi-Fi signal and 'essential' creature comforts (and I don't mean ice and lemons for the G&Ts). The irony remains that still most of the global population does not have such benefits or the perceived 'essentials' of modern life.

We stripped out Daph and re-fitted the original alloys and tyres that we had shipped home. Getting Daph checked out at our local Land Rover specialist was interesting; they loved her. They claimed her OME springs made her drive like a go-cart. This 'test' was driving on the knackered shocks, before we replaced them. Who has heard of a Land Rover described as a go-cart? What they really meant was how Daph asserted herself through corners. All Land Rovers lean through bends, but with the OMEs, Daph would initially lean, then positively reassert herself, so drove flatter around bends, conferring confidence. We needed to retain some weight on the heavy-duty springs and shocks, especially once we stored the rack and roof tent in the garage, so we strapped the six Wolf rims and some gear in the rear.

Sadly, it was evident that Daph was a summer girl; she was not a fan of the cold. Whilst she was extremely spritely and fun in snow, she leaked like a sieve and quickly developed surface rust. Her heater was rudimentary; essentially all the features we enjoyed in the warmth plagued her in the British winter. We, or more precisely Hammy, had drilled one too many holes. She still drove well, especially with the new universal joints transferring the available power, and despite her mileage. But what to do with her? Our options were either keep her, sell her or ship her back to South Africa. We had six months to decide before we needed to pay import tax and VAT, if she was to remain in the UK. To sell her in the UK would also incur import costs; selling her in South Africa would include the cost of shipping and the need for someone to conduct the sale. There was an emotional factor too, beyond the financial considerations. Daph had laboured long and hard to get us home, and she was ours.

Our website (https://.daphneoverland.co.uk) was getting hits and we became linked to an online travel forum. Whilst our site was a crude, basic HTML site, written as we went, we fielded loads of enquiries about overlanding, and now many wanted to acquire some of our gear. The roof tent went to a lovely South African couple, returning home with their trusty Disco after working in the UK. It did seem a slightly one-sided ambition, particularly as the girl had recently found out she was pregnant. We wished them well, but we never heard anything more from them after Spain.

I was speaking to Foleys UK about shipping Daph to South Africa and, through a bizarre set of connections, we unexpectedly sold Daph to a returning South African IT contractor a few months later. He was looking for a fully-prepared, safari vehicle for bush trips, once home. The sale price covered our costs and shipping fees to Cape Town. He paid in sterling, as he was closing his UK account, so neither of us incurred any Forex fees. This was the best outcome we could have hoped for, but losing Daph - the visceral embodiment of our trip - was a wrench. Before you ask, we do not know what became of her. We do know what became of Daphne Number One. A reader of our website sent us loads of photos of the original Daphne frame, stripped clean in a Land Rover graveyard outside Pretoria. The decals made her recognisable, among many other similar, white frames; well done sir, amazing recognition and connection.

Unlike Catherine, my decision to change careers was a thrilling yet risky endeavour; one that had concerned me throughout the journey. In the end, I realised that there was no need to fret. Perhaps the anxiety and self-doubt actually fuelled my performance, but success in one domain often translates to success in others. Venturing into the commercial world felt liberating, although I turned down a tempting offer from two major consulting groups who wanted to place me back in the MoD. I could understand their logic by such a placement, and whilst I would have gathered their commercial toolset and brand values, this was the sort of role I was trying to escape. Instead, I chose to stay small, working in a niche consultancy initially, where I experienced an enjoyable, yet sharp learning curve. Initial concerns around my 'hard, technical' skills were unfounded. On the contrary, my competencies swiftly adapted and shone through. Naturally, I had to build a viable, commercial network, a task best accomplished through work. Engaging with people, networking and collaborating are essentials in any field. Surprisingly, I ended up spending as long in the military as I have as an interim, change and turnaround leader. Interestingly, today's business landscape has given rise to the role of Chief Transformation Officer (CTO), a position that was previously part of the CEO or divisional director's responsibilities.

Drawing upon all previous experiences, I continue to manage people and process. As an interim, I love getting parachuted (no pun intended!) into an organisation or business with an empowered directive for change or restructuring. Being unaligned to company politics, the interim can change the dial objectively, empower and enable a team (s) to deliver, before removing oneself and leaving a sustainable entity. I recently met and delved into Gary Burke's book, Transformation Lens, worthy of comment, as it aptly summarises my commercial thoughts and approach in a balanced and logical way. I was interested to also observe he commented upon a human capital tool called the Game Changer Index (GCI). He and I are both (independently) GC partners, having observed its use within an M&A assessment of teams, through to small company applications. The GCI seeks to objectively identify, then empower effective teams, drive performance and foster team effectiveness. The GCI identifies and nurtures those with the appropriate energy and talent to deliver or have an impact upon the task at hand.

The forces are a microcosm of society; one can find good and bad in all areas. They have always attracted quality, raw talent, who are trained for specific functions to address the country's deterrent; our nation's insurance policy. The outcome of which means the services seek to be prepared for the unexpected. Adaptability remains an implied tenet; we train soldiers for all seasons, grouping and regrouping various assigned teams for support and rehearsals, not unlike today's agile workforce. Aside from the more familiar war-fighting or peace-making roles, I have managed soldiers in support of civil communities, enabling cover for fire-fighters, tanker-driver strikes and foot-and-mouth emergencies. Within a week of joining 2 PARA, I was standing around Gatwick Airport, fully armed and posing in my brand new, red beret. Whilst this was all very swanky and exciting for both the travelling public and the boys, our deterrent effect was perhaps dubious; all sides were questioning our purpose. Plus (and I'll whisper this quietly), thankfully no-one had any ammunition. Flexibility is a mindset and adaptability is baked into military thinking and response.

The Parachute Regiment has long enjoyed the luxury of selecting quality and motivated recruits, from whom it is possible to leverage greater potential and performance. A common misperception implies that selection is based upon a high physical aptitude; selection also focuses on those with the right mental attitude to push that step further. There is no point selecting fit individuals if they cannot act and think clearly under pressure. Character and intelligence is intrinsic; a simple, high-wire assault course identifies those candidates with an ability to assimilate change and act under extreme pressure. There is a raft of aligned sporting analogies that equally apply; Clive Woodward's T-Cup theory comes immediately to mind, within his quest to play 'heads-up' rugby at the highest level. The forces are similarly focused upon team dynamics.

Through collective training, the forces substantiate their deterrent capacity to would-be aggressors, as well as providing the services the luxury of collective, core competency refinement. By comparison, commercial enterprises are engaged in the constant, daily friction of business, so forego the luxury of collective training. Business relies upon the individual. Whilst training is beneficial for the individual, possibly being sent on all manner of courses (successful or otherwise), the individual frequently returns from such excellent courses into the same culture and constraints as before, hence the impact and energy of the training is likely lost. In 2016, Deloitte calculated a potential global waste of $40 billion from, and an estimated $60 billion spent on tertiary education. This approach confers an individualistic mindset, where commercial rewards and benefits become aligned to the individual, which may not always be cordial to those of that business. As a result, commerce is populated by individuals taught to seek attention, as opposed to forging collective endeavour. Again, there are obvious sporting analogies, but when compared to the forces, service personnel subordinate their own goals and ambitions for those of their organisation. Their ambitions are geared to their team and formation (and ultimately, the monarch and country). This tenet of military order and discipline enables the rank system to function. Whilst not infallible, ultimately, when the bullets start flying, it's to the officers and leaders that the soldiers will look. Thus, trust and confidence in the team structure is vital, and such trust is derived through collective training.

I have found it fascinating to learn how such team-based thinking can be transferred to commercial organisations. A first step should be to understand pay and reward. Academically, most acknowledge that money is not an effective motivator, although an American millionaire friend once told me, 'Money will not motivate people, but will sure give you the giggles.' Financial reward has become a social yardstick and an objective sought by employees (trading their time for money), for it confers status and associated living standards. Money may motivate, temporarily, but it can swiftly demotivate. Interestingly, I was involved in running a business that needed to address high absenteeism and poor delivery. By removing team leaders and making everyone collectively responsible for performance (bonus awards, decided by the customer), the team became motivated to self-police and ensure all the team achieved better on-time delivery and standards (a leaderless task).

They self-policed and managed their output.

I turned around another business by applying alternative measures, where leaders from the workforce were offered a greater input to the team decision-making, thereby devolving operational commitment and engagement down. Engaged staff, now with skin in the game, were more committed to their inputs, being motivated to achieve the desired outcomes. So long as the outcomes are cordial to the end state, the business could flourish and achieve greater rewards all round. Ironically, this builds upon something the airborne adhered to: Airborne Initiative (ABI). All airborne troops are briefed and rehearsed on the operational plan; not all commanders can guarantee survival from the parachute insertion, even in training, so lower-level leaders and soldiers are enabled to take the initiative and contemporise, to achieve the higher goal. It's about doing more with better people.

In my experience, the 'softer/enabling' military leadership skills translate to industry. I was part of a business seeking to harness the 'energy from a crisis' to turn their business around, which thankfully was achieved. A core principle adopted was clear communication and openness. Once the business understood the challenges, the approach and required tasks (the vision and mission), staff were both energised, motivated and engaged across all functions. The military refer to this as unifying behind a mission. Commercial organisations ironically rarely operate in a joint and coordinated manner; people shelter within their specialism or silo. Despite the observation that it's essential to interoperate with one another, it's the application of transformational mapping tools that becomes a handrail for change, interoperability and enhancement. Unity of effort fosters a sustainable and more dynamic business. The military have long applied Mission Command: we are conducting X to achieve Y. If staff appreciate why they need to act in a certain manner, they can appreciate the environment and associated risks, as espoused by Simon Sinek and others. One simple way to appreciate Mission Command is to read David Marquet's book, Turn The Ship Around!, who summarises the approach admirably.

Business is about shaping and enabling leaders, empowering the team, identifying and enabling those to lead, encouraging them to achieve, with the right resources and support to overcome challenges. Thereafter it's essential that teams are monitored and sustained on course (not veering off on tangents) and encouraged to exploit successes (the profit motive). Today's yearning for better data and smarter analysis has always been present, yet only once it is assessed, visualised and applied can information become actionable intelligence. Whether it adhered to my military mindset or not, I was surprised to observe that accountability for people and process was commercially fragmented. This was a concern, for the military commander is accountable for current and future operations (unit performance) and administration, whilst remaining accountable for the training and welfare of their people, at all times (the services wrapper).

Commercially, it was common for leaders to delegate people-related issues to another department, in many cases creating and sometimes making work. Whilst this maintains fairness, objectivity and ensures workers' rights and welfare, none of which I am challenging or questioning, it divorces control from those directing resources, i.e., the manager. You may even argue that such an action disempowers the manager; worse, it requires an unengaged, technical manager to rule on matters in which they were neither engaged, aware, nor present. At best, team cohesion and alignment is lost. This is common across most industries. Naturally, this is not to denigrate the technical manager whose technical skills are essential to advise and enable the operational manager to make and take the best course of action. It calls to mind the German military philosophy, 'Schwerpunkt'. Whilst there is no direct translation, it calls for the identification of a main effort, through which all resources are channelled upon that main effort. This really helps focus a turnaround business. I guess the point I make here is that the leader needs to harness and empower all those technical elements to forge the team. After all, the sum of the whole is greater than the constituent parts. To be effective in such enablement requires experience, knowledge and training. What were the chances that 20 years or so after our trip I would find myself in Gaydon, delivering some business thinking and support in Jaguar Land Rover's HQ? Aside from some smart artwork and cool pictures around the offices offering the sole nod to the marque's heritage, the modern, electric models and half-built chassis on display in the huge, glass, modern headquarters were a world away from me throwing Series Threes and Wolfs out of aircraft. It was enticing to see the skunk works vehicles creeping around the compounds, however disconnected they were from our work. The company thrives and the New Defender has been well-received. It made me reflect on the circularity of life.

Today, our garage holds the Oztent, our winch gear, jerry cans and assorted camping bits and pieces, but still no Daph replacement. We did have a Land Rover Discovery in Seattle when we joined the NW Pacific Land Rover Club. This Disco had a lively four-litre petrol engine, as 'gas' prices were low and diesel was not readily available in the US. The extra horsepower completely transformed the Disco's performance, not unlike Simon Mann's Range Rover. We ended up with the Disco by accident, for I was seeking an old, Classic Range Rover, yet Land Rovers generically were very expensive in the US. Whilst fun, that was our last flirtation with Land Rovers and off-road adventure.

As for the African continent 20 years on, it still remains subject to the superpowers' great game - a modern-day 'scramble'. Today, China owns significant chunks of African, mineral-rich resources. Two decades on from 9/11, AIDS has left a significant legacy. Kids are being raised by grandparents, with a generation taken or lost. Ebola and SARs had a limited regional effect, but nothing like the ever-present killers, drought and famine. There was a different urban and rural response to COVID, although the continent fared relatively well, possibly given their SARs and related prior exposures.

Regional instability is increasing, notably the AQIM threat in the Sahel, despite the discussed French/EU/AU intervention and subsequent withdrawal. Whilst our route through Africa could be replicated today, the Sahel remains a dangerous lottery. Westerners here are discouraged; I still shudder to think about the poor Swiss couple caught out in the Ténéré. Yet Libya has opened, despite its civil war; the Arab Spring has rattled across the Maghreb, yet opportunity for independent travel remains easier than before. Travelling south from Kenya, the passage is as easy as ever, although Mozambique has threatened strife. As already discussed, the Congo is a ticking time-bomb, yet a western, coastal passage is now possible, proving that there are constant opportunities within Africa.

Over the next 30 years, according to UN forecasts, half the world's population growth will occur in nine countries, five of which are African. Africa is expected to grow by almost 1.1 billion people (or 100,000 people every day) for the next three decades, assuming a linear growth profile. But we know growth will be exponential, swamping the current resources and competition. This would lead to an increased, urbanised population of digitally-aligned souls in mega cities, the likes of which we cannot imagine. It's probable that Africa will remain at the crossroads of an East-West paradigm, assuming that Chinese and US ideologies remain. Not only in Africa but globally, the World Health Organisation (WHO) will struggle to deal with the next, more virulent pandemic or related health crisis, with or without significant investment and improved governance, to counter corruption and extant issues. Poverty remains the next killer. Climate change alone will hamper the continent through dramatic and unforeseen consequences; drought, floods and famine will increase competition for food and the fauna are less likely to fair well. Within the mix of population pressures, poor governance and corruption, terrorism and non-state actors can thrive within an unchecked world. How do the G7 countries reach out and become active, rather than the current post 9/11 trajectory of 'withdrawal within borders'?

We have recently witnessed the humiliating extraction from Afghanistan. And in Sahel, one wonders if Western powers are ever capable of harnessing the lessons from history? As for the $1 trillion bill for Afghan operations, questions are circulating around the opportunity cost and impact that such sums might have had upon the UK alone. Financial investment would be very welcome if used in a positive manner within the developing world; if only the G7 countries could foresee the benefits of coordinated interaction. Yet sadly, we have 'parked' Afghanistan whilst we address the next drama, today in Ukraine and Palestine (not unlike the Congo for the Balkans in the 1990s).

EPILOGUE
Catherine Stratta's 2024 reflection on the circularity of life

I still think a lot about our African trip, twenty years on. As I write these notes, I recognise that, all these years later, I still hold some anger and resentment from our crash. The trip had become an overriding passion for me (well, us), not just to experience the different countries and wildlife but all that it stood for: freedom and adventure, different perspectives and challenges. Adrian and I could reconnect again. My anger revolves around the stupidity of the accident. I really enjoy driving; I was good at it and was excited about being off the beaten track. I felt our hopes were snuffed out.

So, I was determined not to be robbed of our dream. When Dr Joe DeBeer said I'd need six weeks' recuperation, I was determined to fulfil that goal. He honoured that commitment, but wisely advised that for full recovery, off-road driving would take longer. Should one untoward jerk on the wheel from an uneven surface arise, it could wrench the shoulder and set me be back months. As the passenger, I was in considerable pain on the uneven surfaces; the pain seemed to ricochet up through my shoulder. This implied I would not be able to drive until we reached Kenya, should everything go to plan - I needed to apply myself to other areas of our trip.

Hindsight tells me now that I never really admitted this to myself, let alone expressed my disappointment in not being able to fully participate. Today, I watch my dogs with interest as they seem to allow emotions such as fear and worry to pass through them, and simply shake them off. Sadly, humans frequently hold on to emotions; we trap energy in our bodies, which may eventually cause us harm. Writing this epilogue has helped me to bring my suppressed feelings forward, so now at last I can acknowledge and release them. Interestingly, this process has propagated some pain in my right shoulder and stiffness across my upper back (reminiscent of that post-accident travel), whilst feeling release at my wider admission.

All of us are on some form of life journey, and we are no different. My father hated it if any of us kids cried; so from an early age, I learnt to suppress my emotions. I can now appreciate this is not a healthy strategy, but it has taken me years to 'unlearn' this. I still draw great strength from our trip and use my resilience learnt from our journey within my coaching business. Since COVID (and other events at the time), I have used our African experience as a vehicle to help me speak out about my own health issues.

I have suffered from mood swings since the age of 12, but it was not until I was 25 that I was diagnosed with what was then called 'manic depression'. Today, it is less alarmingly referred to as 'bipolar disorder'. I attended medical school, but there, I suffered two episodes, resulting in months of hospitalisation for severe depression. I needed to pass a psychological assessment before I could re-start my studies. I carried on for a year, but after working on the wards, I began to get depressed again. This time, I decided it was time to leave; my dream was shattered. I only ever wanted to be a doctor and giving up was not in my nature, so it was a very difficult decision. Retrospectively, it gave me time and space to work on my health; I managed to see a consultant psychiatrist who 'understood' my position and suggested that I take lithium. This was not what I wanted to hear, but with nothing else working, what did I have to lose?

Lithium stabilised my mood in weeks. My life was transformed. My first thought was, 'Wow, this must be how normal people feel!' Remaining stable meant I could rebuild my life on solid foundations instead of shifting sands. I sustained a great career in clinical research for over 25 years, allowing me to leverage my medical knowledge. But I had never spoken about my diagnosis until recently, when I started my own coaching business. To paraphrase something Kay Jamieson once said, 'When you tell people you have bipolar, you have to realise that they will never look at you in the same way again.'

I suffered a setback in 2018 when my GP warned me of potential damage to my kidneys and asked me to come off lithium. This was the drug that held me stable for 30 odd years! Being menopausal, I was convinced that I would be fine, but within two months of stopping, my weight plummeted from 70kg down to 53kg and I was suicidal. The antidepressant I was prescribed did not work (common for bipolar people); I sank lower.

Appallingly, there was no available psychiatrist for me to see. My GP sought advice that ended up with me being prescribed lamotrigine, an epilepsy drug. I experienced severe side effects, losing feeling in my fingertips which meant I kept dropping things (having quarry tiles on our kitchen floor wasn't helpful); I was chewing the inside of my mouth; my toenails started peeling and I had a rash on my face. It was too much. Eventually,

I saw a psychiatrist, but he refused to put me back on lithium. Instead, I was prescribed a second-generation antipsychotic, quetiapine. Thankfully, the first thing this did was to help me sleep - something depressed people struggle with. My resilience was to be tested further, for around this time, my mother was given a stage 4 bowel cancer diagnosis out of the blue. This was a shock: my mother and I were very close and she was the glue that held our family together. She had an operation and a colostomy, but radiotherapy did not help; she was given months to live. She died, peacefully at home, a few days after her 89th birthday. Losing her just six months after the diagnosis was hard for us all.

Unsurprisingly, my father took this particularly badly. He had always been a great planner and convinced us all he would pass first, but he survived Mum by a couple of years. He lived at home, was still driving, but one night he suffered a serious stroke that meant he was hospitalised. He then contracted COVID and died two weeks later, in 2021, at the grand age of 94. Dad had risen from a colliery family in Yorkshire to eventually become a chief government scientist. He had always wanted to be a doctor, so in many ways, my medical ambition was partially down to him. He used to say, 'All life starts and ends in a hospital.' Dad was never a fan of the military, especially after (in his words) 'enduring National Service'. He used to say his National Service delayed his ascent to university, but we subsequently learnt that he was funded there by an ex-serviceman's grant. I believe it is a family trait to never accept any orders - especially without questioning them - so one can only imagine Dad's face when I introduced Adrian to the family. Evidently, Adrian was no doctor (it was expected that I should marry a fellow doctor); at the time, he was a potential young officer with the Parachute Regiment. To be fair to Dad, he never said anything untoward. As the years rolled on, Dad still said nothing about Adrian's chosen profession and was happy to tag along to hear various talks and presentations. One memorable talk was from Major John Howard, the commander of D Company Ox and Bucks Light infantry, who famously captured Pegasus Bridge just prior to D-Day in a historic 'coup de main' action. This talk at Depot PARA, Aldershot was memorable for Dad for we took one of his friends along, Geoff Barkway. Geoff had taught me to drive. Mum couldn't drive and Dad was away a lot doing fieldwork during the summer prior to my driving test, so Geoff (despite only having one arm) gallantly offered. He was calm personified and used to say, when advising me to check my rear-view mirror, to 'ensure you are not surprised by a Messerschmitt 109 on your tail'.

Geoff rarely spoke of the war, but it transpired he had flown one of the six gliders that landed on Pegasus Bridge. Geoff was one of the many glider pilots who stood up as John Howard entered the room, along with other notables like Richard Todd, the actor. Poor old John Howard was quite taken aback. Richard Todd had been a young lieutenant in 7 PARA, who had landed to the east of the canal. Richard's task was to be the spearhead force to reinforce Pegasus Bridge, before Lord Lovat's commandos arrived from the breeches. In the film, The Longest Day, Richard played the role of John Howard. All the glider pilots performed an amazing feat of airmanship, but poor Geoff became one of the first casualties that day, getting shot in the arm on landing. Geoff maintained that the loss of his arm saved his life, for had he survived, he would have flown into Arnhem, from where few glider pilots returned. Dad loved the evening, being in Aldershot and it was only a month later that Adrian parachuted onto the original 7 PARA DZ as part of the 50th anniversary commemorative drop, from where he ran to meet Geoff at Pegasus Bridge, with his comrades.

I was still depressed at the loss of my mother when a few months later, I was diagnosed with breast cancer. I had not started processing the grief at losing Mum and was now facing multiple surgeries. Thankfully, I was referred to a wonderful psychologist, whom I saw weekly for a year. We discussed holistic ways to deal with grief, depression and cancer and she encouraged me to research the treatments. After a year, I started to come around and, in the process, I had compiled a comprehensive remedy toolkit. I could speak from knowledge as I had tried the various modalities. Part of my drive to be a doctor was to help people, and now I could be of use to other people with bipolar disorder, for (as I found) there was not much support around at the time. I started to talk openly about our crash in South Africa and the resilience needed to pull myself out of the black hole. It was a spark for my new business and for Adrian to put pen to paper.

Today, I am better, healthy and living a full life. I now leverage my story and experiences to help others, as I describe on my website www.movebeyondbipolar.com. In the UK today, it currently takes nine and a half years to get a bipolar disorder diagnosis, which is shameful. The incidence of bipolar is 1 in 50 (i.e. 2% of the population), so it is not that uncommon, and for the nine and a half years to be an average, there are people who fail to receive a diagnosis for much longer. It is my mission to try to reduce this wait time, and to abolish any stigma by educating people where and how to get help. Whilst medication is important, as I have learnt, there are many holistic methods to help stabilise and manage this affliction, enabling people to live a happy and fulfilled life. I have managed to turn being bipolar into my superpower!

I guess with all this nascent positivity and toolkit, and the absence of my father's negativity about Africa, I subconsciously felt free to explore and express my inner thoughts about our trip. I am immensely proud of completing our journey, my resilience and exercising strength through adversity. I realise it was our dream and I did not want to let us down. I understand Dad was of his generation, who believed Africa to be a dark and foreboding place. I was determined to travel but making that call home from Cape Town to inform my parents of our accident was the hardest thing I have ever done. Thankfully, Mum understood, and Dad was supportive, but I knew it only reinforced his entrenched views.

So, imagine our surprise when my sister, Helen, and I were clearing out Dad's chaotic study, we found a few 1948 passport-sized headshot photos of Dad, posing as a new young officer, wearing Parachute Regiment uniform and red beret. Talk about a shock - Dad had never said! I questioned Adrian – he was amazed. Adrian knew a little more context of Dad's national service. He only admitted to being a driver in an artillery unit in post-war Germany, although he did admit to Adrian that he had spent a few months deployed to Palestine. Whilst in Germany, Dad was selected to attend a six-week Officer Training (OCTU) school in Mons, Aldershot, which was near Adrian's base. We are still staggered as to why he chose to keep such a thing to himself, especially considering it was Adrian's regiment? Whilst Dad never parachuted or ostensibly served in the regiment, Adrian said he could check records to investigate, but we have chosen not to do so. That was his secret and not for us to judge. But just when you thought you knew someone... That's why, for so many reasons, we are total advocates for people following their dreams, or as Adrian might say, Utrique Paratus.

ACKNOWLEDGEMENTS

There are two broad groups of people I'd like to thank, although the majority of those in the first group have already been acknowledged/name-checked within the text for getting and sustaining Catherine and I during our safari. We documented our journey as we travelled, maintaining both written diaries and wrote our initial website (https://daphneoverland.co.uk) as we travelled. We carried a laptop and a new digital SLR camera, for neither modern smartphones, the necessary wireless cover or social media was then available.

We never really envisaged a book; our journey was more about finding ourselves. We initially asked a few key people about sponsorship and writing articles, but the lack of uptake left us content to shelve any such ambition in favour of getting on with our travels and finding new careers.

Years later, COVID hit, along with the first lockdown. I was working in the aviation sector, which effectively shut down overnight, shedding all extraneous cost. With time on my hands, I picked up the diary and reviewed our photographs; fatal. Interestingly, time and reflection had presented an interesting perspective and value. I also reviewed Dr Christopher Everett's diary again, having met him over the years in the village (as a founding member of the Holybourne Sand Club). An initial draft took shape, still with few thoughts of publication.

Catherine had been tackling some tough health issues around COVID, as well as the loss of her parents, which she described so openly and bravely in the Epilogue. During this time Catherine was also starting her coaching business and was discussing our journey and her resilience. That Catherine was discussing and leveraging the trip, subconsciously it gave licence for the book to develop. A key tipping point was her father's death and our subsequent discovery about his early life that totally shocked us.

Hence my appreciation and gratitude for the numerous people who helped bring this publication to fruition. Primarily, I was introduced to Pru Alexander Cooper (from PAC Copywriting); she immediately understood the project, my hesitation and asked to see the initial draft. She had experience of Africa, of similar authors and adventure travel, plus her brother (Ash) was also writing his book, having recently left the Forces. Four edits later, I am grateful for her support, insight and shaping - Pru, thank you.

I now had a manuscript, but no route to market. Again I am grateful to Pru and her initial contacts in this regard; for I have spoken to so many across the publishing industry. It struck me that the predominant business model centred around the industries desire to re-engineer the book (without having seen it, as that is where they had their talent), before taking it to market. One even thought to give the Land Rover a voice?

As ever, I am grateful to the Young Hertfordians Golf Society; my school buddies who use the pretence of a golf weekend to catch-up, at least annually. It was Paul Whelan who introduced the notion of self-publishing, a sector that is growing exponentially. I am in debt to Kevin Walker, graphic design supremo and owner of KW Creative, who created the design and artwork for the book cover and inner pages. As the old army maxim implies, never volunteer, we are truly grateful you did Kev, outstanding. A further host of advisors and meeting, too many to name check everyone, although those who stood out were Harry Bucknall, Neil Springall, Steve Hill, Shelley Wilson, Tony Rushmer (notable for his introduction to Damian Lewis and his team, Suzy Quinn) that ultimately lead to Vickie Boff (VickieBoffConsulting). I am grateful to Nairobi Dorta from Seaflow Studios for the web landing page and Alison Essex (hashtagprcompany) for the social media guidance, support and creation.

As for all the military connections – thank you for the laughs, graft and insights, they still continue, despite having left 20 odd years ago. Notably, I am grateful to David Higginbottom and Alf Vickers, two erstwhile paratroopers supporting Sheffield University OTC who pushed me towards pre-RCB with the Regiment and set the ball rolling. It is to the Regiment that I desire to add back, through the vetrans charity Support Our PARAs, led by 'Little Jacko' Jackson and his team.

Finally Top Spotter Catherine, for her unwavering focus, passion and partner in our adventure.

www.ingramcontent.com/pod-product-compliance
Ingram Content Group UK Ltd.
Pitfield, Milton Keynes, MK11 3LW, UK
UKHW020217100625
459483UK00002B/3